RASHBAM'S COMMENTARY ON LEVITICUS AND NUMBERS

An Annotated Translation

Program in Judaic Studies
Brown University
Box 1826
Providence, RI 02912

BROWN JUDAIC STUDIES

Number 330

RASHBAM'S COMMENTARY ON LEVITICUS AND NUMBERS

An Annotated Translation

edited and translated by
Martin I. Lockshin

RASHBAM'S COMMENTARY ON LEVITICUS AND NUMBERS

An Annotated Translation

edited and translated by
Martin I. Lockshin

Brown Judaic Studies
Providence

RASHBAM'S COMMENTARY ON LEVITICUS AND NUMBERS

An Annotated Translation

edited and translated by
Martin I. Lockshin

Library of Congress Cataloging-in-Publication Data

Samuel ben Meir, 11th/12th cent.
[Perush ha-Torah. Va-yikra. English.]
Rashbam's commentary on Leviticus and Numbers : an annotated translation / Martin I. Lockshin.
p. cm. — (Brown Judaic studies ; no. 330)
Includes bibliographical references.
ISBN 1-930675-07-0 (cloth : alk. paper) — ISBN 1-930675-26-7 (paper : alk. paper)
1. Bible. O.T. Leviticus—Commentaries. 2. Bible. O.T. Numbers—Commentaries. I. Samuel ben Meir, 11th/12th cent. Perush ha-Torah. Ba-midbar. English. II. Lockshin, Martin I. III. Title. IV. Series.

BS1255.53.S26 2001
222'.13077—dc21 2001043280

Printed in the United States of America
on acid-free paper

Dedicated to
my mother
Sylvia Lockshin
and my mother-in-law
Rita Mendelsohn,
with love and gratitude.

TABLE OF CONTENTS

Acknowledgements ix

Introduction 1

Table of Abbreviations 7

Commentary on Leviticus 11

ויקרא	Leviticus 1–5	11
צו	Leviticus 6–8	35
שמיני	Leviticus 9–11	47
תזריע	Leviticus 12–13	69
מצורע	Leviticus 14–15	77
אחרי מות	Leviticus 16–18	87
קדושים	Leviticus 19–20	97
אמור	Leviticus 21–24	115
בהר	Leviticus 25:1–26:2	131
בחוקותי	Leviticus 26:3–27:34	139

Commentary on Numbers 155

במדבר	Numbers 1:1–4:20	155
נשא	Numbers 4:21–7:89	167
בהעלותך	Numbers 8–12	181
שלח	Numbers 13–15	205
קרח	Numbers 16–18	225
חוקת	Numbers 19:1–22:1	247
בלק	Numbers 22:2–25:9	263
מטות	Numbers 30:2–32:42	285
מסעי	Numbers 33–36	293

Bibliography 299

ACKNOWLEDGEMENTS

The research for this book was financed in part by generous grants from the Social Sciences and Humanities Research Council of Canada and from York University's Faculty of Arts. I am very grateful for their help.

Professor Shaye Cohen of the Brown University Judaic Studies Series has been a great help to me, has encouraged my scholarly writing and has made helpful comments about the manuscript of this book at different stages of its composition. I am also grateful to Leigh Andersen of the Society of Biblical Literature for her useful suggestions and advice.

In my research I have been helped by the librarians at York University and at the National Library of the Hebrew University in Jerusalem. I would also like to express my gratitude to Pearl Berger and the library of Yeshivah University for allowing me access to the manuscript, *Quntres tiqqune ṭa'uyot ha-defus beferushe ha-Rashbam zaṣal 'al ha-Torah* by Jacob H. Berzinsky.

My debt to York University goes far beyond the research grants that I occasionally receive. York has provided me with a stimulating and exciting intellectual environment, a friendly workplace, supportive colleagues and eager students. All of these have enriched my life and contributed to my scholarship.

I am very grateful to all of the students who helped me test my theories, at times challenging them intelligently and effectively—my students at York, at the Bible Department at Bar Ilan University, and at the "Beth Haminyan Chumash Group."

A number of students served as research assistants. I am most grateful for the help that I received from Michael Berk, Abigail Brown, Israel Doron, Jutta Raithel and Sharone Tayar. I enjoyed working with each of them and I hope that they too benefited from the collaboration.

York University's Centre for Jewish Studies has been a convivial and supportive home for me. I am grateful to my colleagues there for their friendship and for their role in creating a vibrant intellectual community of Jewish scholarship. Colleagues such as Sara Horowitz, Eric Lawee, Alex Pomson, Ahouva Shulman, Sol Tanenzapf and Rachael Turkienicz were willing to listen to my ideas, and to share theirs with me. I owe an immense debt of gratitude to Michael Brown, the Director of the Centre of Jewish Studies for the last few years, and to his predecessor, Sydney Eisen. I feel blessed that I have been able to work under the supervision of true friends like them.

One of my greatest pleasures is studying Torah with my children. Thanks to Channa, Shoshanna, Noam and Reva for being tolerant when I inevitably bring Rashbam into the material that we study. I think that they too have come to appreciate his greatness and his daring.

My greatest debt is to my wife, Ruth Mendelsohn Lockshin. Aside from providing me with a warm and loving environment, and with four wonderful children, Ruthie is also my editor-in-chief, who corrects my overly heavy prose and forces me to strive for readability. I thank her for that and for everything else too.

I have dedicated this book to two other women, my mother, Sylvia Lockshin, and my mother-in-law, Rita Mendelsohn. Their love and support have made my life so much more pleasant and have allowed me to pursue a life of scholarship and learning.

INTRODUCTION

Rashbam's Commentary on Leviticus and Numbers is the third in a proposed series of four volumes. This series helps English-speaking students of the Hebrew Bible to gain access to one of the great traditional Jewish commentators. Although Rashbam (Rabbi Samuel ben Meir) was a twelfth-century Jew who lived in Northern France, his commentary on the Torah seems oddly modern in its extreme dedication to the pursuit of *peshaṭ*, the plain meaning of the biblical text.

Rashbam's commentary on Leviticus and Numbers has one obvious characteristic that makes it very different from his commentary on the first two books of the Bible: brevity. Roughly speaking, the commentary on the third and fourth books of the Bible is about a third of the length of the commentary on the first two books. It is hard to know why. Was Rashbam tiring of his project? Did he perhaps feel that he had taught his exegetical methodology sufficiently in the commentary on the previous books, and that now he could be more terse? Are the books of Leviticus and Numbers of less exegetical interest? Could the different commentaries on the different biblical books have undergone different editing processes? Any one of these answers is possible.

Rashbam's commentary to the two books in this volume is vintage Rashbam, even if the style is more laconic. Readers who are interested in the plain meaning of the biblical text, in Rashbam's fledgling attempts to interpret the Bible in a literary manner, in the tensions between Rashbam and his grandfather Rashi, or in the tension between *peshaṭ* and midrash will find, I hope, much of interest in the current volume.

In the next and final volume of this series, *Rashbam on Deuteronomy*, I plan to offer in addition to my translation and notes, some summary essays about *peshaṭ*, about Northern French Jewish exegesis and about the interaction between Jewish and Christian Bible interpreters.

Rashbam and Rashi

Rashbam's ambivalent attitude to his grandfather is often apparent in this volume. Rashbam begins his commentary to Leviticus with a paean to Rashi's commentary. Rashbam's commentary is also filled with passages where he offers the same explanation that his grandfather apparently had already offered.

Yet the astute reader will see that Rashbam pointedly targets Rashi's commentary many times, directly undermining Rashi's approach. For example, in his Leviticus commentary Rashi adopts the standard midrashic explanation of the word לאמר, saying that it means "go and tell this to some third party." Even though the word לאמר appears dozens of times in these books, Rashi offers this explanation only twice: in the commentary to Leviticus 1:1 and 11:1. Rashbam opposes this midrashic understanding of לאמור twice in his Leviticus commentary—precisely at the same points that Rashi promotes the midrashic reading. One must conclude that Rashbam is not simply advocating *peshaṭ* over midrash in these passages. He is advocating his commentary over that of his grandfather.

Readers who would like to find further examples of Rashbam opposing or, at least, playing off of Rashi's commentary, should examine Rashbam's commentary on such passages as Lev. 5:13 (and note 85 there), 19:6 (and note 21 there), 19:20 (and note 41 there), 23:27 (and note 30 there), 25:11–12 (and notes 4, 5 and 8 there) and 26:19 (and notes 8–10 there).

The possibility of Rashbam influencing Rashi's commentary is discussed at various points in this book. See, for example, note 21 on Lev. 19:16 and note 4 on Num. 19:16.

Rashbam and *halakhah*

Rashbam is one of the few traditional exegetes who offers interpretations of biblical verses that do not conform with standard Jewish law. For example, in his commentary to Lev. 19:13, s.v. לא תלין, he writes that that biblical verse is referring to a worker who works at night. But the Talmud had explicitly considered and rejected that interpretation, ruling instead that the verse refers to a daytime laborer. Rashbam's interpretation is clearly incompatible with the accepted *halakhah* concerning this verse. (See further the discussion in note 16 there.)

Rashbam does this often. See, for example, his commentary to Lev. 4:3 (and note 70 there) to Lev. 6:11 (and note 9 there), to Lev. 11:40 (and notes 85 and 86 there) or to Lev. 19:13 (and note 16 there). At times his opposition to the standard halakhic reading is pointed and perhaps even has an edge to it. In his commentary to Num. 30:11 he interprets the verse in a manner and in language that is the precise opposite of the standard rabbinical reading. See note 16 there.

Yet here too Rashbam's approach can only be described as inconsistent. Sometimes he studiously avoids an obvious *peshaṭ* reading and interprets as *halakhah* would suggest. See for example commentary on Lev. 6:3–4 (and note 7 there), on Lev. 13:2 (and note 20 there) or Lev. 23:11 (and note 24 there). There does not seem to be a discernible pattern of when Rashbam defers to tradition and when he allows himself to interpret in a heterodox manner.

The same tension can be found in his commentary even when legal issues are not at stake. Rashbam surprisingly portrays Balaam in a much more positive light than the classical midrash does. I argue (in note 58) that the commentary on Num. 24:1–2 seems to be pointedly mocking the midrashic approach or, at a minimum, that it is written in a way that Rashbam knows will scandalize the reader who likes midrash. Yet Rashbam surprises his readers from time to time by adopting a *midrash 'aggadah* approach to a biblical text, for example when he writes (commentary to Num. 21:14) about the miracles that took place at Wadi Arnon, miracles that are mentioned nowhere in the text.

In fact, here in the commentary to Leviticus and Numbers Rashbam shows a surprising interest in midrash. More than once he explains to his readers how a specific midrash derives from the biblical text. (See e.g. his commentary to Num. 5:10, Num. 11:35 and Num. 34:6.) At one point in the Leviticus commentary (to 17:15) Rashbam offers his own *midrash halakhah* on a biblical verse. (See note 25 there.) But this does not mean that he has relaxed his standards about what is and what is not *peshaṭ*. For example, in his commentary to Num. 13:22 he discusses at length a famous *midrash*—that claims that Caleb was the only spy to visit the city of Hebron. He explains how that midrash is grounded in the biblical text and how one might erroneously think that that interpretation qualifies also as *peshaṭ*. Then he explains why that midrash is only midrash, and does not qualify as *peshaṭ*.

Rashbam and literary analysis of the text

In his commentary to these biblical books Rashbam shows a great deal of literary sensitivity. He interprets many verses as examples of the principle that "the text generalizes and then provides examples" (כולל ואח״כ מפרש). (See e.g. his commentary to Lev. 12:1, 16:6, 25:10 and 25:39 and Num. 1:47.) The classical rabbis also considered such structural issues. But when, for example, the rabbis used a phrase like "פרט וכלל ופרט—the text makes a general statement, then provides the details and then repeats the general statement," they attributed halakhic significance to the fact that the Torah used that particular pattern at a specific point in the text. In Rashbam's commentary, though, פרט וכלל ופרט in the Bible is nothing more than a literary or rhetorical device. (See his commentary to Num. 16:14 and note 17 there.) At times it is clear that Rashbam's literary sense causes him to read a biblical phrase (such as לא תעולל, in Lev. 19:10, generally understood as meaning "do not harvest the unripe grapes") in a way that differs from traditional halakhic understanding. (See commentary and note 9 there.) In the commentary to Leviticus 19:11–12, Rashbam offers unusual and unique interpretations of some common biblical words. I believe that this is because of his literary sense that a list of restrictions ought to proceed from the more obviously forbidden to the less (לא זו אף זו). See notes 10–13 there.

Rashbam and the image of the wandering Israelites

The book of Leviticus and particularly the book of Numbers are filled with the complaints of the Israelites as they wandered through the wilderness. Rashbam sheds a much more positive light on those complaints than most commentators do. Perhaps he is defending the Israelites against the criticisms of Christian anti-Jewish polemicists of his own time. In any case he often tries to point out the legitimate concerns that might have been behind his ancestors' griping. For examples, see the commentary to Lev. 17:5 (and note 23 there), to Num. 10:33 (and note 25 there), to Num. 11:1 (and note 29 there), to Num. 11:7 (and note 31 there), to Num. 16:29 (and note 25 there), to Num. 17:27–28 (and note 53 there) and to Num. 21:5 (and note 31 there).

Rashbam: a critic before his time?

We know from his Talmud commentary and from other contemporary medieval sources that Rashbam was a great talmudist and a pious rabbi. So some of his comments seem surprisingly heterodox. In his commentary to Num. 23:2 Rashbam proposes an unattested conjectural emendation of the vocalization of a biblical word. (See note 26 there.) He demonstrates admirable "reader awareness," when he writes that the biblical text must have been more understandable to the Israelites who left Egypt than to readers in later generations. (See commentary to Num. 13:22 and note 41 there.) Finally, in his commentary to Num 22:1 (although the text is presumably garbled) Rashbam appears to take a heterodox approach (or at least what we would consider today a heterodox approach) to the question of the authorship of the Torah. (See note 61 there.)

Many contradictions remain in Rashbam's work. He is firmly committed to *halakhah*; yet he sometimes proposes literary readings that do not conform to *halakhah*. At times he opposes Rashi; at other times he accepts him.

Rashbam does not explain how he works out the contradictions or if they bothered him. In his Talmud commentary (to BB 131a, s.v. ואל תגמרו), he remarks at one point that people who construct logical arguments are essentially like judges. Judges can judge only on the basis of the evidence before their eyes (אין לדיין אלא מה שעיניו רואות). So, Rashbam says, when it comes to any form of logical analysis—and biblical interpretation for Rashbam is surely a form of logical analysis—and all you can do is follow what your mind tells you (והוא הדין לדבר התלוי בסברא דאין לו אלא מה שלבו רואהו).

Rashbam followed what his mind told him; he called them as he saw them. I hope that my readers will find Rashbam's idiosyncratic and independent approach as interesting and as novel as I do.

Note: The text of Rashbam's commentary that underlies the translation is, except when otherwise noted, the best available printed edition, produced by David Rosin (Breslau, 1882). Translations of biblical verses into English usually follow the New Jewish Publication Society version. Often I have used my own translation, especially when Rashbam's understanding of the verse demands a different rendering.

TABLE OF ABBREVIATIONS

Andrew of St. Victor	*Commentary on the Heptateuch*, in *Corpus Christianorum*, vol. 53, edited by Charles Lohr and Rainer Berndt
BDB	*Hebrew and English Lexicon of the Old Testament*, edited by F. Brown, S. R. Driver and C. A. Briggs
Be'ur	Moses' Mendelssohn's translation of the Torah in his *Netivot Ha-shalom*, including commentary on Leviticus (written by N. H. Wessely) and on Numbers (written by Aaron Yaroslav)
Ben-Yehuda	*Thesaurus Totius Hebraitatis*, ed. by Eliezer ben Yehuda
BH	*Biblia Hebraica*
BR	*Bereshit Rabba'*
BT	Babylonian Talmud
D. Berger	*The Jewish-Christian Debate in the High Middle Ages*, by David Berger
Ehrlich	*Mikra ki-pheshuto*, by A. Ehrlich
EJ	Encyclopaedia Judaica
Esh	S. Esh, "Variant Readings in Medieval Hebrew Commentaries: R. Samuel ben Meir (Rashbam)", *Textus 5* (1966), 84-92

G.-K.	*Gesenius' Hebrew Grammar*, as edited by E. Kautzsch and revised by A. E. Cowley
Gray	*A Critical and Exegetical Commentary on Numbers* (ICC) by George Gray
Gerstenberg	*Commentary on Leviticus* by Erhard S. Gerstenberger, translated by Douglas W. Stott
Harrison	*Numbers: An Exegetical Commentary*, by R. K. Harrison
Hizq.	*Ḥizquni*
Hoffmann	David Hoffmann's commentary on Leviticus
iE	Abraham ibn Ezra
Japhet-Salters	*The Commentary of Rabbi Samuel ben Meir (Rashbam) on Qoheleth,* ed. by S. Japhet and R. B. Salters
JBS	Joseph Bekhor Shor
Kasher	*Torah Shelemah*, by M. M. Kasher
Krinski	Y. Krinski's *Ḥumash meḥoqeqe Yehudah*
Licht	*Perush 'al sefer Bemidbar* by Jacob Licht
Levine	*Numbers 1-20: a New Translation with Introduction and Commentary* by Baruch Levine
LT	*Midrash Leqaḥ Ṭov*
LXX	Septuagint
Mendelssohn	See *Be'ur*

Milgrom	*Leviticus 1-16: a New Translation with Introduction and Commentary,* by Jacob Milgrom
Mish.	Mishnah
MT	Masoretic Text
Nahm.	Moses Naḥmanides
NJPS	The New Jewish Publication Society Translation of the Bible
NJPSC	*The New Jewish Publication Society Torah Commentary* [to Leviticus by Baruch Levine and to Numbers by Jacob Milgrom]
Noth	M. Noth's volumes on Leviticus or Numbers
NR	*Numbers Rabba'*
Onq.	Targum Onqelos
PAAJR	Proceedings of the American Academy for Jewish Research
PDRE	*Pirqe derabbi 'Eli'ezer*
PG	J. P. Migne, ed., *Patriologiae Cursus Completus Series Graeca,* (Paris, 1844-65)
PL	J. P. Migne, ed., *Patriologiae Cursus Completus Series Latina,* (Paris, 1844-65)
Ps.-Jon.	The targum attributed to Jonathan ben Uzziel

Qara	Joseph Qara
Qimhi	David Qimḥi
Rosin	Rashbam's Torah Commentary as edited by David Rosin (Breslau, 1881/2)
RSBM	David Rosin's *Rabbi Samuel ben Meir als Schrifterklärer*
RSV	Revised Standard Version
Shapira	Y. L. Shapira's *Ha-rekhasim leviq'ah*
Tanh.	*Midrash Tanḥuma*
Tanh. B.	*Midrash Tanḥuma ha-qadum veha-yashan*, ed. by S. Buber
VR	*Vayyiqra' Rabba'*
Wessely	Commentary on Leviticus by N. H. Wessely, found in Mendelssohn's *Netivot ha-shalom*

COMMENTARY ON LEVITICUS
פירוש לספר ויקרא

ויקרא (Leviticus 1–5)

Rashbam's Introduction to his Commentary on Leviticus

There are many laws [in this book]. Scholars should study the interpretations of my grandfather [Rashi],[1] for I will elaborate only on passages where the plain meaning of the text requires explanation.[2]

1:1 ויקרא אל משה THE LORD CALLED OUT TO MOSES: Since it says above at the end of the book [of Exodus] that "Moses could not enter the Tent of the Meeting [because the cloud had settled on it, and the presence of the LORD

---

[1]Rashbam's commentary on Leviticus appears to pick up right where the Exodus commentary left off. Rashbam's final comment on Exodus reads:

> Whoever is loyal to God's words should never depart from the commentary of my grandfather, Rabbi Solomon . . .. "It is best that you grasp the one"—my commentary—"without letting go of the other one" (Eccl. 7:18).

Rashbam's appraisal of his grandfather's works is more nuanced and more conflicted than these two comments imply. He does not simply see the two Bible commentaries as complementary; he criticizes and takes issue with Rashi, often in very strident language, on a regular basis. See further discussion of this issue in my Genesis volume, pp. 17–23, and in my Exodus volume, in the notes on pp. 225–226.

[2]A similar disclaimer appears in Rashbam's introduction to his commentary to Exodus 25:

> If I write in brief concerning the [next] sections of the text dealing with the Tabernacle and the breastpiece and the ephod, [more] details may be found in the commentaries of Rabbi Solomon—may the memory of the righteous be a blessing!—my mother's father.

As I noted there (p. 303, note 2), the statement seems out of place at the beginning of Exodus 25, where Rashbam does elaborate at rather uncharacteristically great length about "the Tabernacle and the breastpiece and the ephod." Here, though, Rashbam's warning does make sense; he now begins to write much more tersely than he did in his commentary to Genesis and Exodus. Perhaps when it comes to the rules of sacrifices and the like—the major content of Leviticus—Rashbam feels that there are greater limits to what *peshaṭ* exegesis might say. Midrashic interpretations are almost all that are needed. When he reaches the rules of "leprosy," he says this more directly. See commentary to Lev. 13:2, and note 11 there.

filled the sanctuary]" (Exodus 40:35); accordingly [this book, Leviticus, opens by saying that] God called out to him from within the Tent.[3]

The interpretation[4] of the verse is: "He called out to Moses from the Tent of Meeting, and spoke to him, saying . . .."[5] [The phrase] "from the Tent of Meeting" should be understood as modifying "He called."[6] [The verse describes the place from which God called out to Moses,] just like the verse, "The LORD called to him from the mountain, saying . . ." (Ex. 19:3).

[So also] "he would hear the Voice speaking to him from above the cover" (Num. 7:89). [Moses heard the Voice speaking] from above the cover. [So here also] he heard the Voice [speaking] from the Tent.[7]

---

[3]Rashbam's comment here continues his discussion of the closing verses of the book of Exodus. There he explains that the cloud over the Tent of Meeting was temporary, keeping Moses away from the Tent for a while; when it lifted, he was able to enter. Here Rashbam adds that the meaning of our verse is that God called to Moses to invite him into the Tent, perhaps to let him know that the coast was now clear. iE makes the same connection between our verse and Ex. 40:35, both in his commentary here and in both versions of his commentary to Exodus 40. The explanation can also be found in a number of midrashic sources, e.g. Tanh. *Va-yiqra'* 1. For a more complete list of midrashic sources, see Krinski's *Qarne 'or* here, note 5.

Rashbam's interpretation opposes that of Rashi, here, s.v. ויקרא, who argues (following Sifra) that God *always* called to Moses before speaking to him (not just here because of the problem of the cloud over the Tent of Meeting), and that He did so because of the special relationship that they had with one another. JBS, who interprets the verse the same way that Rashbam does, specifically points out the contrast between these two understandings.

[4]Or "the proper syntactical reading." As explained below, Rashbam's reading restructures the wording of the verse.

[5]Instead of a literal understanding of the verse's syntax: "He called out to Moses, and God spoke to him from the Tent of Meeting, saying . . .."

[6]I.e. the adverbial phrase "from the Tent of Meeting" modifies the verb ויקרא, and describes the place from which God "called out to Moses"; it does not modify the verb וידבר, which would mean that it was describing the place where God "spoke" to Moses. Rashbam's interpretation opposes that of Rashi, s.v. מאהל מועד לאמר, who sees this phrase as explaining where the conversation between God and Moses took place.

Rashbam does not say why he is attracted to this syntactical restructuring of the verse. (Shapira, *Ha-rekhasim le-viq'ah*, argues that Rashbam's interpretation even contradicts the cantillation signs.) Perhaps it is because it highlights more clearly the connection between this verse and the end of Exodus—that Moses hesitated to enter the Tent until God called him from within the tent; then Moses entered and then God spoke to him. Nahm. labels the reading offered here by Rashbam as a reading that conforms with midrashic understandings of this verse. He feels that a *peshaṭ* reading (ושיעור הכתוב כפי פשוטו ומשמעו) would, naturally enough, connect the phrase, "from the Tent of Meeting" with the verb "spoke."

[7]I have translated this section of text according to Rosin's conjectural emendation, although I am not pleased with it.

In the manuscript that Rosin used, the reading apparently was: וישמע את הקול מדבר אליו מאהל שמע את הקול. Rosin tells us that he then emended the text in a significant way to read: וישמע את הקול מדבר אליו מעל [הכפרת, מעל הכפרת שמע את הקול, אף כאן מן] האהל

So also "God called to him from within the bush" (Ex. 3:4).[8]

לאמר: [simply] restates the same idea as "he spoke" (וידבר), as I explained in the Torah portion *Noaḥ*.[9] Just as a verse would say [redundantly] "Speak to the children of Aaron and say to them,"[10] so also [our verse means that God] spoke to Moses, saying (לאמר) to Moses.[11]

שמע את הקול. Even if we accept this emendation, it is not clear why Rashbam would say what Rosin attributes to him. Rashbam is arguing here that the phrase "from the Tent of Meeting" must modify "called," not "spoke." The other two prooftexts that Rashbam cites, Exodus 19:3 and 3:4, are examples of an adverbial phrase showing where the place was from which God *called* to Moses. The verse in Numbers does not prove that same point; in that example, the phrase "from above the cover" explains where it was that God *spoke* to Moses. (This difficulty was recognized by Ashkenazi in *Qeren Shemuel*, here.)

My own preferred conjectural emendation would be: וישמע את הקול מדבר באהל שמע את הקול, or perhaps: ושמע את הקול מדבר באהל שמע את הקול. The text would then be translated: "When he heard the Voice speaking, he was in the Tent." In other words, Rashbam is saying that God called out to Moses from within the Tent to invite Moses in. Moses came in and then God spoke to him. At that point, Moses was located in the Tent.

Yet another conjectural emendation is offered by Berzinsky. His reading involves much changing of the words and the word order, but ultimately it arrives at the same suggestion: that Rashbam explains that God called to Moses to come into the tent, then Moses came in, and then God spoke to him. He suggests reading Rashbam's text as:

"ויקרא אל משה" . . . כמו ויקרא אליו ה' מן ההר לאמר ויקרא אליו א-להים מתוך הסנה. "וידבר ה' אליו" כמו וישמע את הקול מדבר אליו מעל הכפרת.

THE LORD CALLED OUT TO MOSES: . . . just like the verse, "The LORD called to him from the mountain, saying . . ." (Ex. 19:3) or the verse "God called to him from within the bush" (Ex. 3:4). THE LORD SPOKE TO HIM: as in the verse, "he would hear the Voice speaking to him from above the cover" (Num. 7:89).

[8]Again Rashbam cites a verse where an adverbial phrase, "from within the bush," describes where God called out from.

[9]In a lost section of Rashbam's Torah commentary. Rashbam makes this same point a number of other times in his Torah commentary: ad Gen. 32:5, ad Ex. 1:22 and ad Lev. 11:1, and see note 49 on that last passage.

[10]In fact, there is no verse like that in the Bible. Presumably a mental lapse or a copyist's error led to this misquotation. The text perhaps should read, "Speak to Aaron and say to him" (Num. 8:2).

[11]In other words, the verse means " . . . the LORD spoke to Moses . . . saying." Rashbam's repetitive language, וידבר למשה לאמר למשה, is meant to make his opposition to Rashi's reading (following Sifra) perfectly clear.

In general Rashbam objects to the common rabbinic explanation that the word לאמר means that the person being spoken to was asked to pass the message on to someone else. He is also taking issue with the specific interpretation of Rashi here (following Sifra) that the word לאמר in this verse means that Moses is to deliver the message to someone else. (Rashi writes: לאמר - צא ואמור להם.) Rashbam chooses to make his exegetical point twice in his commentary to Leviticus, here and ad 11:1, presumably because Rashi offered the midrashic interpretation of לאמר twice in his commentary to Leviticus, at those two precise points.

1:2 כי יקריב WHEN [ANY OF YOU] OFFERS [AN OFFERING]: When someone offers a sacrifice voluntarily, not a sacrifice which is required [to atone] for a sin.[12]

1:3 אם עולה IF [HIS OFFERING IS] A BURNT-OFFERING: I.e. he took the obligation upon himself using the word ["עולה—burnt-offering"].[13] Below (3:1), the text explains [the other possibility,] "if his sacrifice is a sacrifice of well-being (שלמים)."[14]

לרצונו FOR ACCEPTANCE: If someone "offers a male without blemish" and [brings it] "to the entrance of the Tent of Meeting,"[15] then the offering will be "accepted" on his behalf.[16] But concerning the offering of a sickly or maimed

---

[12]So also Rashi (following Sifra). Rashbam here follows standard rabbinic exegesis. His explanation does not relate to the phrase at the end of verse 4, "that it may be acceptable on his behalf, as an expiation for him," which seems to indicate that the sacrifices described here *are* being brought as a result of some sin.

A simpler *peshaṭ*-oriented approach to our verse may be found in Nahm., who comments that this verse is an introduction to sacrifices in general, teaching us that all animal sacrifices (voluntary or obligatory) are to come from cattle or sheep.

On Rashbam's interpretation of the verb להקריב, see below, commentary on 2:12, s.v. תקריבו, and note 49 there.

[13]Rashbam again follows standard rabbinic exegesis in saying that a burnt-offering (עולה) is generally offered not because of a specific obligation, but because a person said "הרי עלי עולה—I take upon myself the obligation of bringing a burnt-offering."

Halakhah also recognizes the idea of an עולת חובה—an obligatory burnt-offering. See e.g. *Beṣah* 20a.

[14]Rashbam may be explaining that, after vs. 2, which (following his understanding) introduces the concept of voluntary animal sacrifices, the two major sub-categories—עולה and שלמים—follow, the first one here and the second one at the beginning of chapter 3.

[15]In other words, if he fulfils all the conditions stipulated previously in the verse.

[16]Rashbam offers a non-standard interpretation of the word לרצונו. Generally in the halakhic literature this word is seen as a further stipulation about the proper offering of a sacrifice. See e.g. *'Arakhin* 5:6. According to this explanation, offering a sacrifice properly requires, among other things, offering it לרצונו, i.e. out of the free will of the person offering the sacrifice. Rashi also explains the word along these lines here, s.v. יקריב אותו.

Interestingly, in his Talmud commentary, Rashbam uses the rabbinic understanding of לרצונו. See e.g. ad BB 48a, s.v. יקריב. However, here in his Torah commentary he offers the interpretation preferred by most moderns—that לרצונו describes the *result* of bringing a proper sacrifice, not a further *stipulation* about how to bring a proper sacrifice. See e.g. NJPSC: "The sacrifice counts in his favor; it is accredited to him." Rashbam is not the first Jewish exegete to explain the word this way; see Onq.: לרעוא ליה. So also JBS and Luzzatto.

I disagree with N. Leibowitz's contention (*'Iyyunim*, p. 33), based on Rashi's comments on other passages, that Rashi also accepts the understanding of לרצונו found here in Rashbam. I also differ with her when she labels this approach "דעת רוב המפרשים—the opinion of the majority of the [traditional] commentators."

animal, it is written (Mal. 1:8), "Will he accept you (הירצך)? Will he show you favor?" So also[17] (Mal. 1:10) "I will accept (ארצה) no offering from your hands."

1:5 והקריבו [AARON'S SONS] SHALL OFFER [THE BLOOD]: [This refers to] "receiving the blood" (קבלת הדם) and "bringing" it (הולכתו) to the altar, in order to dash it against the altar.[18] My teachers[19] also explained it this way.

אשר פתח אהל מועד [THE ALTAR] WHICH IS AT THE ENTRANCE OF THE TENT OF MEETING: Not the silver altar, which is inside the Tent of Meeting.[20]

1:8 הפדר: means "the fat."[21]

See also Rashbam's comment to 19:5, below, and note 6 there.

[17]I.e. another example of the use of the verb ר-צ-ה to refer to the acceptance of a sacrifice.

[18]In other words, although *halakhah* says that the slaughtering of the sacrificial animal may be done by any Jew, whether a *kohen* or not, all of the subsequent steps involved in the sacrifice, beginning with the receiving of the blood, must be performed by a *kohen*.

Rashbam offers here another interpretation that follows the standard understanding in rabbinic literature and is not the simplest reading of the text. The verse does say explicitly that the sons of Aaron would be the ones who would "bring the blood close (והקריבו) to the altar." To that extent, it is correct to say that the text really does teach us that הולכה—bringing the blood to the altar—must be done by a *kohen*. But the conclusion that קבלה—the receiving of the blood—must also be performed by a *kohen* is based on midrash, not on *peshaṭ*. See Rashi s.v. והקריבו, following Zev. 4a and Sifra. On Rashbam's interpretation of the verb להקריב, see note 49 on 2:12 below.

[19]Rosin suggests emending רבותי to רבותי' (= רבותינו). In that case, the translation would read: "The rabbis also explained it this way." Either way the text makes sense, as this interpretation is found both in Rashi's commentary (= רבותי) and in classical rabbinic literature (= רבותינו). See note 18.

[20]Here Rashbam chooses to take the more *peshaṭ*-like approach. The text specifies that the altar is "at the entrance of the Tent of Meeting." This is because there are two altars associated with the Tabernacle, the "outer altar" described in Exodus 27:1f., and the "inner altar" described in Exodus 30:1f. The phrase, "at the entrance of the Tent of Meeting," tells us that it is the former that is described here. So also iE.

Rashbam's interpretation opposes that of Rashi, who follows the midrashic tradition of Sifra, which claims that the phrase "at the entrance of the Tent of Meeting" teaches us that the sacrifice can be offered only when the Tent of the Meeting is fully assembled; if it has been disassembled, then the sacrifice may not proceed. See JBS who offers both alternatives.

[21]The word פדר appears only three times in the Bible (here, 1:12 and 8:20) and its meaning is uncertain. Rashbam, like iE and Onq., says simply that פדר is a synonym for חלב, "fat." In rabbinic literature, פדר is commonly used that way. See for example the phrase: "איברין ופדרין—[sacrificial] limbs and fats" (Zev. 111a). Other commentators, both medieval and modern (e.g. Nahm. and NJPSC), suggest that פדר is the name of one specific type of fat, e.g.

1:9 וכרעיו: means "its legs."[22]

1:15 ומלק PINCH OFF [ITS HEAD]: The rabbis explained how this was done.[23]

Since the text says "ומלק את ראשו—he should *m-l-q* its head," and not "ומלק אותו—he should *m-l-q* it" (in the manner that "ושחט אותו—he should slaughter it" is written), Dunash explained that that constitutes proof for the correctness of the interpretation [of this verb] offered by the rabbis, who [after all] were witnesses to the service in the Temple.[24] [They explained] that the priest,

---

fat on the liver on or some other internal organ. Still others suggest that פדר is a name for the body of the animal or for many of its internal organs (see Krinski's *Yahel 'or*, note 51).

[22]The word כרעים is problematic. In 11:21, in a description of edible insects, the word (in the phrase כרעיים מעל לרגליו) is not synonymous with "legs." Still, in descriptions of mammals, as in our verse, many commentators, like Rashbam, insist that כרעים does mean "legs." (See e.g. Qimḥi *Shorashim*, s.v. כרע.) Others suggest that כרעים must mean the lower part of the leg (or the lower part of the front legs only), or the joint of the leg. For sources and arguments, see Wessely in the *Be'ur*, here, Mendelssohn in the *Be'ur* to Ex. 29:17, and Hoffmann, here. From a survey of the traditional sources, it seems that Rashbam has adopted the more common position.

[23]See e.g. Hul. 21a.

[24]Rashbam argues for the correctness of the standard rabbinic understanding of this phrase on the basis of tradition and on the basis of close reading. The nature of the interpretation against which he and Dunash are polemicizing is not clear. Dunash argues in his *Teshuvot* (p. 75) that Menaḥem follows the alleged position of Anan the Karaite, that the verb *m-l-q* is essentially synonymous with *sh-ḥ-ṭ;* it refers to slaughtering the bird, with a knife, rather than with the priest's fingernail. It is doubtful, as Rabbenu Tam notes in his *Hakhra'ot* there, that Menaḥem is guilty of this heresy. In any case, both the argument from tradition and the argument from close reading offered by Rashbam originate in Dunash.

The argument from tradition is that the early rabbis were eyewitnesses to the Temple service. As such, their interpretation must be considered authoritative. See similarly Hoffmann, on this verse: "For us it suffices to note that the rabbis of the Mishnah, some of whom actually lived during the days of the Second Temple, unanimously interpret the word ומלק in the manner that we did above."

The argument from close reading—that the verse reads "ומלק את ראשו—he should *m-l-q* its head," and not "ומלק אותו—he should *m-l-q* it"—appears in greater detail in Dunash, *ibid.*:

> They [=the rabbis] said that מליקה is not the same as slaughtering (שחיטה); it involves cutting through the backbone and the shoulder bone by hand, not with a knife. The verse demonstrates that מליקה is not like slaughtering as it says, "ומלק את ראשו—he should *m-l-q* its head," and not "ומלק אותו—he should *m-l-q* it" . . .. Perhaps you might say: "Slaughtering is done at the neck. The neck is close to the head. [So there is nothing strange about the phrase 'he should *m-l-q* its head' even if the reference is to slaughtering with a knife.]" In that case, I would answer: "Even if slaughtering were done on the head itself, that answer would be worthless to you. Because even if the verb 'slaughter' referred to an action focused on the head, still the object of the verb is always the dead body [not the head]. Referring to slaughtering, it always says: 'he shall slaughter it' (e.g. Lev. 1:11) . . . or 'he shall slaughter the bull' (Lev. 1:5) or 'he shall slaughter the living bird' (ושחט את הצפור החיה; a misquotation of Lev. 14:5)."

with his fingernail, would cut through the backbone and the shoulder bone,[25] from the back, down to the [area of the] neck. Then he would continue downwards to the *simanim*[26] and would cut them.[27]

ונמצה [ITS BLOOD] SHALL BE DRAINED OUT: When speaking of a thin [liquid],[28] it is appropriate to use this verb. Similarly (Is. 51:17), "You have drained (מצית) the bowl, the cup of reeling" and (Ps. 75:9) "draining (ימצו) it to the dregs."[29]

1:16 מראתו ITS CROP: [The word מראתו should be understood] similarly to "and make a spectacle (ראי) of you" (Nah. 3:6) or "Ah, sullied (מוראה) and polluted" (Zeph. 3:1).[30] They all are connected to the idea of "filth." The Targum reads "זפקיה (its crop)," which is like feces or manure.[31]

Accordingly we say that if מליקה were a form of slaughtering, the text would not say "he should *m-l-q* its head," but rather "he should *m-l-q* it."

[25] מפרקת. Rashi ad Zev. 65b, s.v. מפרקת, explains that the word means "shoulder bone" (עצם הצואר).

[26]The *simanim* are the vital signs of the animal, i.e. the windpipe and the gullet. Both had to be severed as part of the *meliqah* process.

[27]Much of Rashbam's language in the detailed description of *meliqah* is the same as that of Rashi, following classical rabbinic texts (e.g. Hul. 21a).

[28]The phrase Rashbam uses here, בדבר רך, is unusual in this context. I have translated it following the usage of the word in Mishnah *Nedarim* 6:1 where רך appears as an antonym of עבה—thick, when describing different kinds of cooked dishes.

It is possible that Rashbam's comment is meant to explain why the only uses of this verb in the Torah are in contexts of the blood of bird sacrifices (here and ad Lev. 5:9), never in reference to the thicker blood of mammal sacrifices.

[29]Rashbam's interpretation opposes that of Rashi who connects the word ונמצה to מיץ (in Prov. 30:33) and מץ (in Is. 16:4). Those words (as Wessely points out in the *Be'ur* here) are from the hollow root *m-y-ṣ* or *m-v-ṣ*, while Rashbam, and so also iE, argue that our verb should be connected to the root *m-ṣ-h*. The issue is mostly one of grammar; the roots, to be sure, are very similar in meaning, although there might be a slight difference between them. BDB defines *m-y-ṣ* as "to squeeze or press," and *m-ṣ-h* as "to drain."

[30]Rashi, both in his commentary to Nah. and in his commentary to Zeph., connects those verses to ours. iE here connects our verse to the one in Zeph.

[31]Rashbam does not explain distinctly what he sees as the meaning of the Hebrew word מראתו, a *hapax legomenon*. He does say that the word is related to the idea of "filth," and that the Targum translates the word as זפקיה. Most likely, Rashbam believes that the word means "crop." (As defined by NJPSC, the crop is "a pocket in the bird's throat where food was detained during digestion."). If Rashbam thinks this is the meaning, then he is citing the Targum because he agrees with it and because he believes that the Aramaic word זפקיה means "crop."

Rashi's comment to this verse is just as hard to understand and the precise text of Rashi's commentary is hard to establish. The reading quoted by Nahm. begins: מראתו—מקום הרעי זה הזפק ("the word מראתו means the place of the feces, the זפק"). The problems with this reading are many, but the most obvious one is that the crop does not contain feces.

בנוצתה: means that the נוצה should also be removed together with the crop.[32]

2:1 מנחה *MINḤAH*: I already explained in [my commentary to] Genesis that a *minḥah* is a present.[33] The word comes from [the root *n-ḥ-h* ("to lead" or "to bring"),] the same root as "Go, lead (נחה) the people" (Ex. 32:34).[34]

Rashbam, too, says at the end of his comment that זפקיה is כרעי, i.e. "*like* feces," but perhaps all that he means by that is that it is a filthy part of the animal ("*like* feces"), which for that reason is discarded and not sacrificed.

Wessely, in the *Be'ur* here, reads Rashbam's comment as concluding with the words "זפקיה והוא רעי חבל". This small change of one letter means that Rashbam would be saying (and this is how Wessely understands him) that the word מראתו here and the related words that he identifies in Zeph. and Nah. all refer to excrement, not to a place where excrement or filth collects. Wessely then proceeds to argue against such an understanding.

[32]Again Rashbam's comment fails to clarify the difficult word, נוצה, here. Some interpret it as "the feather attached to the crop"; some interpret it as "all the feathers of the bird"; yet others interpret it to mean "the contents of the crop." (For sources, see the commentaries of Hoffmann and Milgrom, here.) Rashbam's comment does not shed any light on that question; he points out only that the preposition *be* at the beginning of the word בנוצתה should be understood as meaning "together with." That is the way that Rashi understood the preposition and it is also the understanding that underlies all three opinions about this phrase in Zev. 65a.

See, on the other hand, Milgrom (p.171) who offers an entirely new anatomical understanding of this phrase which allows him to conclude: "thus the preposition *be* finds its most natural, and, indeed, most obvious resolution: it is the *bet* of means."

[33]Rashbam's comment here is not controversial; in numerous biblical passages it is clear that a מנחה is a present of any sort. See e.g. Gen. 32:18. From there it came to be applied to sacrifices, and specifically to grain sacrifices. See note 34.

[34]Rashbam refers to a lost section of his Torah commentary, presumably to a comment ad Genesis 4:3. In his commentary to Gen. 32:18 he also refers to that same passage. Rashbam gives a detailed explanation of the word מנחה in his grammar work, *Dayyaqut* (Merdler's edition, pp. 59–60), where he uses our verse to prove his interpretation.

His explanation begins with a grammatical argument. He rejects the possibility that מנחה has a hollow root (*n-v-ḥ*), an explanation that is common in Jewish sources. (See e.g. Nahm. ad Ex. 12:6, and Wessely in the *Be'ur* here.) Rashbam argues that if the root were hollow, there would not be a *sheva* under the *nun*. He claims that the *sheva* makes sense according to his explanation that the root is *n-ḥ-h*; the noun form would then follow the pattern of many final-*heh* verbs. (From *b-n-h*, the noun is *mivneh*; from *q-v-h*, *miqveh*.) A similar explanation is offered by Rashbam's younger contemporary, Joseph Qimḥi, in *Sefer zikkaron*, p. 13 (cited by Ben Yehudah, p. 3094, note 2; see also Talmage, *Apples of Gold*, pp. 373–374). Rashbam then proceeds to a contextual argument:

> [מנחה] . . . should be understood as having the same meaning as "Go, lead (נחה) the people" (Ex. 32:34). Because it is brought before someone of high rank it is called a מנחה, something which is brought. Generally the verb "to bring (הבאה)" is used with the word מנחה. . . . The proof of my interpretation can be found in the verse "When one offers a *minḥah* offering to the LORD, the offering shall be of choice flour . . ." (Lev. 2:1). Until this point [i.e. throughout Lev. 1] the text described animal sacrifices, which a person could not carry by hand. Rather, we make the animals walk in front; for that reason they are called an offering (קרבן), but they are not called a *minḥah*. But this [offering, the one in 2:1,] is [a *minḥah*, i.e. it is] described as

2:2 מלא קמצו A HANDFUL: In tractate *Yoma'*,[35] the rabbis explained that the priest scoops out with his three middle fingers.[36]

אזכרתה ITS REMEMBRANCE: It is common to use [words with] the root *z-k-r*—to remember, when speaking of [the burning of] frankincense, because of the fragrance that ascends [from the burning].[37] Thus it is written, "who offer (מזכיר) frankincense" (Is. 66:3),[38] and "[you shall place pure frankincense,] which shall be a remembrance (לאזכרה) for the bread" (Lev. 24:7).

> being offered by hand. And [then the text elaborates,] what should he bring [by hand]? "The offering shall be of choice flour," but not of fruit, as the text continues to explain, "No leaven or honey . . ." (Lev. 2:11).

In other words, the word *minḥah* is most appropriately applied to a meal offering, because the noun implies that it is something that might be carried.

iE must have read or heard of this explanation, as he criticizes it roundly, arguing that Gen. 4:3 and 32:21, passages where the word *minḥah* refers to gifts or sacrifices of animals, disprove Rashbam's explanation. (See iE's *Shiṭṭah 'aḥeret* on Genesis [p. 152 in Weiser's edition].)

At least one modern commentator, Baruch Levine (in NJPSC here) claims that the root of *minḥah* is "probably" *n-ḥ-h*, as Rashbam would have it. Other moderns (e.g. BDB) prefer the explanation offered by ibn Janaḥ and David Qimḥi (both cited by Ben-Yehudah, *ibid.*) that the root of *minḥah* is *m-n-ḥ*, an otherwise uninstantiated root.

[35] 47a.

[36] Again Rashbam gives the standard rabbinic explanation, offered here also by Rashi. iE, who also defers here to the rabbinic definition of a "handful," uses this opportunity to reassert his loyalty to rabbinic explanations.

As Wessely and Milgrom both note, this is not the simple meaning of the word. There is even an opinion in the Talmud (Men. 11a) that the fistful described here is made with all of the priest's fingers, or as the Talmud puts it, "כדקמצי אינשי—the way people [standardly] make a fist." See also Rashi, there, and Maimonides, *Ma'ase ha-qorbanot* 13:13.

[37] Rashbam is explaining why the text uses this unusual word, אזכרה, when speaking specifically of the part of the grain offerings that is burned on the altar. He explains that since frankincense is used with these offerings, the text uses a verb that is appropriate for describing sweet smelling items. Rashbam's explanation appears to be original, and is opposed to that of Rashi (following Sifra) that the אזכרה is so called because it leads to the offerer being "remembered" for good. Rashi's interpretation does not explain why this term is used specifically for grain offerings, and never for the parts of animal offerings that are burnt on the altar, which presumably are also offered in order for the offerer to be "remembered" for good. In his commentary to Leviticus, it seems that iE knows of Rashbam's interpretation (or some interpretation like it) but prefers that of Rashi. However, in his commentary to Hos. 14:8 he appears to be more in agreement with Rashbam, explaining that the word זכרו there, like אזכרתה here, refers to smell.

Both Wessely and Luzzatto suggest, as Rashbam does, that the root *z-k-r* is apt for discussing the sense of smell.

[38] Rashi in Isaiah, there, connects that phrase to our verse in Lev. 2, and to the verse that Rashbam cites from Lev. 24. See also the note to Is. 66:3 in the NJPS Bible.

In tractate *Menaḥot* there are detailed explanations of the different types of *minḥah* offerings that are described in this text[39]—the number of loaves for each,[40] the amount of frankincense[41] and the amount of oil[42] for each, and the difference between a מחבת and a מרחשת. A מרחשת is a deep [frying] utensil, [so called because] its contents "move around" (רוחשין)[43] [when fried]; a מחבת is [a frying utensil that is] not deep.[44]

All [of the loaves of the *minḥah* offerings] are unleavened, as it is written in [the Torah portion,] *Ṣav 'et 'aharon.*[45]

2:11 וכל דבש NO HONEY: "Honey" means fruit of the trees. Dates are referred to as honey.[46]

---

[39]There are five separate *minḥah* offerings that are described in Leviticus 2: vss. 1–3, 4, 5–6, 7–10 and 14–16. In the middle there are three verses (11–13) that describe general rules of all *minḥah* offerings.

[40]Mishnah *Menaḥot* 6:5 and BT *Menaḥot* 76a.

[41]Mishnah *Menaḥot* 13:3 and BT *Menaḥot* 106b.

[42]Mishnah *Menaḥot* 9:3 and BT *Menaḥot* 106b.

[43]Following the understanding of רוחשין in Rashi ad Zev. 9b, s.v. מחבת, or in Qimḥi's *Shorashim*, s.v. *r-ḥ-sh.* Alternatively one could translate the last phrase in Rashbam, "because its contents 'whisper' when fried." In his commentary ad vs. 7, iE understands רוחשין in that way. The Hebrew word רוחשין could sustain either meaning—noise or movement—and one might reasonably say that deep frying pans make more noise and have more movement than shallower ones. The "movement" explanation may be found in Sifra and in Men. 5:8 and BT Men. 63a. It is also quoted here by Rashi ad vs. 7. It is only one of the rabbinic explanations of the difference between these two frying utensils.

[44] Rashbam, unlike Rashi, does not go into any details concerning the laws of the *minḥah* offerings. As he mentioned in his introduction to Leviticus, when dealing with the technicalities of the sacrifices, "scholars should study the interpretations of my grandfather [Rashi]." Here Rashbam also refers his readers to the primary sources in classical rabbinic literature. See similarly Rashbam's commentary below to 7:12, and note 28 there.

After intimating that he will not explain any details, it appears that he cannot resist (or perhaps some later copyist cannot resist?) telling us one detail about the difference between the two types of frying pans, perhaps because the explanation seems well grounded in the meaning of the words.

[45]Lev. 6:7–10: "These are the rules of the *minḥah* offering . . . it shall not be baked with leaven." Rosin notes the difficulty in the fact that Rashbam refers his readers to chapter 6 for a rule that is unambiguously explicit right here in chapter 2, verse 11: "No *minḥah* offering that you offer to the LORD shall be made with leaven." He suggests that Rashbam might have preferred the verse in chapter 6 as it is the prooftext cited by the Talmud (Men. 53a) to prove that all *minḥah* offerings have to be unleavened.

[46]Rashbam follows the standard halakhic understanding, found in Rashi here, that when this verse says that "honey" may not be sacrificed to God, it means that no fruits shall be offered as sacrifices. Most moderns would concur that here and in almost all other biblical passages the word "honey" means the extracted sweetness of fruits. As Milgrom writes (p. 189), that

2:12 קרבן ראשית [YOU MAY BRING THEM] AS AN OFFERING OF FIRST [FRUITS]: [This refers to] the two loaves that are offered on *Shavuot*, which are called "a new *minḥah*" (Lev. 23:16), and [to] the first fruit offering [*bikkurim*] that is described in [the Torah portion,] *Ki tavo'* (Deut. 26:2f.).[47]

תקריבו אותם לה' YOU SHOULD BRING THEM TO THE LORD AS AN OFFERING: You should bring them to the courtyard [of the Tabernacle/Temple] for them to be "lifted up,"[48] but not for them to be sacrificed on the altar.[49]

---

view "is supported on scriptural and philological grounds . . . [and] is supported by comparative philology."

It is possible that Rashbam is taking issue with Rashi here, who writes that the word דבש may refer to *all* fruit extracts. In other passages (e.g. Rashi ad Ex. 13:5, s.v. זבת) Rashi says that דבש refers to the extracted sweetness of dates and figs. Rashbam consistently says (see his commentary ad Deut. 8:9 and 32:13) that דבש refers specifically to dates. In that, he follows the standard rabbinic interpretation, particularly of the list of the "seven species" in Deut. 8:8, where the rabbis see דבש as a specific reference to dates. See e.g. Ber. 41b, and Rashi ad Ex. 34:26, s.v. ראשית.

[47]The previous verse outlawed *minḥah* sacrifices of leaven and of "honey." This verse gives one exception in each category. Leaven is brought as an offering on *Shavuot*, in the form of two loaves, and those loaves are specifically referred to as a "new *minḥah*" (in Lev. 23:16). "Honey" (see note 46) is also brought to the Temple as a sacrifice in the form of a first-fruit (*bikkurim*) offering.

Rashbam's comment here is virtually identical to that of Rashi, following Men. 58a. Rashbam adds to Rashi's comment that the first exception, "the two (leavened) loaves," are specifically referred to in the text as a "new *minḥah*"; accordingly it makes sense for them to be mentioned here after vs. 11, which said that a *minḥah* must *not* be made of leaven. To be sure, *bikkurim*, the first fruit offering, the second exception listed here, is never referred to as a *minḥah* offering. But it is called the offering of "first" fruits (ראשית; e.g. in Ex. 23:19), a phrase which resonates with the words "קרבן ראשית" in our verse.

In his reworking of Rashi's comment, Rashbam also removes a reference to the "honey" of "figs and dates." See note 46.

[48]Or perhaps "waved." See note 13 on pp. 377–78 of my Exodus volume.

The "lifting up" of the two loaves is explicit in the biblical text; see Lev. 23:20. The "lifting up" of the *bikkurim* is found in Mishnah Bik. 3:6. See also Men. 61b. See a full discussion in Tos. Suk. 47b, s.v. *ha- bikkurim*. See also the end of Nahm.'s comment ad Num. 5:9.

[49]In other words, even these two exceptions—sacrifices of leaven and fruit—are brought to the Temple only to be "lifted up"; they are not placed on the altar.

This is the third time in his Leviticus commentary that Rashbam has commented on a form of the Hebrew verb להקריב. The most common meaning of להקריב is "to perform a sacrifice." But all of Rashbam's comments show that he believes that it can mean other things too: "to volunteer to give a sacrifice" (1:2), "to bring something towards the altar, before it is actually placed on the altar" (1:5), or "to bring something to the Temple/Tabernacle" (here). See also commentary below ad 7:16, s.v. ביום הקריבו.

2:14 ואם תקריב IF YOU OFFER: I.e. when[50] you offer the *minḥah* of the *'omer*.[51]

גרש GRIST: [גרס means that it is to be crushed,] as in the phrase (Lam. 3:16), "He crushed (ויגרש)[52] my teeth on gravel." It was ground up in gristgrinders' (גרוסות) mills.[53]

3:1 שלמים: Because this sacrifice is not called an *'olah*,[54] it is not burned *in toto*. Rather it is called שלמים, which means payment (תשלומים), i.e. a person who made a vow and has to fulfill (לשלם) his vow.[55] The following shall therefore be the rule for that sacrifice.

---

[50]In other words, one should not interpret the word ואם as implying that this sacrifice is optional. It is not. So also Rashi, following Sifra. See note 51.

[51]In other words, the *minḥah* sacrifice described here is the same *minḥah* sacrifice mentioned in Lev. 23:16, "You shall offer a new *minḥah* to the LORD." So also Rashi, following Sifra and Men. 84a.

As Milgrom describes at some length, Karaite exegesis insisted that the sacrifice described here could *not* be the compulsory communal sacrifice of Lev. 23:16; it is rather an optional (hence "ואם—if") offering that the individual Israelite farmer might choose to bring. It appears that both iE and Luzzatto also offer that heterodox reading. See Milgrom's argument in favor of the rabbanite position of Rashi and Rashbam.

[52]Rashbam quotes the word in Lamentations as ויגרש, instead of MT's ויגרס. See the discussion in Esh, p. 92.

[53]So also Rashi, with the same biblical and mishnaic prooftexts.

The phrase בריחיים של גרוסות is part of the Mishnah's description (Men. 10:4) of how the *minḥah* of the *'omer* was to be prepared.

[54]Rosin adds a number of words to the text of Rashbam's comment here, unnecessarily, in my opinion. According to Rosin's suggested text, the beginning of Rashbam's comment would read as follows:

> [IF HIS SACRIFICE IS A שלמים OFFERING: I.e. if he said, "I take upon myself the obligation to bring] a שלמים offering," then—since [he did] not [use] the language of *'olah* and it is not burned *in toto*, but rather [he used] the language of שלמים, which implies the idea of payment (תשלומים), i.e. "a person who made a vow and has to fulfil (לשלם) his vow"—the following shall be the rule for that sacrifice.

Rosin's emendation would make Rashbam's comment here parallel to his comments to 1:3, 7:12 and 7:16. However, Rashbam's comment as we have it is understandable on its own.

[55]Rashbam's explanation of the term שלמים (here and ad 7:16) appears to be original. Milgrom (pp. 220–221), who offers seven possible explanations of this term, points out that Rashbam's explanation finds support in the parallelism of Proverbs 7:14: "I had to make a sacrifice of well-being (שלמים)/Today I fulfilled my vow." See Wessely who uses grammatical arguments (in the *Be'ur*, here and ad 7:16) against Rashbam.

Rashi, like Rashbam, offered both an ostensibly *peshaṭ*-oriented interpretation of שלמים and a midrashic one. While Rashbam in the continuation of this comment offers the same midrashic explanation as Rashi, Rashbam proposes his own, independent *peshaṭ* interpretation

The rabbis, [however,] connected the word שלמים to the idea of שלום (peace or good-will). [This sacrifice leads to good-will] because everyone gets a share of it: the *'emurin*[56] [are offered on the altar] to God, the chest and the thigh are given to the priests and the [rest of] the meat is eaten by the owners of the animal.[57]

3:4 היותרת THE PROTUBERANCE [ON THE LIVER]: That which extends (שמייתר) and grows on the liver.[58]

3:9 לעומת העצה [THE FAT] CLOSE TO THE עצה: I.e. the kidneys.[59] In

---

of שלמים. Rashi had suggested that שלמים means a sacrifice that brings peace to the world. That explanation may be found in a number of midrashic sources; see e.g. Tanh. *Toledot* 1.

[56]I.e. those parts of a sacrifice that are not to be eaten but are burnt on the altar. In this case, the reference is to the various fats and body parts listed in vss. 3–4.

[57]This rabbinic explanation may be found in Sifra and in a number of other midrashic sources. It was so well known in twelfth-century Northern France that it appears even in the Leviticus commentaries attributed to Hugh and Andrew of St. Victor, *ad loc*. This comment is found in Andrew's commentary on page 163 of the *Corpus Christianorum*, vol. 53. I will cite all quotations from Andrew's commentary from that collection.

The Leviticus commentaries attributed to Hugh and Andrew in PL are basically identical. G. Dahan has suggested (*Les intellectuels chrétiens et les juifs au moyen age*, p. 283) that the author of the commentary was really Andrew, not Hugh. Since editors could not find Hugh's commentary, they published Andrew's in its place. For simplicity's sake, I will adopt Dahan's thesis and when the same explanation is found both in the commentary attributed to Hugh and in the commentary attributed to Andrew, I will cite it simply as Andrew's.

[58]Lengthy discussions about the history of interpretation of this phrase may be found in Hoffmann's commentary here, and in Julius Preuss' *Biblical and Talmudic Medicine*, translated by Fred Rosner, pp. 96–98. There are two traditions of interpretation of this word. The most common explanation, found both in traditional rabbinic and in modern critical sources, is that the יותרת is the caudate lobe (*lobus caudatus*), "a fingerlike projection from the liver, close to the right kidney" (Milgrom). Others identify it with some membrane or "separating wall" on or near the liver, either the animal's reticulum or its diaphragm. It seems that Rashi subscribes to the latter theory. (See his commentary here, and ad Ex. 29:13 and ad Ber. 44b, s.v. יותרת הכבד.) Possibly Rashi relates the word יותרת to the meaning of "something stretched out," one of the meanings of the Hebrew root *y-t-r*.

It is hard to say what Rashbam thinks the meaning of יותרת is. His etymological explanation is that יותרת is related to the other meaning of the root, *y-t-r*, to be additional or extra. Hoffmann suggests hesitatingly that Rashbam would interpret the יותרת על הכבד as the caudate lobe.

[59]Almost all commentators, ancient and modern, understand עצה as meaning the "spine," (Onq.: שדרתא) or perhaps the bottom of the spine (ibn Janaḥ, *Shorashim*; Qimḥi, *Shorashim*; Hoffmann and many others). Practically speaking, if the phrase means "close to the bottom of the spine," then it also means close to the kidneys. But Rashbam's dubious identification of the word עצה as *meaning* kidneys appears to originate with Rashi, who got it from the

Sheḥiṭat ḥullin [60] the rabbis explained how it [= the fat close to the עצה] was to be removed.

3:17 בכל מושבותיכם כל חלב וכל דם לא תאכלו IN ALL YOUR SETTLEMENTS YOU MUST NOT EAT ANY FAT OR ANY BLOOD: I.e. even in your settlements [away from the Temple] where your meat is eaten as *ḥullin* [= non-sacrificial meat] as there are no sacrifices there and the blood and fat are not offered upon the altar.[61]

4:2 אשר לא תעשינה [IN REGARD TO ANY OF THE LORD'S COMMANDMENTS] ABOUT THINGS NOT TO BE DONE: The rabbis explained in *Keritot*[62] and *Horayot*[63] that this verse refers to sins of commission that incur the penalty of *karet*,[64] but not to [refraining from] circumcision or offering the paschal sacrifice, which are sins of omission.[65]

---

midrashic etymology in Hul. 11a. Since the kidneys are the source of "counsel—עצה," they are referred to as העצה. See Rashi there, s.v. מקום.

[60] *Sheḥiṭat ḥullin* is the name that Rashbam and many medieval rabbis used for the Talmudic tractate that is generally referred to now as *Ḥullin*. Rashbam may be referring his readers to the discussion in Hul. 11a. A more detailed description of the removal of that fat may be found in Tos. Hul. 9:13.

[61] Rashi's comment to this verse simply directs the reader to the Sifra, which explains that the rules of not consuming fat and blood apply "in all your settlements," meaning both inside and outside of Israel, whether or not the Temple is standing.

Rashbam does not take issue with that approach but explains the context a little more. Since it might have been supposed that the consumption of blood and fat was outlawed only because those sections are to be burnt on the altar, one might have then concluded that when eating *ḥullin* [= non-sacrificial meat] the prohibition would not be in force. (See such arguments in iE ad 7:20.) That is why the Torah had to tell us that these laws apply "in all your settlements." Rashbam appears to be the first to give this explanation. It is found later in Malbim, Wessely and many others. See also Rashbam's commentary below ad 7:25 and 7:26, and notes 37 and 38 there.

[62] Ker. 3a and 7a.

[63] I am unable to find any reference in *Horayot* to the fact that a *ḥaṭṭat* offering would not be offered in a case of someone who fails to circumcise himself or fails to bring a paschal sacrifice. The idea is found in Mak. 13b and in the sources listed in note 62.

[64] Being "cut off" from the people. See e.g. Ex. 12:15.

[65] The punishment of *karet* generally applies to sins of commission. The only two sins of omission that warrant the punishment of *karet* are refraining from circumcising yourself and refraining from offering a paschal sacrifice. Rashbam is saying that the *ḥaṭṭat* offering described in the following verses is offered only by someone who accidentally *committed* a sin which would have received the *karet* penalty had it been done on purpose.

This is the standard rabbinic explanation. See similarly Rashi here. Rashbam adds only that the phrase, "commandments about things *not to be done*," constitutes the exegetical

מאחת מהנה [WHO SINS BY DOING] ONE (מאחת) OF THEM: The rabbis explained[66] that [the apparently unnecessary letter *mem*, on the word מאחת, is the partitive *mem*,[67] meaning that even if the sinner did] only part of one of those sins, for example writing only the letters שם, part of [an attempt to write the complete word] שמעון.[68]

4:3 לאשמת העם [IF THE ANOINTED PRIEST SINS] TO THE DETRIMENT OF THE PEOPLE: In *Horayot*,[69] the rabbis explained that [the phrase, "to the detriment of the people," teaches that some of] the rules regarding the sinning priest are equivalent to the rules regarding sins of the people. However, following the plain meaning of Scripture, the verse means: Since it says concerning the priests [in general] that they are the ones who "will teach Your laws to Jacob, and Your Torah to Israel" (Deut. 33:10)—and how much more so does this apply to the High Priest, who is considered by the public to be an expert—accordingly, if that priest sins in his teaching, causing the people also to sin with him, then HE SHALL OFFER FOR THE SIN . . . .[70]

---

source for the rabbis' claim that this sacrifice would not be brought for a sin of omission. See similarly Sifra on this verse.

Moderns also often note that only sins of commission lead to a *ḥaṭat* offering. See e.g. NJPSC and Milgrom here.

[66]Sifra, Shab. 103a-b and Sanh. 62a.

[67]The textual difficulty here is a real one. The text would read more smoothly had it said ועשה אחת מהנה, instead of ועשה מאחת מהנה. Rashbam offers the standard midrashic solution. It is found here in Rashi and in many classical rabbinic sources, such as those listed in the previous note.

Rashbam's explanation, so far from the simple meaning of the text, seems out of character. For another approach to the problem, see G.-K. 119w, note 2 (cited by Milgrom), who argues that the *mem* here could mean "*any* one of those sins." And see also Rashbam's commentary below, ad 5:13, where he offers a straightforward *peshaṭ*-like explanation of the phrase מאחת מאלה, a phrase very similar to our מאחת מהנה.

[68]This specific example is given in Mishnah Shab. 12:3: Some person was accidentally writing on the Sabbath. While intending to write the word, שמעון, the offender succeeded in writing only the first two letters. The law says that even though what was accomplished was not what was planned, the sin of writing on the Sabbath took place, since a meaningful word was written. The offender is then obliged to offer a *ḥaṭṭat* offering.

[69]Hor. 7a.

[70]Rashbam's comment here follows the precise pattern of Rashi's comment to this phrase. Rashi also begins by citing the same rabbinic explanation: that the phrase לאשמת העם teaches us that we should compare the laws of the sins of the people (vs. 13f.) with the laws of the sins of the anointed priest, here. Then Rashi proceeds to offer his own interpretation which he labels *peshaṭ*: When discussing sins of High Priests, the verse teaches us, *en passant*, that when a High Priest has been sinful, the people suffer spiritually. The one who is supposed to atone for them and pray for them is found to be spiritually lacking. In other words, Rashi reads this first part of the verse as an "if-then" phrase: *If* the High Priest sins, *then* that sin

4:12 אל שפך הדשן TO THE ASH HEAP: As it is written in the Torah portion, *Ṣav 'et 'aharon*, "He shall carry the ashes outside the camp" (Lev. 6:4).[71]

4:17 את פני הפרכת IN FRONT OF THE CURTAIN: According to the plain meaning of Scripture, this means [the same as the slightly variant phrase,] "את פני פרכת הקדש—in front of the curtain of the Holy" (vs. 6), i.e. the curtain that separates the Holy from the Holy of Holies. The reason the text elaborated there [using the ostensibly redundant words] "the curtain *of the Holy*" was to teach that the sprinkling of blood [described in that verse] should be opposite the middle of that curtain on the outside, [the place on the outside of the curtain that is] opposite where the Holy Ark (ארון הקדש) would be found on the inside of the curtain.[72]

---

leads to the detriment of the people (לאשמת העם). As is often the case, even on the *peshaṭ* level Rashi finds a didactic message in the biblical words.

Rashbam characteristically tries to compete with Rashi on the *peshaṭ* level, while not objecting to the midrashic reading. Rashbam suggests that the simple meaning of the verse is that a priest sinned and that sin led לאשמת העם, i.e. to some sin committed by the people. Since priests are meant to be instructors of Torah, he argues, priests who teach improperly lead the people to sin. Accordingly, the phrase לאשמת העם should be read as a restrictive phrase. Concerning which sins of the priest are we speaking? Concerning those sins that lead לאשמת העם, to the sin of the people.

Rashbam's *peshaṭ* interpretation does seem simpler and more contextual than that of Rashi, but, as is often the case, its drawback is that it conflicts with the *halakhah*. Mishnah Hor. 2:1 makes it clear that the sacrifice would be brought even if the High Priest's sin involved only himself. Kasher, here (p. 157, note 23*) notes the halakhic difficulties involved with the explanation that Rashbam offers. Still he assembles an impressive list of exegetes, after Rashbam, who offer this heterodox interpretation (e.g. iE, Hizq. Qimḥi and Abarbanel). Andrew of St. Victor (p. 164) also explains the verse this way.

[71]So also Rashi. Since there is also a "place for ashes" (מקום הדשן) right beside the altar, according to 1:16 (referred to in the Mishnah [Zev. 6:5] as בית הדשן, as opposed to שפך הדשן of our verse), it is necessary to explain that the "ash heap" mentioned here is the one outside of the camp, the one mentioned in 6:4. See also commentary ad 6:3–4, and note 7 there.

[72]Rashbam's explanation takes issue with a didactic midrash offered by Rashi (following Zev. 41b) who understands the word הקדש adjectivally ("the holy curtain") and who explains that the curtain was referred to as "holy" above in verse 6, because at that point only one person's sin was being expiated with a sacrifice. In our verse, since the text is describing the sacrifice brought for a sin of the whole community, it is as if the curtain has lost its holiness. Rashbam says more simply that both verses refer to the same curtain, and that the stylistic variation teaches a law about the placement of blood on the curtain, and not a moral lesson.

The halakhic lesson that Rashbam derives from the word הקדש (in vs. 6) is found also in Rashi, there, following Sifra. Rashbam may be trying to ground the *midrash halakhah* more firmly in the text's language. The midrash itself simply says that from the word הקדש we learn that the sprinkling should be done "מכוון כנגד [בין] הבדים—in the direction of 'between the poles'," i.e. towards the Ark that has poles on either side. (See Ex. 25:13f.) Rashbam's language suggests that the *halakhah* may be based on the connection between the

4:22 אשר נשיא יחטא: [The words should be transposed and read נשיא אשר יחטא, A CHIEFTAIN WHO SINS,] just like the phrase (Est. 6:8) ואשר ניתן כתר מלכות בראשו. [Those words should also be transposed to] וכתר מלכות אשר ניתן בראשו, i.e. "a crown which was placed on his head."[73]

מצות ה' א-לוהיו [SINS CONCERNING . . .] THE LAWS OF THE LORD HIS GOD: [The phrase *his* God is used] to say that [this rule applies only] if he feared God, and sinned accidentally, not on purpose.[74]

---

phraseology, "the curtain of the Holy," and the common late Hebrew name of the Ark (once in the Bible, in II Chron. 35:3) "the Ark of the Holy."

Kasher (p. 189, note 116) points out that there is a dispute in the classical rabbinic sources whether all sprinklings of blood in the direction of the curtain must be to the spot opposite the Ark, or whether that rule applies only when the text specifies פרכת הקדש, the curtain *of the Holy*. Perhaps Rashbam's comment here implies that he would follow the latter approach.

[73]There is an anomaly in this verse: the word אשר is used when one might expect that the clause, "If a chieftain sins," would be introduced with the word כי or אם. Again Rashbam's comment takes issue with the didactic midrashic solution offered by Rashi here (following Hor. 10b), which connects the word אשר to the word אשרי, and argues homiletically that the Jewish people are truly "happy" or "blessed" (אשרי) when they have chieftains who admit to having sinned.

While Rashbam's approach fails (as Leibowitz notes [*'Iyyunim*, p. 47]) to explain why an anomalous form appears precisely at this spot in the text, Rashbam argues that there is precedent in biblical Hebrew for this type of syntax. Rashbam appears to have been the first to suggest this solution. Aside from Leibowitz's criticism, both Hoffmann and Luzzatto also express doubts about the validity of the comparison to the verse in Esther.

The phrase in Esther, is also difficult. (See e.g. BDB who suggests deleting the whole phrase.) Most moderns follow iE's interpretation that the reference is to a horse upon whom the king has ridden and upon whose head a crown was placed. Rashbam understands that the request is for: (1) a horse upon whom the king has ridden and (2) a crown that has been placed on the king's head. Rashbam's reading fits nicely with the famous midrash (quoted by Rashi ad Est. 6:9, following PDRE 50 and many other sources) that says that Haman originally requested both a horse and a crown, but changed his request (in vs. 9) and omitted the mention of a crown when he sensed the king's negative reaction.

The interpretation offered by Rashbam here is also found in Ḥizquni here, and in the Esther commentary published by Jellinek (Leipzig, 1855) which he sees as a compilation of commentaries by Rashbam and a number of his Northern French colleagues.

[74]Of all the sin offerings, only this one makes reference to a sin against *his* (the sinner's) God. Rashbam says that the phrase is appropriate; the sinner here has sinned unwittingly. God is then still appropriately called *his* God.

This interpretation is apparently original. Wessely writes that he does not understand it; if the text already says that the sin was done "בשגגה—unwittingly," then why does one need in the same verse a further reference to the fact that the sinner is not at fault? For alternate explanations, see Wessely (so also Hoffmann) and Nahm.

4:23 או הודע אליו: Like "אם הודע—IF HE IS INFORMED." That is how the phrase is generally explained.[75]

But I say [that the word או should be understood in its standard meaning of "or" and verse 23 continues the thought of vs. 22: "He sinned . . .] and he learned of his guilt (ואשם) *or* he was informed of his guilt" by others.[76]

4:25 מזבח העולה THE ALTAR OF BURNT OFFERING: The [blood sprinkling ceremony is performed for the sacrifice for the sin of a chieftain on the altar] outside [the Tent], as opposed to the inner altar, [which is where the blood sprinkling ceremony is performed for sacrifices] for [the sin of] the High Priest (vs. 7) or the entire community (vs. 18).[77]

4:35 כאשר יוסר חלב הכשב [AND HE SHALL REMOVE ALL ITS FAT] IN THE SAME WAY THAT THE FAT OF THE SHEEP [IS REMOVED]: I.e. (3:9) "the fat, the whole broad-tail, [which shall be removed] close to the kidneys (העצה)."[78]

---

[75]The reference is surely to Rashi, who argues here that או is often used in biblical Hebrew in the sense of "if" or "when." Most moderns also interpret the verse in that way, either because they agree with Rashi's claim or because they remove the word או from the text through emendation. (See e.g. BDB.)

[76]Rashbam appears to be the first to offer this interpretation, which was later taken up by quite a number of Jewish commentators (e.g. Nahm., Seforno and Luzzatto). Milgrom also asserts, like Rashbam, that "MT is punctiliously correct. Either the chieftain discovers his error (and regrets it) or someone else informs him." On Rashbam's understanding of ואשם, see commentary below ad 5:2, and note 79 there.

[77] The words of the verse, מזבח העולה, are understood by several *midreshe halakhah* (e.g. Sifra here and Zev. 51a-52a) as the source for various halakhic teachings. Rashbam says simply that the words are necessary to point out that a different altar is used for this specific *ḥaṭṭat* offering than the one used for the previous *ḥaṭṭat* offerings in this chapter. His understanding is also found in the beginning of the Sifra's discussion of this verse (*Ḥova* 6:9: ונתן על קרנות מזבח העולה ולא על קרנות מזבח הפנימי).

In fact, the words *are* somewhat redundant; they appear twice in our verse when one mention would do. See Nahm.'s comment that this type of repetition is not remarkable; it is דרך הלשון—standard style. And yet, Nahm. adds, the rabbis often use *midrashim* to interpret such redundancies because God's Torah should be seen as perfect, with nothing lacking and nothing redundant (ולדבותינו בהם מדרשים, כי תורת ה' תמימה אין בה חסר ויתר).

[78]Rashbam simply provides a footnote here to explain what verse the text is referring to when it says that the fat is removed in the same way that the fat is removed from the sheep of the *shelamim* offering. Rashi understands the phrase in the same way, but does not provide the reference to the earlier verse.

I translated העצה here as "kidneys" based on Rashbam's commentary to 3:9. See note 59 there.

5:2 ונעלם [ממנו] והוא טמא ואשם THE FACT HAD ESCAPED HIM THAT HE WAS IMPURE AND [THEN LATER] HE FELT GUILTY: about the fact that he had forgotten that he was impure, and had entered the Temple or eaten sacred food, both of which are sins that would incur the penalty of being "cut off" (*karet*) if they were done intentionally.[79]

5:3 והוא ידע ואשם AND HE KNEW AND HE FELT GUILTY: He found out now that he was impure and he knows that he is guilty.[80]

---

[79]As Nahm. notes, the difficulty in this verse is that, following the simplest reading, the person's infraction in the verse consists of touching something impure. However, both rabbinic traditions and the simple meaning of many other biblical passages rule out that possibility; in rabbinic Judaism it is not forbidden to touch something impure. What then is the infraction? Rashbam's answer, also found in Rashi (following Shav. 14b and Sifra) is the standard rabbinic one. People in a state of impurity are prohibited from doing such things as entering the Temple or eating sacred food. The sinner described in this verse touched something impure, forgot about the impurity and then disobeyed one of those prohibitions. (Rashbam makes this same point twice more in his Leviticus commentary, ad 11:8 and 17:16.) See Wessely's adamant statement here: "This [the rabbinic reading] is the *peshaṭ* of the verse; the Israelites were never commanded to avoid touching impure objects.")

Rashi's comment (on this verse, s.v. ואשם, and on vs. 3, s.v. ואשם) implies that he thinks that this infraction is hinted at in the verse itself. The word ואשם, for Rashi, means something like "incurs guilt" or "commits some sort of crime," which Rashi then sees as an allusion to entering the Temple or eating sacred food while impure. Nahm. notes the difficulty with Rashi's understanding of ואשם here: the word often appeared previously in Leviticus and was *not* interpreted in that way. Milgrom (pp. 339–345) argues that the word ואשם, when not followed by the preposition *le*, consistently means "to feel guilt." It seems to me that Rashbam, in his commentary above ad 4:23 and below ad 5:3, 5:17 and 5:24, also understands ואשם as meaning "to feel guilt."

I have translated Rashbam's comment to this verse based on the assumption that he is interpreting the word ואשם here in a manner consistent with the other passages (and is thus positioning himself as opposed to Rashi's understanding). The words of the comment here (והוא טמא ואשם על ששכח שהוא טמא ונכנס למקדש) allow such an understanding, but do not require it. They could mean "BEING IMPURE, HE INCURRED GUILT: in that he forgot that he was impure, and then entered the Temple." Rashbam's super-commentator, *Qeren Shemuel,* argues the merits of both of these possible understandings of Rashbam's words and opts for the second one.

[80]It seems certain that Rashbam is offering an alternative to Rashi's understanding of this phrase. The problem is that there are two versions of Rashi's comment with a small but significant difference between them. The text of Rashi's commentary should read here either: "ונעלם" ולא ידע, ששכח הטומאה (THE FACT ESCAPED HIM: he did not know; he forgot that he was impure) or "ונעלם והוא ידע" ששכח הטומאה (THE FACT ESCAPED HIM AND HE KNEW: that he had forgotten that he was impure). In the continuation of his comment Rashi writes: "ואשם" באכילת קדש או בביאת מקדש (HE INCURRED GUILT: by eating sacred food or by entering the Temple.)

5:8 ולא יבדיל WITHOUT SEVERING: He should cut one of the *simanim* but not both of them.[81]

5:9 והזה מדם החטאת HE SHOULD SPRINKLE SOME OF THE BLOOD OF THE SIN OFFERING: He holds the body[82] and squirts [the blood] from a distance, then the rest of the blood is drained [onto the base of the altar].[83]

Rashbam is clearly opposed to the second part of Rashi's comment. As explained in note 79, while Rashi feels comfortable interpreting ואשם as meaning "he incurred guilt," Rashbam sees it as meaning "he felt guilty."

Rashbam, I feel, is also opposing the first part of Rashi's explanation of this phrase. If we take the second of the two formulations above for Rashi's comment ("ונעלם והוא ידע" שכח הטומאה), the reading preferred by Berliner, Krinski, Luzzatto and others, then the difference between Rashbam's reading and Rashi's is most easily understood. Rashi addresses the problem: how could the text say ונעלם, which means that he did *not* know, but also say והוא ידע, which means that he *did* know? His solution is שכח הטומאה, he *forgot* that he was impure. In other words, at first he did know that he was impure but then he forgot. (Later, of course, he was reminded of his impurity; otherwise he would not be bringing a sacrifice.) Rashi then is trying to read into our verse (following Shev. 4a-b and Sifra) the halakhic principle that the sacrifice described here is brought only if the person *had* originally known of his impurity and then forgot and entered the Temple. If he had *not* originally known, but had found out that he had been impure only *after* he entered the Temple, the sacrifice would not be required. In other words, the words והוא ידע teach us that the person *had* originally known of his impurity.

Rashbam does not accept that understanding of והוא ידע. He emphasizes the distinction between his reading and Rashi's when he writes: "שנודע לו עכשיו שהוא טמא— he found out *now* that he was impure."

[81]The *simanim* are the vital signs of the animal, i.e. the windpipe and the gullet. According to the rabbis, both had to be severed as part of the *meliqah* of the bird sacrifice in 1:14–17. Here Rashbam says, in accordance with rabbinic teachings, that the added words ולא יבדיל teach that this bird sacrifice is different.

Rashbam's explanation is essentially identical to Rashi (following Mishnah Hul. 2:1; BT Hul. 27b and Rashi there s.v. בסימן אחד, and Tos. there, s.v. מה עוף בסימן אחד).

[82]Based on Rosin's conjectural emendation (בגוף, instead of the manuscript's reading בכף). See the language of the Talmud (Zev. 64b): והזה . . . אוחז בראש ובגוף ומזה. See also Rashi's language describing this same sprinkling in his commentary ad Men. 2b (cited in note 83).

[83]Both Rashi (ad Men. 2b) and Rashbam (here) try to explain the difference between draining and sprinkling of the blood. Their explanations appear to be similar; in fact the language is so similar that it is likely that Rashbam is playing on Rashi's wording. However there is one significant difference. Rashi writes in Men.: " הזאה - אוחז בגוף העוף ומעלה ומוריד בכח והדם ניתז מעצמו מיצוי סוחט בין אצבעותיו ונצוק הדם הולך למרחוק—'Sprinkling' means holding the bird's body and moving it up and down with force so that the blood drips out on its own; 'draining' means squeezing [the bird's body] between his fingers so that the blood pours out and flows for a distance." In other words, "draining" causes the blood to go farther than "sprinkling." Rashbam's comment here says the opposite—that it is "sprinkling" that causes blood to go farther than "draining." (The explanation quoted is not the only explanation of "draining" blood that Rashi offers. Ad Zev. 64b, s.v. היה מתמצה, and in his commentary ad

However, an *'olah* bird offering requires only draining, not sprinkling.[84]

5:13 מאחת מאלה [FOR THE WRONG THAT HE COMMITTED] IN ANY OF THESE MATTERS: [This refers to] one of the three types of sins mentioned above: "he heard a public imprecation" (vs. 1) or [the sin of] an uttered oath (vs. 4) or [the sin of] impurity concerning the Temple or sacred food (vss. 2–3).[85]

5:15 מקדשי ה' [WHEN A PERSON COMMITS A TRESPASS] CONCERNING THE HOLY THINGS OF THE LORD: by misappropriating Temple property.[86] This [sacrifice, i.e. the sacrifice required for such an infraction] is an *'asham me'ilot.*[87]

Lev. 1:15 Rashi says the draining is accomplished by crushing the bird's body against the wall of the altar.)

[84]So also Rashi here. The comment is based on a comparison of the simple meaning of our verse and the simple meaning of Lev. 1:15. See also Mishnah Zev. 6:4–5.

[85]Rashbam disputes Rashi's understanding of the phrase (which presumably follows Rashi's understanding of the Sifra here). According to Rashi, מאחת מאלה is a reference to any one of the three types of expiatory sacrifices listed here (sheep [vs. 6], birds [vs. 7] or flour [vs. 11]). The verse would then mean: "The priest shall make expiation מאחת מאלה—i.e. in one of the ways outlined above—for the sin that he [= the sinner] committed."

Rashbam argues that מאחת מאלה must be seen as a reference to the types of sins, not to the types of expiatory sacrifices. In order to make his opposition to Rashi as clear as possible, Rashbam writes "one of the three types of sins," playing on Rashi's language "one of the three types of expiation acts." (He does this despite the fact that one could easily argue that more than three types of sins are listed in vss. 1–4. Cf. e.g. Ps.-Jon. ad vs. 5: "one of these four [sins]." But Rashbam's language "three types of sins" is chosen to highlight his opposition to Rashi.) Rashbam's understanding of the text is clearly the simple meaning of the text (with the phrase מאחת מאלה in the closing verse of this section of text being parallel and equal to the phrase לאחת מאלה which appears in vss. 4 and 5, the opening verses of the section). Most moderns follow Rashbam, although Wessely predictably tries to defend Rashi.

[86]So also Rashi, verbatim.

Perhaps Rashbam felt the need to explain the phrase מקדשי בני ישראל because the word מקדשי has a number of meanings in different contexts. See e.g. Rashbam ad Lev. 22:2 where he explains it as meaning sacrificial food.

[87]I.e. a guilt offering for misappropriating sancta. *'Asham me'ilot* is the standard rabbinic name for the sacrifice described here. See e.g. Mishnah Zev. 5:5 and Rashi's commentary ad Zev. 54b, s.v. אשם מעילות.

Here and ad vss. 17 and 21, Rashbam introduces three separate types of special *'asham* offerings (in addition to the standard ones, which he summarizes in his commentary to vs. 13) and identifies them by name: *'asham me'ilot*, *'asham taluy*, and *'asham gezelot.*

5:16 ונתן אותו לכהן HE SHALL GIVE IT TO THE PRIEST: He shall give the ram of the guilt offering to the priest to make expiation on his behalf.[88]

5:17–18 ולא ידע ואשם HE DID NOT KNOW AND [THEN] HE FELT GUILTY: These verses speak of the *'asham taluy*[89] sacrifice,[90] as it says (vs. 18), " . . . for the error he committed when he did not know . . .."[91] [This sacrifice applies] when he mistook prohibited fat (*ḥelev*) for permissible fat and he ate it.[92] "HE DID NOT KNOW" that it was prohibited fat. Later when he heard that what he had eaten may have been prohibited fat or may have been permissible fat, "HE FELT GUILTY" (ואשם).[93] [In such a case (18)] HE SHALL BRING A RAM FROM THE FLOCK AS A GUILT OFFERING (*'asham*). [The expiation of this sacrifice would then be "suspended'] until he found out that what he had eaten was certainly prohibited fat. In such a case he would then bring a sin offering (*ḥaṭṭat*).[94]

---

[88]The syntax of the verse allows two possible readings: (1) "he shall . . . give *it* [the amount of money for restitution] to the priest"; or (2) "he shall . . . give it [the sacrificial ram] to the priest." Rashbam prefers the second reading, although almost all other commentators who relate to the phrase prefer the first understanding. See Wessely who criticizes Rashbam's explanation.

Perhaps Rashbam's unusual reading can be understood in light of an issue raised by Milgrom. Milgrom observes (p. 330) that this section seems to break with the standard biblical pattern that "man can seek reconciliation with God" through a sacrifice "only after he has made the required restitution." (See similar concerns in Malbim, note 357.) The standard reading of vss. 15–16 has the opposite order—the sacrifice first in vs. 15, followed by the restitution, in vs. 16. In Rashbam's understanding that is not the case; the sacrifice is not "given" to the priest until the end of vs. 16, after restitution has been made.

[89]Rashbam continues to identify the various types of special *'asham* sacrifices. See note 87 above.

[90]So also Rashi. This is also the standard rabbinic term for this type of *'asham* (see e.g. Mishnah Zev. 5:5) and the standard rabbinic understanding of these verses (e.g. Ker. 19b), i.e. that they describe an *'asham taluy*, a guilt offering that was to be brought only if the offender was uncertain whether he actually had offended. See iE here who offers an alternative understanding—that the *'asham* offering described here is brought by a person who did something and knows what he did but does not know the rule about whether such a thing is forbidden.

[91]Rashbam reads the verse the same way that R. Joshua did (in Ker. 19b), i.e. that the phrase ולא ידע teaches us that if the sinner now knows of the sin with certainty then he does not bring this particular sacrifice. So also Rashi.

[92]This is the standard rabbinic description of the events that would lead to an *'asham taluy*. See e.g. Ker. 5:5 and Rashi here.

[93]On ואשם, see note 79 above.

[94]Even if he had already brought an *'asham taluy* offering. So also Rashi. This is the standard rabbinic understanding. See e.g. Ker. 24b.

5:21 וכחש בעמיתו AND DEALS DECEITFULLY: This section deals with the *'asham gezelot*.[95]

5:24 ביום אשמתו ON THE DAY WHEN HE REALIZES HIS GUILT: When he makes his confession in order to repent[96] for one of those infractions written above [concerning] a pledge or theft or fraud or a lost object.[97]

---

[95]Rashbam continues to identify the various types of special *'asham* sacrifices. See note 87 above. The term *'asham gezelot* is the standard rabbinic term for this type of sacrifice. See e.g. Mishnah Zev. 5:5.

[96]Rashbam again emphasizes that the root *'-sh-m* does not mean to commit an infraction but to realize one's guilt. See note 79 above.

Rashbam's understanding opposes that of the Sifra here, and of BM 43b, where the classical rabbis seem to agree that ביום אשמתו means "on the day when he committed the infraction." The only question that the rabbis discuss is whether the infraction was committed on the day that the object was originally purloined or on the day that that action was later denied in court. According to Rashbam's *peshaṭ* understanding, neither of these days was meant.

[97]The list of infractions here is selected from vss. 21 and 22.

צו (Leviticus 6–8)

6:2 זאת תורת העולה THIS IS THE RITUAL OF THE BURNT OFFERING (*'OLAH*): The text reviews and completes the discussion of the laws of all the sacrifices that were described in the Torah portion, *Va-yiqra'*.[1]

היא העולה THAT IS THE BURNT OFFERING: which is incinerated during daytime,[2] as it is written (19:6) "on the *day* of your sacrifice," and (7:16) "on the *day* that he offers his sacrifice."[3] You may complete its incineration כל

[1]A helpful comment on the structure of the beginning of Leviticus. See similarly Baruch Levine in NJPSC, who writes that chapters 6 and 7 "present the *torah*, the 'ritual,' for each of the several types of sacrifices already outlined in chapters 1–5." See also commentary ad 7:35 below, and note 40 there.

A number of classical exegetes say that this verse is actually using the word '*olah*, in an unusual manner, not as a reference to the burnt offering of Lev. 1 (which would be Rashbam's point of view), but as a reference to the daily sacrifice, specifically to the sheep that was offered each evening. See e.g. JBS and LT. See also Andrew of St. Victor, p. 167: "*de quotidiano intendit holocausto . . . de vespertino*—the text refers to the daily sacrifice . . . the one offered in the evening."

[2]Since the simple meaning of this verse could be that the '*olah* is appropriately offered at night, and since that is not the accepted halakhic position, Rashbam says emphatically that the '*olah* is to be offered by day. According to him, our verse teaches that the incineration may continue and be completed at night. See also iE who says that our verse hints that '*olah* sacrifices are offered only by day (ובכאן רמז שלא יעלה עולה בלילה). Cf. LT who says that our verse teaches that the last sacrifice of the day, the one closest to the night, must be the evening sheep of the daily sacrifice.

[3]The prooftext cited most often in rabbinic literature to establish that sacrifices are to be offered only by day is Lev. 7:37–8, where, at the end of the rules of all the sacrifices, the text says, "Such are the rituals of the burnt offering, the meal offering . . . (38) with which the LORD charged Moses . . . on the *day* when He commanded . . . ." See e.g. Hul. 22a and Rashi there, s.v. מביום צוותו נפקא. The midrash is based on the alleged redundancy of the word "ביום—on the day." Rashbam attempts to find prooftexts that are less midrashic in nature. His prooftexts—unlike the one just cited, a verse which refers to the day when the *command* about sacrifice was given—at least refer to the day of the sacrificing itself. Rashbam's prooftexts are also occasionally used in rabbinic literature to prove that sacrificing, or that some steps of sacrificing, are to be done by day. For the proof from 19:6, see Zev. 56a; for the proof from 7:16, see Meg. 20b-21a.

הלילה, ALL NIGHT LONG. THE ALTAR FIRE IS KEPT BURNING ON IT at night just as during the day.[4]

6:3 מדו: [The letter *vav* at the end of מדו should be seen as an "extra" *vav*,] just like [the *vav* in the word] (Num. 23:18), "בנו צפור—Zipor's son," or [the *vav* in the word] (Num. 24:3), "בנו בעור—Beor's son."[5] [The word מדו should be understood in the same way as the word מדיו, in the phrase,] "ומדיו—i.e. his clothes—were torn" (I Sam. 4:12).[6]

6:3–4 והרים את הדשן HE SHALL TAKE UP THE ASHES: [This refers to *terumat ha-deshen*—the clearing of the ashes.] The law is that that is to be done every morning, [before] the daily offering of the morning. But (4) HE SHALL REMOVE THE ASHES refers to something that is done less frequently, when one has to remove it from the altar because of the excess of ashes on it.[7]

---

[4]Rashbam connects our verse to the prescription of vs. 6: "Fire shall be kept burning on the altar perpetually." This perpetual fire, says Rashbam, will complete at night the incineration of sacrifices offered earlier. See JBS on this verse, who says that the honor of the Temple requires that the altar be perpetually in use.

[5]Both Rosin and Ashkenazi had an impossible reading before them: מדו כמו בנו בנו ומדיו קרועים לשון בגד. I have translated above following the conjectural emendation offered by Rosin: מדו כמו בנו צפור בנו בעור ומדיו קרועים לשון בגד, although to my mind Ashkenazi's suggested reading—without Rosin's words בנו צפור—is just as good and perhaps simpler.

The difficulty in this verse is that if מדו is understood in the standard manner ("*his* raiment"), the syntax of the phrase makes little sense. As Milgrom notes, some commentators have understood the phrase as appositional: "his raiment, the linen one." Others who do not emend (see e.g. Milgrom and BDB), see an extra *vav* here. As Rashbam notes in *Dayyaqut* (Merdler's edition, p. 54), such extra *vavs* generally appear at the end of the first element of a construct (מצינו ווין יתירין בסוף הדבוקה). See similarly G.-K. 90k and 90o.

Exegetes use the phrase בנו בעור as the parade example of an "extra" *vav* in biblical Hebrew. See e.g. Rashbam's commentary to Gen. 1:24 and his *Dayyaqut*, *ibid.*; iE ad Ex. 1:16 (longer commentary), ad Eccl. 4:12 and *passim*; Qimḥi to Is. 56:9. See also Rashi ad Num. 24:3.

[6]Unlike Rashi, Rashbam does not attempt to identify which particular garment is meant by the word מדו. For Rashbam it simply means clothing. Rashbam is also distancing himself from the *midrash halakhah* that Rashi cites (following Sifra and *Yoma'* 23b) that connects מדו to the word מדתו, deriving from here the rule that the priest must wear clothing that fits properly.

[7]So also Rashi. This distinction—between "clearing" and "removing" ashes—represents the more common rabbinic interpretation. See the sources cited by Kasher, p. 148, note 54, and see especially the discussion in *Mishneh la-melekh* ad MT *Temidin u-musafin* 2:13. As noted there, there is also another possibility: whenever ashes were cleared, they were also removed. As *Mishneh la-melekh* argues, that appears to be Maimonides' position. Since the Mishnah (*Yoma'* 1:8) says explicitly that ashes were to be cleared daily, that means, according to Maimonides, that they are also to be removed daily. As Milgrom and others suggest, it does seem

6:9 בחצר אהל מועד IN THE ENCLOSURE OF THE TENT OF MEETING: [This sacrifice must be eaten] within the enclosure [surrounding the Temple]; [it is] not [one of those sacrifices that may be eaten anywhere] in Jerusalem.[8]

6:11 יקדש [ANYONE WHO TOUCHES THESE] IS HOLY: i.e. should purify himself before touching.[9]

6:13 זה קרבן אהרן ובניו THIS IS THE OFFERING THAT AARON AND HIS SONS SHALL OFFER: According to the plain meaning of Scripture, [the meaning of "AND HIS SONS" is that] Aaron's descendants, the High Priests

---

that the verses here are describing just one ceremony: the priest clears the ashes, changes his clothes that presumably became soiled, and then moves the ashes outside of the camp. JBS suggests here that that is the *peshaṭ* reading of this passage—that whenever needed (not necessarily daily) the ashes are cleared and removed.

So Rashbam here opts for the explanation that is more standard halakhically but farther from the simple meaning of the biblical text.

[8]In the rabbinic system, there are sacrifices that must be eaten within the confines of the Temple area and other sacrifices that may be eaten anywhere in Jerusalem. Rashbam notes here that the *minḥah* sacrifice falls into the first category. This represents the unanimous halakhic opinion. See e.g. Mishnah Zev. 6:1. When the verse says that this sacrifice must be eaten "in the courtyard," Rashbam interprets this as meaning that the farthest that the priest may take it is to the courtyard, not outside of the Temple compound. (On this, he would disagree with Milgrom, who interprets it to mean "in the courtyard, but nowhere else in the Temple grounds.") Ad 19:24 Rashbam points out that a different holy item, "second tithe" food, may be consumed anywhere in Jerusalem.

As Baruch Levine notes in NJPSC, the phrase חצר אהל מועד is not common; it appears in the Bible only in our chapter (here and in vs. 19). Presumably that is why Rashbam feels the need to comment on it. Rashbam takes this unusual term, which relates to the wilderness experience of the wandering Israelites, and "translates" it into the geography of the Jewish commonwealth in the land of Israel.

[9]Rashbam offers an interpretation that differs radically from the standard rabbinic understanding. This novel interpretation appears four separate times in Rashbam's commentary: here, ad Ex. 29:37, Ex. 30:29 and ad Lev. 11:8.

The standard halakhic understanding is that, in some way, "holiness is contagious" (NJPSC, ad Ex. 29:37) and that something that touches a holy item יקדש, will itself become holy. See e.g. Rashi ad Ex. 29:37 (following Zev. 9:1, BT Zev. 83b, Sanh. 34a-b and other sources). Rashbam interprets יקדש to mean "shall purify himself [beforehand]," and does not follow the standard rabbinic understanding, that יקדש means "shall [itself] become holy." Hoffmann (here) pays Rashbam a left-handed compliment and calls his interpretation the one that is relatively best of all the many heterodox interpretations that have been offered to this verse.

For a fuller discussion of this exegetical issue, see commentary to Ex. 29:37, and note 22 there. See also NJPSC and Milgrom here (the former similar to Rashbam, the latter emphatically not).

who will follow him, [will each bring one of these sacrifices "ON THE OCCASION OF HIS ANOINTMENT"]. The rabbis, however, explained midrashically that every rank and file priest had to dedicate himself by means of a grain offering (*minḥah*) on the occasion of beginning his service [in the Temple].[10]

6:14 מרבכת: Based on context,[11] the word means "softened in oil."[12] Because it is to be baked in an oven, it is to be softened[13] beforehand with oil.

תופיני: is related to the meaning of "baking," [i.e. to the root *'-p-h*, even though the word תופיני lacks the initial root letter, *'aleph*]. The *'aleph* has elided, as often happens; for example (Is. 13:20), "No Arab shall pitch his tent (יהל) there. [The word יהל should be understood as if] יאהל [were written, and the word וימש in] (Ex. 10:21) "let darkness fall (וימש) [should be understood as if] ויאמש [were written].[14]

---

[10]The standard rabbinic understanding of these verses may be found in Rashi here, following Sifra and Men. 51b. According to this understanding, our verse teaches that every priest inaugurates his service in the Temple with the *minḥah* sacrifice described here. However verse 15 teaches us that the High Priest offers this same *minḥah* sacrifice on a daily basis. The Talmud and the Sifra both consider and reject the interpretation suggested by Rashbam; nevertheless, he is clearly correct when he labels his interpretation the *peshaṭ*.

As Milgrom notes (p. 396), other old traditions, similar to Rashbam's understanding of these verses, do exist. See Ps.-Jon here. Milgrom also argues that this understanding is reflected in the way that the verse was understood in Sirach 45:14 and in Hebrews 7:27. To my mind, both of those sources may be read as consonant with the traditional rabbinic understanding.

[11]Rashbam often uses this phrase to mean that while there is no certainty about the meaning of the word, contextual considerations suggest the meaning that he offers.

[12]Or perhaps Rashbam's Hebrew phrase here, רכה בשמן should be translated "thinned out with oil." See Rashbam ad 1:15 s.v. ונמצה, and note 28 there. In any case, it appears that Rashbam is offering a different interpretation from the more traditional one found in Rashi (following Sifra) "חלוטה ברותחין כל צרכה—scalded sufficiently in boiling water." Rashbam's explanation appears original. iE later interprets the same way.

As Milgrom notes, the word מרבכת is difficult and its meaning is still disputed. Milgrom says, however, that Rashbam's explanation "has no philological support."

[13]As Rosin notes, the manuscript reading here, להרכיבה, is obviously a mistake. Rosin suggests reading להרביכה, in which case Rashbam is creating a Hebrew neologism here. Krinski quotes Rashbam as reading לרככה.

[14]Standard rabbinic exegesis sees the word תופיני as a reference to baking. See e.g. Sifra and Rashi. Rashbam attempts to provide some linguistic grounding for that explanation. Ultimately the meaning of the word is "as yet unexplained," as NJPSC notes.

Rashbam also identifies the phenomenon of eliding *'aleph*s in his commentary to Ex. 10:21.

6:20 תכבס [IF ANY OF ITS BLOOD IS SPATTERED ON A GARMENT] YOU SHOULD WASH [THE BESPATTERED PART]: so that the garment shall not be considered forbidden, under the category of *notar*.[15] This would require that it be burnt.[16]

6:23 וכל חטאת NO SIN OFFERING [MAY BE EATEN] FROM WHICH BLOOD IS BROUGHT [INTO THE TENT OF MEETING]: This refers to the "internal" sin offerings (חטאות הפנימיות):[17] the bull of the anointed priest,[18] the bull when the community forgets,[19] the bull and the goat of the Day of Atonement[20] and the goats [that are offered for sins] of idolatry.[21] Concerning all five of these it is written that the "placements" [of the blood of those sacrifices]

---

[15] I.e. "left over" sacrificial meat that has not been consumed within the allotted time period.

[16] Arguably a garment that had sacrificial blood sprinkled on it could be considered to have *notar* status and then it would have to be burned. So Rashbam argues that our verse teaches us that that need not be the case; if one washes the garment in due time, then the rules of *notar* will not apply.

Perhaps Rashbam is reacting to the difficulty that Milgrom notes, that the ceremonial washing outlined here is more often and perhaps more appropriately found when a garment comes in contact with something impure (e.g. Lev. 11:25, 28 and *passim*), not when it comes in contact with something holy. So Rashbam provides a rationale as to why washing is appropriate for contact with sacred items.

See Wessely who argues at length against Rashbam's explanation and attempts to prove that, according to standard rabbinic understanding, the sacrificial blood sprinkled on this garment could *not* have *notar* status.

[17] As Rashbam noted already in his commentary to 4:25, there are two categories of *ḥaṭṭat* offerings: ones that are not eaten and that have their blood sprinkled on the "internal" (or "incense") altar, and ones that are eaten and whose blood is sprinkled on the "external" altar (or "the altar of the burnt offering"). Our verse then applies only to the former category.

[18] 4:3–12. See especially vs. 7.

[19] 4:13–21. See especially vs. 18.

[20] See 16:27.

[21] Num. 15:22–29. See Rashbam's comment there. He accepts the standard rabbinic explanation of that passage—that the sinner who "failed to observe one of the commandments" is to be understood as an idolater. See notes 82 and 83 there.

Concerning the other *ḥaṭṭat* offerings listed here by Rashbam, there are explicit biblical verses (listed in the previous notes) that prove that they are defined as "internal" *ḥaṭṭat* offerings. However, nowhere does it say explicitly in Numbers that the *ḥaṭṭat* offerings described there are from that category. Rashbam is relying on the standard *midrash halakhah* exegesis in Sifra and in Zev. 39b to establish that "שעירי עבודת כוכבים—goats of idolatry" (Rashbam's phrase here and the phrase used in Zev. *ibid.*) are to be defined as "internal" *ḥaṭṭat* offerings.

should be *inside* the *hekhal*[22] on the curtain[23] and on the golden altar. This is the plain meaning of Scripture.[24]

7:10 וחרבה A DRY [MEAL OFFERING]: The meal offering of the sinner and the meal offering of the suspected adulteress.[25]

7:12 אם על תודה IF HE OFFERS IT FOR THANKSGIVING: I.e. if he took the obligation upon himself using the word "תודה—thanksgiving," and he did not mention it in terms of a שלמים ("well-being") offering.[26] Generally a person

---

[22]Rashbam, as he often does, uses the standard rabbinic word here for the part of the Tabernacle that is not the Holy of Holies. See e.g. his commentary ad Ex. 25:12, s.v. על צלעו, and note 27 there.

[23]That separates the *hekhal* from the Holy of Holies.

[24]Rashbam is offering an alternative explanation to the standard *midrash halakhah*, which reasons as follows: It seems that our verse is superfluous. Since there are already verses that tell us that "internal" *ḥaṭṭat* offerings are to be burned *in toto* (e.g. 4:11–12), there is no reason for our verse to tell us that a *ḥaṭṭat* offering whose "blood is brought into the Tent of Meeting" may not be eaten. Of course one may not eat that which must be burned. So the *midrash halakhah* argues that our verse refers to *ḥaṭṭat* offerings whose blood was *incorrectly* brought into the Tent of Meeting, i.e. to external *ḥaṭṭat* offerings that were by mistake performed in the manner that internal *ḥaṭṭat* offerings are to be performed. The verse teaches us that, if such an error occurred, then the meat of that *ḥaṭṭat* offering, which would have been edible before the error, now becomes forbidden to eat. That explanation is the one offered by Rashi here, following Sifra and Zev. 82a.

Rashbam says that there is a simpler explanation—that the verse tells us explicitly not to eat meat of "internal" *ḥaṭṭat* offerings, even though it had already told us that the meat must be totally burned. Later this explanation was offered also by Nahm. as a *peshaṭ* alternative. Nahm. points out that in the Talmud (*ibid.*) and in the Sifra one can find this explanation reflected in the minority opinion of R. Jose the Galilean. He argues that our verse does refer to "internal" *ḥaṭṭat* offerings whose blood was *correctly* brought to the Tent of Meeting. The purpose of the verse is to teach us, by giving us a specific negative commandment ("it may not be eaten"), the severity of eating the meat of such a *ḥaṭṭat*.

Like Rashbam, see also iE, Hoffmann and Wessely.

[25]So also Rashi. The explanation is based on the simple meaning of the texts in Lev. 5:11 and in Num. 5:15. Moderns explain the phrase the same way. See e.g. Milgrom.

[26]The simple meaning of the verses here (11, 12 and 15) and the view of the halakhic literature is that the "thanksgiving" offering is a subset of the larger category of "well-being" offerings. What then makes some, but not all, "well-being" offerings into "thanksgiving" offerings? Rashi and Rashbam disagree about this question. Rashi (s.v. אם על תודה) says that if, after being saved from a specific disaster, one volunteers to bring a "well-being" offering, that offering is, apparently automatically, defined as a "thanksgiving" offering. In other words, context defines whether or not an offering is "thanksgiving." See similarly iE on verses 12 and 16.

Rashbam, on the other hand, suggests that language defines the difference: if the sacrificer mentions the word תודה, the sacrifice becomes a "thanksgiving" offering and the rules of

offers a thanksgiving offering after being saved from some type of distress, as the rabbis said (Ber. 54b), "Four are obligated to offer thanksgiving . . .."

The rabbis explained that the total of [the different kinds of] "cakes" [described in vss. 12–14] was forty.[27] They also explained how much their oil was to be and how many *'esronim* [a measure of volume] they were.[28]

7:16 ואם נדר או נדבה IF [THE SACRIFICE IS] A VOW OR FREE-WILL: I.e. if he said "I hereby take upon myself the obligation to bring a *shelamim* offering." As I explained above,[29] that [formulation, using the word *shelamim*] refers to a vow and its payment (*tashlumim*). In other words, this sacrifice is being brought because of a vow, and not because of thanksgiving.[30]

---

verses 12–15 apply. But if he mentions the word שלמים, then (Rashbam writes ad vs. 16) it is a regular offering of "well-being" and the rules of verses 16–18 apply.

It is the common halakhic opinion that a "thanksgiving" sacrifice is required in specific situations and presumably the context of those situations would determine the sacrifice's definition. Still, as Rosin notes, Rashbam can draw support from a text such as Mishnah Men. 7:5 (and many similar texts) that refers to a person saying "הרי עלי תודה—I hereby obligate myself to bring a thanksgiving offering."

A further distinction between the way Rashi and Rashbam understand our verse involves the word תודה. For Rashi, it refers to the *concept* of "giving thanks." I.e. "If he offers his sacrifice for the sake of giving thanks . . .." For Rashbam, the word תודה in this verse is a technical term, the name of a type of sacrifice. I.e. "If he offers his sacrifice as a *todah* sacrifice." Cf. Hoffmann and Milgrom (p. 413) who write here explicitly that one should not see the word תודה in this verse as the name of a sacrifice, but as a word that means "giving thanks." N. Leibowitz also argues similarly and criticizes Mendelssohn's translation for seeing תודה in the beginning of our verse as the name of a sacrifice (צום דאנק-אפפער ברינגען ווייל). Like Rashbam, see Ehrlich.

[27]See e.g. Men. 77b. Rashbam's words stand in contrast to iE's apparently heterodox explanation. In the beginning of his comment, iE suggests that the general, unspecified language here, "cakes," implies that the sacrificer may bring any number of cakes (two or more) that he wishes. But, in his commentary to vs. 14, iE apparently retreats from that position and accepts the standard rabbinic explanation.

[28]Men. *ibid.* and 89a. Rashi here provides his readers with some details of this information. Rashbam simply suggests that we consult the sources for further information.

See similarly Rashbam's commentary to 2:2 above, and note 44 there.

[29]See commentary to 3:1, and note 54 there.

[30]Another common explanation of the word "vow" (נדר) here is that while in vs. 12 the תודה sacrifice is brought *after* the individual was saved from distress, the נדר of vs. 16 means that a person who is *currently* in distress vows to bring a sacrifice if God intervenes. See similarly iE, Hizq. and Wessely. Rashbam, on the other hand, explains that if a vowed sacrifice was designated for thanksgiving, then it is defined as a תודה. Otherwise the "default" position is that it is defined as a "well-being" (*shelamim*) sacrifice. See commentary above ad vs. 12, and note 26 there.

ביום הקריבו ON THE DAY WHEN HE OFFERS: On the day when he has already offered HIS SACRIFICE IT SHALL BE EATEN, after the offering.[31]

7:18 ואם האכל יאכל IF IT SHALL BE EATEN: The rabbis uprooted this verse from its plain meaning[32] and explained it as referring to someone who, while performing [in an appropriate manner] one of the four sacrificial duties— while slaughtering, or bringing the blood [to the altar], or collecting [the blood][33] or

---

[31]The two main steps in the sacrificial process are the slaughtering (זביחה) and the offering at the altar (הקרבה). Our verse says that the eating of the sacrificial meat is allowed on the same day that the blood of the slaughtered animal (זבחו) is brought (הקריבו) to the altar. Theoretically "on the day of the offering" could mean that one could eat the meat at any time after the sacrificing, even before the blood was placed on the altar, as long as the blood was to be placed on the altar later that same day. (*Halakhah* in fact requires that the blood be placed on the altar on that same day; see Zev. 56a-b). Rashbam suggests that our text teaches that only *after* the blood has been placed on the altar may the meat be consumed. This is the unanimous halakhic opinion. See Mak. 17a and Maimonides, *Ma'aseh ha-qorbanot* 11:4, where this restriction is derived from Deut. 12:17.

In Zev. (*ibid.*) the Talmud discusses (and offers several midrashic answers to) the question of why our verse says "on the day of the *offering* of his *sacrifice*." What would have been missing had the text read simply "on the day of his sacrifice"? (Note also the simpler language in vs. 15: "ביום קרבנו יאכל—shall be eaten on the day that it is offered.") Rashbam may be suggesting that this ostensibly redundant language teaches us that both the slaughtering and the offering are required before the sacrificial meat may be consumed.

Rashbam's interpretation of the word הקריבו here is similar to the one he suggested ad 1:5. See also commentary ad 2:12, s.v. תקריבו, and note 49 there.

[32]Rashbam uses strong language here to tell us that the *midrash halakhah* to this verse uproots the *peshaṭ* understanding. He uses similar language, albeit quoting a talmudic text, in the introduction to his commentary on Ex. 21, in a generalizing manner, not about any one specific *midrash halakhah*. See p. 226, note 4, of my Exodus volume.

One can find an example in the Talmud (Yev. 11b) of referring to a specific explanation as one that uproots a text from the *peshaṭ*. Similarly one can find one example of Rashi using this formulation in his Talmud commentary (Sanh. 15b, s.v. הניחא) and one example of a similar phrase in his commentary to Hos. 13:10 ("י"ת איה מלכך ואני אומר אינו צריך לעקרו ממשמעותו—Yonatan translated . . . but I say that there is no need to uproot it from its meaning"). However, I am not able to find another example of an exegete before or contemporaneous with Rashbam taking an accepted *midrash halakhah* from classical rabbinic literature and labeling it, based on his own independent assessment, as one that uproots the plain meaning of the text, as Rashbam does here.

[33]Rashbam's listing of "bringing" (הולכת הדם) the blood to the altar before "collecting" (קבלה) it, is very strange and may simply represent a copyist's error. Cf. his commentary to 1:5 where he lists these two actions in the standard order.

sprinkling [the blood]— thought[34] that he would eat the sacrificial meat on the third day.[35]

7:19 כל טהור יאכל בשר ANYONE WHO IS PURE MAY EAT MEAT: which is pure.[36]

---

[34]From a halakhic perspective it is possible that Rashbam's words here "במחשב לאכול מבחו ביום השלישי" ought to be translated as "[he] *said* that he would eat the sacrificial meat on the third day." See Tos. BM 43b, s.v. החושב.

In part the rabbinic understanding—that our verse describes the מחשב, the one who thinks or speaks inappropriately—is based on a midrashic reading of the phrase לא יחשב in our verse. That phrase is generally understood on a *peshaṭ* level as meaning that the sacrifice will not be "counted" or "accredited" to the person who offered it. But, as Milgrom (p. 421) explains: "Because the basic meaning of *ḥ-sh-b* (*qal*) is 'think,' the word may have provided the ground for the rabbinic rule of intentionality . . .. [It] could imply that the offender actually planned to eat of the sacrifice after the time limit had expired. Hence, he did not think properly . . .."

[35]The simple meaning of our text is that if the meat is eaten on the third day—i.e. after the permitted time period—the sacrifice is disqualified. As the Talmud argues (Zev. 29a, citing Sifra, here), the problem with that explanation is that it is hard to imagine that an action performed two days after the blood was properly placed on the altar would have the power to annul the efficaciousness of the sacrifice retroactively. So also Rashi here; see also iE. Accordingly the rabbis say that our verse teaches that an inappropriate thought concerning the eating while performing the sacrificial duties would disqualify the sacrifice. See also Rashbam's commentary below ad 19:7, and notes 7 and 8 there.

It is noteworthy that modern traditionalists such as Hoffmann, Wessely and Malbim all try to find textual reasons why the ostensibly obvious *peshaṭ* reading cannot be sustained. A medieval traditionalist like Rashbam feels no need; for him it suffices to say that the rabbinic explanation uproots the *peshaṭ*. Luzzatto's comment to our verse is particularly interesting:

> For a number of years I have been wondering why the rabbis would, as Rashbam put it, uproot this verse from its plain meaning. Today, Purim 1847, I have finally understood what motivated them. So also whenever the rabbis deviated from the plain meaning of Scripture—not when their interpretation is just one man's opinion but when it is accepted unanimously—it is not because they made an [exegetical] error. Rather it is some enactment (תקנה) that they legislated according to the needs of later generations. Who can match them as Reformers? (מי כמוהם ריפורמאטור) But their enactments were always based on deep wisdom, fear of God and love of humanity; never were they for the sake of self-interest or self-aggrandizement, nor in order to find favor in the eyes of people.

[36]The difficulty with our verse is that the formulation, "anyone who is pure may eat meat," suggests that someone who is impure is not allowed to eat *any* meat, a rule that contradicts standard *halakhah*. Rashbam proposes reading the phrase in context. The first part of our verse says that sacrificial meat that became impure may not be eaten by anyone. The verse continues, והבשר—i.e. other sacrificial meat that remained pure—may be consumed by anyone who is pure.

Rashbam's explanation is opposed to that of Rashi (following Sifra) who interprets our verse as teaching that not only the person who offered a *shelamim* sacrifice may eat it; the sacrificer is allowed to invite anyone pure to join in. See Wessely who argues for the superiority of Rashi's reading over Rashbam's. Like Rashbam, see Hizq. and Milgrom.

7:25 מן הבהמה אשר יקריב [ANYONE WHO EATS OF THE FAT] OF AN ANIMAL FROM WHICH THERE MAY BE MADE: from that species of animal, AN OFFERING TO THE LORD, even if [the meat of that animal is] *ḥullin* [= non-sacrificial meat].[37]

7:26 בכל מושבותיכם [YOU MUST NOT CONSUME ANY BLOOD] IN ANY OF YOUR SETTLEMENTS: Even though they [the animals being eaten] outside of Jerusalem are certainly *ḥullin* [= non-sacrificial meat].[38]

7:35 זאת משחת אהרן ומשחת בניו THIS IS THE ANOINTING OF AARON AND THE ANOINTING OF HIS SONS: I.e. this is the recompense[39] for the

---

[37]One might read this verse to mean that only the fat of sacrificed animals is forbidden to be eaten and that fat of animals that are not sacrificed is permitted. See iE (ad vs. 20) who explains the verse that way (although his explanation may be meant as an anti-Karaite polemic, and not as serious exegesis). A number of modern critics have also explained the verse in that way. See the discussion in Hoffmann here. Rashbam explains our verse in a way that is consonant with *halakhah*. He says that it means that the rules about the consumption of fat apply also to *ḥullin*, provided that the animal being consumed is of a species from which sacrifices may be made. So also Nahm. and Hizq. here. See also Rashbam's commentary above ad 3:17, and note 61 there, and commentary below ad vs. 26, and note 38 there.

[38]In other words, the phrase, "בכל מושבותיכם—in all your settlements" teaches us that the rules against consuming blood do not apply only to sacrificial meat. They even apply outside of Jerusalem, where no sacrifices are offered. See Rashbam's commentary ad Ex. 12:20 (and notes 55 and 56 there) where he makes the same point concerning the phrase בכל מושבותיכם there. See also above ad 3:17 and ad 7:25 where Rashbam makes a similar point about fat and/or blood.

Rashi here also raises the question of why the phrase בכל מושבותיכם appears in our verse. His answer (from Qid. 37b) is that the phrase teaches us that the rule against consuming blood applies even when the Temple is no longer standing. Rashbam's explanation is certainly closer to the simple meaning of the words בכל מושבותיכם.

See also Nahm.'s strident argument (in his commentary to vs. 25) that בכל מושבותיכם is incontrovertible evidence that the Torah applies these laws to meat other than that of sacrifices. He directs this against iE's claim (in his commentary to vs. 20) that the phrase need not mean that, and that context suggests that the whole discussion here concerns sacrificial meat.

[39]I.e. the extra benefits that the priests will receive because of their service and because they were anointed. Rashbam uses the Hebrew word שכר, presumably as an allusion to Num. 18:31, where the text describes the Levites' gifts as "[their] recompense (שכר) for [their] services."

The phrase משחת אהרן is difficult. While the word משחה, especially when applied to priests, would usually be translated as "anointing," that explanation makes little sense here. There are also two more passages in the Torah (Ex. 29:29 and Num. 18:8) where a similar word, למשחה, is used in a context that, arguably, describes extra benefits accruing to priests, not the act of anointing.

Most commentators have attempted to explain משחה as meaning something other than anointing here. Some say that since the root *m-sh-ḥ* can mean to "measure," the noun משחה

anointing of Aaron and his sons, as it is written in [the Torah portion,] *Ṣav 'et 'aharon*:[40] the "skin of the burnt offering" (7:8), the meat of the sin offering (6:19) and of the guilt offering (7:7), the cakes of the thanksgiving offering

---

here might mean "allotment" or "share." (See Levine, here.) Alternatively some follow Onq.'s translation, לרבו, claiming that it means "perquisite." (See e.g. Milgrom, here.) However, this may be a misunderstanding of Onq. As Rashi points out (in his commentary to Ex. 29:29, s.v. למשחה), Onq. virtually always uses a form of the Aramaic root *r-b-y* to translate the root *m-sh-ḥ*, when referring to political or religious anointing. So Onq. does not seem to be suggesting that the word משחה means anything different here from what it generally means.

Rashi curiously does not comment here. Perhaps he feels confident that his interpretation is already known, since he has written a number of times that the root *m-sh-ḥ* can imply "greatness" or "honor" (e.g. commentary ad Ex. 29:29, 30:29 or Num. 18:8).

In his commentary to Ex. 29:29, Rashbam seems to follow Rashi, interpreting the word למשחה figuratively. See notes 14 and 15 there. Here and ad Num. 18:8, Rashbam does not do that. He does see למשחה as meaning "anointment," but posits the understood word שכר in our verse. In other words, Rashbam does not change the meaning of the word למשחה but assumes that the phrase is to be seen as elliptical. Hence the verse describes the recompense that Aaron and his sons will receive in exchange for their anointing. So also NJPS which adds in a footnote that the word "anointment" here implies "accruing from anointment." Like Rashbam, see also iE and Ehrlich, and see Hizq. who offers two explanations, Rashbam's and one that would be consonant with Rashi's.

The idea that the root *m-sh-ḥ* need not be connected to anointing must have been commonly taught by Jews in Northern France; it even appears in the commentary of Andrew of St. Victor. He writes (p. 167) that even though the Vulgate translates למשחה here as *unctio* (the Latin word for anointing), the Hebrew really means "*augmentum*," (i.e. "increase," or some other similar idea related to Rashi's theories). See the discussion of the passage in Dahan's *Les intellectuels chrétiens*, p. 283. Curiously, Rainer Berndt suggests ("*Les interprétations juives*," 230, number 174) that Andrew's comment here is in some way dependent on or similar to Rashbam's. Rashbam, though, would hardly agree, as explained in the previous paragraph. In all of Andrew's Leviticus commentary this is the only interpretation that Berndt sees as possibly dependent on Rashbam. I believe, however, that there are a number of places in Leviticus where the commentaries of Andrew and Rashbam bear striking similarities. See e.g. notes to Lev. 10:1–3, 13:2, 16:10, 17:4 and *passim*.

[40]That Torah portion extends from Lev. 6:1 to 8:36.

It is strange to find an exegete, in the middle of his commentary to Torah portion X, writing the phrase "as it is written in Torah portion X." Perhaps Rashbam is continuing his comment to 6:1, where he noted that there is a great deal of repetition between this Torah portion and the previous one. He may be pointing out that one of the themes explored only in *this* Torah portion is the theme of priestly perquisites. Perhaps the text of Rashbam's comment should read כל מה שאמור ב[פרשת] צו, instead of the version that we have, כמו שאמור ב[פרשת] צו.

Rashbam's interpretation opposes the explanation that the extra rights or rewards being given to Aaron in this verse are simply the rights outlined in the previous four verses—the right to the chest and the thigh of the well-being offerings. (See Milgrom [p. 433] and Mendelssohn [in his parenthetical addition to the *Be'ur*] who argue for that reading.) Rashbam sees our verse not as a summary of the immediately preceding unit of text, concerning the well-being offering, but as a summary of all the laws of chapters 6 and 7.

(7:14), the breast and the thigh of the well-being offering (7:34) [and] "what is left" of the meal offering (7:9).

שמיני (Leviticus 9–11)

9:1 ויהי ביום השמיני ON THE EIGHTH DAY: of the ordination ceremony (*milu'im*), when the Tabernacle was erected and when Aaron and his sons had already been dedicated to perform the [sacrificial] service.[1]

9:4 כי היום ה׳ נראה FOR TODAY THE LORD WILL APPEAR: and will bring forth fire from the heavens to consume the sacrifices.[2]

9:13 ויקטר על המזבח HE TURNED IT INTO SMOKE ON THE ALTAR: He placed them [the parts of the sacrifice that were to be burned] on the altar, so that when the divine fire would come, they would be turned into smoke.[3]

---

[1]Both here and in his commentary to Exodus 29:35, Rashbam views the events of this chapter as occurring on the day immediately following the seven day *milu'im* ceremony which had ordained Aaron and his sons as priests. This follows standard rabbinic exegesis. See e.g. Git. 60a-b, and Rashi there, 60a, s.v. ופרשת אחרי מות. Cf. iE who suggests here that he would prefer (were it not for the rabbinic tradition) to say that "the eighth day" really means the eighth day of Nisan, i.e. one week after the date of the erecting of the Tabernacle. See also iE's longer commentary to Ex. 40:2 where he attempts to show that his explanation makes more sense and may also have some grounding in rabbinic literature. Like iE, see Luzzatto and Milgrom (p. 571). See also the discussions in the *Be'ur* by Mendelssohn (to Ex. 40:2) and by Wessely here.

Rashi here offers generally the same explanation, but Rashbam's language seems to be a more *peshaṭ*-like reworking of Rashi's. Rashi's commentary makes three points: that this day was the eighth day "(1) of the ordination ceremony . . . (2) the very day when the Tabernacle was erected and (3) it [this day] took ten crowns of distinction, which are enumerated in Seder Olam." Rashbam tells us the first two points that Rashi made, using virtually the same language. For Rashi's third, midrashic point he substitutes his own, more contextually relevant, explanation, i.e. that Moses is calling to Aaron and his sons in our verse because this is the day of the completion of their dedication as priests. Similarly to Rashbam, see JBS and Hizq.

[2]Rashi (following Sifra) says that God's "appearance" means that He will "cause His divine Presence to dwell in the works of your hands." Rashbam however sees the appearance as something much more concrete—the divine fire of vs. 24. In his commentary to vss. 23–4 below he emphasizes the point. See note 9 there. See also commentary to Ex. 16:7 (and note 15 there) and to Ex. 29:43 (and note 25 there). Like Rashbam, see iE (ad vs. 6) and Luzzatto.

[3]Rashbam's problem is the apparent contradiction between vs. 24, which says that a divine fire consumed the burnt offering, and our verse, which says that Aaron "turned the burnt offering into smoke." His solution is that Aaron's action here was simply to place the appropriate pieces on the altar, to be consumed later by the fire of vs. 24. See Wessely (ad vs.

9:23–24 ויבא משה ואהרן אל אהל מועד MOSES AND AARON ENTERED THE TENT OF MEETING: to pray that the [divine] fire should descend.[4] THE PRESENCE OF THE LORD APPEARED TO ALL THE PEOPLE: In what way? FIRE CAME FORTH FROM BEFORE THE LORD: from the Holy of Holies[5] [first] to the golden altar,[6] in order to burn the incense offering there. For, as it is written in tractate *Yoma*' (33a-b), the incense is to be offered [regularly in the Temple service] before the daily offering is turned to smoke. The fire found Aaron's two sons there, near the golden altar, and it burned them [to death]. Then the fire went out [of the Tabernacle] to the [copper] altar[7] where it

---

10) who argues against Rashbam, saying that Rashbam has illegitimately stretched the meaning of the word ויקטר, and that there must have been a fire burning on the altar, even before the divine fire appeared. So also Hoffmann, here and ad vs. 24. Still Hoffmann notes that the LXX to our verse interprets as Rashbam does. Milgrom (p. 582) notes further the strange coincidence that both the LXX and Rashbam choose to comment only on ויקטר in our verse, not on הקטיר of vs. 10, which ought to present the same problem. Milgrom (*ibid.*) notes that Targum Neofiti more consistently interprets all these forms of the verb *q-ṭ-r* as meaning "to arrange," not to turn into smoke.

[4]As Milgrom notes (p. 588), a conjectural explanation is required since no reason is given for Moses' and Aaron's entry into the Tent. Rashi offers two explanations (both found in Sifra): (1) Moses went into the Tent to teach Aaron how to offer incense; and (2) Aaron was embarrassed that he had not succeeded in getting the Presence of God to appear. He complained to Moses. Moses went into the Tent together with Aaron, and, when they prayed together, God's Presence descended.

Rashbam's interpretation may be seen as a more *peshaṭ*-like reworking of that second explanation. Like Rashbam, see iE, Hizq. and Wessely. Milgrom also considers this the most attractive conjectural explanation.

[5]Here Rashbam writes that the fire "came forth" from the Holy of Holies. Above ad vs. 4 and below ad 10:1–3 he writes that the fire came from the heavens. Both explanations may be found in rabbinic literature. For the Holy of Holies, see e.g. Sanh. 52a (יצאו מבית קדשי הקדשים). For the heavens, see Sifre Zuta ad Num. 11:2 (אותה אש שירדה מן השמים). Apparently Rashbam does not see these two ideas as mutually exclusive. (Perhaps the fire from heaven entered the Holy of Holies and from there came forth to the altars.) See Hoffmann who opposes Rashbam and says that the fire came from heaven, and not from the Holy of Holies. Like Rashbam, Milgrom writes (p. 590) that "there can be no doubt" that the fire emerged from the adytum" [= the Holy of Holies].

[6]Or the "incense altar," the altar in the Tabernacle, just outside of the Holy of Holies. This is the normal place for the incense offering, and Rashbam writes here and in his commentary to 10:1 that it really was taking place there. Perhaps he emphasizes this because there are opposing opinions that the incense offering on that day was taking place somewhere else, either inside the Holy of Holies or on the outer altar. See e.g. Tos. Eruv. 63a, s.v. מאי דריש. See also iE ad 10:4.

[7]Or the "burnt offering altar," the altar in the enclosure, outside of the Tabernacle itself. Rashbam emphasizes that despite the order of the verses, the fire consumed Nadab and Abihu before it consumed the offerings, i.e. the events described in 10:2 took place before the events described in 9:24. To that end, he emphasizes that the fire followed standard halakhic

CONSUMED THE BURNT OFFERING AND THE FAT PARTS[8] ON THE ALTAR.[9]

---

procedure, burning the incense before burning the animal parts from the sacrifices. Josephus (*Antiquities* 3:117) has the actions taking place in the order described in the text. See also the discussion of Rabad in his commentary to Sifra *Milu'im*.

[8]Both here and in his commentary to 10:1–3, Rashbam misquotes (or the ms. miswrites) השלמים, instead of MT's החלבים, probably because of the similar phrase at the end of vs. 22.

[9]Rashbam makes two interesting and arguable points about the fire described in vs. 24. First he says that the description of the fire here (in vs. 24) is an elaboration of the statement (at the end of verse 23) that God's Presence appeared. According to Rashbam, the verses say that God's Presence appeared in the form of a fire. Secondly, Rashbam says that the fire, which miraculously consumed the sacrifices (in vs. 24), is the same fire that killed Nadab and Abihu (in 10:2). As NJPSC puts it, this same fire "was a blessing to those who pleased God but destructive to those who angered Him."

Concerning the first point—that the verse about the fire gives the details of how it was that God's Presence appeared—this is not the first time that Rashbam has offered such an explanation. In Genesis 18:1, God "appears" to Abraham, but no explanation is given of that "appearance." Vs. 2 says that Abraham saw three men. Rashbam writes that the way that God appeared to Abraham was through the visit of the three men. That explanation opposes a number of midrashic attempts to delineate what the unexplained "appearance" of God there really was. See note 1 on pp. 58–59 there.

Here also it is possible to see the phrase (vs. 23) "the Presence of the LORD appeared" as referring to some (perhaps mystical) theophany, something other than the physical fire that appears in the next verse. See e.g. Nahm. ad Gen. 18:1, (s.v. באלוני ממרא) who argues that both there and here the "appearance" described is "seeing the Shekhinah," a special favor done for Abraham there, and here for Moses and Aaron (and through them for the entire people) as a reward for *miṣvot* that they had performed. See also Rashi ad 9:23, s.v. ויבא ("ירדה שכינה לישראל—the Shekhinah descended upon the Jewish people"), or Qohelet Rabba 4 which argues that when Moses and Aaron blessed the people, God appeared through the Shekhinah that hovered over their hands (שרתה שכינה על ידיהם). Rashbam's explanation—that the Presence manifested itself as fire—achieved much popularity. It is found in Hizq., Abarbanel, Shapira in *Ha-rekhasim leviq'ah* (despite the fact that Shapira generally has a negative attitude to Rashbam), Luzzatto (ad 9:4), NJPSC, and Milgrom (p. 599). See also N. Leibowitz's *'Iyyunim*, p. 96. See Hoffmann who argues against Rashbam, claiming that II Chron. 7:1 ("fire descended from heaven . . . and the Presence of the LORD filled the house") proves that the fire and the Presence are two separate things. Wessely also prefers Nahm.'s understanding to Rashbam's.

The second point that Rashbam makes—that the fire of our verse and the fire of 10:2 are one and the same—is also innovative. A more midrashic formulation of this idea may be found in Sifre Zuta ad Numbers 11:2. There it is argued that the same fire consumed the sacrifices and also incinerated Nadab and Abihu. But it is further argued there that this same fire also miraculously lasted throughout the Israelites' sojourn in the desert and consumed all the sacrifices that they brought during the forty years. (וכל הקרבנות שהיו ישראל מקריבין במדבר היתה האש יוצאה ואוכלת אותן . . . ותרד אש מן השמים ותאכל אין כת' אלא ותצא ואותה האש היא שאכלה נדב ואביהו שנאמר ותצא אש מלפני יי״ ותאכל אותם). Rashbam makes the point in a more *peshaṭ*-oriented manner and provides literary arguments for his reading. See Rashbam's continuation of this explanation in his next comment.

10:1–3 ויקחו בני אהרן נדב ואביהוא AARON'S SONS NADAB AND ABIHU TOOK . . . Before the fire came forth from before the LORD (9:24), they had already EACH taken HIS FIRE PAN to offer incense inside [the Tabernacle] on the golden altar. [This must have happened before the events of 9:24,] for the morning's incense always precedes the [burning of the sacrificial] limbs.[10] Into those pans they put AN ALIEN FIRE, WHICH HE, Moses,[11] HAD NOT COMMANDED THEM [to offer] on this day. Even though on all other days it is written that "the sons of Aaron the priest should put fire onto the altar" (1:7), today [specifically] Moses did not command [that that be done]. He did not want them to bring a "regular" fire,[12] because they were expecting the descent of a divine fire.[13] It would have been inappropriate to bring an alien fire on that specific day; [they should have waited] so that God's Name would be sanctified[14] when everyone would find out that a fire had descended from heaven.[15] Elijah

---

[10]As Rashbam argued above ad 9:23–24, citing a rabbinic prooftext.

See the various arguments of Wessely, Luzzatto and Hoffmann, who offer textual and/or halakhic arguments to show that the incense being offered here could *not* be the regular morning incense offering. Many *midrashim* also make that argument. See e.g. VR 20:8. So also NJPSC.

[11]Rashbam writes that the subject of the verb "צוה—*he* commanded" is Moses. Arguably it might be God. So NJPS. Milgrom writes (p. 598): "The subject is obviously the Lord."

In fact most interpretations see God as the subject of the verb צוה, and the sin of Nadab and Abihu as failure to observe some instruction of God's. Rashbam, though, has to say that Moses is the subject of צוה. According to his explanation, the fire that Nadab and Abihu brought was, generally speaking, an appropriate fire, the one that God *had* commanded that priests should bring regularly. The problem was that Moses had overridden the general instructions for this specific day since he was praying that God would provide a divine fire. Many *midrashim* also see Nadab and Abihu's sin in terms of not listening to instructions from Moses, or of failing to accept Moses' authority.

[12]Rashbam's argument—that the ritual actions of Nadab and Abihu would have constituted proper behavior on any other day—may be found in a number of classical rabbinic sources. Some of those sources even cite this same verse from Lev. 1 to explain their reasoning. See e.g. Eruv. 63a and Yoma 53a. Rashbam uses the phrase "a 'regular' fire— אש של הדיוט," the same phrase that is used in those sources.

However Rashbam is taking issue here with a perhaps more common rabbinic tradition that the fire was brought in a manner that would have been improper at any time. See e.g. Onq. and VR 20:8. So also Milgrom (pp. 598–599).

[13]As Rashbam wrote above, in his commentary to 9:4. See similarly Andrew of St. Victor who writes (p. 176) that the fire was "alien" because it was an earthly fire, not the heavenly one (*ignem alienum terrenum et non illum qui de caelo missus a Domino descendit*).

[14]Miracles are often understood in rabbinic literature as vehicles for "sanctifying God's Name." See e.g. Tanh. B. *Va-yeṣe'* 14.

See also the end of Rashbam's comment to vs. 3 below, and note 32 there.

[15]Midrashic and exegetical literature provide a variety of explanations of what precisely Nadab and Abihu did wrong. Rashi says, in his commentary to Ex. 24:10, that their sin was that they "saw the God of Israel," an action that Rashbam there sees as meritorious, not a

said similarly, "Apply no fire" (I Kings 18:25), because he wanted to sanctify God's Name through the descent of a fire from above.[16]

The verse (2) ותצא אש מלפני ה' ותאכל אותם, FIRE CAME FORTH FROM THE LORD AND CONSUMED THEM, is referring to the same fire as in the verse (9:24) above, "Fire came forth . . .." I already explained this concerning the [repeated] verse, "Moses brought back the people's words to the LORD."[17] Similarly the phrase "He returned the silver to his mother," appears twice (Judges 17:3 and 17:4) in the story of Micah's idol and the two [verses] are [referring to] one [and the same action].[18]

Here also the two verses (9:24 and 10:2) are [referring to] one [fire].[19] The fire came forth to "consume the burnt offering and the fat parts" on the outer altar.

---

capital crime. (See p. 300, note 12, of my Exodus volume.) Here in Leviticus (ad 10:2) Rashi offers two more explanations: that Nadab and Abihu were intoxicated (following VR 12:5) or that they made a halakhic decision concerning the fire without consulting Moses (following Sifra and Eruv. 63a and many other sources). For further midrashic explanations, see Kasher, vol. 28, pp. 2–5.

Rashbam's explanation appears similar to that last explanation from Sifra and Eruv. cited by Rashi. See however Wessely who argues with great passion that Rashbam's explanation could not be correct and that the various midrashic sources (and Rashi in their wake) understood the sin of Nadab and Abihu as taking place *after* the divine fire descended. Nadab and Abihu, caught up in the joy of the divine appearance and acting out of genuine religious motives, but without consultation, did something that was not specifically commanded. The language of the Sifra (*Milu'im* 32, the source that Rashi is citing) supports that understanding: "כיון שראו אש חדשה עמדו . . .—after they saw the new fire, they arose . . .."

Rashbam appears to be the first medieval exegete to suggest that impatience was the problem. However, as Mendelssohn points out (in his parenthetical additions to the *Be'ur*), Rashbam's position does appear in an alternative understanding found in Sifra (*Milu'im* 22): "When Aaron's sons saw that all the sacrifices had been offered and all the deeds had been done and the Shekhinah had not yet descended, Nadab said to Abihu, 'Does anyone cook a meal without fire?' Immediately they took an alien fire . . .." Rashbam's explanation achieved a certain following. See e.g. JBS, Hizq. and *Da'at zeqenim.*

[16]Rashbam's comparison of our chapter to the Elijah story appears to be his innovation, as does his explanation that the sin of Nadab and Abihu was that they lost an opportunity for God's Name to be sanctified. Rashbam's description of their sin sounds similar to the language of Num. 20:12 "because you did not believe in me sufficiently to sanctify My Name," concerning the sin of Moses and Aaron. (See Rashbam ad Num. 20:10, and note 20 there. See also Rashi ad Deut. 32:51.)

[17]The wording of that verse is repeated virtually verbatim in the next verse in Exodus (19:8). Rashbam explains there that though the words are written twice in two separate verses, only one action took place. According to him, Moses reported the people's words to God just once.

[18]On Rashbam's explanation of the verses in Exodus and the verses in Judges, see his commentary to Exodus 19:8 and notes 8, 9 and 11 there (pp. 203–205).

[19]As noted above concerning 9:23, Rashbam's explanation here—that there was one fire, not two—appears to be his own new insight, or at least his own reworking of an old midrashic point using literary arguments. He claims, both here and in Exodus 19, that at times a

Aaron's sons had taken[20] an alien fire and offered it on the internal altar. THE FIRE CAME FORTH FROM BEFORE THE LORD to burn the incense [at the internal altar,] inside [the Tabernacle] first. There it struck down Aaron's sons and they died. Then the fire went out from there and came to the outer altar where it consumed the burnt offering.

So THEY DIED BEFORE THE LORD: Immediately when Aaron heard about their deaths, he wanted to cease performing the service and begin mourning for his sons. (3) BUT MOSES SAID TO AARON . . .: "Do not mourn or cry. Do not cease performing the service.[21] For what I am saying to you now is THAT WHICH THE LORD HAD SAID, 'בקרובי אקדש—I WILL SANCTIFY MYSELF THROUGH THOSE WHO ARE CLOSE TO ME'": [This means that Moses said, "God had said to me,] 'through those High Priests that are close to Me I wish to be sanctified; I do not want My Name and My service to be desecrated.' That is what God said to me (Lev. 21:10–12), 'The priest who is greater than his fellows . . . should not let his hair grow long[22] or tear his clothing

---

particular phrase appears twice, in close proximity, within the same narrative, when the phrase really is describing something that happened only once. Rashbam may have learned this literary principle from Joseph Qara, or perhaps they came to this conclusion together. See the discussion in the notes to my Exodus volume and in my forthcoming article, "Rashbam as a 'Literary' Exegete," in *With Reverence for the Word*, edited by Jane McAuliffe and Barry Walfish.

A number of exegetes follow Rashbam's lead, arguing that it was the same divine fire in 9:23 and 10:2. See e.g. JBS, Hizq. and NJPSC. See Luzzatto, Hoffmann and Milgrom (p. 599) who argue against Rashbam. Luzzatto's claim—that if Rashbam were right, 10:2 would have to read ותצא האש instead of ותצא אש—appears to disregard Rashbam's argument that proper biblical style allows the repetition of the phrase verbatim in a situation like this.

[20]The syntax of Rashbam's comment as it is printed in Rosin's edition is unusual: כשיצא האש ותאכל . . . כשלקחו בני אהרן. I have done my best to render the sense of the remark. Perhaps Rashbam is saying, "At the time that the fire came forth to consume the burnt offering, at that very time Aaron's sons were offering an alien fire . . .."

[21]Rashbam appears to be the first Jewish exegete to suggest that Moses' remarks to Aaron constituted instructions, or perhaps even chastisement for the fact that Aaron wanted to desist from performing the sacrificial service. Nowhere in the text does it say that Aaron wanted to stop. Still, Rashbam's speculative explanation that Moses was addressing Aaron's hesitancy about continuing to perform priestly duties fits in well with the tone of the discussion between Moses and Aaron below in vss. 16–20.

The standard explanation is that Moses is addressing words of comfort, not of chastisement, to Aaron in this verse. See e.g. the midrashic explanation which Rashbam himself cites and dismisses below. JBS offers a few interpretations to our verse, the first of which is the same as Rashbam's. Wessely, as is his wont, dismisses Rashbam's interpretation (ואין פירושו נראה לי); Ehrlich rejects it caustically (ואין פירושו פירוש).

[22]It is hard to know what Rashbam thinks the verb פרע means in this context. I am assuming that he understands it in the standard halakhic manner, as meaning to refrain from cutting one's hair. See e.g. Sifra and Rashi ad Lev. 21:10, and Rashi here, vs. 6. For other instances

[even when a relative of his dies.] . . . He shall not go out of the sanctuary and profane the sanctuary of his God.'[23] This means that if he does *not* go out,[24] he will sanctify[25] [God's service]."

([I am offering this interpretation—that Moses here, in chapter 10, is referring to a speech from God that is not recorded until chapter 21—because] there is no chronological order in the Torah.[26])

"Accordingly do not set the service aside, for you are the High Priest. Do not go out and do not desecrate [the service]. Rather let God and His service be sanctified by you."

---

of the verb פרע associated with hair, see Rashbam's commentary to Ex. 5:4 (and note 4 there), and commentary to Deut. 32:42. See also commentary to Ex. 32:25, and notes 32 and 33 there.

[23]Concerning the phrase, "that which the LORD had said," in our verse, Milgrom writes (p. 600), "But where did he say it?" The most common rabbinic explanation, the one that Rashbam dismisses below, is that the reference is to Ex. 29:43. Others (e.g. the opinion of Rabbi Judah the Prince in Zev. 115b) suggest that it is Ex. 19:22. Some (e.g. iE) suggest that not all of God's speeches to Moses need to be recorded in the text; if Moses said here that God previously told him something, then God did, even if it was never recorded in the Torah. Others (e.g. Nahm. and Luzzatto) argue that what God "said" means that God "decreed," in other words that God's actions here "tell" us that "I will sanctify . . .."

Rashbam's interpretation, that "that which God said" is a reference to Lev. 21:10–12, appears to be original. It is also offered by his younger contemporary JBS.

[24]Rashbam interprets the words "לא יצא—he shall not go out" in Lev. 21 as meaning "he shall not refrain from performing his sacrificial duties." That is the standard rabbinic explanation. See e.g. Sanh. 84a and Rashi there, s.v. ומן המקדש.

[25]Rashbam offers an alternative to the talmudic "close reading" of this verse, perhaps even playing with the language of the Talmud. In Zev. 16a, the Talmud says that the phrase, "*he* [= the High Priest] should not go out, and *he* will not desecrate," implies "if some other [priest] refrains from going out, he *will* desecrate (הא אחר שלא יצא חילל)." In other words, the verse teaches that any other priest who is a mourner should stop serving in the Temple; he would desecrate God's Name if he continued the service. Rashbam's close reading of the phrase is that "he should not go out and he will not desecrate," implies that "if he does *not* go out, he will sanctify (הא אם לא יצא קידש)."

Rashbam is also offering an alternative understanding of the word אקדש. Almost all exegetes suggest that the word refers to God being sanctified though the deaths of Nadab and Abihu. Rashbam says that God is described here as being sanctified through the sacrifices of this chapter, if Aaron continues to perform them despite his mourning. See also Rashbam's commentary to Num. 20:10 and 20:13, and notes 20 and 22 there.

[26]The exegetical principle that the Torah does not always record events in the order in which they occurred (אין מוקדם ומאוחר בתורה) is found once in the Talmud (Pes. 6b) and is used many times by Rashi (for example ad Gen. 35:29) and other commentators. The phrase appears in Rashbam's commentary only here.

ועל פני כל העם אכבד AND I WILL [THUS] GAIN HONOR BEFORE ALL THE PEOPLE: This is God's honor, when a man sees his sons dead and yet sets his mourning aside because of the service of his Creator.[27]

וידם אהרן AARON WAS SILENT: about his mourning; he did not cry and he did not mourn. [וידם here means to refrain from mourning;] so it is written in Ezekiel (24:16–17), "O mortal, I am about to take away from you the delight of your eyes through pestilence . . .. Silence yourself (דום) from screaming; observe no mourning for the dead." Here also וידם refers to being silent [and thus refraining] from any mourning or crying.[28] This is the lesson[29] of the text and it is the true plain meaning of Scripture.

[There is] however an *'aggadah*[30] which says that Moses was comforting Aaron by saying to him:

> God had told me [before] (Ex. 29:43), "ונקדש בכבודי—that He would sanctify Himself בְּכְבוּדַי,"[31] through [the death of] someone whom He honors. I had thought that meant either me or you. Now you see that they [Nadab and Abihu] are greater than you or I [since God chose to sanctify Himself through their death].

[That explanation] does not follow the plain meaning of Scripture.[32] Could God have really told Moses, "Make for me a Tabernacle and on the day when it is erected your greatest people will die"?!

---

[27]Again Rashbam explains the word אכבד in an original manner. Most exegetes say that honor (כבוד) will come to God through the lesson that people will learn from the deaths of Nadab and Abihu. (Thus e.g. Rashi.) Rashbam explains that honor will come to God from Aaron's actions. So also JBS and Hizq.

[28]Again Rashbam's explanation is original. Generally the word וידם is interpreted as meaning that Aaron, as NJPSC puts it, "accepted God's harsh judgment." Rashbam argues that the word describes refraining from mourning, and correctly notes that in Ezekiel the word serves a similar function. Milgrom's paraphrase here (p. 604) of Rashbam's position, "Thus, Aaron, on his own initiative did not mourn (Rashbam)," misses Rashbam's central point that it is Moses who makes sure that Aaron will not mourn, following the explicit instruction of Lev. 21:11.

[29]The precise meaning of this part of Rashbam's comment is uncertain. The ms., according to Rosin, reads מותר, which makes no sense here. Rosin emends to מוסר, which is better, but would still be an unusual word for Rashbam to use in this context.

[30]Zev. 115b.

[31]This explanation is based on the *'al tiqre'* method of exegesis. Rashi here reads the proposed *'al tiqre'* "emendation" as בִּמְכֻבָּדַי. In his commentary to Exodus, our text of Rashi reads בִּכְבוּדַי, like Rashbam's text here. Both readings can be found in talmudic manuscripts. See *Diqduqe soferim* ad Zev. 115b.

[32]In his comment Rashbam has offered two separate explanations of how "sanctifying God" took place or was supposed to take place in this text. He writes that miracles—e.g. a miraculous fire from heaven—sanctify God's Name, and he writes that when priests continue to perform the Temple service even when they are mourners that also leads to the sanctification of God. But he rejects the idea of God being sanctified by administering strict punishment to

10:6–7 ראשיכם אל תפרעו DO NOT LET YOUR HAIR GROW: This is what he [= Moses] said to Eleazar and Ithamar: "Even though you are only rank-and-file priests, and the commandment to refrain from cutting one's hair[33] and from tearing one's clothes applies only to *High* Priests,[34] still today you have the status that, in the future, only High Priests will have. Why? FOR THE LORD'S ANOINTING OIL IS UPON YOU. I.e. because you are being anointed anew with your father."[35] That same reason [i.e. the anointing] is written (Lev. 21:10–12) concerning the [restrictions on the way that a] High Priest [mourns for a relative], "He should not let his hair grow . . . he should not go outside the sanctuary and profane the sanctuary of his God for upon him is the distinction of the anointing oil of his God, I am the LORD."[36]

10:10–11 ולהבדיל. . . .ולהורות FOR YOU MUST DISTINGUISH . . . AND YOU MUST TEACH: As the rabbis said (Eruv. 64b), "an intoxicated person may not teach (אל יורה)."[37]

---

those who are close to Him. See also Rashbam to Num. 20:10 and 20:13 and notes 20 and 22 there.

[33]See note 22 above.

[34]Lev. 21:10–12. There it is clear that it is only a High Priest who should refrain from mourning when a close relative dies. Other priests have no such restrictions.

[35]Exodus 40:13–15 states that both Aaron and his sons were anointed on the day that the Tabernacle was dedicated, which, according to Rashbam ad 9:1, is the day that the events of this chapter are taking place. Rashbam writes here that they are being anointed "anew" because it says in 8:30 that a mixture of anointing oil and blood was sprinkled on Aaron and his sons. That ceremony took place seven days before the events of chapter 9.

[36]From the point of view of halakhic analysis (and perhaps even from the point of view of the simple meaning of the text), our verses are problematic. Lev. 21 states clearly that a rank-and-file priest, i.e. any priest other than the High Priest, does observe standard rules of mourning when someone to whom he was closely related (e.g. a brother) dies. Why then were Eleazar and Ithamar told *not* to mourn for their brother?

Rashi's answer is that the special celebration of the day led to this ruling. Rashbam instead suggests that Eleazar and Ithamar have special status; they are in some ways like a High Priest. Lev. 21 explains that the status of the High Priest is connected to the anointing oil, so the fact that Eleazar and Ithamar are anointed makes them special too. Hizq., who follows Rashbam's line of interpretation, writes that only on the very day of the anointing would Eleazar and Ithamar have had that status, and he argues further that that position finds support in a (virtually unfathomable) comment in Sifra here. See also lengthy discussions in Nahm. here and in Kasher, vol. 28, note 32.

[37]Or perhaps, "an intoxicated person should not make a halakhic ruling."

So also Rashi. However Rashi offers this interpretation only concerning the word ולהורות in vs. 11. He feels that something else is to be learned (concerning priestly duties) from the word ולהבדיל in vs. 10. The Talmud (Ker. 13b) also suggests that each of these words teaches something different. Rashbam says that these two verses present one theme, the idea that an intoxicated person should not teach. As Milgrom notes (pp. 615 and 617), Ezekiel

10:16 ואת שעיר החטאת THE GOAT OF SIN OFFERING: The rabbis interpreted (Zev. 101a-b) that the reference is to the goat offering that was offered in honor of the New Moon, an offering which applies also in future generations.[38] [That offering was burned and was not eaten;] however the goat brought on behalf of the [entire] people and the goat offered by Nahshon were eaten.[39]

10:17 לשאת את עון העדה [THE SIN OFFERING . . . HE HAS GIVEN IT TO YOU] TO REMOVE THE GUILT OF THE COMMUNITY: [This offering atones for the sin of] impurity of the sanctuary and its holy things, as it is explained in *Shevu'ot*.[40]

10:18 הן לא הובא את דמה אל הקדש פנימה SINCE ITS BLOOD WAS NOT BROUGHT INSIDE INTO THE HOLY: i.e. into the *hekhal*,[41] [accordingly the sacrifice should have been eaten, not burned]. All "internal" sin offerings are [supposed to be] burned, as it is written (6:23), "No sin offering may be eaten from which blood is brought into the Tent of Meeting for expiation in the

---

(44:23) combines the instructions of these two verses into one: "They shall teach (יורו) my people what is sacred and what is profane and inform them what is pure and impure."

[38]The phrase that Rashbam uses here, קדשי דורות, is from Zev. 101a.

[39]According to rabbinic exegesis, since that day when Nadab and Abihu died was the first of Nisan and the first day of the celebration of the erection of the Tabernacle, there were three goats offered as sin offerings: the one described in 9:3 ("Speak to the Israelites: take a he-goat for a sin offering"); the one described in Num. 7:1–16 ("(1) On the day that Moses finished setting up the Tabernacle . . . (12) the one who presented his offering on the first day was Nahshon . . . (16) one goat for a sin offering"); and the one that is required as a sacrifice on any New Moon (Num. 28:15). In Zev. 101b the rabbis explained what logic motivated Aaron's sons to eat two of those sacrifices and to burn the third (the sin offering of the New Moon, the one that was to be a requirement in future generations). See also Rashi here at greater length.

[40]The phrase טומאת מקדש וקדשיו is taken from Mishnah Shev. 1:4, where it says that all sin offerings atone for such sins. The Talmud in Shev. 9b-10a and in Zev. 101b explains that our verse teaches that the specific sin offering being discussed here—the sin offering of the New Moon, as Rashbam told us in his previous comment—atones for such sins of impurity. So also Rashi here, at much greater length.

The talmudic discussion draws a parallel between the functions of the sin offerings and the function of the "frontlet" (ציץ) worn by the High Priest. According to the Talmud, the frontlet also atones for sins of cultic impurity. Curiously, in his commentary to Exodus 28:38 Rashbam distances himself from that interpretation of the phrase there concerning the frontlet, "ונשא אהרן את עון הקדשים—Aaron will take away any sin arising from the holy things," arguing that "following the plain meaning of Scripture, the verse is not referring to sacrifices offered in an impure manner." Here in his commentary to Leviticus, Rashbam offers only the approach of the *midrash halakhah*, even though the words here, "עון העדה—the sin of the community," arguably have even less connection to the problem of impurity of *sancta*.

[41]The standard rabbinic word for the part of the Tabernacle that is not the Holy of Holies.

sanctuary; any such shall be consumed by fire." But this is an "external" sin offering.[42]

10:19 הן היום הקריבו את חטאתם ואת עולתם THIS DAY THEY BROUGHT THEIR SIN OFFERING AND THEIR BURNT OFFERING: This is a reference to the burnt offering and the sin offering of Aaron and his sons that is mentioned above (9:2), "Take a calf of the herd for a sin offering and a ram for a burnt offering, without blemish." [In our verse Aaron appropriately attributes the offering of those sacrifices to his sons, despite the fact that chapter 9 describes Aaron himself as the primary priest performing those sacrifices,] for Aaron's sons assisted with the collection of the blood, as it is written above (9:9 and 9:12).[43]

This is what Aaron said: "Why were you angry with my sons? THIS very DAY my sons and I BROUGHT our sacrifices through which we were dedicated to perform the [sacrificial] service.[44] In the midst of all this greatness, this terrible tragedy occurred; SUCH THINGS HAVE BEFALLEN ME. How could I eat that sin offering which applies also in future generations,[45] on this day when our joy has been destroyed and darkened.[46] [Such behavior would be] similar to

---

[42]See commentary to 6:23, and notes 21 and 24 there, for an explanation of the different rules for the two kinds of sin offerings, the ones whose blood is placed on the internal altar and the one whose blood is placed on the external altar.

Rashbam's explanation is uncontroversial. It is slightly different from that of Rashi (following Zev. 101a). Rashi explains that the point that Moses is making here is that the blood of this sacrifice was not brought *inappropriately* into the *hekhal.* If it had been, then burning was correctly done. Rashbam explains that Moses is saying, "This sin offering is not of the category of sin offerings whose blood is *appropriately* brought into the *hekhal.*" Rashi and Rashbam disagreed in the same way about the interpretation of 6:23. See note 24 there.

[43]Rashbam's explanation is much simpler than the complicated answer that Rashi suggests (following Zev. 16a and 101a) as to why this sacrifice is being referred to here as offered by Aaron's sons, not by Aaron.

[44]This is the same phrase that Rashbam uses to describe that ceremony in his commentary to 9:1.

[45]Rashbam is alluding here to the talmudic attempt to understand Aaron's logic. In vss. 12–15 Moses gave Eleazar and Ithamar specific instructions to eat a number of the sacrifices of the day. The Talmud (Zev. 101a) suggests that Aaron felt that those instructions applied only to קדשי שעה, to sacrifices that were being offered on a one-time basis, because of the events of the dedication ceremony. He thought, though, that the general stricture against a mourner in his first day of mourning (an *'onen*) eating sacrifices would apply to קדשי דורות, to sacrifices like that of the New Moon that were being offered that day but were *not* directly related to the dedication ceremony. Much of this logic is spelled out in Rashi to vs. 16 and here, s.v. הייטב.

[46]Rashbam's phrase, נתערבה שמחתנו, is based on the usage in Is. 24:11, ערבה כל שמחה, rendered there by NJPS, "the sun has set on all joy." A similar phrase is used in VR 20 in connection with the death of Nadab and Abihu. Three times in his Torah commentary, Rashi

[what the rabbis said (Git. 36b)], 'It is an impudent bride who plays the harlot inside her own bridal chamber'."[47]

11:1 לאמר אליהם [THE LORD SPOKE TO MOSES AND AARON] SAYING (לאמר) TO THEM: I.e. "saying to Moses and Aaron." From this passage one may prove concerning every case where לאמר is written in the phrase, "The LORD spoke to Moses לאמר,"[48] that it means, "saying to Moses."[49]

Since above [it is written (10:8) that] God spoke to Aaron alone, the text had to write here that [this time] God spoke אליהם, to both of them.[50]

11:3 מפרסת פרסה THAT GROWS HOOFS: With one nail, like a shoe; not a number of nails on the individual toes, like a hare or a rock-badger.[51] ושסעת שסע

---

uses a form of this phrase in a description of those same deaths (ad Ex. 24:10, Lev. 10:4 and Lev. 10:6).

[47]In the previous parts of his comment Rashbam alludes to the possibility that Aaron's argument here is based, as Rashi would have it, on technical halakhic considerations about the different status of sacrifices that are and that are not part of the special events of the day. Rashi's argument, following the talmudic approach, portrays Aaron as the better student of the laws of mourning, who reminds Moses of laws that Moses had forgotten.

Here Rashbam suggests, in a manner closer to the *peshat*, that Aaron's motivation is not necessarily based on halakhic grounds. Psychological or esthetic considerations make him conclude that eating sacrificial meat while one's children are being buried is inappropriate. See N. Leibowitz's praise of Rashbam's approach in her *'Iyyunim*, p. 116.

[48]Ex. 25:1 and *passim*.

[49]See commentary to Lev. 1:1, and notes 9 and 11 there. Rashbam reiterates his opposition to the midrashic principle that לאמר means "to say to a third party." As noted above, Rashbam makes this point twice in his Leviticus commentary (here and ad 1:1), presumably because Rashi offered the midrashic reading of לאמר twice in his Leviticus commentary, at those two locations. Here Rashi (following Sifra) tells us that לאמר אליהם means "to say to Eleazar and Ithamar." Rashbam apparently considers Rashi's explanation so far-fetched and out of context that he writes that our passage can constitute proof that the midrashic explanation is inappropriate for all passages in which לאמר appears in the Torah.

While Rashbam's approach underlies virtually any Bible translation, some early modern Jews came to Rashi's defense. See e.g. Wessely here. See also Hoffmann, who admits that Rashbam's reading is the simplest sense of Scripture (הפשט הפשוט) but still claims that the midrashic understanding of לאמר is well grounded in the text here.

[50]Rashbam provides a contextual explanation for the appearance here of the unusual phrase, לאמר אליהם.

[51]I have followed Milgrom's translation (p. 643) of ארנבת and שפן. There are many theories about what animals are being described and there is no way of knowing what Rashbam thought.

WITH CLEFTS: The hoof must be split in two; not one undivided hoof, like that of a horse or a donkey.[52]

Following the plain meaning of Scripture and as a [useful] rebuttal of the heretics,[53] [it may be argued that] all the animals (domesticated and not domesticated), birds, fish, locusts and insects which God forbade to the Israelites [were forbidden] because they are repulsive. They damage and heat up the body. That is why they are called impure.[54] Outstanding physicians also concur with this

---

[52]Rashbam's interpretation is opposed to Rashi's. Rashi understands the word מפרסת as meaning "split." מפרסת פרסה for Rashi means that the hoof is split; שסעת שסע means that the split goes through the entire hoof, from front to back. Rashbam's explanation is that מפרסת פרסה simply means that the animal has a hoof, while שסעת שסע means that the hoof is split. This dispute also affects Rashi and Rashbam's different understandings of vs. 26 below. See note 64 there.

Like Rashbam, see iE. Virtually all translations and commentaries agree with the interpretation offered by Rashbam. See e.g. NJPSC and Milgrom. Even some early modern devotees of Rashi prefer Rashbam's explanation here; see Wessely (ופירושו מחוור מאד—his [= Rashbam's] explanation is very clear) and Shapira (. . . ולא נתברר טעם המפרשים ז"ל — the opinion of the commentators [= Rashi] is not clear). See also Mendelssohn's addendum to the *Be'ur,* where he writes that he had translated the verse following Rashi, but after reading Wessely he became convinced that Rashbam's understanding was correct.

[53]Jewish-Christian polemics often dealt with the question of whether it was reasonable to observe the rules of kosher food. See the discussion in David Berger's *Jewish-Christian Debate*, pp. 356–58, and especially the references to Meir of Narbonne in footnotes 13 and 14 there. See also the discussion of the polemical implications of Rashbam's comment here by Touitou in *Milet* 2, 283–285.

[54]Rashbam appears to be the first Jewish exegete to give such a sweeping justification of the rules of kosher food on health grounds. In *Ṭa'ame ha-miṣvot besifrut yisrael* (vol. I, pp. 47–48) Heinemann argues that explanations such as this—of the pragmatic and utilitarian benefits that accrue from the observance of the Torah's laws—are typical of the philosophical schools of Jewish thought. They are found after Rashbam's days in the works of philosophers or philosophically-oriented exegetes. (See e.g. *Guide of the Perplexed* 3:48 or Gersonides' commentary to our chapter.) Generally, members of what Heinemann calls the rabbinical school do not offer explanations like this. (It is perhaps for that reason that N. Leibowitz ['*Iyyunim*, p. 122f.] labels the health-oriented approach to these food laws "the Maimonidean approach," and writes that "Rashbam also followed that approach," despite the fact that Rashbam was at least fifty years Maimonides' senior.) Rashbam, according to Heinemann, represents the exception that proves the rule. "As an ardent *peshaṭ*-oriented exegete, he was closer to the [approaches of] the students of philosophy than to [those of] his colleagues in Christian countries." Heinemann also notes that, as Rashbam himself admits, foremost in Rashbam's mind is the polemical benefit of this explanation when disputing with Christians. See previous note.

The justification of the laws of kosher food on health grounds has been a controversial one in the history of Jewish thought. See e.g. the opposition of Abarbanel, Luzzatto and Hoffmann, all in their commentaries to Lev. 11. See also N. Leibowitz, *'Iyyunim*, pp. 122–128. On the other hand, see Julius Preuss' *Biblical and Talmudic Medicine*, p. 501: "we can conceive of no reason other than sanitary" for the rules of kosher food. See also the discussion

explanation.[55] [It is] also [to be found] in the Talmud, "When non-Jews eat disgusting things and insects, their bodies heat up."[56]

מעלת גרה CHEWS THE CUD: After it eats, it regurgitates its food into its throat (גרגרת).[57]

11:8 ובנבלתם לא תגעו DO NOT TOUCH THEIR CARCASSES: at a time when you have to touch a holy item or eat holy food. So it is written, "Anyone who is to touch these should be in a holy state" i.e. should purify himself [beforehand]. Concerning [people who are about to touch] Temple utensils (Ex. 30:29) or the altar (Ex. 29:37) or the meat of a sin offering (Lev. 6:11 and 20), concerning all of them it is written, "Anyone who is to touch these should be in a holy state," i.e. should make himself holy and pure beforehand. That means that if he touched some carcass or any other source of impurity listed in the Torah, he should make

---

in Milgrom (p. 719f.), where he cites William Foxwell Albright as the modern-day champion of this approach.

JBS, Rashbam's colleague and younger contemporary, also offers a health-related rationale for the rules of kosher food. Arguably, Rashi's comment to vs. 2 might also be read as alluding to a health-related justification for kosher food laws. Rashi sends his readers to a midrash (Tanh. *Shemini* 6) which explains why kosher food laws were given only to Jews through the analogy of a doctor who makes dietary suggestions to the patient who might yet be cured, but makes no dietary suggestions to the patient who is beyond help. Still the analogy might be just an analogy; it need not mean that Rashi sees the kosher food laws as health based.

[55]It is surprising and unusual to find an Ashkenazic rabbi of the 12th century appealing to the authority of scientific knowledge. (The early printed editions of Rashbam's commentary do not have this sentence in them.)

[56]The phrase, [גויים] דאכלי שקצים ורמשים חביל גופייהו, appears three times in the Talmud, in Shab. 86b, Nid. 34b and AZ 31b. While the words חביל גופייהו could, in another context, mean "harm their bodies," when the Talmud uses this phrase it means that eating such foods causes the bodies of gentiles to become warmer. See Rashi in Shab, s.v. חביל.

However, considering the context, especially the context of AZ 31b, the heat of the body of non-Jews resulting from their consumption of insects is, according to the Talmud, something *positive* for them. It does not *cause* disease; to the contrary, it *protects* gentiles from diseases to which Jews might be susceptible. Following that standard understanding of the talmudic passage, the Talmud is hardly a fitting prooftext for Rashbam; it is saying the opposite of what Rashbam is arguing.

Perhaps Rashbam has his own non-standard interpretation of the talmudic phrase.

[57]Rashbam is taking issue with the etymology of the word גרה offered here by Rashi. Rashi says that it is related to the word נגרים (= "poured" or "dragged"; II Sam. 14:14). Like Rashbam, see LT, iE and Qimḥi in his *Shorashim*, s.v. ג-ר-ה and s.v. ג-ר-ר. Like Rashi, see Milgrom (p. 647).

himself holy by purifying himself and immersing [in a ritual bath] before touching holy items.[58]

11:20 ההולך על ארבע [ALL FLYING INSECTS] THAT WALK ON ALL FOURS: Bees, for example.[59]

11:21 לנתר TO LEAP: [The word לנתר is to be understood] as the Targum [explained it: לקפצא—i.e. to leap].[60] [It is from the prima-*nun* root, *n-t-r*,], just like (Hab. 3:6), "וַיַּתֵּר גוים—He made the nations tremble,"[61] which should be understood as [if it were written] וינתר. Just as from the root *n-p-l*, one says וַיִּפֹּל.[62]

---

[58]This verse is problematic for traditional Jewish exegetes, since, unlike the straightforward meaning of this verse, *halakhah* has never claimed that it is forbidden to touch the corpse of a non-kosher animal. See Sifra here, and RH 16b. Rashi explicitly writes that the plain meaning of the verse is not acceptable halakhically. See also the detailed arguments of JBS (here and ad Deut. 14:8) against the literal meaning of the verse. Cf. iE who apparently explains the verse in a heterodox manner, following the *peshaṭ*.

Rashbam's answer is not that different from Rashi's. Rashi says (following the classical rabbinic sources) that our verse is a specific reference to a requirement that Jews refrain from touching impurities on (or perhaps before) a Jewish holiday. Rashbam expands that idea considerably and says that our verse teaches that whenever Jews are about to have contact with *sancta*, the Torah says that they should avoid contact with impure carcasses. See also Rashbam's commentary to Lev. 5:2. Rashbam then connects this explanation to his own novel reading of the phrase, "Anyone who is to touch these should be in a holy state," which he saw also as an instruction about what a Jew should do before contact with *sancta*. See his commentary to Ex. 29:37, and note 22 there, and commentary above ad 6:11, and note 9 there.

Many Jewish exegetes offer the same understanding of our verse as Rashbam's. See e.g. Nahm., Luzzatto, and Wessely.

[59]The example of bees is suggested already in Ps.-Jon. Rashi here provides a different list of four-legged flying insects. See Nahm.'s objections to Rashi's comment.

Bees have six legs, not four. In fact, as Hirsch noted (and later Hoffmann and Milgrom), no flying insect has fewer than six legs. So Hirsch suggests, reasonably, that "four legs" here really means only "more than two legs." Vss. 13–19 deal with the kosher status of flying creatures that have two legs; vs. 20f. deals with flying creatures that have more legs. As Hirsch himself notes, there is a problematic comment in Sifra here (cited by Rashi in his commentary to vs. 23), that suggests that the verse is speaking only about four-legged insects and that any flying insect with more than four legs would be kosher (רבי אומר כל שרץ העוף אשר לו ארבע רגלים טמא הוא לכם, אם יש לו חמש הרי זה טהור).

[60]Unlike Rashbam's, Rashi's long comment on the way that these insects move does not really explain the verb לנתר. Rashbam's explanation is unobjectionable.

[61]Or perhaps, "He made the nations jump." Both Rashi and Qimḥi, in their commentaries to Hab., make the same connection between our verse and the verse in Hab. So also Eliezer of Beaugency in his commentary to Hab., and see the discussion in Harris, p. 88.

[62]Rashbam makes the grammatical point that וַיַּתֵּר is from a prima-*nun* root and the *nun* falls out in the imperfect. He cites the form וַיִּפֹּל as his example of this phenomenon, just as he did in his commentary ad Ex. 15:22.

11:24 ולאלה תטמאו WITH THE FOLLOWING YOU WILL MAKE YOURSELVES IMPURE: if you touch their carcasses. Then the text goes on to elaborate [a list of] impure animals.[63]

11:26 הבהמה EVERY ANIMAL: even though it מפרסת פרסה—HAS HOOFS, but שסע איננה—WITHOUT CLEFTS, i.e. [the hoof is] not split, like a horse or a donkey,[64] OR THAT DOES NOT CHEW THE CUD, WHOEVER TOUCHES THEM [SHALL BE IMPURE], whether these animals have died [on their own] or have been slaughtered. This verse does not say "[whoever touches them] במותם —*when they die*."[65] But concerning a kosher animal it says below (vs. 39), "If an animal that you may eat *dies* (ימות) . . . [he who touches the carcass shall be impure,]" [because it is a source of impurity] only if it dies [on its own]; if it is slaughtered ritually it is not a source of impurity, even if it is [found, after the slaughtering, to be] *ṭerefah*.[66]

---

[63]Rashbam makes two points in this comment: (1) that the verse is saying that you *will* become impure through touch; and (2) that ולאלה means "for the following," not "for the preceding." Both of these points are made also by Rashi to this verse. However both of the points are arguable and at least one of Rashbam's contemporaries disputes each point.

The first point is disputed by JBS who does not interpret תִּטַּמָּאוּ as meaning "you *will* become impure [if you touch them]," but "you *are allowed to* become impure [by touching them]." That is the way this verb is understood in verses such as Lev. 21:3, "for her he may make himself impure (יִטַּמָּא)." JBS argues further that our verse teaches us that vs. 8, "do not touch their carcasses," is not a general injunction against ever touching something impure. (See commentary and note 58 there.) That is the reason that our verse says "you *are allowed to* become impure [by touching them]." One opinion in Sifra (*Shemini* 2:4) understands the verse as JBS does.

Rashbam's second point, that ולאלה means "the following," not "the preceding," is disputed by iE (here and ad vs. 27). iE's interpretation appears to be both heterodox and unsupported by the text. See Nahm.'s strong criticism of seeing לאלה as meaning "the preceding," and the even more forceful criticism in Wessely.

[64]See Rashbam's commentary to 11:3, and note 52 there.

Rashbam is opposing Rashi's comment to our verse. Rashi says that the reference here is to an animal like a camel. He says that because he feels that מפרסת means "split," or, as Rashi writes here, סדוקה. Rashbam, as noted above ad vs. 3, disagrees. Rashbam forcefully writes here that the hoof is not at all split (איננה סדוקה).

[65]If it said "במותם—*when they die*," it might imply that impurity results only from accidental death; in the case of ritual slaughter the animal might *not* be a source of impurity. Rashbam bases his comment here on the distinction that he notes between the language of vs. 31 (כל הנוגע בהם במותם יטמא—whoever touches them *when they die* shall be impure) and the language of our verse (כל הנוגע בהם יטמא—whoever touches them shall be impure).

[66]I.e. if it is a kosher animal and it is slaughtered properly but it is found to have some anomaly in its lung or some other internal organ. Then the meat of the animal is defined as being *ṭerefah* and inedible, but the animal's carcass is still not a source of impurity.

11:27 על כפיו [ALL ANIMALS THAT] WALK ON PAWS: For example, bears and dogs.[67]

11:28 והנושא HE WHO CARRIES [THEIR CARCASSES . . . SHALL BE IMPURE]: [This refers to] someone who moves it from its place, even without touching it.[68] But a person upon whose shoulders a carcass is loaded, and he neither touches the carcass nor moves from his place, is not impure. So we also learned in a Mishnah in tractate *Zavim* (5:3). Even if a dead body is placed on a bed and underneath the dead body there is [something as thin as] paper[69] that keeps the dead body from touching the bedclothes, those bedclothes are still pure. A dead body transfers impurity [through "carrying"] only if the carrying involves moving. So it is taught in the Mishnah there.

Rashbam repeats this halakhic and exegetical argument below in his commentary to vs. 39. The argument originates in Sifra (*Shemini* 10:1) and can be found a number of times in the Talmud (e.g. Hul. 74a). So also LT. A careful reading of those sources shows, as Rashbam himself writes explicitly ad vs. 39, that at least in most of those classical rabbinic texts, the legal conclusion (that a ritually slaughtered kosher animal is "pure" even if it is *ṭerefah*) is derived midrashically from the word מן in vs. 39. So also Rashi ad Shabbat 136a, s.v. לאכלה. Rashbam attempts to ground that *halakhah* more solidly in the simple meaning of the text, reading the two verses closely and comparing them.

Rashbam's comment both here and ad vs. 39 may be seen as opposed to Rashi. Rashi writes here that our verse teaches us about the carcasses of non-kosher animals, while vs. 39 teaches about the carcasses of kosher animals, but Rashi makes no halakhic or exegetical distinction between the two categories.

[67]I.e. animals that have paws, not hoofs. Rashbam's list of examples is virtually identical to that of Rashi and that of LT.

[68]Since the previous verse says that a person who *touches* a carcass is impure, our verse—that says that *carrying* a carcass causes impurity—would be redundant, unless we say that it refers to carrying a carcass without touching it. To be sure, another theoretical solution to the alleged redundancy is available. The person who "carries" the dead body may well have touched it too. But the verse tells us that carrying leads to a more serious form of impurity, requiring washing one's clothes. (See thus Rashi ad vss. 25 and 40.) But Rashbam's point, even if it is not exegetically required, does represent the standard halakhic position, at least among Ashkenazic authorities. It is possible that Maimonides disagrees and claims that "carrying" an item, even without moving it, conveys impurity. See the discussion in Kasher, vol. 28, p. 125, note 96***.

Like Rashbam, both Wessely (to our verse) and Hoffmann (to vs. 25) explain in their commentaries that "carrying" implies "moving." Wessely attempts to prove that that is implied in the Hebrew verb *n-s-'*.

[69]The image of the paper as a barrier is taken from Zav. 5:5.

Rashbam intends his comment here—on the impurity of a dead body—to be read in contrast with his comment below, ad 15:4, on the impurity of a menstruant or of a person with a discharge. See note 16 there.

In the Jerusalem Targum, the word [in our verse], "נושא—carry," is translated as "מסיט—move."[70]

11:32 מכל כלי עץ WHETHER IN A VESSEL OF WOOD [OR CLOTH OR SKIN OR SACKCLOTH]: But not stone or earthenware vessels.[71]

שק SACKCLOTH: A garment made from the hair of goats.[72]

אשר יעשה מלאכה בהם [ANY VESSEL] INSIDE OF WHICH WORK MAY BE DONE: Not the work of covering [another vessel,] for then no work is done *inside* of it.[73]

---

[70]Rashbam's name for the Torah translation attributed to Jonathan ben Uziel is "the Jerusalem Targum." This is the only time in his Torah commentary that Rashbam refers to that translation by name. There is reason to believe, however, that he did use it in discussing other passages. See the discussion in Rosin's RSBM, p. 60, note 8, and in his Hebrew Introduction to the Torah commentary, p. xxiv.

Rosin argues that Rashbam had a different version of that commentary than we have. Here the difference he cites is rather minor: Rashbam says that the translation reads מסיט, while our version of Ps.-Jon. reads ודיוסיט. Either way the word means to move an object.

[71]Rashbam points out that our verse's list of the types of vessels that might become impure is not all-inclusive. Vessels of earthenware and of stone are, according to *halakhah*, not susceptible to impurity. Rashbam's halakhic point is not controversial. See e.g. Maimonides, *Ṭum'at met* 6:4. However, to the best of my knowledge Rashbam is the first exegete to connect this halakhic principle to our verse. In Sifre (Numbers 126 and 157) this halakhic principle is derived from Num. 31:20, a verse that is very similar to ours. See note 72. Like Rashbam, see Wessely.

[72]See similarly NJPSC here: "Hebrew *beged* is defined as something woven of cloth, and *sak*, as something made of goat's hair or the hair of a similar animal."

In Num. 31:20 there is a list of articles that may be purified, a list that is almost identical to the one in our verse. Both lists have four items. Both lists mention a בגד (cloth), wood items and leather items. The remaining item in our verse is שק; in Numbers, the remaining item is called מעשה עזים. Hence Rashbam's claim that שק refers to an item made from goat hair.

Rashbam's phraseology here טלית של נוצת עזים appears unusual. See Milgrom, p. 674: "'cloth of goat feathers (*sic*)' (Rashbam)." But the word נוצת does not mean feathers here. Rashbam is using a common talmudic phrase. See e.g. Hul. 137a. Rashi explains there that goat hair is called נוצה in rabbinic Hebrew because it is generally removed by hand, like feathers, not by shearing. See also Rashi and Rashbam ad Ex. 25:4 and note 7 there.

See Tosafot ad Shab. 27a, s.v. ונוצה של עזים, which appears to be directed against Rashbam's commentary here. There the Tosafot try to distinguish between two different kinds of goat hair and, on the basis of that distinction, argue that a garment made from the kind of hair called נוצה של עזים would *not* fall under the category of sackcloth.

[73]Rashbam's comment is best understood if we consider what he says about the word בהם. Most translators would translate "*with which* work may be done"; Rashbam reads it as "*inside of which* work may be done." He then reaches the halakhic conclusion that the rules described

11:34 אשר יבוא עליו מים יטמא [ANY FOOD] WHICH CAME IN CONTACT WITH WATER [. . . SHALL BE IMPURE]: A person who wishes to give reasons for the commandments[74] in a manner that conforms to the way of the world[75] and that is appropriate for rebutting the heretics[76] [may explain this verse as follows]: God did not attach [the concept of] impurity to any food or drink until they have been rendered usable as food. Bringing them in contact with water is the first step in their preparation and the true way that they are to be "promoted"[77] to the status of foodstuffs.[78]

---

here do not apply to lids of vessels. Those are items with which, but not inside of which, work is done.

Rashbam here may be following Sifra's understanding of the phrase (יכול שאני מרבה את חפויי כלים ת"ל בהם פרט לחפויי כלים), although it is not certain whether חפויי כלים, in Sifra, refers to lids or to some form of coating or overlay. See Kasher, vol. 28, p. 162, note 147. Like Rashbam, see Hizq.

[74]Rashbam's phrase here, "[לתת] טעם במצוות—[to give] reasons for the commandments," may be the first use of the phrase in rabbinic history. The phrase later became a standard one in the slightly different form, טעמי המצוות. Before Rashbam, see the common phrase, טעמי תורה (e.g. Sanh. 21b). Rashi also on two occasions makes reference to the טעם of an individual ***misvah*** ad BM 79a, s.v. והארץ and ad Num. 19:2, s.v. זאת.

[75]On Rashbam's use of the phrase דרך ארץ, see the variety of explanations suggested by Touitou ("*Shiṭato ha-parshanit* . . .," p. 65) and M. Berger (pp. 99–113).

[76]The relevance of this comment to Jewish-Christian polemics is probably similar to that of Rashbam's comments above (ad 11:3) about kosher food. The Christians presumably argued that the rules of kosher food and the rules of ritual impurity make no sense on the literal level. Only an allegorical Christological explanation would make sense of them. Rashbam and other Jews argue, then, that these rules have some form of logic or at least common sense on the literal level.

Touitou (*Milet* 2, 284) suggests a further possible polemical use for Rashbam's comment here. Christians often argued that the whole idea of impurity goes against the approach of Genesis that the entire world that God created is good (Gen. 1:31). Rashbam then, Touitou argues, explains here that nature in its natural state is pure; it is only after people get involved with nature that impurity becomes possible.

[77]The word חשיבות is used in a technical sense related to the rules of impurity. "Thinking" about eating something, "considering" it to be food, promotes that item to the status of being food and renders it susceptible to impurity. Rashbam is saying that the simplest way of doing that is to bring the item into contact with water.

The standard rabbinic Hebrew phrase for this is מחשבת אוכלין. (See e.g. Hul. 102b.) While the form Rashbam uses, חשיבות, is unusual, it has a precedent. See Rashi ad Hul. 16a, s.v. אינו בכי יותן.

[78]The idea that contact with water makes an item susceptible to impurity is, as Touitou explains (*Milet* 2, 284), counter-intuitive: does water not *cleanse*? Rashbam provides one answer. Another common answer, found both in JBS (ad vs. 34) and in Nahm. (ad vs. 37), is that once water is added to some foodstuff, it is easier for the pollution of an impure item to be transferred to that foodstuff by contact.

11:36 אך מעין ובור HOWEVER A SPRING OR A CISTERN [. . . SHALL BE PURE]: Following the plain meaning of Scripture, [this verse means that] water gathered in the ground is not susceptible to impurity. Rather, as it said above (vs. 34), [only] "if it was inside a vessel, a liquid that may be drunk shall become impure."[79]

11:37 אשר יִזָּרֵעַ [ANY SEED] THAT IS SOWN: in the ground, SHALL BE PURE: Anything connected to the ground is not susceptible to impurity.[80]

זֶרַע זֵרוּעַ: means "grain (זֶרַע) of seeds (זֵרְעוֹנִים)." The plural form is [found] in Daniel (1:12), "let them give us some seeds (זֵרוֹעִים)"; the singular form is [the one found here,] זֵרוּעַ.[81]

---

[79]Rashi says that our verse means or teaches two things: (1) that water in pools, where it collects naturally, does not become impure; and (2) that such water may serve as a *miqveh*, rendering impure items immersed therein pure. Rashbam's comment agrees with the first point that Rashi makes, but not with the second. Rashbam argues that the *peshaṭ* requires reading our verse as a continuation of vs. 34. That verse says that water collected in a vessel is susceptible to impurity; our verse says that that is not the case if the water is in its natural location. In passing, one sees that Rashbam is also disputing Rashi's comment to vs. 34. There Rashi provided an extremely long comment on a variety of *halakhot* that may be derived from that verse, but he did not mention the *peshaṭ*-oriented reading that Rashbam offers.

Like Rashbam, see Nahm.

[80]Rashbam's understanding of this verse does not conform to the more standard understanding of the phrase, "the seed that יִזָּרֵעַ is pure." Generally the translation is "a seed that is to be sown" (NJPS and Milgrom, p. 680). Then our verse and the following verse read together mean: (37) Any seed that *is to be sown* (אשר יִזָּרֵעַ) in the future is pure while in its natural state, but (38) once it has been brought into contact with water it is susceptible to impurity. Rashi also understands our verse in that way.

But Rashbam's understanding (following Sifra 11:3) is: any seed that *has been sown* in the ground already is pure. This means that even if the seed had been impure, once it is planted in the ground it ceases to be impure and returns to its state of purity. Then Rashbam proceeds to explain that the principle upon which this law is based is that "anything connected to the ground is not susceptible to impurity." As far as I can tell, the first person to enunciate this halakhic principle in that precise wording was Rashi, in his commentary to vs. 36. Rashbam then disagrees with Rashi about the meaning of both vs. 36 and vs. 37, and yet, as is occasionally his custom, he playfully uses Rashi's phraseology, moving Rashi's phrase from the commentary on vs. 36 to the commentary on vs. 37. He then uses Rashi's phrase to mean something different from what Rashi used it for.

While Rashi's understanding of the imperfect form יִזָּרֵעַ appears to be more standard, Wessely defends Rashbam's explanation here at some length. Luzzatto also concurs with Rashbam.

[81]iE mentions, as one of two interpretations, the possibility that זרוע is to be understood as an adjective or a participle meaning "sown" (as if זָרוּעַ were written). But Rashbam explains the phrase זֶרַע זֵרוּעַ as a construct form, consisting of two nouns, in the way that most ancient and

11:39 וכי ימות מן הבהמה אשר היא לכם לאכלה IF AN ANIMAL THAT YOU MAY EAT DIES [. . . SHALL BE IMPURE]: [It is impure only if it "dies," as the verse says, a natural death;] but if it is slaughtered it does not have the status of *nevelah* [= an impure carcass], even if it was found to be *ṭerefah.*[82] But when discussing the [laws concerning the ritual impurity of a] carcass of a non-kosher animal, the text does not mention "dying," because even if such an animal were to be ritually slaughtered it still has the status of *nevelah* and it transmits impurity. But the rabbis [in order to reach this same halakhic conclusion] interpreted the words "מן הבהמה—**from** the animal" to mean that some such animals are sources of impurity but others are not, for ritual slaughter renders a *ṭerefah* animal pure and keeps it from the status of *nevelah.*[83]

11:40 והאוכל ANYONE WHO EATS OF ITS CARCASS: The rabbis explained[84] (Nid. 42b) that this verse teaches the "amount" [required for impurity to be transferred: in the case of] a person who touches or carries [something impure, if the amount touched or carried is, at the minimum.] an amount worthy of eating, i.e. an olive's size, then he is impure. Following the plain meaning of Scripture, [the verse teaches that] a person becomes impure when he eats something impure, even if he does not touch it with his hands.[85] In the same

---

modern exegetes do. (See e.g. Rashi and Milgrom, p. 680.) Rashbam's comment here is essentially the same as Rashi's—in the explanation of the phrase, in the prooftext from Daniel, and even in the use of the form זרעונים in the explanation, a form more common in rabbinic Hebrew than זֵרֹעִים.

[82]On the meaning of *ṭerefah*, see commentary above ad 11:26, and note 66 there.

[83]Rashbam repeats the interpretation that he offered ad vs. 26. See notes 65 and 66 there.

[84]This verse has been a source of much difficulty from the perspective of standard Jewish law. On the simplest level, the verses here equate the touching and the eating of an impure carcass: both make a person impure. The problem is that, according to standard Jewish law, it is permitted to touch a carcass but it is forbidden to eat a carcass.

[85]This exegetical solution is explicitly considered by the Talmud and rejected. Rashi here quotes the talmudic passage at length, showing why, from a *midrash halakhah* perspective, that interpretation (the one that is offered here by Rashbam) is unacceptable. Then Rashi offers the explanation that our verse teaches the rule concerning the "amount" of impure food required in order to transfer impurity.

The specific impurity being discussed here is the impurity of a kosher animal that dies without ritual slaughter. *Halakhah* says that the person who eats such food, without ever carrying it, would not become as impure as the person who carries such food. His clothes would not require cleansing. Nevertheless Rashbam here says that the *peshaṭ* of our verse is that eating such food does transfer impurity, even if one eats it without touching it or carrying it, and, as the verse says, "anyone who eats of its carcass shall launder his clothes." In other words, Rashbam interprets the *peshaṭ* of our verse in a way that would contradict *halakhah*. This comment is therefore an example of anti-halakhic exegesis, a rare but not unheard of phenomenon in Rashbam. See e.g. commentary to Ex. 22:6–12, and note 18 there.

manner, it is written (Lev. 22:8), "He shall not eat anything that died or that was torn by beasts, thereby becoming impure."[86]

For an alternative *peshaṭ* explanation of our verse—an explanation that is not in conflict with *halakhah*—see Nahm.'s commentary.

[86]Rashbam cites the same text that Rashi and the Talmud cite from Lev. 22, but for a very different purpose. The Talmud and Rashi say that that verse teaches that only the eating of the impure food listed there imparts the stricter form of impurity. Standard halakhic understanding is that Lev. 22:8 refers to impurity from eating a kosher *bird* that was not slaughtered properly and that our verse refers to impurity from eating a kosher *animal* that was not slaughtered properly. The bird's carcass transfers the more serious form of impurity; the animal's does not, according to standard *halakhah*. Rashi and his talmudic sources cite the emphatic language of Lev. 22 (לטמאה בה) as proof that the strict rule of Lev. 22:8 does not apply in Lev. 11. Rashbam, while knowing well the explanation of his grandfather, still tells us that, on the *peshaṭ* level, Lev. 22:8 and Lev. 11:40 both teach that eating carcasses of kosher animals (whether bird or mammal) imparts the same level of impurity.

תזריע (Leviticus 12–13)

12:2 אשה כי תזריע WHEN A WOMAN PRODUCES SEED: I.e. when a woman becomes pregnant, whether with a male or a female child. Following this general statement, the text writes more specifically: if she gives birth to a male child, the following rules shall apply. If she gives birth to a female child, the following rules shall apply.[1]

---

[1]Rashbam's comment opposes the common midrashic interpretation concerning this verse, that says that when a woman reaches orgasm (תזריע) before her husband, the child will be a male. See Ber. 60a and a number of parallel passages. The midrashic assumption about sex determination is also quoted by Rashi in his Torah commentary (ad Gen. 46:15), although Rashi attached the principle to a different prooftext. Even a *peshaṭ*-oriented exegete like iE cites this midrash as a possible reading. So also Nahm., who labels this explanation as משמעותו, the "meaning" of the text. See also Hizq., who uses his commentary to this verse as an opportunity to provide his readers with a lengthy excursus on how to influence the gender outcome of their children. See also Fred Rosner's discussion of this principle in his chapter, "Sex Determination as Described in the Talmud," in his *Medicine in the Bible and Talmud*, pp. 248–253. And see also Rashbam's commentary to BB 127a, s.v. תנא . . . ספוקי מספקא ליה, where, despite the fact that the context does not require it, Rashbam mentions this midrashic explanation as the possible halakhic "lesson" of our verse.

This midrashic explanation finds grounding in the text in two ways. First the word תזריע appears to be anomalous here when referring to a woman. Secondly, the verses appear to be imbalanced. The phrase "אשה כי תזריע—when a woman produces seed" is written only in verse 2, concerning the birth of a boy, not in verse 5, concerning the birth of a girl.

Still the midrash is quite far from the simple meaning of the verse. Most commentators would agree with iE that תזריע means "to give birth," or with Rashbam (following Onq.) that תזריע simply means "to conceive." See the discussions in NJPSC and in Milgrom's commentary here (p. 743). See also Wessely who compliments Rashbam for explaining that תזריע means to conceive. And see Rashbam's commentary to Num. 5:28 (and note 22 there), where he interprets the similar phrase, ונזרעה זרע, as meaning "to conceive."

Rashbam also deals with the perceived imbalance here—that the word תזריע appears only in vs. 2 and not in vs. 5—by having recourse to his principle, "the text generalizes and then specifies." Often Rashbam uses this principle to explain a perceived redundancy in the biblical text. (See note 29 to Ex. 2:15.) Here he uses it to explain the structure of our verses as follows: "When a woman conceives, then one of two outcomes may occur. וילדה זכר—If it is a male child, then . . .. (5) If it is a female child, then . . .."

While Rashbam's explanation fits very well with the text, the midrashic explanation is more in conformity with the cantillation marks.

וטמאה SHE SHALL BE IMPURE FOR SEVEN DAYS: Even if she saw no blood.[2]

כימי נדת דותה: means "like the days of separation for her 'illness'." [She should be impure for the same period] specified below for seeing impure blood, i.e. seeing the blood of menstruation.[3]

The word נדה refers to a woman who must wander away (נדודה)[4] and be separated from her husband.

The word דותה is related to the idea of illness.[5] So similarly (Jer. 8:18) "my heart is sick (דוי)."

12:4 בדמי טהרה [SHE SHALL STAY IN A STATE OF] BLOOD PURITY: [For the blood that she might see in that time period] is not menstrual blood.[6] The plain

---

[2]So also Rashi here. This is also the standard halakhic position. See Nid. 21a and the clear formulation in Maimonides, *'Issure bi'ah* 10:1.

The phrase "to see blood" is technical halakhic language. Essentially it means "to bleed."

[3]This translation is based on the conjectural emendation of Berzinsky who suggests reading ראיית דם נידה instead of the text that Rosin found in the ms., ראיית דם לידה. Rosin's text is very difficult, as it would appear then that Rashbam is contradicting what he wrote in his last comment—that birth impurity is unrelated to the seeing of blood. See Rosin's hesitant attempt to resolve the contradiction, in his note 7 here.

[4]The claim that the word נדה comes from the root *n-d-d,* to wander, is made by a number of exegetes. See e.g. iE. As Wessely points out, there are two possible ways of understanding the "wandering" of our verse: either, as Rashbam would have it, that the woman must wander away from her husband or, as Wessely prefers, that the menstrual blood will wander from her body.

Others (see e.g. Rashi ad Lev. 15:19 or Nahm. ad 12:4) connect the word to the root *n-d-h*, a common root in rabbinic Hebrew (but not very common in the Bible) meaning "to banish." As Milgrom (p. 745) notes, these two roots may not be so different; often final-*heh* verbs and their counterpart geminate verbs have identical or very similar meanings.

[5]The printed texts of Rashi's commentary (but see a different text quoted by Nahm.) have Rashi offering two alternative explanations for the word דותה. The first explains it as meaning "to flow," presumably based on similarity to the Aramaic דבב. Rashbam follows Rashi's second explanation, that דותה is a reference to menstruation as a form of illness. So also iE and Nahm., although Nahm. does note that menstruation itself is not an illness, but is called an illness because of its accompanying symptoms. See also Milgrom's lengthy note (pp. 745–746) which concludes, "Thus philology confirms experience: menstruation is associated with sickness."

[6]Rashbam is following the standard halakhic understanding of the opening verses of this chapter which says that, following Torah law, a woman is considered impure for the first seven or fourteen days after birth, and that following that time there is a period of thirty-three or sixty-six days in which she would be considered pure even if she were to see blood. For an alternate understanding, see Nahm.

meaning of Scripture follows the opinion that "there are two fonts [of blood]." [The blood that flows] during the thirty-three days [described in this verse] comes from the font that is pure.[7]

12:7 וטהרה [SHE SHALL BRING A LAMB FOR A BURNT OFFERING . . .] THEN SHE SHALL BE PURE: I.e. then she shall be pure enough even to eat sacrificial meat (*qodashim*).[8] That is how the rabbis explained the verse. For once [a person has completed all the other steps of purification and] the sun has set at the evening [following the day of the purificatory measures] and [the only thing] lacking is the expiation [that comes from bringing a sacrifice, at that point, he or she] is [considered sufficiently pure to be] permitted to eat [even] *terumah*.[9] But

---

[7]Rashbam is referring to a dispute in the Talmud (Nid. 35b). One opinion says that a woman has two fonts of blood; she is not considered impure when she sees blood in the period of thirty-three or sixty-six days since that blood comes from the pure font. The other talmudic opinion is that even though the blood comes from one source, sometimes the Torah declares it pure and sometimes impure.

It is unusual to find such a strong statement in the works of a medieval Jewish commentator arguing that one of two sides in a talmudic debate finds better support in the *peshaṭ* of the verse. Cf. Rashbam's commentary to Ex. 12:2, and note 12 there.

[8]Rashbam's language here, וטהרה לאכול קדשים, is a virtually verbatim quotation of the Sifra here.

The difficulty in our verse is as follows: When a woman gives birth to a daughter, for example, the mother is impure for fourteen days (vs. 5). For the next sixty-six days she is considered pure (vs. 5). After those days she brings a sacrifice and our verse says that *then* she shall be considered pure (וטהרה). But has she not already been pure for the last sixty-six days?

Rashi does not really address the issue; in fact, Rashi perhaps compounds the problem by simply quoting the talmudic line (Zev. 19b) "וטהרה: מכלל שעד כאן היא קרויה טמאה—the words 'she shall then be pure' teach us that until now she is called impure." Rashbam provides the standard halakhic explanation (implied but not spelled out in Rashi's commentary to the previous verse) that there are different possible levels of purity, and that she reaches the highest level of purity—being allowed to eat sacrificial meat—only after she fulfils her own sacrificial obligations.

The alternative understanding of this passage is that of the Karaites who claim that a mother of a daughter is *not* pure during the period of sixty-six days. They interpret the phrase תשב בדמי טהרה as meaning that during those sixty-six days she is completing the process of purifying herself from her bleeding. (As Milgrom notes [p. 748], Nahm. "draws close" to this Karaite interpretation.) While there is no evidence that Rashbam had significant contact with or knowledge of Karaites, it is distinctly possible that he knew of this line of interpretation, or at least recognized its possibility, and for that reason he has carefully explained his understanding of how the rabbanite reading fits well with the *peshaṭ*.

[9]*Terumah*, or the "heave-offering" given to the priest, may be eaten only by a priest who is pure. See Num. 18:11: "This too shall be yours: all the heave-offerings (תרומת) . . .; anyone of your household who is pure may eat of them."

[that purifying person] may not eat sacrificial meat (*qodashim*) until after the expiation [that comes from bringing a sacrifice].[10]

13:2 אדם כי יהיה בעור בשרו WHEN A PERSON HAS ON THE SKIN OF HIS BODY: When we follow the plain meaning of Scripture or the expertise gained through the ways of the human world, we have nothing [to add] concerning all these sections that describe plagues of humans or of clothing or of houses, the way they look, the way to count their quarantine periods, or the distinctions between white, black and yellow hairs. Rather the truth is found through the exegesis (*midrash*) of the rabbis, their laws and the traditions that they received from the earlier rabbis.[11]

כי יהיה בעור בשרו ON THE SKIN OF HIS BODY: Since it will say below (vs. 29), "[If a man or a woman has] an affection on the head or in the beard," here the text had to say that the affection [described in these verses] is "on the skin."[12]

The idea that a person who is becoming pure may eat of *terumah* after sunset is found in Rashi ad 22:7, following Yev. 74b and many other talmudic passages.

[10]Rashbam is following the law as specified in Neg. 14:3. In Yev. 74b the Talmud discusses how one knows that there is a difference between "purity for *terumah*" and "purity for sacrificial meat." Our verse is then cited there as the prooftext.

[11]Rashbam has provided other disclaimers at certain points in his commentary, disclaimers that emphasize the relative unimportance of his *peshaṭ* enterprise when compared with classical rabbinic midrash, especially when dealing with legal texts. See e.g. the introductions he wrote before his commentary to Ex. 21 or to Ex. 25. Here he seems to argue further that *peshaṭ* exegesis is especially inappropriate when dealing with sections of text like these; since we have no first-hand experience with the "plagues" of these chapters, we cannot really comment on them on the *peshaṭ* level. See also Rashbam's introduction to Lev. 1 and note 2 there.

A very similar disclaimer is found in the commentary of Rashbam's younger contemporary, Andrew of St. Victor (p. 178). Andrew writes that the kinds of "plagues" that the law here deals with are not known to us in these lands these days, and it is difficult to know how to distinguish between what is and is not impure. Naturally, Andrew's disclaimer does not end with a statement that one therefore has to rely on the rabbis.

[12]Rashbam's interpretation is opposed to that of Sifra (so also LT) which attributes halakhic significance to the allegedly redundant phrase "on his skin" (suggesting that from this phrase we learn that even an anomaly on a part of the skin where hair does not grow is considered an "affection"). Rashbam points out that the phrase is, on the *peshaṭ* level, not redundant; it helps us distinguish between the rules of affections here and the rules of affections that are described in vs. 29f.

Like Rashbam, see Hoffmann and Milgrom (p. 773). In the *Be'ur*, Wessely labels Rashbam's interpretation far-fetched (דחוק). Mendelssohn, in his interpolations into Wessely's commentary, defends Rashbam.

שאת: should be understood as connected to the idea of height[13] [and hence means a "swelling." It is referred to as a swelling] because it is not as white[14] as [the other affection in our verse,] בהרת, which is [very] white. So it is written (Job 37:21), "It [the sun] is bright (בהיר) in the heavens."[15] בהרת has a deeper appearance [than שאת],[16] just as the sun appears to be deeper than the shade.[17]

---

[13]I.e. it is from the root *n-s-'*, to lift. Rashbam's explanation is identical to that of Shev. 6b.

[14]Many moderns would concur with Rashbam's explanation that שאת refers to a swelling. See e.g. NJPS. However, Rashbam departs from the *peshaṭ* (to follow rabbinic traditions) when he suggests that the name, שאת—swelling, does not mean that that affection *is* higher, but rather that, when compared to בהרת, it *appears* higher.

[15]This is the same prooftext cited here by Rashi and by iE to explain what בהרת means. That verse was a natural choice, for it is the only example of the root *b-h-r* in the Bible, outside of these chapters of Leviticus. However, Rashbam and Rashi agree neither about the meaning of בהרת, nor about what the prooftext in Job means.

Rashbam understands the root *b-h-r* in the way that it is used in later Hebrew, as referring to brightness. Presumably the Talmud (*ibid.*), which sees בהרת as the brightest type of affection, concurs. Rashi, however, thinks that בהרת means a stain or patch or some other such mark. In his commentary to Job he suggests that בהיר there means a rain cloud, which certainly is not bright white. See also Rashi's commentary to *Ta'anit* 7b, s.v. אפילו, where he writes that the talmudic word בהורין (or perhaps בהירין) is like the word בהרת and means "mottled with clouds (מנומר בעבים)."

In the commentary to Job attributed by Japhet to Rashbam, the exegete explains בהיר as Rashi does there, not as Rashbam does here.

[16]I have taken some liberties with the text in my translation. The text reads: אבל הבהרת לבנה היא ונראית עמוקה יותר מבהרת. It makes no sense to say that בהרת appears deeper than בהרת (even after Rosin's creative attempt to vocalize the second word מְבָהֶרֶת). The text reads well if one simply removes the last word, or if one emends it to משאת.

[17]Rashbam's comment here is predicated on the assumption that bright or white things appear to be deeper than darker colored ones. Rashbam himself spells out this principle of perception in his BB commentary, ad 84a, s.v. עמוק. This assumption is common in rabbinic literature; the final words of Rashbam's comment here (מראה חמה עמוקה מן הצל) are a verbatim quote from the Talmud (Shev. 6b and BB *ibid.*). However, this common rabbinic principle contradicts our standard sense today about depth perception. (We assume that darker shading is the way to indicate greater depth.) See Adin Steinsalz's comment (BB, *ibid., ha-'olam* section), where he argues that assumptions about depth and perception may be culturally dependent; in rabbinic culture perhaps people really did see lighter shading as indicating depth.

In any case, the logic of Rashbam's comment works as follows: There are two major types of "affection" (according to the Mishnah Neg. 1:1), בהרת and שאת. The former (following both etymology and the Mishnah, there) is brighter. That is why the less bright one is called שאת, meaning "elevation"; its darker shade makes it appear more elevated.

Rashbam is virtually forced into this position because of his acceptance of the rabbinic claim that white objects appear deeper. If that is the case, how can שאת mean an elevation? Furthermore, the text specifically says in vs. 3 that these affections appear to be deeper than the skin. His solution is that שאת is white and, like all other items that are white, it looks deeper than the skin. But, in comparison to the much whiter and deeper בהרת, it is appropriate

ספחת: means [an affection that is] secondary to שאת or one that is secondary to בהרת.[18] שאת has a sub-category, and בהרת also has a sub-category that goes along with it. [These sub-categories are called ספחת because] they are attached [to the main category], as in the phrase (I Sam. 2:36), "Attach me (ספחני) to one of the priests' offices."[19] [ספחני and ספחת are] linguistically connected to the idea of being secondary or being attached. That is how the rabbis explained this verse.[20]

לנגע צרעת: [This phrase means] that the spot of the affection is white flesh. So it is written (Ex. 4:6), "as מצורעת as snow." This [i.e. the word, צרעת, or the related adjective, מצורע,] is the name of a white affection.[21]

13:3 ומראה הנגע עמוק THE APPEARANCE OF THE AFFECTION IS DEEP: [because it is] white.[22]

13:4 ועמוק אין מראה AND ITS APPEARANCE IS NOT DEEP: I.e. it is not one of the [shades of] white that are defined in [Mishnah] tractate *Nega'im* (1:1) as the appearances of affections.[23]

---

to call שאת elevated. This same solution is proposed hesitatingly (ואולי נאמר) by Nahm. in his commentary to vs. 3. See also note 23 below.

[18]The Mishnah, *ibid.*, says that there are two major types of white affections—שאת, which is the color of white wool, and בהרת, which is the color of snow. However, there are also other affections in other shades of white that would be considered impure. Those shades are subsumed as sub-categories (or תולדות, divisions) of the two major categories. The word ספחת is seen by the Talmud (Shev. 6b) and by Rashbam as teaching us that both בהרת and שאת have sub-categories attached to them.

[19]This prooftext is the same one that the Talmud (*ibid.*) cites to show that ספחת means a sub-category. iE also cites this phrase to prove his own, non-talmudic explanation of ספחת.

[20]See Shev. 6b. Perhaps the final words of Rashbam's comment here show that he realizes that his explanation is not the *peshaṭ*. Most commentators, at least those who are not bound by the talmudic explanations, would see the phrase שאת או ספחת או בהרת as a list of three separate categories, not as a reference to two categories and their sub-categories. See e.g. iE and NJPS. However Rashbam, as he announced in his first comment to this verse, generally toes the rabbinic line when explaining the rules of affections.

[21]As Milgrom notes at length (pp. 774–776), there is no certainty at all about what the word צרעת means, nor about its etymology. Rashbam suggests that צרעת is yet another word that means "white" (just as he interprets the words שאת and בהרת, and as he will interpret the word עמוק in the following verse). His explanation appears original. See also commentary below ad vs. 8, and note 25 there.

[22]So also Rashi here (following Shev., *ibid.*). Rashbam reiterates the point that he made above ad vs. 2, s.v. שאת.

[23]On the phrase, "its appearance is not deep," Rashi writes that he doesn't know what it means. There is much literature on that humble assertion, both attempting to explain what it is that made this phrase so hard to understand and trying to find some solution to Rashi's problem.

13:8 צרעת היא IT IS *ṢARA'AT*: And he is a "confirmed"[24] [carrier of the disease]. "He shall dwell apart" (13:46) until he is healed and then he should bring his bird sacrifice (14:4f.).[25]

13:10 ומחית בשר חי WITH QUICK RAW FLESH: A piece of flesh was growing in the affection. That flesh was raw, not like cooked flesh.[26]

13:18 שחין AN INFLAMMATION: Our rabbis interpreted [that our verses (18–23) refer to the rules of an inflammation that is] caused by the heat from a beating that was inflicted on the person; on the other hand, [the next unit of text (vss. 24–28) refers to] an inflammation of "מכות אש" (vs. 24), one caused by the heat of fire.[27]

In his commentary to vs. 3, Nahm. explains Rashi's problem well. Since Rashi told us in the previous verse (s.v. עמוק) that white things always appear deeper than dark objects, and since our verse says specifically that it is dealing with a white affection, then how could the verse say that this affection does *not* appear deep?

This seems to be the question that Rashbam is addressing in his comment, too. His solution is that our verse means that the affection in question is a non-standard shade of white. Hence it is appropriately called לבנה but its appearance is not עמוק. See Nahm. for a much more complicated solution.

[24]Rashbam uses the word מוחלט, the standard rabbinic terminology (see e.g. Mishnah Meg. 1:7) to distinguish between the suspected carrier who is confined (מוסגר) pending determination, and the confirmed (מוחלט) carrier.

[25]Rashbam's comment is almost identical to that of Rashi, s.v. וטמאו.

Here Rashbam interprets the word צרעת as the name of a halakhic category. Above ad vs. 2, s.v. לנגע צרעת, he explains that the word צרעת means "white," i.e. that it is the description of a physical reality. The explanations need not be seen as contradictory.

[26]The more common understanding of בשר חי here among Jewish exegetes is that it means healthy flesh. In other words, although (or perhaps, even because) there is some healthy flesh in the middle of the affection, the affection is impure. (See e.g. Rashi here.) In rabbinic literature the words בשר חי often mean healthy flesh. See e.g. Sifre Numbers 12 (commenting on Num. 5:19), where בשר חי is used as the antonym of מכה—a wound.

Rashbam is correct that בשר חי can mean raw flesh. In fact, in the only other biblical example of the adjective חי modifying the noun בשר (I Sam. 2:15), בשר חי unambiguously means uncooked, raw, flesh. So Rashbam's comment here may be an example of his penchant for, whenever possible, interpreting the Bible using the Bible, not using rabbinic Hebrew. (On this issue, see the discussion in my Genesis volume, pp. 422–424.) But it is difficult to see what sense Rashbam makes of our verse if he sees חי, here, as meaning "uncooked." As Wessely writes, Rashbam's comment is hard to fathom (לא ידעתי טעמו).

[27]Rashbam's comment agrees with that of Rashi and expands slightly on it. Both of them are following the standard rabbinic explanation; see Neg. 9:1.

Rashbam's language here—אבל שחין של מכות אש—is somewhat clumsy, as it implies that מכוה is a sub-category of שחין. The Mishnah that serves as Rashbam's source sees שחין and מכוה as discrete categories.

13:30 נתק: *Ṣara'at* on a hairy part of the body is called a נתק, because the affection causes the hair to detach (מתנתק).[28]

13:31 ושער שחור אין בו והסגיר IF THERE IS NO BLACK HAIR IN IT, THE PRIEST SHALL ISOLATE [THE PERSON . . . FOR SEVEN DAYS]: For if there were black hair in it, then the person would be entirely pure and would not require [even] isolation. So it is written below (vs. 37), "If black hair has grown in it, the scall is healed, he is clean; the priest shall pronounce him clean."[29]

13:51 צרעת ממארת A MALIGNANT AFFECTION: [The word ממארת should be understood] like [the word ממאיר in the phrase] (Ezek. 28:24) "prickling (ממאיר) briers and lacerating thorns." So also [one should understand the word מארה in the phrase] (Deut. 28:20) "calamity (מארה) and panic," as being related to the idea of curse or loss.[30]

13:55 פחתת A FRET: פחתת refers to a type of curse, which diminishes (מפחית) or causes a loss [to the affected object].[31]

---

[28]Rashbam's comment here should be seen as an attempt to improve on Rashi's. Rashi writes here simply that נתק is the Torah's name for an affection on a hairy part of a body. Rashbam adds an etymological grounding for that. Nahm. explains the etymology in this same way and argues that Rashi was wrong when he claimed that נתק is just the name of a type of affection. Like Rashbam, see also iE, Hizq., Seforno, Milgrom (p. 792) and others.

[29]Rashbam's explanation is identical to that of Rashi in content, and very similar to his in language. The explanation is the clear plain meaning of the text and is found also in Sifra here.

[30]Rashbam's comment here seems dependent on Rashi's. The first part of Rashbam's comment (the comparison to the verse in Ezekiel) is found in Rashi here. The second part of Rashbam's comment (the comparison to the verse in Deuteronomy) is found in Rashi's commentary to Deut. Still Rashbam's comment may be seen as partially opposed to that of Rashi, who (following Sifra here) offers a midrashic interpretation of the "curse" of this verse ("see the affected person as cursed and have no 'benefit' from him").

See iE here who argues that the comparison that Rashbam (and Rashi in Deut.) make between מארה and ממארת is unjustified, as ממארת has a *mem* in its root while מארה does not. So also Milgrom (pp. 811–812). That grammatical point is, however, arguable. In ibn Janaḥ's *Sefer ha-shorashim* (in Bacher's edition, but not in ibn Tibbon's) מארה is connected to the root *m-'-r*.

[31]Rashbam, like Rashi and most Jewish commentators, connects the word פחתת to the root (more common in rabbinic Hebrew) *p-ḥ-t*, which most often means to lessen or diminish. Rashi (following Sifra) sees פחתת here as being a physical description of the affection; פחתת means that it is deep. Rashbam understands the word as evaluative, not descriptive: פחתת means that the affection is a form of curse. See Wessely's criticism of Rashbam.

מצורע (Leviticus 14–15)

14:7 והזה שבע פעמים על HE SHALL SPRINKLE IT SEVEN TIMES ON: the aforementioned (vs. 2) person WHO IS BEING CLEANSED OF his ERUPTION.[1]

14:11 ואותם AND THEM: I.e. the lambs.[2]

14:37 שקערורות: is the name of some color;[3] the words that appear beside it in this context, "ירקרקות—green" and "אדמדמות—red" prove that that is the case.[4] So we also find in the Twelve Prophets (Zach. 6:3), [that the words] "אמוצים" and "ברודים" [are to be interpreted as the names of colors, even if we do not know precisely what they mean].[5]

---

[1]Rashbam has rearranged the word order of the verse. The verse, literally translated, actually reads: "He shall sprinkle it on him who is to be cleansed of the eruption seven times." Technically speaking, the verse could mean that the person is to be cleansed of his eruption seven times. Rashbam tells us that the adverbial phrase "seven times" modifies the verb "sprinkle," not the verb "cleansed." He does that by moving the words around so that his rephrasing reads: "he shall sprinkle it seven times . . .."

Rashbam's comment appears to be original and unobjectionable.

[2]The word "אותם—them," in our verse could refer either to all of the items mentioned in verse ten (the lambs, the flour and the oil) or just to the lambs. Rashbam explains that it refers only to the lambs, and presumably he does so because of the way that he understands the verb והעמיד in this verse. If one were to understand והעמיד as "to present" (NJPS) or "to place" (Milgrom, p. 849), then אותם could have the wider meaning. Rashbam apparently thinks that it means "to cause to stand"; animals and humans may be caused to stand, but not oil and flour.

Like Rashbam, see iE and Wessely.

[3]The word that Rashbam uses here, מראה, might simply mean "appearance." I am more comfortable translating it as "color," based both on the context, and on the use of the word by Rashbam in other passages. See his commentary to Gen. 29:17, Ex. 24:10 and, especially, BB 84a, s.v. מדקתני. See also commentary to Num. 11:7, and note 30 there.

[4]The more common understanding of שקערורות is that it is a noun, modified by the adjectives ירקרקות and אדמדמות. There is however no agreement as to what that noun would mean ("depressions"? "streaks"?). Rashbam is not the only exegete to suggest that it is, like ירקרקות and אדמדמות, another adjective, the name of a color; see e.g. Qimḥi, in his *Sefer ha-shorashim*. See Milgrom (p. 870) and Wessely who both argue (on different grounds) against seeing שקערורות as the name of a color.

[5]Rashbam's prooftext is well chosen. In that passage the horses of four different chariots are described. After writing the colors of the horses of the first three chariots (אדומים—red,

14:41 יקציע: means "to scrape," just like the verse (Is. 44:13), "He forms it with scraping tools (במקצועות)."[6] And [the word also appears] in the Talmud (Mishnah *Kelim* 27:4), "He who scrapes (המקצע) a hand's breadth from any of them."

[While יקציע has the root *q-ṣ-'*, other similar verbs in this text,] אשר הקצו (in our verse) and הקצות את הבית (vs. 43) have [a different root; they are from a] weak final-*heh* root (*q-ṣ-h*). But it would appear that those verbs [from that second root] should *also* be understood as meaning "to scrape." Since it says below (vs. 43) "after scraping (הקצות) the house" [and that word does not have the letter *'ayin*] while the language used before that [in our verse] is "he shall scrape (יקציע) the house," [written with an *'ayin*], this shows that the verbs *q-ṣ-'* and *q-ṣ-h* mean the same thing.[7]

14:56 וְלַבַּהֶרֶת: The [guttural] letters *heh, ḥet* and *'ayin* [when preceded by an *a* vowel][8] cause the word to change[9] at [a pausal cantillation sign, such as] an

---

שחורים—black, and לבנים—white), the text says that the horses of the fourth chariot were אמוצים ברודים. While no one is quite sure what those words mean (Rashi, for one, writes there that he does not know what אמוצים means), many exegetes conclude based on the context that the words must be the description of a color or colors. See e.g. ibn Janaḥ's *Sefer ha-shorashim* and iE's commentary to Zach.

[6]The interpretation of יקציע as meaning "to scrape" is universal. The comparison to the verse in Isaiah is also common; see e.g. iE commentary here, and ibn Janaḥ's *Sefer ha-shorashim.*

[7]Like Rashbam, many ancients and moderns consider these two verbs to be equivalent. See e.g. Onq., Hoffmann and Milgrom (p. 872). Others attempt to distinguish between the two verbs; see e.g. Qimḥi in his *Sefer ha-shorashim.* It appears to me that Rashi, too, distinguishes between the two verbs and learns something different from the use of each. According to Rashi (s.v. הקצו), "they scraped (קצעו) at the edges (בקצות) of the affection." Hence Rashbam's comment may be seen as opposed to Rashi's. See also iE who interprets as Rashi does. And see Wessely who dismisses Rashbam's attempt to see the two verbs as equivalent ("ואינו כן—this is not the case").

[8]The text of Rashbam as printed in Rosin's edition is difficult: ולבהרת: ה"י א"ח ה"ע גורמת להפוך . . .. The parallel passage in Rashbam's grammar work, *Dayyaqut* (Merdler's edition, pp. 31–32), is much easier to understand. There he cites examples almost identical to the ones he cites here, in order to discuss the vowel changes that occur in letters "with an *a* vowel (בהברת אה)" that occur before the gutturals *ḥet*, *'ayin* and *heh.* I have emended our text so that it reads the same as Rashbam's text in *Dayyaqut.*

[9]Perhaps the word להפוך which Rashbam uses here should be translated as "cause the [vowels of the] word *to switch places*," meaning that the "*a-e*" vowel pattern of בַּהֶרֶת becomes an "*e-a*" vowel pattern in the word בָּהָרֶת. In the parallel passage in *Dayyaqut* (Merdler's edition, pp. 31–2), Rashbam writes explicitly that this stress change at a pause causes the vowels to "switch places" (להפוך למפרע). On the other hand, in the passage here not all the examples that Rashbam cites are cases of the vowels "switching places."

Rashbam often talks about the changes that guttural letters effect in vocalization—and almost always uses some form of the verb "to cause (*g-r-m*)" to describe those changes. See

'etnaḥta or a *sof pasuq*. The word בָּהֲרָת becomes בָּהָרֶת. Similarly, [while in a context position, the form is (Lev. 16:21)] "הַשָּׂעִיר הַחַי—the living goat," [in a pausal form, e.g.] at an *'etnaḥta*, [it] becomes (Lev. 16:20) "הַשָּׂעִיר הֶחָי." [While the proper context form would be הַחֶרֶב (e.g. Gen. 3:24), the pausal form is] הֶחָרֶב, as in the phrase (II Sam. 11:25), "the sword (הֶחָרֶב) always takes its toll." The form without an *'etnaḥta*[10] is וְהִטַּהֲרוּ (e.g. Gen. 35:2); [at a pause the form becomes וְהִטֶּהָרוּ, as in the phrase (Num. 8:7),] "wash their clothes and cleanse themselves (וְהִטֶּהָרוּ)."[11]

15:2 זב מבשרו A DISCHARGE FROM HIS FLESH: The rabbis have explained[12] [and distinguished between] the appearance of this discharge and the appearance of semen.[13]

15:3 רר בשרו את זובו WHETHER THE DISCHARGE RUNS FROM HIS FLESH: [The word רר is to be understood] like [the word ריר in the phrase (I Sam. 21:14)] "he let his saliva (רירו) run down his face." In other words [the verse means] whether the discharge is thin, like semen, and is dribbling and dripping from his "flesh,"[14] or if the discharge החתים, HAS HARDENED, i.e. it has solidified and is sticking to his "flesh."[15]

---

e.g. commentary to Gen. 34:10, Ex. 8:25 and 14:16, Num. 11:28 and Deut. 3:24. See my Exodus volume, p. 83, note 26.

[10] I.e. the context form.

[11] The points that Rashbam makes here concerning vowel changes after gutturals at a pause are well grounded. See similarly G.-K. 27q and 29k.

[12] See e.g. Nid. 35b.

[13] Rashbam's comment here should be seen as similar to his comment to Lev. 13:2 and to his introductory comment to Leviticus. He asserts here that there is no need for him to provide details about the differences between male discharges (זוב) and semen (קרי); that information is contained in rabbinic literature and does not belong in a *peshaṭ* commentary.

Rashbam's comment implicitly criticizes Rashi for introducing such information into his commentary here, s.v. זובו טמא.

[14] While he does not say so explicitly here, Rashbam apparently agrees with the majority of ancients and moderns who see "בשר—flesh" here as a euphemism for the male member. (See e.g. the explicit comments of iE and of Milgrom.) From Rashbam's commentary to vs. 11, one sees that he interprets the phrase החתים בשרו in our verse (referring to the hardening of the discharge) as meaning that "החתים פי האמה—the opening of the penis was stopped up."

[15] See also Rashbam's commentary below ad vs. 11.

Rashi offers two interpretations of this verse, the first of which he labels the *peshaṭ*, while the second (following Meg. 8a; see also Rashi there, s.v. שלט) he labels the midrash. As often occurs in such situations, Rashbam presents only one interpretation, similar to Rashi's, the interpretation that Rashi labels *peshaṭ*. This understanding is the one commonly shared by most exegetes, traditional and modern.

15:4 אשר ישכב עליו [ANY BEDDING] ON WHICH [THE ONE WITH THE DISCHARGE] LIES [SHALL BE IMPURE]: Even if it [= the bedding] is underneath a rock[16] and [the person with the discharge was lying on top of the rock, such that] he did not touch the bedding at all. The general rule is that a man or a woman with a discharge or a menstruant woman all impart to items underneath them—even if they did not touch those items[17]—such a strict level of impurity that those items [in turn] impart impurity to a person [who touches them] and to the clothing [that that second person wears].[18] This is the case only if the items underneath [the person with the discharge] are specifically used for sitting [or for lying upon].[19]

15:11 וידיו לא שטף במים AND HE DID NOT SCRUB HIS "HANDS" IN WATER: The rabbis interpreted this to refer to the person who is impure because of a discharge and did not immerse himself [in a *miqveh*].[20]

To me it appears that, following the plain meaning of Scripture, [the word "יד—hand" is to be interpreted as a euphemism for the male member]. It says

---

[16]In rabbinic literature, the example of the impure person seated or lying on top of a rock, which in turn is on top of a bed or chair, is often used to illustrate the specific stringency attached to the impurity of the menstruant and of the person with a discharge. See *Kelim* 1:3 and Sifra, here, ad vs. 6. See also Sifre on Num. 5:2, where it is stated specifically that this is a way in which these types of impurity are even more stringent than the impurity of the dead body (generally considered to be the most stringent form of impurity).

Rashbam's comment here should be read together with his comment above on 11:28 where he writes, "Even if a dead body is placed on a bed and underneath the dead body there is [something as thin as] paper that keeps the dead body from touching the bedclothes, those bedclothes are still pure." Here he writes that, by contrast, the impurity of the menstruant and of the person with a discharge would be transferred to the bedclothes even if those bedclothes were separated from the impure person by a barrier as thick and as heavy as a rock.

[17]Rashbam often makes the point that impurity may be transferred without touching. See e.g. his commentary above ad 11:28 and 11:40.

[18]Rashbam's point—that impurity is transferred even to the clothing of the second person—is the undisputed halakhic position. It is also the simple meaning of verses 5 and 6.

Below, in his commentary to vs. 23, Rashbam continues (and refines) his discussion of the question of imparting impurity to clothing.

[19]Again Rashbam's comment follows the undisputed halakhic position. See also Rashi here, ad vs. 4, who (following Shab. 59a and Sifra here) makes the same point: the item underneath the impure person becomes impure only if it was an item intended for sitting or for reclining. Perhaps it is because of Rashi's comment that Rashbam feels required to add his refinement: Yes, Rashi is right that impurity would be imparted only if there was some real bedding or some real chair beneath the impure person. However, Rashbam adds, that bedding or chair need not be directly underneath the impure person; there could even be a barrier as solid as a rock separating that item from the impure person.

[20]This is the common halakhic explanation. See Sifra here. Rashi also interprets the verse in this manner.

above (vs. 3) "whether the discharge runs from his 'flesh' or has hardened on his 'flesh'," meaning that it has solidified and is sticking to his "flesh." That is why it now says, euphemistically, that "he did not scrub his 'hands' with water." [This means] that if he did not scrub his flesh, including the opening of the penis over which the discharge had hardened[21] (as it is explained in tractate *Niddah* [43b]), then he would remain impure even if he immersed (in a *miqveh*). [22] This is because he did not scrub well before immersing. Accordingly, anyone who touches him becomes impure.[23]

Since it is the opening of the penis through which the discharge comes out and which requires scrubbing, the text euphemistically uses the wording "scrubbing one's *hands*."

---

[21] So also Rashi ad vs. 3, s.v. או.

[22]This last sentence of Rashbam's comment could be translated differently. Rosin's notes would support the following translation:

[This means] that if he did not scrub his flesh, including the opening of the penis over which the discharge had hardened, then he would (as it is explained in tractate *Niddah* [66b]) remain impure even if he immersed (in a *miqveh*).

The question is whether Rashbam's reference to tractate *Niddah* is to a text there (66b) that says that immersion without scrubbing is not efficacious (Rosin), or a reference to a text there (43b) that says that a male discharge stops up the opening of the penis. I feel that the Hebrew syntax is marginally smoother in the wording that I have used.

[23]The problem that our verse poses for the *peshaṭ*-oriented traditional exegete is described well by iE. The verse, in its simplest sense, says that the impure person who has not "washed—שטף" his hands, transfers impurity to someone else. This implies that if he *has* washed his hands, he would not transfer impurity. But that is not what the *halakhah* says. A person impure because of a discharge does not become pure again until he has immersed his entire body in a *miqveh*. Even aside from the halakhic problem, it would be unusual if the text were read to say that a person impure from a discharge imparts impurity to a chair he sat on, even if he didn't touch it, but does not impart impurity to an item he touched, as long as he washed his hands. See, however, Milgrom who argues for the logic of that position. In any case, this solution is not available to the halakhically-minded exegete.

Rashi's solution is to say that "washing your hands" really means immersing your entire body in a *miqveh*. Rashi's explanation involves a midrashic reading both of the verb *sh-ṭ-p* and of the word ידיו—hands. Rashi then offers a *midrash halakhah* explanation of why the text would use the word "hands" when it really meant the entire body.

Rashbam, without having recourse to the heterodox explanation (that hand washing is sufficient to remove the impurity resulting from a discharge), offers an explanation that conforms more to what he considers to be *peshaṭ*. He does not interpret "hands" literally, but argues that the word is being used here euphemistically. He argues further that the verb *sh-ṭ-p* is used in contexts of vigorous washing or very strong flows of water.

While Rashbam's *peshaṭ* explanation is not found in the classical rabbinic sources, it is in conformity with *halakhah*. *Niddah* (66b) and other classical sources prove that immersion is not considered valid if a person has not cleansed well beforehand.

See iE who offers another attempt to interpret our verse in a *peshaṭ* manner (as not referring to *miqveh* immersion) yet in such a way that it does not conflict with *halakhah*.

Similarly [i.e. another example of euphemistic wording is found in the phrase] concerning a harlot (Prov. 30:20), "She 'ate' and then wiped off her 'mouth' and said, 'I have done no wrong'." Or when it says concerning relieving oneself (Jud. 3:24), "he is 'anointing his legs'."

Here also "scrubbing one's hands" refers to the scrubbing of that place from which the discharge comes out.[24]

The use of the verb *sh-ṭ-p* also proves that the reference is to the removal of a stain from something. For example when the verse says (Lev. 6:21), "it shall be scoured and scrubbed (ושטף) with water," the reference is to the removal of the fat of the *ḥaṭṭat* that is [stuck] on the vessel. Similarly [one sees that the verb *sh-ṭ-p* refers to vigorous action of water in the phrases] (Is. 28:2) "massive, torrential (שוטפים) rain," or (Job. 14:19) "Torrents wash away (תשטף) earth." So also here [one must interpret that verb as referring to scrubbing] in order to remove [all traces of] the discharge from his flesh.[25]

15:19 דם יהיה זובה HER DISCHARGE BEING BLOOD: I.e. she becomes impure through a red flow, unlike the white flow of the male discharge or of semen.[26]

---

[24]The examples that Rashbam cites from Proverbs and Judges are universally seen as being euphemisms. See e.g. Rashi to both those passages and Milgrom here. The question is whether it is reasonable to argue further, as Rashbam does, that ידיו here should also be seen as a euphemism.

Hoffmann says that the word ידיו never appears in such a euphemistic manner. Although Milgrom calls Rashbam's explanation "interesting but bizarre," he nevertheless cites ancient near Eastern examples of other uses of יד as a euphemism for penis (including Is. 57:8 and 10). One might also add that the common rabbinic word for penis, אמה, is simply a synonym of יד.

Perhaps Rashbam's interpretation would be somewhat easier to accept if the text read "ידו—his hand," in the singular.

[25]This is the strongest element of Rashbam's argument. The common rabbinic explanation (e.g. Rashi), that שטף means to immerse, and even the common modern explanation (e.g. Milgrom) that שטף means to rinse, both stretch the meaning of the verb. Wessely, who does not like Rashbam's contention that ידיו is a euphemism, still writes that Rashbam is correct about what שטף means. He, too, sees our verse as the source for the rabbinic principle that a person who is about to immerse in a *miqveh* must first scour away the dirt and stains from his body. Nahm. also interprets שטף in a manner similar to Rashbam's explanation.

[26]Rashbam's comment appears to be an attempt to improve on Rashi's. Rashi explains the phrase, "her discharge being blood," by saying: "her discharge is not considered a[n impure] discharge unless it is red." There are, however, halakhic problems with that statement. The Mishnah in *Niddah* 2:6 says that there are five different colors of blood that constitute an impure flow for a woman—only one of which is "red." To be sure, the other four colors are all similar to red. However, the Talmud (*Niddah* 19a) discussing that Mishnah specifically considers and rejects the possibility that only red blood constitutes an impure flow, the position that Rashi seems to be advocating.

15:23 ואם על המשכב הוא IF HE IS ON THE BED: I.e. if he is lying or sitting on something that is [impure because of] her[27] *midras*,[28] even if he is not touching it.[29] בנגעו בו יטמא עד הערב ON TOUCHING IT HE SHALL BE IMPURE UNTIL EVENING: I.e. *or* even if he touched an item which is impure because of *merkav*.[30] [In such a case] he shall be impure until evening, but not so impure as to make his clothing impure. For when dealing with *merkav* impurity, there is a distinction between someone who touches the impure item and someone who carries it. He who carries it becomes impure, and so does his clothing; he who touches it becomes impure but his clothing does not.[31]

Rashbam's explanation, while similar to Rashi's, explains that the word "blood" does imply redness, but that the redness of the discharge is in contrast to the previously listed (male) flows that are all shades of white. Rashbam's formulation is more in consonance with the talmudic position. Like Rashbam, see also Milgrom ("[the phrase is] an explanatory asyndeton, requiring the addition of the word *dam* 'blood' to distinguish the nature of her discharge from that of the male") and Wessely. (For further understanding of Rashi's position, see his commentary to *Niddah* 19a, s.v. למימרא.)

[27]Rosin helpfully emended the manuscript's reading שלו (his) to שלה (her).

[28]I.e. because of the *midras* of the woman with a discharge.

Midras is the technical halakhic term for an item that became impure because it was underneath someone impure, i.e. an item upon which the impure person sat or reclined or stood.

[29]The text that I have translated is difficult. It is Rosin's abbreviation of what he found in the manuscript. The section that Rosin omitted from the commentary, labeling it an interpolation from the hand of some mistaken copyist, is harder yet to fathom. It reads: עד הערב יטמא לטמא אוכלין ומשקין בנגעו בו יטמא עד הערב כמו ששנינו במסכת נדה שעליונו של זב מטמא אדם לטמא אוכלין ומשקין. See Rosin's note here, and RSBM, p. 56, note 10. In addition to the various objections that Rosin raised to the text he considered interpolated, one might add one more. The final words of that text say ". . . [a blanket] on top of a person impure because of a discharge will impart impurity to another person . . . ." That statement is halakhically inaccurate and directly contradicts what Rashbam says in his commentary to vs. 24. See note 35 there.

[30]*Merkav* impurity is impurity that is imparted to an item upon which someone impure "rode." The precise distinction between impurity that is imparted through riding and impurity that is imparted through sitting (*moshav*) is a matter of some halakhic debate. See e.g. Rashi's commentary to vs. 9, above, or P. Kehati's note at the end of his commentary to *Kelim* 23:2.

[31]Verse 23 presents many difficulties both for the traditionalist and for the modern exegete. Milgrom, for example, writes that there are five possible antecedents for the pronoun הוא in our verse.

Rashbam (as long as one accepts Rosin's emendation described in note 29 above) appears to interpret the verse in the same manner that Rashi does, although the comment is not phrased as clearly as Rashi's.

Rashbam and Rashi both interpret the verse as saying two separate things. First it tells us that anyone who lies or sits on the *midras* of a menstruant, even without touching it, becomes impure to the extent described in the previous verse—requiring even the laundering of clothing. This interpretation requires, as Rashi says explicitly, reading the first half of our

The rabbis interpreted [that the topic being discussed here is] *merkav* impurity, based on the words אשר היא יושבת עליו—UPON WHICH SHE SAT.[32]

15:24 אשר ישכב עליו יטמא [AND IF A MAN LIES WITH HER (i.e. the menstruant) . . .] ANY BEDDING ON WHICH HE LIES SHALL BECOME sufficiently IMPURE: that it imparts impurity to food or drink.[33] In chapter

---

verse, "If he is on the bed . . .," as a continuation of the previous verse, "he shall wash his clothes . . . and remain impure until evening." Then, in the middle of our verse, a new rule begins: "He who touches it (an object with *merkav* impurity) shall be impure," but shall not require laundering of clothes. The first half of the verse then teaches us a stringency about the menstruant's bed or chair (even without touching it, the one who sits on it becomes impure and so does his clothing); the second half of the verse teaches us a leniency about her *merkav* (although the person who carries it has to launder his clothes, the person who touches it does not). This last point is explicit in *Kelim* 23:3.

Cf. iE's attempt to find a more *peshaṭ*-oriented interpretation of this verse, and see also the criticisms of his position both by traditionalists like Wessely and moderns like Milgrom.

[32]As Rosin notes, Rashbam's comment is slightly inaccurate. The Sifra (and so also Rashi) see the word "כלי-vessel" in our verse (and not the words "upon which she sat") as the reference to *merkav* impurity.

Perhaps Rashbam either subconsciously or consciously is attempting to improve on the traditional *midrash halakhah.* Aside from other problems with that traditional reading, the problem of the order of the clauses is irksome. The Sifra's reading sees four clauses in our verse: (1) ואם על המשכב—a reference to bedding impurity; (2) על הכלי—a reference to *merkav* impurity; (3) אשר היא יושבת עליו—a reference to chair impurity; and (4) בנגעו בו יטמא עד הערב—a clause that means that the level of impurity is relatively less stringent, as the impure person's clothing remains pure. The midrash (and so also Rashi) then combines the clauses in an unusual manner. Clauses 1 and 3 are attached to the previous verse: i.e. bedding and chair impurity are said to be part of the stringent rules (including laundering of clothing) of vs. 22. The leniency of clause 4 is seen to apply only to *merkav* impurity—i.e. clause 4 refers only to clause 2. So Rashbam's "correction"—that sees clause 3, not clause 2, as the reference to *merkav* impurity—smoothes over one of the roughest elements of the syntactical reading of the verse proposed by the midrash.

[33]In other words, there is a lower level of impurity attached to the bedding upon which this man, who had intercourse with a menstruant, slept. A person who touched that bedding would not become impure. Only foodstuffs and drinks that came in contact with that bedding would become impure. This is the standard halakhic position.

Perhaps Rashbam's comment should be seen as a refinement of Rashi's. Rashi writes that a man who has intercourse with a menstruant becomes as impure as the menstruant, and transfers impurity to another human through touch. While not rejecting that claim (which is also the simple meaning of the verse), Rashbam clarifies that, halakhically speaking, the man who has intercourse with a menstruant is not quite as impure as she. If *she* slept on a bed, that bed would transfer impurity to a person who touched it; if *he* slept on a bed, it would not. For a clear formulation of the distinction between the impurity of the menstruant and that of the man who had intercourse with her, see Maimonides, *Meṭamme'e mishkav umoshav* 3:1–2.

Benot kutim[34] [the rabbis explain that the level of impurity imparted to items] *underneath* the man who had intercourse with a menstruant is equivalent to [the level of impurity imparted to items that are] *on top of* the man who is impure because of a discharge.[35]

15:25 בלא עת נדתה [WHEN A WOMAN HAS HAD A DISCHARGE] . . . NOT AT THE TIME OF HER MENSTRUATION: I.e. after the days of her menstruation, as it is explained in tractate *Niddah.*[36] A woman is not considered [the type of] *zavah* [a woman impure because of a discharge] who is required to bring a sacrifice[37] unless she sees blood for three consecutive days after her seven days of menstrual impurity, during the next eleven days thereafter, whether at the beginning or at the end [of that eleven day period].[38] [Such a woman] requires seven "clean" days followed by a sacrifice on the eighth day [as elements of her purification process].

---

[34]The fourth chapter of tractate *Niddah*. See *Niddah* 32b.

[35]A person who touches bedding underneath a person who is impure with a discharge or underneath a menstruant becomes impure. A person who touches blankets on top of the menstruant or on top of the person with a discharge, does not become impure; only food and drink can become impure in that manner. When it comes to the man who is impure because of having intercourse with a menstruant, the rule for bedding *underneath* him is similar to the rule for blankets *on top of* the menstruant.

[36] See e.g. *Niddah* 73a.

[37] Rashbam chooses his language carefully as he knows well that there are different categories of women with discharges (*zavot*). It is only the most serious *zavah*, the one who must bring a sacrifice, that he is defining in this comment.

[38]When menstruation begins, any blood that the woman sees on that day or on any one of the following six days is defined as "menstrual." When that seven-day period concludes, any subsequent blood that she saw would be considered "menstrual" only if there had been a "clean" intervening period of at least eleven days after the first seven. It is blood that is seen during the eleven-day interval period following each seven-day menstrual period that is potentially defined as "discharge" (זבה) blood.

The explanation that Rashbam gives is the standard halakhic position and is found also in Rashi and in Sifra.

אחרי מות (Leviticus 16–18)

16:1 אחרי מות AFTER THE DEATH [OF THE TWO SONS OF AARON]: God then warned Aaron, so that he too should not die like his sons did for entering the Temple[1] in an unauthorized[2] manner.[3]

16:2 כי בענן אראה על הכפרת FOR I APPEAR IN A CLOUD OVER THE COVER: According to the plain meaning of Scripture, this verse means "because it is through a pillar of cloud that I appear regularly over the cover [of the Ark, inside of the Holy of Holies]." So it says (in Exodus 25:22), "[There I will meet with you,] and I will speak to you from above the cover, from between the

[1]The reference to "the Temple (מקדש)" in this comment might be anachronistic. Alternatively, the word could be translated here as "the Holy precinct."

[2]Rashbam uses the phrase, שלא כדת, to describe an unauthorized entry, playing with the language of Est. 4:16, a text that describes another unauthorized entry (Esther's entry into the king's inner chamber without being summoned) that could lead to death. Rashbam's younger contemporary, JBS, who interprets our verse in the same way as Rashbam, peppers his comment here with a series of allusions to the language of that chapter in Esther.

[3]The explanation that Rashbam offers is similar to that offered here in Sifra. So also Rashi, iE, Nahm. and others. In the oldest sources, this point is made in a more general way: Aaron is warned not to enter the Holy of Holies and is reminded about the severe punishment that his sons received (although not necessarily for the same crime). Rashbam was the first exegete to make the point clearly that, since the sin of Nadab and Abihu involved some unauthorized entrance or action inside the Holy precinct, it is appropriate for God to refer to their death before giving Aaron rules about entering the Holy precinct. Why did earlier sources refrain from making this connection? Perhaps they felt that the two sins were different. It is generally not felt that Aaron's sons entered the Holy of Holies, whereas here Aaron is warned not to enter the Holy of Holies.

iE actually uses our verse as proof that the sin of Aaron's sons did take place within the Holy of Holies. (This is also the position of R. Jose the Galilean in the Sifra here. See also Tos. Eruv. 63a, s.v. מאי.) Rashbam, as we have seen in his commentary to chapters 9 and 10 (see e.g. note 6 there), does not agree. He feels that their sin took place at the "inner altar," which is inside the Tabernacle, but not inside the Holy of Holies. See also Nahm., ad vs. 2, who argues against iE's claim. Rashbam and Nahm. can still see our verse as connecting Nadab and Abihu's unauthorized action/entry with the instructions to Aaron, even if Nadab and Abihu had been punished for entering a different location. As Luzzatto writes here, "even though they [= Nadab and Abihu] had not entered the Holy of Holies, in any case they died because of their disregard of the proper honor and reverence that are appropriate for God's sanctuary and for his service."

two cherubim [that are on the Ark]." If the priest were to see [this pillar of cloud], he would die.

Accordingly God commanded that, when he enters [the Holy of Holies] on the Day of Atonement, he should offer incense there beforehand, inside the Holy of Holies, so as to darken the Temple with a cloud of incense. [Only] then would he bring the blood of the bull and the blood of the goat [into the Holy of Holies].[4]

16:6 והקריב אהרן AARON SHALL BRING HIS OWN BULL FORWARD: into the courtyard, וכפר בעדו—and he shall immediately make a confession upon it. [This is the traditional rabbinic interpretation.] However, according to the plain meaning of Scripture [the verse means that] Aaron shall bring it into the courtyard in order to sacrifice it [later] לכפרה—to make expiation. And so it is

---

[4]The traditional rabbinic reading of this verse was that Aaron was to create a cloud of incense smoke when he entered the Holy of Holies. According to *Yoma'* 53a, both the Pharisees and the Sadducees agreed that the cloud described here is the cloud of incense smoke prepared by Aaron. They differed only about how and where that cloud was to be prepared. Rashi also offers that rabbinic interpretation as his second, midrashic option. iE too suggests that reading, apparently as his preferred reading of the verse. See, however, Hoffmann who is so convinced that this interpretation is wrong that he posits that it must have originated with the Sadducees. Milgrom, on the other hand, finds this understanding perfectly acceptable.

Rashi also offers a *peshaṭ*-oriented interpretation—that the cloud described in our verse is the cloud that hovers regularly over the Ark in the Holy of Holies. That idea is found in Ex. 25:22 and see also Rashbam's commentary to Ex. 40:35.

Here Rashbam follows the basic pattern of Rashi's *peshaṭ* explanation, with some twists. First, Rashbam adds that the reason that Aaron would die for entering beyond the normal limit is that he would see the Presence of God hovering over the Ark. According to Rashi's formulation, Aaron's potential sin is not connected with sight. On Rashbam's attitude to seeing God hovering over the Ark, see also commentary to Ex. 24:11, and note 17 there, and commentary to Num. 4:20, and note 37 there.

Rashbam's second innovation in his commentary here is that he appears to combine the midrashic view of the "cloud" of our verse with the *peshaṭ* understanding. According to Rashbam, Aaron cannot enter lest he see the ***cloud*** *of God's Presence*. So, on the Day of Atonement, in order to avoid that problem he creates his own ***cloud*** *of incense*. However, when Rashbam uses the word "cloud" for the second time, describing the incense cloud, he is not, in my opinion, agreeing with the traditional rabbinic opinion that the word "cloud" in this verse refers to the cloud of incense. Rather, punning on the word "cloud," which he believes refers, in this verse, only to the cloud of God's Presence, he is paraphrasing the continuation of the chapter. Since our verse says that Aaron is not authorized to see the standard divine cloud, later verses say that, on the Day of Atonement, he should create his own cloud as a form of camouflage.

written below (vs. 11) "Aaron shall then offer his bull of sin offering [to make expiation]."[5]

16:10 לשלח אותו לעזאזל המדברה TO RELEASE IT TO AZAZEL, TO THE WILDERNESS: According to the plain meaning of Scripture [this means] "to release it alive to [let it go graze with] the [other] goats[6] in the wilderness." This

---

[5]Rashbam is dealing with a redundancy. The first half of vs. 11 is a verbatim repetition of our verse. Both verses say that Aaron should והקריב (either "sacrifice" or "bring in") the bull offering and should make expiation (וכפר) with it. But in the second half of vs. 11, Aaron is told to slaughter the bull. Thus Rashbam and others understand that והקריב means "bring the bull forward" in both verses. See also Noth, and Milgrom, who writes: "The verb must be rendered 'bring forward,' a meaning frequently attested in ritual."

But what about the repeated phrase, "וכפר בעדו ובעד ביתו—he shall make expiation for himself and for his household"? The standard rabbinic solution (Sifra here, *Yoma'* 36b, Rashi here) is that "expiation" here means "confession." The first "expiation" described in our verse refers to a confession that the priest makes as soon as he brings the bull into the Temple's courtyard, a confession for his own sins and for those of his family. The second expiation, the one in verse 11, refers to a second confession that the priest will make later, just before the slaughtering, a confession concerning the sins of his clan, the priests. The Mishnah, which describes in tractate *Yoma'* the actions of the priest in the Temple on the Day of Atonement step by step, writes in 3:8 about the first confession over the bull and then in 4:2 about the second confession ("בא לו אצל פרו שניה—when he comes back to his bull the second time [then he makes his second confession]").

Rashbam begins his comment here by citing the beginning of the rabbinic explanation. Then he offers his own more *peshaṭ*-oriented solution. The "expiation" of our verse has nothing to do with confession. Slaughtering the sacrifice in the correct manner effects expiation. The redundancy is explained as follows: Aaron, according to our verse, is to bring the bull into the courtyard now in order to offer it later, at the appropriate time, as a sacrifice that will effect expiation. See also NJPSC: "This statement is anticipatory. This is what Aaron would do at the appropriate time."

Both the Sifra and the BT (*Yoma'* 36b) explicitly reject this solution that Rashbam offers. They claim that וכפר could not refer to expiation through the sacrificial ceremony, but must refer to two separate confessions.

Rashbam's explanation here may be seen as an example of his use of the exegetical principle of "the text generalizes and then specifies." (On this exegetical principle, see notes to 12:2 above and to Ex. 2:15.) Our verse tells us that the bull sacrifice is intended for expiation. Later verses will explain in detail how that expiation is effected.

Like Rashbam, see iE. In the *Be'ur*, Wessely polemicizes at length against Rashbam's understanding of the verse ("ותמה אני על הרשב"ם . . . ואין דבריו נראין . . . ולמה ירחיק לפרשו על וידוי דברים—I am amazed by Rashbam's comment . . . it does not make sense . . . why does he reject the interpretation that it refers to a confession?"). However, Mendelssohn interpolates into Wessely's *Be'ur* a lengthy and passionate defense of Rashbam's position, saying that "אעפ"כ איני זז מפשוטו של מקרא—in spite of everything [that Wessely wrote], I shall not abandon the *peshaṭ* of the verse." He argues that the exegetical methodology of "the text generalizes and then specifies" constitutes an acceptable, orthodox rabbinical way of interpreting.

[6]See Rashbam's next comment, on the word Azazel, and note 12 there.

is just like what is done with the bird offerings of the "leper," that purify him from his impurity; [concerning one of the two birds] it is written (Lev. 14:7),] "he shall set the live bird free (וְשִׁלַּח) in the open country." So here also, in order to purify the Israelites from their sins, he sets the goat free in the wilderness (מדבר).[7]

[The word מדבר means] a place where animals graze. So it is written (Ex. 3:1) that Moses "led the sheep to the מדבר." So also in rabbinic literature [one speaks of two kinds of animals], "מדבריות and ביייתיות—domesticated."[8]

---

[7]Rashbam offers an innovative and audacious reading of the ceremony with the goats. In rabbinic tradition it was unanimously understood that the second goat, the one that was not sacrificed, was killed by pushing it off a cliff. See e.g. *Yoma'* 6:6, Sifra here, Rashi here, and virtually all traditional Jewish exegetes. Classical rabbinic literature considers and explicitly rejects the possibility that the goat was not killed. See Rashi here, vs. 10 (following Sifra).

Rashbam argues reasonably that this ceremony parallels the bird ceremony of the "leper" in chapter 14. In both texts there are two animals that are brought to a priest. In both cases the purpose is to effect purification. In both cases one of the animals is sacrificed. The *piel* form of the verb *sh-l-ḥ* is used in both texts to describe the fate of the second animal. In chapter 14 it is universally understood that the word וְשִׁלַּח means that that bird is "set free" and will continue to live. So, Rashbam argues, when our text says concerning the second goat לְשַׁלַּח אותו, it means that the goat is to be set free. So also (after Rashbam) Baḥya here, and Hizq. ad vs. 22. This analogy between chapters 14 and 16 is popular among exegetes who do not feel bound by the interpretive traditions of classical rabbinic Judaism. See e.g. Ehrlich who offers Rashbam's understanding (without attribution) as the sense of the text, and see Milgrom, who draws a number of parallels between the goats of chapter 16 and the birds of chapter 14.

As might be expected, many traditionalist Jewish exegetes were not pleased with Rashbam's explanation. See e.g. Wessely. Even iE in his commentary to vs. 8 quotes and dismisses an unnamed exegete who explains the verse as Rashbam does.

Although Rashbam's interpretation can be understood on its own terms, Touitou argues (*Milet*, 288) that there is an anti-Christian polemical purpose to this comment. Touitou feels that Rashbam's interpretation was meant to undermine the Christian claim that the scapegoat of our chapter prefigures Jesus' death which was also intended to lead to atonement for sins. If, as Rashbam interprets, the scapegoat of Lev. 16 never died, the text could not serve as a prefiguration of atonement through the crucifixion.

[8]Rashbam is opposing the suggestion that the fact that the goat was released into a מדבר proves that the goat was intended to die. (See e.g. Luzzatto, who offers that argument.) A מדבר, Rashbam argues, is not a desert, or at least is not always a desert. Moses took his father-in-law's sheep to a מדבר to graze. Animals in the Mishnah are divided into two categories: domesticated and מדבריות—not domesticated. Wherever non-domesticated animals graze must be a place that can sustain life.

Moderns would agree with Rashbam's contention that מדבר does not (or need not) mean a desert. See BDB, where the first definition of מדבר is: "tracts of land used for the pasturage of flocks and herds." The root of the word is generally seen to be *d-b-r* in the sense of "to lead," yielding the idea of leading sheep to pasture. (See e.g. Sarna, NJPSC, Exodus, p. 240.)

עזאזל [The word] AZAZEL: [should be understood as if its final letter] *lamed* were [an] *extra* [added, but insignificant letter].[9] So also [one should interpret] the *lamed* in [the phrase] (Hos. 10:14), בית ארבאל. [The word *Arbel* there actually derives from the root *'-r-b* "to lie in wait,"] as in the phrase (in Deut. 19:11) "וארב לו—lies in wait for him."[10] Similarly the [final] *mem* in words like ריקם (empty) or חנם (free) are extra letters, [i.e. they are not letters of the root. They were added to the root letters] to create an [abstract?] noun [or adjective],[11] just like the final *nun* in words like שגעון—madness, עצבון—sadness or עשרון—a tenth.[12]

Other Jews in pre-modern times also interpreted מדבר as a grazing place. See Onq. to Ex. 3:1, who claims that when the verse says that Moses led Jethro's sheep to the מדבר, it means that he led them "לאתר שפר רעיא—towards good grazing." Qimḥi often makes the point that מדבר means a grazing place. See e.g. his commentary to Josh. 8:15 and see also his commentary to I Kings 2:34, where he argues that a מדבר might even be in a settled area; any place that is not cultivated may be called a מדבר.

[9]Rashbam often discusses "extra" letters in biblical words. These letters are not part of the root, they do not appear because of some grammatical necessity and they do not convey any particular meaning. See e.g. his commentary to Gen 1:24.

[10]This strange interpretation of the word Arbel (presumably simply a place name, as Dunash points out [p. 49]) has a long history among Jewish exegetes. It may be found in Menaḥem, in Ps.-Jon., in Qara and as one of two alternatives in Rashi (the last three *ad loc.* in Hos.)

[11]It is difficult to know the precise meaning of Rashbam's phrase here, לתיקון פעולה. On פעולה, see Rashbam's commentary to Ex. 21:2 (and note 10 there), and see Rosin, RSBM, pp. 140–141, and notes there. See also Rashbam's grammar book, *Dayyaqut* (*passim*, especially p. 8 and p. 51 in Merdler's edition). In her M.A. dissertation, Merdler writes (p. 137) that Rashbam uses the word פעולה as the equivalent of the modern Hebrew grammatical term שם פעולה. I am not certain that that definition applies whenever Rashbam uses the term.

In his commentary to Gen. 27:33, Rashbam uses the word תיקון as he does here—in the sense of (in that case) an entire word which he sees as not adding meaning to the sentence, i.e. a stylistic flourish.

[12]Rashbam discusses the use of an "extra" *nun* or *mem* at the end of a word in a number of places, e.g. in his commentary to Gen. 49:24.

There are dozens of theories about what Azazel means, with no clear consensus opinion—neither in rabbinic literature nor among moderns. As Ehrlich puts it, "no one knows who or what Azazel is."

Rashbam's explanation of the word Azazel is not the strongest element of his comment on this verse. The assumption that the *lamed* at the end of the word is "extra" is unconvincing. As noted here by Rashbam's supercommentary, *Qeren Shemuel*, generally only the Hebrew letters ה-א-מ-נ-ת-י-ו can be seen as candidates for being declared "extra." To be sure, even a commentator like iE who tried to limit the use of the principle of "extra" letters (see e.g. his commentary to Amos 3:12 or Est. 8:17) still found a number of examples of extra *lamed*s in the Bible. His parade example, לאבשלום in I Chr. 3:2, is cited many times in his Bible commentaries (e.g. ad Mal. 3:7). iE even identified one "extra" *lamed* in the middle of a word (שלאנן; commentary to Job 21:23). But it is a long way from there to Rashbam's position that Azazel simply means "the place of the עזים—goats." See however Qimḥi in his

[Below (vs. 22), the place to which the goat is sent is called] ארץ גזירה, which means an arid land in which there are no [cultivated] crops, a land which is cut off (גזורה) and separated from anything good.[13]

16:21 ביד איש עתי: [means that the goat was sent] in the care of some person who knows the roads and the pastures,[14] someone whom people would regularly send [to do various tasks].[15]

16:32 וכפר הכהן אשר ימשח אותו THE PRIEST WHO HAS BEEN ANOINTED [IN PLACE OF HIS FATHER] SHALL MAKE EXPIATION: [This verse had to be written] since it said above (vs. 3), "Thus shall *Aaron* enter . . .." If Aaron is no longer [alive], then [our verse tells us that] the priest anointed in his place performs the ceremony of the Day of Atonement.[16]

16:34 ויעש HE: Aaron, when the Day of Atonement arrived, DID WHAT THE LORD HAD COMMANDED MOSES.[17]

Sefer ha-shorashim who suggests that Azazel is a combination of the Hebrew word עז—goat, and the Aramaic word אזל—to go, so called because it is the place to which the goat goes. See Milgrom who suggests that the Vulgate's reading, *caper emissarius*, may reflect that same understanding. Andrew of St. Victor (p. 178) says that the Vulgate's term *caper emissarius* actually means "*in desertum emittendo*—[the one] let loose in the desert," an interpretation very similar to Rashbam's.

[13]Rashbam's comment is directed against Rashi, who, in his commentary to verse 8, cites the word גזירה from vs. 22 to prove his own explanation of Azazel. Rashi interprets Azazel in a way that conforms with the Mishnah's explanation (*Yoma'* 6:5–6) of what one does with this goat. Rashi says that Azazel is a cliff (using the Mishnah's word צוק to define Azazel). Rashi then says that Azazel is called "the land of גזירה" in vs. 22 because of the steep way that the cliff has been cut. Rashbam, in opposing Rashi's explanation of Azazel here, offers his own explanation of why this land is considered "cut off." See JBS who uses almost the same language as Rashbam in explaining the phrase, but tries to harmonize that understanding with Rashi's.

[14]On מדברות as "pastures," see commentary on vs. 10, and note 8 there.

[15]Rashi (following Sifra and *Yoma'* 66b) interprets איש עתי as meaning someone who had been appointed to the position on the previous day. Rashbam opposes that explanation, claiming that it means someone who is regularly chosen for such tasks because of his special skills. As Milgrom notes, an איש עתי, as Rashbam understands the term, has the advantage that he is sufficiently knowledgeable about the terrain that he would be able to return without the goat following him back to civilization. See similarly to Rashbam, Qimḥi, *Shorashim*, s.v. *'-y-t*.

[16]Rashbam's explanation is the same as that of Rashi (following Sifra and PT *Yoma'* 5:1). It is also the plain meaning of the text.

[17]The syntax is unclear. After the text outlines all the instructions concerning the Day of Atonement, we have half a verse that says that *he* did what God had commanded Moses. What is the subject of the verb ויעש? *Who* did what God had commanded?

17:4 דם יחשב לאיש ההוא דם שפך IT SHALL BE CONSIDERED BLOOD-GUILT FOR THAT MAN, HE HAS SPILLED BLOOD: That man shall be considered to be liable for the death penalty at God's hand,[18] because of the blood that he spilled when he slaughtered[19] [an animal] outside [of the permitted place for slaughtering].[20]

Rashbam adopts the explanation of Rashi (following Sifra) that the phrase means that Aaron, at the appropriate time (the next Day of Atonement), followed the instructions listed above. This explanation appears to me to be the plain meaning of Scripture. So also iE and Nahm. (with a small twist; Aaron fulfilled what God commanded even before the Day of Atonement, as he observed the restrictions legislated above concerning entry to the Holy of Holies). Among moderns see, e.g., Milgrom who explains that the reference is to Aaron.

See, however, NJPS, which translates "*Moses* did as the LORD had commanded him." So also RSV. Baruch Levine, when explaining, in NJPSC, the NJPS translation for this verse, writes that even though the syntax is clumsy, "the sense is clear"—that Moses is the one who fulfils God's instructions.

[18]Many Jewish exegetes interpret the words "דם יחשב—it should be considered as blood" as meaning that the actions of this sinner should be considered tantamount to the spilling of human blood. (See e.g. Rashi, Nahm. and Seforno.) Rashbam understands it differently—that "blood" here means "bloodguilt." See also Rashbam's comment to Ex. 22:1.

Rashbam, as a careful halakhist, adds that the "death penalty" of this verse is not enforced by a Jewish court; the verse means only that God will exact the ultimate penalty. That is also, from the perspective of halakhic exegesis, the meaning of the end of the verse that says that the sinner will be "cut off."

[19]Here also Rashbam disputes Rashi's comment. Rashi argues (following one opinion in Zev. 107a) that the words "דם שפך—he has spilled blood" teach us (presumably because of their perceived redundancy) that *sprinkling* the blood of a sacrifice is yet another action forbidden outside of the holy precinct. Rashbam explains more simply that the spilling of blood referred to is that blood which is spilled when one slaughters. So also Sifra.

[20]The standard understanding of most halakhic exegetes is that the opening verses of chapter 17 are directed to the Israelites traveling through the Sinai wilderness. For them, any slaughter of animals for meat, even for personal consumption, is prohibited if it takes place away from the Tabernacle. When the book of Deuteronomy permits such slaughter (e.g. Deut. 12:15), that is seen as a change in legislation, a new rule that applies to the Jews entering the land. See Nahm., Wessely and Luzzatto who all argue that this opinion represents the simple meaning of the text.

Rashi, however, follows the opinion in rabbinic literature (R. Aqiva's position in Hul. 17a and the opinion of the Sifra here; according to Nahm., this is the minority opinion among the rabbis) that interprets our text as forbidding only *sacrifices* taking place in the wilderness away from the Tabernacle. Slaughter for personal consumption away from the Tabernacle was always permitted.

It would appear that Rashbam follows Rashi, at least with respect to this exegetical issue in our verse. When Rashbam uses the words שחיטת חוץ to describe the infraction in these verses, he is using the technical term that describes *sacrifices* that have been offered outside of the permitted area. See e.g. Zev. 69a. See also the related term שחוטי חוץ which appears even more often in rabbinic literature and which is, as far as I can tell, invariably used for the prohibited slaughter of *sacrifices* outside of the permitted area. See, for example, the

17:5 אשר הם זובחים על פני השדה [IN ORDER THAT THE ISRAELITES MIGHT BRING] THE SACRIFICES WHICH THEY HAVE BEEN MAKING IN THE OPEN . . . [(vs. 7) THAT THEY MAY OFFER THEIR SACRIFICES NO MORE TO THE GOAT-DEMONS]: For some of them err[21] and sacrifice to the goat-demons[22] instead of to God.[23]

17:13 וכסהו בעפר [HE SHALL POUR OUT ITS BLOOD] AND COVER IT WITH DIRT: So that it will no longer be edible.[24]

---

discussion in BB 120a and Rashbam's commentary there, s.v. זה הדבר and s.v. שאני התם, where the Talmud and Rashbam both consider it obvious that the term שחוטי חוץ and the laws of Lev. 17 refer to an infraction that applies in all generations, not just during the time of wandering in the wilderness. See also Andrew of St. Victor who writes (p. 178), presumably after being convinced by some Jew(s) to interpret this way, that the text is *not* referring to slaughter for the purpose of eating, but only to slaughter for sacrifice. Andrew adds further that the intent of this text is to cut back on the amount of private sacrifice.

[21]In his commentary to Ex. 20:20, Rashbam uses a very similar phrase, "for there are those who err and think that they are real divinities." According to Rashbam, there, too, the Torah legislates a precaution to minimize the possibility of idolatry occurring.

[22]It is difficult to know what Rashbam thinks the word שעירים means. From his comment to Deut. 18:13 it is apparent that he thinks that שעירים were used for divination. Perhaps Rashbam would agree with Rashi's definition (ad Deut. 32:17) that a שעיר is a devil (שד). So also iE here. The translation I have used here is from NJPS.

[23]Rashbam's comment seems to be defending the Israelites wandering through the wilderness from the accusation that they were all idolaters or worshippers of demons, as the verse seems to imply. (See e.g. Maimonides, *Guide* 3:46, who concludes from our verse that the biggest religious problem for the Israelites in the wilderness was the worship of שעירים.) Rashbam says that the words "that they may offer their sacrifices no more to the goat-demons," imply only that *some* of the Israelites mistakenly were doing (or perhaps might do) that. See similarly Seforno who also tries to explain our verse in such a way that the Israelites are not seen as evil idolaters.

See Rashbam's younger contemporary, JBS, who offers the fascinating explanation that this verse teaches that the value of sacrifices is not intrinsic; they are rather a protective measure to keep people away from idolatry (in a manner similar to Maimonides' theory of sacrifices in *Guide* 3:32).

[24]Rashbam gives another (see e.g. commentary and notes to 11:3, above) explanation that would fall into the category of *ṭa'ame ha-miṣvot*, an attempt to provide a rationale for a commandment. This time he does not claim that his explanation is תשובה למינים—an argument appropriate for anti-Christian polemicizing. As is often Rashbam's custom, he provides a practical and prosaic purpose for the legislation here. Much more edificatory and uplifting explanations have been offered, either suggesting that blood, as the animal's "soul" or life force, requires special treatment (Nahm., here; *Sefer ha-ḥinukh* #187), or that blood left exposed might be used for illicit divination or might make the country appear to be full of bloodshed (both explanations in Luzzatto here). See Wessely who dismisses Rashbam's comment here ("ואיו זה נכון") and concludes that one should not try to figure out the reasons for commandments unless they are required for an understanding of the *peshaṭ*. Like Rashbam, see Hizq.

17:15 אשר תאכל נבלה [ANY PERSON] WHO EATS AN ANIMAL THAT HAS DIED: I.e. even a minor who eats it, SHALL BE IMPURE.[25]

17:16 ונשא עונו [BUT HE (THE IMPURE PERSON) WHO DOES NOT WASH . . .] SHALL BEAR HIS GUILT: If he eats holy food or enters the Temple.[26]

18:5 וחי בהם [YOU SHALL PRACTICE MY LAWS] AND LIVE THROUGH THEM: But if you do not practice them, then (vs. 29) "all those who practice [those abhorrent things] shall be cut off from their people."[27]

See also JBS's impassioned tirade (ad 17:11) against exegetes (Karaites?) who interpret the verse even more prosaically than Rashbam—not as a commandment but as either good housekeeping advice or as descriptive, not prescriptive language ("when you slaughter at home, the blood will spill out and be swallowed up by the ground").

[25]Halakhists, from the days of the Sifra until modern times, have struggled to explain the need for this verse when there are many other verses that teach that eating animals or birds that have died leads to impurity. (See e.g. Lev. 11:40 and 22:8; see also Rashbam's commentary and notes to those passages.) See e.g. Rashi who (following Sifra) explains that this verse does contain new information, if we assume that the carcass described here is the carcass of a kosher bird.

Rashbam says that this additional verse, with its emphatic phrase, "כל נפש—**any** person," teaches that even children would become impure from eating such a carcass. As far as I can tell, Rashbam is offering his own new, independent halakhic midrash of our verse. There are other examples of halakhic *midrashim* which deduce from the word נפש that a particular law applies to a minor, not just to an adult. But I have found no source before Rashbam to offer this explanation of our verse. Like Rashbam, see Hizq.

[26]This verse is problematic for all halakhic exegetes since it implies that there is a sin involved in being or remaining impure. That is not the standard halakhic position. The solution that Rashbam offers (following Rashi and Sifra) is the standard halakhic solution: the impure person "bears guilt" for impurity only if he or she does something that requires ritual purity. This is the third time in his Leviticus commentary that Rashbam has made this same point; see above ad 5:2 and 11:8.

[27]As Rosin notes, Rashbam's comment here may be seen as directed against Rashi's midrashic question and answer. Rashi (following Sifra; see also Onq.) asks, rhetorically, how the Torah can guarantee that we will "live" if we observe the commandments; do we not all die eventually? Rashi answers that the "life" guaranteed by the Torah as a reward for observance is the life of the world to come.

Rashbam explains the phrase in a more contextual manner: the "life" promised to those who follow God's practices is in comparison to the punishment of *karet* (being "cut off," often understood as meaning death at a premature age; see e.g. Rashi ad Gen. 17:14) that will be the lot of those whose practices are abhorrent. This interpretation of our verse may also be found in Mishnah Mak. 3:15, at least the way that Mishnah is interpreted in the Talmud commentary (ad Mak. 23a-b) of R. Yehudah b. Natan. (Rabbi Yehudah b. Natan was married to Rashbam's aunt Miriam, Rashi's daughter, and completed Rashi's commentary to the last few folios of Mak.)

18:9 מולדת בית או מולדת חוץ [YOUR SISTER . . .] WHETHER BORN IN THE HOUSEHOLD OR OUTSIDE THE HOUSEHOLD: [The phrase, "מולדת חוץ—born outside the household," means that she is the daughter of your father and] an unmarried woman. To my mind that is the plain meaning of Scripture.[28]

18:18 לצרור [DO NOT MARRY A WOMAN] AS A RIVAL [TO HER SISTER]: [The word לצרור, "as a rival,"] should be understood just like [the word צרתה, in the phrase (I Sam. 1:6),] "her rival (צרתה) would make her miserable." The two wives of the same man are called "צרות—rivals" to each other.[29]

A number of later exegetes offer new twists on Rashbam's reading, arguing that people will live longer if they practice appropriate sexuality, the theme of this chapter. That is either because they will avoid the dangers of avenging cuckolds (JBS) or because society will remain safe because of stable family units (Luzzatto). See also the fourteenth-century exegete, Nissim of Marseilles (*Ma'ase Nissim*, ed. by H. Kreisel, pp. 382–3) who says that society will be stronger if the rules of incest are observed. If families intermarry, people will see each other as one big happy family and will cooperate more.

Rashbam's explanation of this phrase may also be seen as opposing the very common midrash on this verse, that says that the words וחי בהם teach us that (with rare exceptions) one may transgress the rules of the Torah if that is the only way of staying alive. In other words, the verse is read: "These are the commandments that a person should practice, וחי בהם—as long as observing the commandments will still allow him to stay alive." See Sifra here, *Yoma'* 85b (where this phrase is labeled as the best proof that saving a human life overrides the requirement of observing Torah) and many other rabbinic sources.

[28]Rashbam disputes the interpretation of Rashi, who says that the phrase, "מולדת חוץ—born outside the household," refers to your sister who is the product of a liaison between your father and certain women with whom your father is forbidden to have a liaison. See Nahm. who criticizes Rashi for being insufficiently loyal to his talmudic source (Yev. 23a) in listing which forbidden women are referred to here. Then Nahm. offers another interpretation "according to the *peshaṭ*," the same interpretation that Rashbam offers. So also LT and iE. See also Andrew of St. Victor (p. 169) whose interpretation here is very similar to that of Rashbam. Wessely defends the talmudic understanding, dismissing Rashbam's explanation.

[29]So also Rashi, iE, Nahm. and others. The NJPS translation, "as a rival," also reflects this understanding. See Wessely who rejects this explanation, citing Qimḥi's *Shorashim*, to argue that צרה and לצרור have two separate roots (*ṣ-v-r* and *ṣ-r-r*, respectively). In ibn Janaḥ's *Shorashim* both words have the same root (*ṣ-r-r*).

קדושים (Leviticus 19–20)

19:2 קדושים תהיו YOU SHALL BE HOLY: [This phrase is written here] because there are many commandments [in the following verses; accordingly] they [= the Jewish people] were exhorted to make themselves holy[1] and observe them.[2]

19:3 ואת שבתותי תשמרו [YOU SHALL EACH REVERE YOUR MOTHER AND FATHER] AND KEEP MY SABBATHS: Following the plain meaning of Scripture, [these two commandments], honoring parents and observing the Sabbath, were juxtaposed[3] here for the same reason that they were juxtaposed in the Decalogue:[4] to teach us that the honor of parents is equated with the honor of God.[5]

---

[1]Another possible translation of Rashbam's comment here would be:

> YOU SHALL PREPARE YOURSELVES: [This phrase is written here] because there are many commandments [in the following verses; accordingly] they were exhorted to prepare themselves in order to observe the commandments.

Rashbam often writes that forms of the Hebrew root *q-d-sh* mean "to prepare oneself." See his commentary to Gen. 38:21, Ex. 19:10, 29:37, 30:29, Lev. 6:11 and 11:8.

[2]There are a variety of approaches among Jewish exegetes as to how to understand an instruction "to be holy," and why it is placed specifically here. Rashi sees it as a summary statement to the laws about forbidden sexuality in the previous chapter; "being holy" means living a life of sexual control. Nahm. sees this instruction as an independent commandment; aside from all the other commandments, Jews are commanded to be "holy," to refrain from being Torah-observant scoundrels.

The precise meaning of Rashbam's short comment is unclear. I understand Rashbam as saying that our verse is an introduction to the laws that follow, exhorting people to become holy (or to prepare themselves) in order to observe the vast number of laws that follow. This is then another example of Rashbam's willingness to interpret a verse in such a way that it has rhetorical and exhortative purpose alone, and does not "teach" us anything.

[3]Rashbam's language here, "סמכו הכתוב—the text juxtaposed," shows clearly that he is taking direct issue with Rashi who wrote here: "סמך שבת למורא אב לומר—the text juxtaposed the rules about the Sabbath to rules about revering parents in order to teach us . . . ." See note 5 below.

[4]Comparisons between chapter 19 of Leviticus and the Decalogue are very common in midrashic and exegetical literature. See e.g. VR, LT, iE and NJPSC here.

[5]Rashbam's comment is opposed to that of Rashi who (following Sifra and Yev. 5b) explains the juxtaposition in another manner. According to Rashi and the midrash, our verse is the source for the halakhic principle that observance of Torah laws overrides the requirement to honor parents. If a parent asks for something that can be done only by desecrating the Sabbath, the child should ignore the request.

19:5 לרצונכם FOR ACCEPTANCE: [I.e. in order that the sacrifice be "accepted" on behalf of the person who offered it. To that end,] it should be without blemish and there should be the proper laying on of hands [etc.]; all of the rules of sacrifices should be observed, as the text continues to explain [in vss. 6–8].[6]

The order in which the laws are recorded in this verse— revering parents followed by observing the Sabbath—is often seen as the basis for that midrash. The order then conveys the message: "revere your parents, but still observe the Sabbath." Rashbam's comparison between our text and the Decalogue undermines that point, for in the Decalogue the order is reversed.

Rashbam's own explanation of the juxtaposition is, in turn, based on another midrash (Mekhilta *Ba-ḥodesh* 8) which cites both our verse and the verse in the Decalogue about parents in order to prove that the two types of honor are comparable. The argument in the Mekhilta is formulated in a slightly less *peshaṭ*-oriented manner. It is based not on juxtaposition, but on *gezerah shavah* exegesis—the fact that the Bible uses (in passages from different books) the same words about honoring God and honoring parents. Rashbam cites that same midrash in his commentary to Ex. 20:7. See note 8 there. Here he seems to rework that source to make it conform more to his understanding of *peshaṭ*.

Rashi offers a number of midrashic interpretations to different parts of our verse. JBS, Rashbam's younger colleague, also takes strong issue with some of the *midrashim* about honoring and/or revering parents which Rashi cites here.

[6]While the language of Rashbam's comment is a little clumsy (and Rosin suggests a conjectural emendation), his point is clear. Rashbam is reiterating his comment from 1:3, s.v. לרצונו. There he explained that the word לרצונו should not be understood in the standard way that it is interpreted in rabbinic literature, as a further stipulation about how to offer a sacrifice (meaning "have the proper intentions when offering the sacrifice"). Rather it means "offer the sacrifice in such a way that it will be 'accepted'." One does that simply by observing all the rules about sacrifices. For further discussion of the interpretive issue, see notes 15 and 16 above ad 1:3.

See also *Qeren Shemuel* who points out that our text is discussing a *shelamim* offering. He notes that previous texts (Lev. 3:1–2) have legislated that a *shelamim* offering must be without blemish and hands must be laid upon it, but nowhere has the Torah previously described *shelamim* as לרצונכם. So Rashbam points out that the previously legislated requirements (in addition to the new ones in these verses) also lead to this sacrifice's "acceptance on your behalf."

It is possible that Rashbam reiterates his comment here because of Rashi, who here again offers the interpretation that Rashbam opposes. In chapter one, Rashi offered only one interpretation of the word לרצונו. Here Rashi offers two explanations of the word לרצונכם, labeling one the *peshaṭ* and the second the midrash. Rashbam rejects both of Rashi's explanations, because according to both of them לרצונכם teaches us something about the intentions that the sacrificer ought to have; in other words, according to both of Rashi's interpretations there is some new regulation about sacrifices that we derive from the fact that the sacrifice is supposed to be לרצונכם. In order to combat that approach Rashbam reemphasizes that, following the *peshaṭ*, לרצונכם conveys no *further* law about sacrifices; rather, if you follow all the *other* sacrificial regulations of the text, you will find that your sacrifice was "accepted," i.e. לרצונכם.

19:7 ואם האכל יאכל IF IT IS EATEN [ON THE THIRD DAY . . . IT WILL NOT BE ACCEPTABLE]: The rabbis explained[7] that this refers to a person who, [at the time of the slaughtering of the sacrifice,] had in mind that he would eat its meat outside of the permissible area.[8]

19:10 לא תעולל: refers to [harvesting] the corners [of the vine], as it is written (Jer. 6:9), "Let them glean as a vine."[9]

---

[7]Sifra here, Zev. 28a-b, and Rashi here. The rabbis do not accept the apparent meaning of the text, namely that a sacrifice is unacceptable if it is eaten after a three-day period of time. (Their logic is explained in note 35 to the parallel verse, Lev. 7:18.) Instead they conclude that both this verse and Lev. 7:18 refer to someone who had improper intentions at the time of the sacrifice. In order to avoid the redundancy of interpreting two verses the same way, the rabbis interpret 7:18 as a reference to a worshipper who illicitly intended to eat the sacrifice outside of the permissible *time*; and they interpret our verse as a reference to the worshipper who illicitly intended to eat the sacrifice outside of the permitted *area*.

[8]It is not Rashbam's custom simply to reiterate midrashic readings found in standard classics of rabbinic literature and in the works of his grandfather. His comment here should be seen as the continuation of his comment to 7:18 where he wrote:

> ואם האכל יאכל IF IT SHALL BE EATEN: The rabbis uprooted this verse from its plain meaning and explained it as referring to someone who, while performing one of the four sacrificial duties— while slaughtering, or bringing the blood [to the altar], or collecting [the blood] or sprinkling [the blood]— thought that he would eat the sacrificial meat on the third day.

Since there Rashbam began a discussion of how the rabbis uprooted the verses on this topic from their straightforward meaning, here he finishes the discussion.

See also notes there.

[9]Rashbam's comment is hard to understand. He is offering an interpretation that flies in the face of standard rabbinic exegesis and he does not explain why.

The standard rabbinic understanding of תעולל is that it means to harvest the grapes that are not yet ripe. See e.g. Rashi here, following *Pe'ah* 7:4 and Sifra here. Most moderns interpret the word as meaning to pick every last grape off the vine. In that case, the words could mean either "to glean even the corners," as Rashbam would have it, or "to glean even the unripe grapes," according to the traditional interpretation. It is unclear why Rashbam is attracted to his explanation; the words, and indeed the verse that he cites (Jer. 6:9), would seem to support either explanation.

Rosin (in note 9, here) offers, in my opinion, a fine explanation of Rashbam's thinking. (Rosin himself did not, ultimately, think much of his explanation. After offering this explanation of Rashbam's thinking, Rosin writes that Rashbam was just wrong [ואיו דעתו נכונה].) Rashbam may be reading vs. 10—rules about not harvesting all the grapes—as parallel to vs. 9—rules about not harvesting all the grain crops. Each of the two verses outlaws two categories of "overharvesting." In vs. 9 the two restrictions concerning crops (פאה and לקט) are interpreted respectively as "gathering the corners" and "gathering the fallen crops." Then vs. 10 outlaws two forms of "overharvesting" of the vine—עוללות and פרט. The second restriction in vs. 10, "do not pick up the *grapes* that fell to the ground during harvest," is traditionally interpreted as paralleling the second restriction of vs. 9: "do not pick up the *sheaves* that fell to the ground during harvest." (See Sifra, *Pe'ah* 7:3 and Rashi here.) So Rashbam claims that the first rule in vs. 10 "do not take עוללות from your grape harvest,"

19:11–12 לא תגנבו DO NOT STEAL: money.[10]
ולא תכחשו DO NOT DENY: do not deny that money has been entrusted to you, as it is written (Lev. 5:21–2) "[dealing deceitfully . . . in the matter of a pledge . . .] or denying (וכחש) it."[11]
ולא תשקרו DO NOT LIE: about money that was lent to you.[12]
ולא תשבעו DO NOT SWEAR FALSELY BY MY NAME: even in cases that do not involve the denial of money.[13]

---

should also be interpreted as parallel to the first rule in vs. 9, "do not harvest the corners of your field."

Rashbam's explanation is not reconcilable with the standard halakhic understanding (e.g. Tosefta *Pe'ah* 2:13 and Hul. 131a). Standard *halakhah* says, as Rashbam says, that פאה laws do apply to vineyards. But *halakhah* says also that so do עוללות laws, and they are two discrete categories of restrictions. I have found no other exegete who interprets as Rashbam does.

[10]Rashbam follows the standard rabbinic interpretation of this phrase. See Rashi at greater length (following Sanh. 86a and Mekhilta *Ba-ḥodesh* 8), who explains that the restriction against "stealing" in the Decalogue refers to kidnapping; our verse is the source for the commandment not to steal money. Rashi is trying to explain why, from a halakhic perspective, two verses seem to say the same thing. Rashbam does not address that issue directly. See also notes 11, 12 and 13.

[11]Rashbam's comment is again very similar to that of Rashi (following Sifra). Both cite the same prooftext. There are, however, two distinctions between them.

First, Rashi's comment again (see note 10) reflects, this time explicitly, the technical halakhic approach, answering the question of why our verse appears to repeat an idea from Lev. 5.

Secondly, Rashi does not identify what it is that one is, according to our verse, not supposed to "deny." If our verse is to be read along with Lev. 5:21–2, it would seem that one is not supposed to "deny" a long list of things: " . . . in the matter of a deposit or a pledge or through robbery or by defrauding his fellow or by finding something lost *and denying it*." Rashbam, though, says that the phrase in our verse, "do not deny," refers specifically to a pledge. See notes 12 and 13.

[12]Here Rashbam's different approach to our verse becomes clearer. Rashi (following BQ 105b) says that this phrase, "do not lie," is the source for the commandment not to swear falsely about a monetary matter. Again Rashi follows the technical halakhic approach. To paraphrase his comment:

> We have learned previously what the punishment is for swearing falsely on monetary matters. Where, though, does it explicitly say that such behavior is forbidden? In this phrase, "do not lie."

Rashbam, on the other hand, says that while the previous phrase in our verse referred to denying a pledge, this phrase refers specifically to denying a loan. Hoffmann writes that there is no basis for the distinction that Rashbam makes (אין יסוד לביאורו של הרשב"ם). For an explanation of why Rashbam might make this distinction, see note 13.

[13]See notes 10, 11 and 12. Here Rashbam finally diverges completely from Rashi's approach. Again Rashi (following Sifra) takes the technical halakhic approach. To paraphrase his comment:

19:13 לא תעשק DO NOT CHEAT: This refers to those who (Mal. 3:5) "cheat laborers of their hire . . . and subvert [the cause of] the stranger."[14]

ולא תגזל DO NOT STEAL: [The verb *g-z-l* refers to brazen theft,] as in the phrase (II Sam. 23:21), "He stole (ויגזל) the spear from the hand of the Egyptian."[15]

Other verses say that swearing falsely by God's Name is forbidden. What new restriction is, then, added by our verse? It tells us that such swearing is forbidden no matter what name of God is invoked by the person swearing.

Rashbam, however, says that the verse simply means that one may not swear falsely by God's Name. This restriction, Rashbam adds, applies even if no monetary issue is involved.

Rashbam has now explained the four restrictions of vss. 11 and 12 as follows: (1) stealing money (i.e. taking into your possession something to which you have absolutely no claim); (2) denying a pledge that was entrusted to you (i.e. stealing something that came into your possession legally, but which you were never entitled to use); (3) denying a debt that you owe (i.e. stealing something that came into your hands legally and that you were entitled to use as you wish, but that ultimately you were required to return); (4) swearing falsely when no money is involved.

The progression of the clauses in Rashbam's understanding is now clear—from theft, to more subtle forms of fraud involving false statements in a court of law, to crimes that involve false statements in a court of law without any theft. The progression suggested by Rashbam is in contradistinction to that of Rashi, which Rashi identifies in his final comment to vs. 11. According to Rashi's understanding, each of the crimes of our verse will lead to the next (perhaps more serious) crime: theft will lead to denials which will lead to lying which will lead to swearing falsely by God's Name. See also JBS and iE who see a similar progression to worse crimes, especially in vs. 12.

For Rashbam, on the other hand, the progression is from the more serious or obvious crimes to the more subtle. This is an example of Rashbam's fondness for the לא זו אף זו style of interpretation that argues that biblical (and rabbinic) texts often progress from the more obvious to the less obvious. "Not only is the first item forbidden, even the subsequent items are too." On this type of exegesis in Rashbam, see my Exodus volume, note 48 on pp. 178–9.

See also N. Leibowitz, *'Iyyunim*, p. 232, for a lengthy discussion of Rashi's comment here. Leibowitz argues that what really troubles Rashi (particularly in his comment that sees the infractions as leading one to the other) is that the verse does *not* progress in a לא זו אף זו manner, the manner that one would expect. Rashi then had to arrive at another logical way of connecting the four restrictions of the verses. If Leibowitz is correct, then Rashbam (whom Leibowitz does not mention) is addressing the issue that troubles Rashi here and solving Rashi's problem in a different way.

[14]Rashi and LT (following Sifra) also write that the verb "cheat" refers to the withholding of wages. Rashbam agrees and cites the verse in Malachi as a prooftext.

[15]The verse that Rashbam cites is the common verse used in rabbinic literature to explain what the verb *g-z-l* means. See e.g. BQ 79b, BR 54, Rashi ad RH 22a (and *passim*) and iE ad Lev. 5:21. See also the NJPS translation of the verse in II Sam.: "wrenched (ויגזל) the spear from the Egyptian's hand."

Rashi does not comment here on what לא תגזל means in this verse. In his commentary to BM 111a, s.v. משום, Rashi says that the Talmud teaches (*ibid.* 61a) that the words לא תגזל

לא תלין [THE WAGES OF A HIRED LABORER] SHALL NOT REMAIN WITH YOU [UNTIL MORNING]: [The text is referring to the wages of] an employee who is working at night.[16]

19:14 לא תקלל חרש YOU SHALL NOT CURSE THE DEAF: The text describes the most likely occurrence.[17]

---

in our verse should not be interpreted literally, but should be seen as a further restriction against withholding the wages of a worker. Perhaps Rashbam is opposing that explanation of Rashi's and, for that reason, he states here that our verse, following the *peshaṭ*, is simply about brazen theft.

In Rosin's edition, Rashbam quotes the verse in II Sam. as מידו, instead of MT's מיד המצרי. See the discussion in Esh, p. 89.

[16]Rashbam's explanation directly opposes the talmudic tradition of interpretation of this verse.

There are two verses about withholding wages in the Torah. Here the verse says that laborers' wages must be paid before morning. Deut. 24:15 says that wages should be paid before sunset. Rashi here (following BM 110b) offers the standard rabbinic explanation, that one verse refers to a worker on a night shift and one to a worker on a day shift. When a worker finishes a shift, the employer has 12 hours grace to pay that worker's wages. Accordingly, our verse, which refers to paying before morning, refers to a day laborer whose shift finished the previous evening. The verse in Deut. refers to a night laborer, who finished working at dawn and must be paid before dusk.

Rashbam feels that that is not the *peshaṭ*, presumably because there is no hint in the text that employers are to be given a twelve-hour grace period to pay workers' wages. (See also Nahm. who, ad Deut. 24:15, interprets the words differently from Rashbam and defers to *halakhah* on this issue, but still writes that a worker expects to get paid immediately after completing the shift and expects to take the money to buy food.) Rashbam's explanation of this verse was explicitly considered by the Talmud ("ואימא אפכא"; *ibid.*) and rejected. This is an example of Rashbam offering an interpretation that is not only non-halakhic, but anti-halakhic, as he attributes to the verse a *peshaṭ* meaning that is not reconcilable with *halakhah*. (For another such example, see Rashbam's commentary above to 11:40 and note 85 there.)

[17]Rashbam uses a variation of the common rabbinic phrase דיבר הכתוב בהווה. He means that although the text says only that one should not curse a deaf person, actually it is forbidden to curse anyone. According to Rashbam, the text said that one should not curse the deaf since they are the most likely people to be cursed. Rashbam wrote the same idea in his commentary to Ex. 22:27, "Do not revile a judge and do not curse a chieftain among your people." There he explained at greater length why it is more likely that someone would curse a monarch or a judge specifically. In my notes there (notes 75 and 77 on pp. 270–271), I outlined how Rashbam's understanding of these two verses about cursing differs from traditional halakhic exegesis and from Rashi, specifically from Rashi's comment here. On Rashbam's use of the principle, "the text describes the most likely occurrence," see note 55 on p. 264 of the Exodus volume.

Rashbam was, as far as I can tell, the first exegete to explain our verse in this way. After Rashbam this explanation achieved some popularity. See e.g. the commentaries of JBS, Nahm. (יזהיר בהווה—the text warns about the most common occurrence) and Wessely (מדרך האדם להקל בקללת חרש—people tend to be lax about cursing the deaf).

The word חֵרֵשׁ--deaf, has stress on the final syllable,[18] since it is from the dageshized construction (*piel*), just like עִוֵּר—blind and גִּבֵּן—hunchback.[19]

19:16 לא תלך רכיל DO NOT "CIRCULATE LIKE A PEDDLER": someone who goes from city to city [hawking merchandise]. [The phrase means "do not be a gossip"; a gossip is referred to as a רכיל] because he goes around from one person to another to tell tales.[20]

The Targum for this phrase, לא תיכול קורצין, means "do not broadcast gossip." Similarly [the Aramaic phrase] in Daniel (3:8), אכלו קורציהון דיהודאי, means "they broadcast [slander about the Jews]." So also the phrase (II Sam. 22:14), "ירעם מן שמים—He thundered from heaven" is translated into Aramaic as אכלי מן שמיא. It means to make one's voice be heard.[21]

---

[18]S. Kogut, in his *Ha-miqra' ben ṭe'amim lefarshanut*, p. 55, points out that from Rashbam's comment here one may learn something about his readers. From the fact that Rashbam has to make this comment about the stress, one sees, he suggests, that he does not expect his readers to have access to a vocalized text of the Bible. Alternatively, he suggests that one might see from here that Rashbam's readers did not distinguish between the vowel *ṣere* and the vowel *segol*. That is why Rashbam was concerned that they might confuse the word "חֵרֵשׁ—deaf" here with the similar word "חֶרֶשׁ—secretly" (with penultimate stress) in Josh. 2:1.

[19]Rashbam's grammatical point is uncontroversial. See similarly G.-K. 84^{b}d who writes that the intensive stem (i.e. what Rashbam calls משקל דגש) is used for "a considerable number of adjectives which denote a bodily or mental fault or defect," and cites (among other examples) all three words that Rashbam mentions here.

[20]Rashbam disagrees with Rashi's explanation of why a gossip is called a רכיל. Rashi says that the word is really connected to the root *r-g-l*, meaning to act like a spy. He claims that the root *r-k-l* is just a variant of *r-g-l*. A peddler is called a רכיל, according to Rashi, because he goes around to many different locations other than his own home, just as a spy does. A gossip is also like a spy, according to Rashi, because he gathers negative information about others.

These two roots may indeed be connected. See e.g. II Sam. 19:28 and Ps. 15:3, and Qimḥi's commentary to both passages. See also Rashi ad AZ 22b, s.v. מכתבא. Rashbam, however, does not see *r-k-l* as a variant of *r-g-l*. In a passage like ours where the noun רכיל is used as metaphor, it seems forced to say that the text alludes to a "spy" instead of a "merchant." So Rashbam says that when the text calls a gossip a "peddler" the allusion is to the way in which a gossip disseminates stories (like a peddler) not the way in which a gossip might gather information (like a spy).

Rashbam's explanation is the common one among Jewish exegetes: see e.g. Sifra, iE and Nahm. (I think that NJPSC errs when it writes here: "Many traditional commentators, among them Ibn Ezra, Ramban, Rashbam and Rashi, relate the verbal root *r-kh-l* to *r-g-l*, 'to spy'.")

[21]The second half of Rashbam's comment here is not directly about the biblical text but is disputing with Rashi's commentary to this verse. Rashi gives a long explanation of why the common Aramaic translation of "gossip," both in the Targum here and in other passages, is אכל קורצין. Rashi argues that the Aramaic verb *'-k-l* in that phrase is simply the well-known Hebrew and Aramaic verb, "to eat." Rashi speculates that the phrase originated with the

לא תעמוד על דם רעך DO NOT STAND BY THE BLOOD OF YOUR FELLOW: Do not stand idly by [if your fellow is being attacked]; you may save his life even by taking the life of his attacker.[22]

---

custom of gossiping people who allegedly eat something together as a sign of accepting the gossip.

Rashbam says that that is not the meaning of the Aramaic verb *'-k-l* here or in other contexts that relate to speech. He gathers a number of examples of the use of this Aramaic root to mean to broadcast, or announce or disseminate. See similarly Nahm. here, who interprets in the same way and who claims that there is no sense to what Rashi says about the Targum here (ואין במה שפירש בתרגום הזה טעם או ריח).

Curiously, in his commentaries to prophetic books and in his commentary to BB, Rashi advocates the same interpretation that he ignores here—that the Aramaic root *'-k-l* means to announce or broadcast. See his commentary to Is. 1:4, Zach. 2:10 and BB 5a, s.v. ולאו גברא. In that last text, Rashi even writes that "Jonathan [ben Uziel]" always translated verbs of announcing using the Aramaic root *'-k-l*.

It is tempting to speculate that perhaps Rashi, later in life, came to the conclusion that Rashbam offers here. This change in Rashi's position might be understood if we posit that he commented on the Prophets after writing his Torah commentary, and if we accept the traditional view that Rashi's final literary project was his BB commentary, the project that he never finished. (See the note in the Pesaro ed. of BB ad fol. 29a: "כאן מת רש"י—here Rashi died." See also Tos. BQ 23b, s.v. ולא ישמרנו, where Tos. assumes that Rashi's BB commentary is one of his later works.) Rashbam claims in his commentary to Gen. 37:2 that he often argued with Rashi and convinced him of new ways of interpreting biblical works and that Rashi told him that he would have revised his Torah commentary if he had had the time. So perhaps Rashi's commentaries on Isaiah, Zachariah and BB reflect a later stage of his thinking about this Aramaic word, a position that he might have adopted after discussing the issue with his grandson.

Still, the order of Rashi's works suggested above should not be considered an established historical fact. See Grossman's *Ḥakhme Ṣorfat*, pp. 216–18. For further opinions on the relative order of Rashi's works, see B. Gelles, *Peshaṭ uderash*, pp. 142–146. Gelles argues that a draft of the Talmud commentary was Rashi's first work, followed by the Torah commentary and then the commentary on the rest of the Bible. Rashi spent his final years revising his Talmud commentary and did not manage to finish the revision of BB before he died. (This postulated order would still fit with what I suggested in the previous paragraph.) See also Isaac Maarsen, "*Raschis Kommentar zu Sprüche und Job,*" MGWJ 83 (1939; reprinted 1963), 442–443 and the sources cited there.

[22]Sifra here offers two possible explanations of this difficult and unclear phrase: (1) go help your neighbor who is in danger of drowning or being attacked by an animal; (2) go save your neighbor from a רודף, a human attacker, even if that involves killing that attacker. Rashi offers only the first option in his commentary and Rashbam offers only the second option in his. The Talmud in Sanh. 73a considers the question of how two *halakhot* could be derived from this one phrase. The Talmud concludes that it is only the first *halakhah*, the one that Rashi quotes, that is derived from this verse. (The second is derived from a different verse.) Presumably that is why Rashi offers only that first explanation. Rashbam does not tell us why he prefers the second. But his comment demonstrates well that Rashbam does not consider himself bound by exegetical conclusions of talmudic passages. Cf. Wessely who quotes both explanations of the Sifra and claims that both are part of the *peshaṭ* of our verse.

19:17 לא תשנא את אחיך בלבבך YOU SHALL NOT HATE YOUR BROTHER IN YOUR HEART: If he did something wrong to you, do not try to appear to him as if you are still his friend, [like a person who "speaks to his fellow in friendship,] but lays an ambush for him in his heart."[23] "The thing you are doing is not right."[24] Do not hate him[25] in your heart; rather הוכח תוכיח REPROVE him for what he did to you.[26] The result will be that you will have peace with him ולא תשא עליו חטא, AND YOU WILL NOT BEAR A GRUDGE AGAINST HIM in your heart.[27]

---

[23]Using the language of Jer. 9:7.

[24]Using the language of Ex. 18:17.

[25]Rashbam paraphrases the words of the verse, לא תשנא, as אל תשנאהו.

Rosin suggests (note 7) that Rashbam writes at such great length here in order to clarify that לא תשנא here should be understood as an imperative, not a future indicative. I do not believe, however, that Rashbam's paraphrase has any significance. There are dozens and perhaps hundreds of commands in the Torah which are expressed through the word לא followed by the imperfect, where Rashbam does not feel bound to explain that usage.

[26]Nahm. explains well the two options for interpreting this verse. One might interpret our verse as saying that the Torah is forbidding all forms of hatred of one's brother; the reason the Torah uses the phrase "in your heart," is because the more common way of hating is to hide the hatred, keeping it "in your heart." Then the Torah offers a further, unrelated instruction (in Nahm.'s language: מצוה אחרת) that one should rebuke people who transgress the laws of the Torah. In rabbinic literature the second phrase of our verse, הוכיח תוכיח, is commonly interpreted that way, as a general instruction to watch out for your fellow Israelite's spiritual well-being by chastising him or her when necessary. According to this understanding, the second clause of the verse is unrelated to the issue of hating. (See e.g. Arakh. 16b.)

Nahm. then says that he prefers to see the rules of this verse as being connected to each other. Then he offers essentially the same reading as the one found here in Rashbam. The verse is not a general admonition against hating; it is a specific instruction to the person who has a (perhaps legitimate) grudge against his neighbor. "Don't brood with anger against your friend in your heart; confront your friend and explain what troubles you." Rashbam was not the first to explain the verse this way; the interpretation is already found in *Seder Eliyyahu Rabba*, chapter 18, where it is attributed to Rabbi Elazar b. Matya. After Rashbam, this interpretation achieved much popularity. See e.g. Hizq., JBS and NJPSC.

[27]This last phrase of the verse may be the most difficult. Rashi comments only on this clause of the verse. He connects it with the previous clause, which he presumably interprets in the traditional manner as referring to rebuking a sinner (and not as referring to someone against whom you have a grudge, Rashbam's interpretation). Rashi's understanding (following Arakh. 16b) is, to paraphrase: "Rebuke your neighbor, but לא תשא עליו חטא, do not do it in a sinful manner by chastising him in public."

Others (e.g. Onq.) feel that the phrase ולא תשא עליו חטא teaches that if I refrain from rebuking my friend I will be punished for his sin. Others yet (e.g. iE) interpret that if I fail to discuss my grievance with my friend, it might be the case that I will fail to find out reasons why I should *not* have a grievance; I would then be liable for punishment for continuing my grievance. (N. Leibowitz [p. 290] suggests that this is also the way Rashbam understands the phrase, but I disagree.)

19:18 לא תקום DO NOT TAKE VENGEANCE: Paying him[28] back evil for evil.[29] ולא תטור AND DO NOT BEAR A GRUDGE: even in your heart.[30] Rather give in.[31]

ואהבת לרעך כמוך LOVE YOUR FELLOW AS YOURSELF: If he is really your fellow, i.e. if he is good. However, if he is evil, [you should hate him,[32] as it is

---

Rashbam says that the third phrase, simply means, "do not carry (לא תשא) around a grudge (חטא) concerning him in your heart." Rashbam interprets two words of the phrase in a different manner: for him חטא means a grudge or a grievance (not "punishment') and תשא means to carry (not "to receive").

Rashbam, typically, feels no need to interpret this final phrase of the verse as teaching something new. For him it is enough to view it as rhetorical, an emphatic repetition of the idea in the first clause of the verse. "Do not bear a grudge against him in your heart" means the same thing as "do not hate your brother in your heart." See similarly Gerstenberger who suggests (among other interpretations) that "the sense of the double prohibition may have been: 'Do not hate your brother in your heart; do not falsely impute guilt to him'."

As Leibowitz notes (*ibid.*), the simple meaning of the phrase in Num. 18:32 " ולא תשאו עליו חטא—you will incur no guilt through it," suggests that the similar phrase here refers to a punishment that one might incur (as Onq. or iE would have it).

[28]Rashbam is interpreting this verse as the continuation of the previous one. "If you have a grudge against your friend, do not hate him. Talk it out with him. And do not try to repay him evil for evil."

[29]The phrase רעה תחת רעה originates in BR 38. It is a play on the biblical phrase, " רעה תחת טובה—to repay good with evil." See e.g. Gen. 44:4 and Prov. 17:13.

[30]Rashi here quotes the standard rabbinic explanation (e.g. Sifra here, and *Yoma'* 23a) of the difference between לא תקום and לא תטור. Both refer to someone who has to decide whether to do a favor for someone who did not do him or her a favor. The first person, the נוקם, takes vengeance by refusing to do the favor. The נוטר, on the other hand, does the favor in a self-righteous manner, pointing out to the recipient of the favor how undeserving he or she is.

Rashbam's explanation is considerably less vivid than Rashi's, but not at odds with it. According to both of them, the נוטר is someone who remains angry and remembers grudges, but does not act on them. This is also the simple meaning of the text. See e.g. NJPSC: "The sense is that one ought not to keep alive the memory of another's offence against him."

[31]The phrase עובר על מידותיך is hard to translate into English. It is a common rabbinic phrase (more often with the *hifil* form of the verb, מעביר) and it means to be willing to forgo something that is due to you, to renounce the claim for vengeance or for recompense. See the explanation of the phrase offered by Rashi in his commentary to RH 17a, s.v. המעביר על מידותיו.

[32]Rashbam's comment here is connected with the last few sections of his commentary: "Do not have a grudge against your neighbor. Even if he did you something wrong you should be willing to forgo vengeance. But the commandment to *love* a neighbor applies only to good people."

Rashbam offers a very limited interpretation of the commandment to "love one's neighbor." One has to love only the type of neighbor who is deserving of love. This interpretation is not Rashbam's innovation; there are many similar classical rabbinic sources. See e.g. Sifre Deut. 89.

written (Prov. 8:13),] "To fear the LORD is to hate the evildoers."[33]

19:19 בהמתך לא תרביע כלאים YOU SHALL NOT LET YOUR CATTLE MATE WITH A DIFFERENT KIND: [An explanation that is] in conformance with the way of the world and that is appropriate for rebutting the heretics[34] [is]:

In the history of the Jewish exegesis of this famous phrase, the greatest controversy has centered around the question of whether the word רעך includes non-Jews. See e.g. *Sefer ha-ḥinukh*, number 243, where this commandment is paraphrased as "to love every Israelite (לאהוב כ"א מישראל)." Kasher, p. 71, also cites two old midrashic sources that say explicitly that the commandment applies only to Jews. On the other hand, many (particularly modern and early modern) exegetes insist that רעך must include non-Jews. See e.g. N. Leibowitz (*'Iyyunim*, p. 301) who argues that the fact that an Egyptian is described in Ex. 11:2 as the רֵעַ of an Israelite proves conclusively that the commandment here to love one's רֵעַ includes non-Jews. The context of our verse, however, "Do not take vengeance . . . against the members of your people (בני עמך)," might suggest otherwise.

Joseph Klausner (p. 202) notes that Rashbam here studiously avoids that form of limiting the commandment. He does not distinguish between Jews and non-Jews; he provides a different form of limitation, not based on national/religious identity. Klausner argues further that Rashbam's comment is directed against the Christian morality that preached love of everyone, even of people who strike one of your cheeks or steal your coat. In other words, Klausner suggests that Rashbam chose not to explain this verse in a way that would devalue his Christian neighbors; rather he explained it in a way that opposed Christian morality.

See Rashbam's comment below ad 20:10 where he interprets the word רֵעַ in that verse as a word that applies only to Jews, not to gentiles.

[33]While most Jewish exegetes see the verse in Proverbs as saying that one should hate *evil*, Rashbam's explanation, that it is the *evildoer* whom people must hate, is found in classical rabbinic sources. See e.g. Pes. 113b.

Perhaps Rashbam is punning between the word רֵעַ (neighbor) and the word רָע (evildoer).

[34]Rashbam uses these or similar phrases to introduce "reasons for the commandments" in his commentary above to 11:3 and 11:34. See notes 53, 74 and 76 there. The polemical necessity of dealing with these laws in the 12th century was real. As Touitou notes (*Milet* 2, 285), Christians, such as Gilbert Crispin, often mocked the Jews for interpreting laws like these in a literal manner.

Rashi here presents the old rabbinic claim (e.g. *Yoma'* 67b) that the "statutes (חוקים)" of the Torah, such as those listed in this verse, have no rationales and they are therefore mocked by the nations. Accordingly Rashi makes no attempt to explain them. Rashbam, on the other hand, does present rationales for these commandments, and specifically says that his explanations are appropriate ways of neutralizing non-Jewish criticism. This dispute between Rashi and Rashbam about whether חוקים is a technical word for a law without an obvious reason affects their interpretations of a number of biblical passages. See their commentaries to Gen. 26:5 and Ex. 15:25 (and note 77 on pp. 166–167 there). See also commentary to Num. 19:2, and note 1 there.

See also Nahm.'s criticism here of Rashi's approach. Nahm. offers a rationale for these laws that is very similar to Rashbam's. So similarly *Sefer ha-ḥinukh*, number 244. This rationale is also found in many moderns. See e.g. Noth: "At the basis of this . . . prohibition

Just as Scripture in the creation story (Gen. 1:11) commanded[35] each species to produce fruit "according to its own kind (למינו)," so it commanded that we conduct the affairs of the world in a similar manner when it comes to animals or fields or fruit-trees[36] or ploughing with an ox and an ass[37] (two separate species) [together].

Similarly [one should explain the restriction against wearing] wool and linen[38] [together; it is outlawed] because [it is an illicit combination of two categories, as] the former is from an animal and the latter is from the category of things that grow in the ground. To the heretics [= Christians] I said that the text outlawed clothing of two different colors,[39] for wool is [generally] colored, but linen is not. They accepted this explanation.[40]

---

lies the idea that the union of heterogeneous stock is against the divine ordinance." Presumably Rashbam was the first rabbinic exegete to interpret these laws in this way. Perhaps such an understanding also lies behind the rephrasing of our verse in PT *Kilayim* 1:7, חוקים שחקקתי בעולמי (or, as quoted here by Nahm. from some unknown source חוקים שחקקתי בהם את עולמי). But the PT passage probably means something else entirely. See *Pene Moshe*, there. See also Wessely here, who criticizes Rashbam and Nahm. for their explanation.

Outside of the rabbinic tradition, see, like Rashbam, Philo (*Special Laws*, 4:39) who labels these laws "laws of nature."

[35]In his Genesis commentary, Rashbam interprets in a more *peshat*-oriented manner. There he says that the Torah describes the trees and animals as being *created* to replicate themselves, rather than being *commanded* to replicate themselves. See commentary there, and note 5 on p. 42. Here, for polemical and apologetical purposes, Rashbam adopts the explanation that just as the species were commanded to preserve their identities, human beings are required to preserve the discrete species that God established in this world.

[36]While our verse does not mention hybrids of trees specifically (and there is no other specific injunction against such hybrids in the Torah), the rabbis saw our verse as including that restriction. See e.g. Sifra, here, and Qid. 39a, and Rashi there, s.v. חקותי תשמרו.

[37]Rashbam reasonably suggests that Deut. 22:10, "You shall not plough with an ox and an ass together," is of the same category of restriction as those listed in our verse.

[38]Along with virtually all exegetes, Rashbam uses Deut. 22:11 to explain the difficult word שעטנז in this verse.

[39]I have translated the word מראות as "colors." See note 3 above ad 14:37.

[40]As Nahm. notes, the more problematic law of this verse—the one which the rabbis specifically said was hard to explain—is the law about a garment from wool and linen. The other restrictions of the verse outlaw the *generating* of some new plant or animal through hybridization. Improving on God's world through the creation of some new species could be seen as an act of hubris and for that reason might be forbidden. (See e.g. JBS's reformulation of Rashbam's argument in that way.) It is harder to sustain that same argument about mixing wool and linen.

Rashbam accordingly offers two explanations—one seeing this restriction as having the same rationale as the hybridization laws, and one offering another approach. When Rashbam writes, "to the heretics I said (ולמינים אמרתי)," I assume that indicates that he thinks that this second explanation has no value other than to silence Christian criticism.

19:20 נחרפת [A WOMAN WHO IS A SLAVE WHO IS נחרפת]: i.e. handed over and set aside for one [particular] Jewish slave. So it is written [concerning a Jewish male servant (Ex. 21:4)], "If his master gives him a wife." A similar usage [of the verb *ḥ-r-p*] is (Jud. 5:18) "[Zebulun is] a people that belittled (חרף) its life to die." The Targum understood the word the same way.[41]

לא נפדתה SHE HAS NOT BEEN REDEEMED: i.e. she has not been freed.[42] Accordingly she does not have the status of a [standard Jewish] married woman, where the punishment [for her and for the man who had intercourse with her] would be [death by] strangulation.[43]

בקרת תהיה THERE SHALL BE AN INVESTIGATION: [The phrase is to be understood] like the phrase (Lev. 13:36) "the priest need not investigate (יבקר)." That is how both Dunash and Menaḥem explained the word.[44] The court shall

---

The second rationale that Rashbam offers is unique to him. He says (as Touitou explains, *ibid.*, p. 286) that when the Torah forbade clothes of wool and linen what it really meant is that common people ought not to wear clothing of two different colors. High Priests do that, but regular people do not. JBS offers another related rationale, explaining how this restriction ensures that common folk will not dress like priests.

[41]The Targum here reads אחידא—attached.

Rashbam's comment here is a gloss on Rashi, who says that נחרפת means "designated and set aside for," but says that he can find no such usage in the Bible. Rashi also says that this woman is "half a [Canaanite] slave and half a free woman who is betrothed to a Jewish slave."

Rashbam disagrees with Rashi in three ways: (1) Rashbam says that this woman is a full-fledged Canaanite slave (following the more *peshaṭ*-oriented opinion of R. Ishmael in Sifra), not the half slave that Rashi says (following the opinion of R. Aqiva there). (2) While Rashi refers to this woman as "designated (מיועדת)" for the Jewish slave and as "betrothed (מאורסת)" to him, Rashbam says that she has already been "handed over (מסורה)" to the slave. The Targum's language, "אחידא—attached," supports Rashbam. Similarly Ker. 11a says that this woman must have already been sexually active for the rule of this verse to apply. In the PT (Qid. 1:1), R. Ishmael describes the woman as נשואה—married, while R. Aqiva describes her as מאורסת—betrothed. (3) Rashbam feels, as opposed to Rashi, that it *is* possible to find a similar use of the verb *ḥ-r-p* in the Bible. His interpretation of the verse in Judges is debatable, but see Qimḥi and Ps.-Jon. there, who both use the verb "*m-s-r*—to give over" in their explanation of the verb חרף. See iE, Hizq. and Nahm., who all offer different explanations of the etymology here. See Wessely who prefers Rashbam's explanation to the others.

[42]Rashbam takes issue with Rashi who (following the opinion of R. Aqiva; see note 41) says that the doubling of the Hebrew phrase והפדה לא נפדתה shows that this woman is half freed and half slave. Rashbam reiterates that the phrase simply means an unfreed slave woman. Presumably he, like R. Ishmael (*ibid.*), sees the doubling as insignificant, as an example of "the Torah speaking in common human language."

[43]See Sanh. 11:1.

[44]See Menaḥem's *Maḥberet*, s.v. *b-q-r*, and Dunash's *Teshuvot*, p. 53.

investigate and, if [the judges find that] she has not yet been freed [i.e. that she is still a slave], they should not impose the death penalty as they would in the case of a married woman [who is not a slave].[45]

19:23 וערלתם ערלתו YOU SHALL REGARD ITS FRUIT AS *'ORLAH*: I.e. as closed or shut up or removed. [Similarly one should understand the phrases] (Jer. 6:10), "their ears are blocked (ערלה)," or (Ezek. 44:9) "of closed (ערל) heart," or (Hab. 2:16) "Drink, you too, and be blocked off (והערל)."[46]

19:24 קדש הלולים HOLY[47] FOR PRAISE: [This fruit which grows on trees in their fourth year] shall be as holy as *ma'aser sheni* ("second tithe"); it should be eaten in Jerusalem[48] and, [while it is being eaten,] one should praise the Creator.[49]

---

[45]The word בקרת is difficult, and has been interpreted in many ways. Some Jewish exegetes (e. g. Sa'adyah) see it as a reference to the type of punishment that the slave woman would receive for her sexual misconduct. (See also NJPSC, here, which interprets the details in a very different manner, but still sees בקרת as referring to a type of punishment.) Nahm. and Luzzatto see the word as a description of the (relatively) "unattached" nature of the woman. A midrash in the Talmud (Ker. 11a) derives from this phrase a rule about the way in which a Jewish court administers the punishment of flogging.

Rashi offers two interpretations of the word. The second is the midrash of the Talmud on this verse. It is not certain what Rashi meant by his first explanation, but most later readers of Rashi interpret his explanation as being the same as the one later offered by Rashbam. (See e.g. Nahm. and Wessely.) If that is the case, then Rashbam has chosen, as he often does, to support the *peshaṭ* interpretation offered by Rashi and not the midrashic one. Cf. JBS who cites only the midrashic one. Many later exegetes follow the explanation offered here by Rashbam (and presumably by Rashi). See e.g. Hizq. and Wessely.

[46]Many explanations exist for why the Torah used the standard word for "foreskin" to describe these forbidden fruits. Rashbam explains the use of the root *'-r-l* essentially in the same way that Rashi does, both here and in his commentaries to Jer., *ibid.*, and Hab., *ibid.* So also Rashi ad Ex. 6:12. Rashbam adds only the word "הרחקה—removal," to Rashi's explanation. In that he is following Onq. here (ותרחקון).

The verse that Rashbam quotes from Hab. is difficult and has been explained (and emended) in many different ways. Again Rashbam's explanation is the same as that of Rashi.

[47]Or perhaps, "prepared for praise." (See note 1 on Lev. 19:2.)

[48]See note 8 above ad 6:9.

[49]The phrase קדש הלולים is unusual and was explained in the Talmud (Ber. 35a) as meaning that fruit of the fourth year, if not brought to Jerusalem, remains holy (קדש), and therefore inedible, until it is redeemed. This explanation is based on punning between the word חלולים (redemption in rabbinic Hebrew) and the word הלולים. (So Rashi there, s.v. האי מבעי ליה.)

Rashi's explanation of the verse here is a combination of midrashic and *peshaṭ* exegesis. Rashi discusses the necessity of redeeming fruit outside of Jerusalem, but does not connect that idea to any particular word or phrase in the verse. Then he explains the word הלולים essentially in the way that Rashbam does. Performing this commandment leads to praise (הלולים) of God. Rashbam explains the verse using only the *peshaṭ* part of Rashi's

That is what we find [also] concerning *ma'aser sheni*, that it is to be eaten (Deut. 14:23) "in the place that the LORD shall choose . . . so that you will learn to revere the LORD your God forever."[50]

19:25 להוסיף לכם תבואתו THAT ITS YIELD TO YOU MAY BE INCREASED: That is the reward that you will receive if you do what I commanded.[51]

19:26 לא תאכלו על הדם DO NOT EAT UPON BLOOD: Following the plain meaning of Scripture, this phrase should be interpreted on the basis of its context,[52] [namely the restrictions outlined at the end of the verse,] "do not practice divination or soothsaying." So also this [restriction, "do not eat upon blood,"] means acting according to the customs of the gentiles.[53] [It may refer to a gentile

---

comment. He does not even mention the concept of "redemption," which is not part of the plain meaning of the words of the verse.

Rashbam's interpretation of the verse conforms to the standard halakhic explanation about what one should do with fruit from the fourth year. Cf. e.g. iE, who writes a heterodox comment that troubled all his super-commentaries—that the verse means that fruit from the fourth year is given to the priest who is the only one who is allowed to eat it.

[50]The comparison, on the halakhic level, between the rules of *ma'aser sheni* and the rules of the fruit of the fourth year is common throughout rabbinic literature. To the best of my knowledge, Rashbam was the first to extend that comparison to the theological level, by saying that the Torah teaches us that both of these types of food are to be taken to Jerusalem and eaten there in order to strengthen our relationship with God. See Sifre Num. 5, where the midrash claims that the only purpose of *ma'aser sheni* is to lead to Torah study and fear of God. See also Tosafot ad Qid. 24a, s.v. ה"ג רש"י and ad BB 21a, s.v. כי מציון.

The assumption that Deut. 14:23 is referring to *ma'aser sheni* is universal in halakhic literature. See e.g. Pes. 36a, Tem. 21a and Rashi in Deut., *ad loc.*

[51]Like most exegetes, Rashbam says that the words להוסיף לכם תבואתו mean that God promises those people who refrain from use of fruit in the first few years that they will receive a bonus in coming years. So also Rashi and NJPSC, for example. For other explanations of the phrase, see JBS and Wessely.

[52]Although much of Rashbam's *peshaṭ* exegesis is based on using context to determine meaning, this passage is one of only two times in his Torah commentary that he refers explicitly to this traditional principle, the twelfth of the thirteen principles of midrashic exegesis (found in the introduction to the Sifra), דבר הלמד מעניינו, i.e. using context to understand a word or phrase. The other time Rashbam cites this principle is in his commentary to Ex. 21:13. There he is simply following the lead of the Talmud and of Rashi in saying that that specific verse should be interpreted "דבר הלמד מעניינו—on the basis of the context."

Here Rashbam's explanation is an innovation. He is the first to suggest that context determine meaning here. See later Nahm. (here) and Qimḥi (ad I Sam. 14:32), who both use some version of this same phrase, דבר הלמד מעניינו, to explain our verse in a manner that is very similar to Rashbam's explanation.

[53]The Hebrew phrase that Rashbam uses, חוקות הגויים, has become a technical halakhic term (based on Lev. 18:3 and 20:23) for a wide variety of activities that are forbidden because

custom] to eat at the grave of someone who has been murdered, for purposes of sorcery, to keep [the spirit of that dead person] from seeking vengeance.[54] Or it may refer to some other form of sorcery, such as the one that we discuss [in Mishnah Shab. 6:10], "a nail from a hanged person."[55]

In tractate *Sanhedrin* the rabbis explained [the phrase, "eating upon blood,"] in a number of [other] ways.[56]

19:29 להזנותה [DO NOT DEFILE YOUR DAUGHTER] BY LEADING HER TO DEBAUCHERY: This refers to [leading her to a life of] promiscuity as an unmarried woman, making her like a harlot.[57]

---

they are things that gentiles do, things that a Jew ought not to do. The term is used often in later halakhic literature but this passage of Rashbam may be the first such recorded usage of this precise wording.

[54]It is possible that Rashbam has simply postulated the existence of such a custom among the idolatrous nations in biblical times. Alternatively, he may be describing some superstition from his own time period. In Hizq.'s rewriting of Rashbam's comment one finds that he calls this behavior "מנהג הערלים—a custom of the uncircumcised ones," a phrase that when used by a medieval Jew would generally be describing a medieval Christian custom.

[55]In that Mishnah and in the talmudic discussion that follows (Shab. 67a), it is explained that a nail that was used in a hanging (or perhaps in a crucifixion) was believed by many people to have curative powers. The opinion of the Sages in the Mishnah is that making use of such a nail is forbidden not only on the Sabbath, but even on a weekday because such a practice constitutes "דרכי האמורי—the ways of the Amorites," a phrase that is essentially equivalent to Rashbam's phrase here, חוקות הגויים.

[56]Rashbam's comment here is opposed to that of Rashi. Rashi cites two of the rabbinic explanations from Sanh. 63a, acknowledges that there are others and does not attempt his own *peshaṭ*-oriented explanation. Rashbam, on the other hand, acknowledges the variety of midrashic traditions, but explains the verse only according to its "plain" contextual sense.

As previously mentioned, both Nahm. and Qimḥi independently reached conclusions similar to Rashbam about the meaning of this verse. (Presumably neither of them had ever read Rashbam's commentary.) See also Hoffmann, Luzzatto and Wessely who all explain the phrase as related to a practice done for superstitious or divining purposes.

The phrase "do not eat upon blood" remains difficult and there are many opinions among moderns about what it means.

See also Rashbam's commentary to Gen. 37:28 where he himself uses the phrase לאכול על הדם in a manner that differs somewhat from his explanation here.

[57]Rashbam's explanation of this phrase is very similar to that of Rashi. Both say that the crime of the father is encouraging (or forcing?) his unmarried daughter to have intercourse before she is married.

Nahm. has a lengthy criticism of Rashi's explanation. Essentially, Nahm. argues that in halakhic Hebrew the word זונה is *not* a reference to a woman who has intercourse without being married. Nor does it mean "harlot" for the halakhist. Rather it is a technical term for a woman who has intercourse with someone to whom she could never be married.

Rashi and Rashbam explain the term in a manner closer to the simple meaning of the word in the Bible. See Wessely's rare compliment of Rashbam here (יפה אמר הרשב"ם). See

19:35–6 במדה [YOU SHALL NOT FALSIFY MEASURES OF] מדה: which refers to the measurement of land, or משורה, which refers to measurement of liquid. So they say,[58] "drink water by measure (במשורה)."[59] A הין [in vs. 36] is a measurement of liquid.[60]

20:9 דמיו בו HIS BLOODGUILT IS UPON HIM: [This phrase means the same thing as the phrase (Josh. 2:19),] "his blood will be on his head." In other words, he himself brought about his own death.[61]

---

also Maimonides, *Na'arah betulah* 2:17, who explains our verse in the same manner. Maimonides realizes that, from the point of view of standard *halakhah*, his reading is innovative. He prefaces it with the words: "אני אומר שזה שנאמר בתורה—*I say* that the meaning of what is written in the Torah is . . .." There is much discussion in traditional circles about whether the interpretation of Rashi, Rashbam and Maimonides can find some support in the Sifra here.

It is possible that Rashbam's comment represents a slight modification of Rashi's. The simplest reading of Rashi's comment is that a father who causes his daughter to have intercourse, even with *one* person, without the benefit of clergy has made her a זונה. But Rashbam's comment implies that the daughter in our verse is a זונה because she is having intercourse with *many* people, like a קדישה, a term which Rashbam defined already (in his commentary to Gen. 38:21) as a loose woman who has intercourse with many people. However, when one examines the commentaries of Rashi and Rashbam on the word קדישה in Deut. 23:18, it is not clear that the distinction that I am suggesting can be sustained.

Many moderns see our verse as referring specifically to cultic prostitution. See e.g. Luzzatto, Hoffmann and Noth.

[58]The quotation, "drink water by measure," first appears in Ezek. 4:11. But (as noted by the author of the notes in the *Torat ḥayyim Miqra'ot gedolot*) Rashbam's language, "כמו שאמרו—as *they* say," leads one to think that here he is referring to the use of the line in *'Avot* 6:4. To be sure, below (in his commentary to Lev. 26:26) Rashbam quotes the phrase as part of the verse in Ezekiel.

[59]Rashbam follows Rashi's comment fairly closely, but he disagrees about one point. Rashi (if one follows the reading in the better texts) sees the word משורה as referring to any measurement of volume—whether solid or liquid. Rashbam says that it is just a term for volume of liquid. In his Talmud commentary (ad BM 61b, s.v. משורה), Rashi also follows the opinion found in Rashbam here and explains משורה as "מידת הלח—a measurement of liquid."

Like Rashbam, see NJPSC, here. Like Rashi, see Luzzatto (who also explains why Rashi had to explain the term differently in his Talmud commentary). See also Wessely who had a different (and presumably inaccurate) text of Rashi's commentary, that read the same as Rashbam's. Wessely then argues against the text that he thinks is Rashi and suggests understanding the word משורה as a measure of volume of liquid or solid, i.e. the same way that our texts of Rashi read.

[60]See similarly iE, who says that the text uses the phrase "הין צדק—an honest *hin*" here (and *hin* clearly must be seen here as a measure of liquid, as even Rashi writes here) because it refers back to the משורה of the previous verse.

[61]The idea is explained at greater length in Rashi. The court would be guiltless if it put such an evildoer to death; the responsibility for his death is his alone.

Rashi offers two explanations for this phrase. The first (following Sifra) is that the phrase דמיו בו should be read as a code phrase, meaning that the type of death penalty

20:10 את אשת רעהו [IF A MAN COMMITS ADULTERY WITH A MARRIED WOMAN . . .] WITH THE WIFE OF HIS FELLOW: Not with the wife of a gentile.[62]

20:17 חסד הוא: [The word חסד is to be understood as meaning "disgrace,"] as in the phrase (Prov. 25:10), "Lest he who hears it reproach you (יחסדך)," or the phrase (*ibid.* 14:34), "The חסד of nations is sin," which means that disgrace comes upon nations through sin. Yosef[63] also [understood the phrase that same way and therefore] translated it "חיסוד דעמא חטאוהי—the disgrace of a nation is its sins."[64]

20:20 ערירים ימותו THEY WILL DIE ערירים: means that [God] will neither allow [any] children [that they already have] to survive nor [will He allow them] to bear [other] children.[65]

---

imposed for this infraction is stoning. Then Rashi offers his second explanation which he labels פשוטו של מקרא—the plain meaning of Scripture. As often occurs, Rashbam presents only the explanation that Rashi labels the plain meaning. Both commentators use the same prooftext from Joshua and they use very similar language in their explanations. See also iE here who offers the same *peshaṭ* explanation and subtly criticizes Rashi's midrashic reading.

[62]As Rosin notes, the apparent redundancy of our verse, "with a married woman, with the wife of his fellow," is the reason for Rashbam's comment, which is an abridged version of Rashi's, following Sifra.

[63]This is the standard way that the Aramaic translation of the Prophets (and not the Hagiographa) is cited in classical rabbinic literature. (See Melammed, *Mefarshe ha-miqra'*, vol. 1, pp. 142–143.) Rashbam uses the phrase twice in his Torah commentary (here and ad Ex. 15:2, citing "R. Yosef's Targum" of Job 4:15), both times citing the Aramaic Targum of the Hagiographa (and not of the Prophets).

Curiously, in the commentary on Job that Japhet attributes to Rashbam, the commentator makes no reference to any Aramaic translation on Job or on any other work of the Hagiographa, while he does cite the Aramaic translation of the Torah nine times, according to Japhet's count. See the discussion in her *Rashbam on Job*, p. 49, and notes 2 and 3 there.

[64]Again Rashi writes two explanations, first a *peshaṭ* explanation and then a midrashic one. Rashbam offers only the first of those, and expands Rashi's comment by adding more prooftexts. Both Rashi and Rashbam support their explanation of the Hebrew word חסד by noting that the Aramaic word חיסודא means disgrace.

This explanation is adopted by most moderns. See e.g. NJPS and Gerstenberger. Cf. Nahm.'s lengthy criticism of this interpretation.

[65]My translation is based on Rosin's minor emendation, reading להחיות או להוליד בנים, instead of the clumsy ms. reading, להחיות להוליד בנים. If Rosin is right, then Rashbam is simply offering the traditional explanation of ערירים, found here in Rashi (following Sifra and Yev. 55a).

אמור (Leviticus 21–24)

21:1 לנפש לא יטמא בעמיו NO ONE SHALL DEFILE HIMSELF בעמיו: [This means] no one from the company (עם) of priests should defile himself for [i.e. through contact with] any [dead] human body.[1] [The word בעמיו in this verse is not a reference to the person who died, but to the subject of the sentence, the priest, and his "עם—company,"] as in the phrase (vs. 14), "he shall take a virgin מעמיו as a wife."[2]

If the word read לעמיו, then it would [be a reference to the person who has died; the verse would then] mean "he should not defile himself for anyone from his [=the Jewish] people (עמו)." [References to the bodies that are the source of defilement are always introduced by the letter *lamed*,] as in the phrase (in this verse), "לנפש לא יטמא—he shall not defile himself *for* (ל) any body." [So also in the verse] (Num. 6:7), "for his brother (לאחיו), for his sister (ולאחותו), he shall not defile himself להם—*for* them." The text [of those verses] does not read בהם.

---

[1]Aside from those relatives listed as exceptions in the following verses.

Rashbam understands the syntax of the verse in a manner that differs from almost all exegetes. Most exegetes explain that the priest is to separate himself from a human body (נפש) who is part of the Jewish people (בעמיו). See e.g. Rashi, iE, NJPS, Gerstenberger and many others. Rashbam insists (at least in his first explanation) that the word בעמיו is modifying the subject of the sentence, the priests, the sons of Aaron. Any person בעמיו, i.e. from the company of priests, should not defile himself.

Aside from the linguistic argument that Rashbam himself makes in the continuation of his comment, his explanation solves another problem in the verse. As Noth notes, there really is no description in the verse of who is required to observe this law. Rashbam's explanation solves that problem to some extent by saying that the law—which, the text says, is to be told to Aaron and his sons—is specifically directed to people that are בעמיו, from the company of the priests.

Like Rashbam, see Heidenheim and Luzzatto.

[2]Rashbam's comment here is radical from the halakhic perspective. He "proves" his explanation of this verse through a non-halakhic reading of vs. 14, which says that the High Priest is allowed to marry only a virgin מעמיו. *Halakhah* says that a High Priest is allowed to marry any Jewish virgin. Rashbam's proof—that בעמיו means "from among the priests," is based on a heterodox *peshaṭ* reading, according to which a High Priest is allowed to marry only a virgin from his own tribe of priests. See Luzzatto who argues that Rashbam is right that that is the *peshaṭ* of verse 14. See also Gerstenberger, "a virgin from his clan."

See Rosin here, note 1, who says that Luzzatto misunderstood Rashbam. Rosin offers a convoluted reading of Rashbam's comment that defends Rashbam's orthodoxy.

It is also possible to interpret the phrase as meaning, "he should not defile himself *for* any body (לנפש) that may be found בעמיו—among his people."[3]

21:4 לא יטמא בעל בעמיו NO בעל FROM THE COMPANY [OF PRIESTS] SHALL DEFILE HIMSELF: No husband from the company of priests shall defile himself by [becoming impure through contact with the dead body of] his wife, להחלו—for that would render him unfit for the priesthood.[4] But according to the rabbis, [the verse means that] he should not defile himself by [becoming

---

[3]Rashbam now seems to retreat from his innovative position and to say that it is also possible to read the verse the way most exegetes have.

The phrase, "גם יש לפרש—it is also possible to interpret," is rare in Rashbam's commentary. It, and the similar phrase, "גם יש לומר—it is also possible to say," (commentary to 26:26) appear only twice in the Leviticus commentary. In that second passage too, after explaining each phrase of a verse in a manner that does not conform with Rashi's exegesis, he writes that, concerning the last phrase in the series, "it is also possible to explain it" the way Rashi explains. Perhaps in these two passages Rashbam is displaying rare tolerance of others' opinions. More likely a later hand has interpolated these two more orthodox readings into Rashbam's words. See also commentary to Num. 5:31 (and note 25 there) and Num. 7:3, s.v. צב (and note 52 there). And see also Sara Japhet, *The Commentary of Rabbi Samuel ben Meir (Rashbam) on the Book of Job*, pp. 305–306, where Japhet identifies six such interpolated passages—all beginning with wording such as ויש לפרש or ויש לומר—in the commentary which she claims is Rashbam's commentary to Job. See the discussion in my article, "'Rashbam' on Job: a Reconsideration," *Jewish Studies Quarterly* 8 (2001), 80–104.

[4]Rashbam offers a radical explanation, from the halakhic perspective, explaining the *peshaṭ* of the verse in a manner that contradicts the *halakhah*. The *halakhah* says that a priest may (in fact, must) defile himself by going to his wife's funeral and burial. Rashi writes here that that halakhic explanation is פשוטו של מקרא, the plain meaning of Scripture. Rashbam says that the *peshaṭ* of our verse is the precise opposite—that the priest is forbidden to defile himself when his wife dies.

One might contrast Rashbam's approach with that of one of his younger contemporaries and fellow *peshaṭ* enthusiasts. iE mentions the *peshaṭ* understanding (= Rashbam) as something that someone might have thought or that he used to think (היה נראה לנו). Then, after noting that that explanation contradicts *halakhah*, iE says that the *peshaṭ* explanation is therefore nullified (בטל הפירוש הראשון). Rashbam can and does tolerate the idea that the *peshaṭ* contradicts *halakhah*, forbidding something that *halakhah* requires; iE does not tolerate that tension. See further discussion in my article, "Tradition or Context."

See also the commentary of Eliezer of Beaugency to Ezek. 44:25, where Eliezer interprets our verse in Leviticus the way that Rashbam does here. See the discussion in Harris, pp. 45–6.

See criticism of Rashbam's explanation in the commentaries of Shapira and Wessely. Although they cite contextual and linguistic arguments against him, their true objections to Rashbam's comments are doubtless based on orthodoxy.

See also Maimonides (*'Evel* 2:7) who argues that the rule that a priest should defile himself at the death of his wife is of rabbinic origin. Apparently Maimonides finds the rabbinic exegesis here to be so far from the plain meaning of the text that he cannot see the law as being of Torah origin.

impure through contact with the dead body of] his unfit or disqualified wife. But he may defile himself by [becoming impure through contact with the dead body of] his legitimate wife.[5]

21:5 לא יקרחו THEY SHALL NOT SHAVE [THEIR HEADS] SMOOTH: [As a sign of mourning] for someone who died. This same rule applies to an Israelite.[6]

21:7 וחללה: [The word חללה means] the daughter of [the union between a priest and] one of the women concerning whom it is written [that a priest should not marry them,] (21:15) "lest he profane (יחלל) his offspring."[7]

21:9 ובת איש כהן WHEN THE DAUGHTER OF A PRIEST [PLAYS THE HARLOT]: When she is betrothed, as it is explained in *Sanhedrin*.[8]

---

[5]Rashbam here presents the standard halakhic understanding of the verse, using language that is very close to that of the Sifra here. This explanation is that if the priest married a woman whom he was not supposed to marry (e.g. a divorcee), then he may not defile himself through contact with her dead body. This explanation is based on understanding the word להחלו adjectivally, as modifying the [implicit] noun "wife." The only wife for whom the priest is not allowed to defile himself is an illegitimate wife (אשתו מחוללת).

[6]In other words, even though the verse here says only that priests are not allowed to shave their heads as a sign of mourning, the same restriction applies to Israelites who are not priests. In this way, Rashbam harmonizes our verse with Deut. 14:1. See Rashi who reaches the same conclusion after a very long comment that explains why two verses were necessary if the same rule applies in both cases. See also JBS who writes that the *peshaṭ* would seem to suggest that there are distinctions between the rule for priests here and the rule for Israelites in Deuteronomy, but the *peshaṭ* must be abandoned in the face of the rabbinic explanation (ואין להעמיד על הפשט מפני הגזירה שוה).

It is difficult to know why Rashbam simply toes the rabbinic line in his commentary to this verse, when he was willing to offer an interpretation that contradicted *halakhah* in his commentary to the previous verse.

[7]Rashi here (following the standard rabbinic position; see e.g. Qid. 77a) lists two types of women who are considered חללה: (1) women who are the daughters of a relationship between a priest and a woman with whom he should not have had intercourse, and (2) women who had sexual relations with certain inappropriate partners. Rashbam lists only the first category here but his interpretation should not be seen as heterodox. The Talmud itself (*ibid.*) considers the question of what kind of חללות are described explicitly in the Torah. It concludes that only the first category is explicitly described. The second category, according to the Talmud could not be derived from the Torah without rabbinic exegesis. (חללה, שעיקרה מדברי תורה ואין צריכין לפרש מדברי סופרים). Rashi there (s.v. כל שנולדה) explains that the first category of women are considered to have been explicitly identified by the Torah as חללות because of vs. 15, i.e. precisely the argument found here in Rashbam.

[8]In his commentary to 19:29, Rashbam explains the word להזנותה as a reference to the promiscuity of an unattached woman. Here he has to note, then, that the rule of this verse

21:18 חרום ושרוע: These words are explained in *Bekhorot*.[9]

21:20 מרוח אשך: means that his testes are crushed.[10]

22:2 וינזרו LET THEM SEPARATE THEMSELVES [FROM THE SACRED DONATIONS OF THE ISRAELITES]: I.e. from eating holy food[11] when they are impure.[12]

---

about the woman who plays the harlot (לזנות) does not apply to single women, only to betrothed ones.

Both Rashi and Rashbam refer their readers to *Sanhedrin* (50a-51b). Rashi says that the Talmud presents a dispute about whether this verse applies to a betrothed woman or to a married woman (or to both). Rashbam seems to see the issue as settled, and writes that the Talmud says that the rule applies only to betrothed women (whose promiscuous behavior would have led to the death penalty even if they were not daughters of priests. The verse teaches us that because they defamed the priesthood they will receive the stricter death penalty of "burning.") Ultimately they both agree on the most important point—that the rule does not apply to unmarried women. See Hoffmann who writes that that is not the *peshaṭ* meaning of the text, and that Philo and Josephus understood the text in the *peshaṭ* manner as referring to the punishment of the unmarried daughter of a priest who brings dishonor on the priesthood through her promiscuity. The earliest rabbis argued against this harsh treatment and I have found no instance of Philo's interpretation within rabbinic circles. See also Nahm.'s commentary to Gen. 38:24.

[9]The Mishnah in *Bekhorot* 7:3 defines חרום as a person who has a nose that is so shrunken that his two eyes seem to be connected. The word שרוע, in reference to an animal, is defined in BT *Bekhorot* (40a) as an animal with a dislocated thigh. In *Bekhorot* 3b the word שרוע is used in relation to humans and animals. It is not defined, but from the context it means a person with organs that are mismatched (e.g. one larger eye and one smaller one). Rashi on our verse goes into details about the meaning of the words, and combines the two explanations of שרוע into one. Rashbam says more simply that details may be found in *Bekhorot*.

There is no consensus among modern scholars about what these words mean.

[10]So also Rashi, at much greater length. That is the common understanding of the phrase both in rabbinic literature and among moderns.

It is unclear why Rashbam chose to comment specifically on three of the many defects listed in vss. 18–20. He does not seem to be adding anything new or saying anything controversial about them.

[11]Rashbam explains the word מקדשי here in a manner that differs from the way that he explained it in 5:15. See commentary and note 86 there.

[12]Read on its own, our verse is problematic for it says that priests should separate themselves from the holy donations of the Israelites. But are priests not the very ones who are supposed to take care of those donations?

Rashbam solves the problem in the simplest manner, the same way that Rashi and most other exegetes do. Our verse is seen as a general statement ("There are situations in which a priest should avoid the Israelites' sacred donations") and, as NJPSC puts it, "the verses that follow provide details of what such avoidance entails." Specifically, it is the impure priest who is to avoid contact with the Israelites' sacred donations.

See also commentary to Numbers 18:32, and note 63 there.

22:3 אשר יקרב [ANY PERSON . . .] WHO APPROACHES [THE SACRED DONATIONS]: In order to eat thereof.[13]

22:8 נבלה וטריפה לא יאכל HE SHALL EAT NOTHING THAT DIED OR THAT WAS TORN BY BEASTS: [It is necessary for the text to restate that priests are not allowed to eat animals that were not ritually slaughtered, because] one might think that [priests were allowed to do so,] since they were permitted to eat birds that were put to death by pinching off their heads (i.e. through *meliqah*),[14] which is somewhat like eating animals that were not slaughtered ritually.[15]

---

[13]The word יקרב, to approach, could mean many things. The simplest explanation here might be that the verse is outlawing all forms of contact between the impure priest and sancta. Rashbam, however, concurs with Rashi, who argues that the reference must be to the impure priest who *eats* holy food, since contact with sancta short of eating would not, according to *halakhah*, entail the punishment of being "cut off." See also Rashbam's commentary to Num. 17:27–28.

See NJPS here, which translates in accordance with the traditional Jewish understanding "who . . . partakes," and Baruch Levine's comment in NJPSC that it would be better to translate more literally, "'who shall approach.' . . . The purpose of this law was to prevent impure priests from having physical contact with consecrated offerings, lest they defile them."

[14]On *meliqah*, see Lev. 1:15 and Rashbam's commentary there.

[15]This verse is problematic for it implies that only priests (and not other Jews) are commanded to refrain from eating animals that were not ritually slaughtered. There is a verse in Ezekiel (44:31) that might lead to a similar conclusion. Furthermore, one might conclude from Lev. 17:15 that when an Israelite (who is not a priest) eats some animal that was not slaughtered ritually, he or she has not committed a crime, but has simply become impure. And see Noth here who suggests precisely such a conclusion.

Such an interpretation not only opposes the standard *halakhah*; it also contradicts the simple sense of other biblical verses (e.g. Ex. 22:30 and Deut. 14:21). Halakhists assume accordingly that the law against eating animals that were not ritually slaughtered must apply to all Jews. Some moderns agree. See e.g. NJPSC here: "There is no basis for concluding that . . . [these restrictions] . . . once applied only to priests and were later extended to all Israelites, as some modern students of biblical religion maintain."

In that case, one has to explain why there would be a need for a specific rule against *priests* eating animals that were not ritually slaughtered, when no Jew is allowed to eat them. Rashi (following Sifra) gives a complicated halakhic explanation—that our verse teaches a further detail about how the rules of impurity for eating *a bird* that was not slaughtered properly differ from the rules of impurity for eating *an animal* that was not slaughtered properly. (Using midrashic exegesis, our verse is understood to be speaking only of birds.) See Rashi and Rashbam ad 11:40 (and notes 85 and 86 there) for another instance where Rashi offers an explanation for a problematic verse about impurity (which he solves by reading into the text a distinction between birds and animals) and Rashbam seeks a simpler way of dealing with the problem.

22:10 וכל זר לא יאכל קדש NO OUTSIDER [= non-priest] SHALL EAT OF THE HOLY THINGS: I.e. of *terumah*.[16]

22:14 כי יאכל קדש IF A MAN EATS OF THE HOLY THINGS: I.e. of *terumah*.[17]

22:16 באכלם WHEN THEY: I.e. lay people,[18] EAT SUCH HOLY THINGS, i.e. *terumah*.[19]

Here Rashbam uses a solution that is found already in the Talmud (*Menaḥot* 45a), as an explanation of the verse in Ezekiel (44:31), "Priests shall not eat anything, whether bird or animal, that died or was torn by beasts." The Talmud's solution, and Rashbam's, is that there is a theoretical reason to believe that priests might be exempted from the general restriction against eating meat from animals that were not slaughtered. Rashi offers that same explanation in his commentary to Ezekiel. A more common explanation is to say that the restriction against eating such meat is reinforced concerning priests for they would be doing something even worse than other Israelites if they consumed such food. See e.g. Shapira and NJPSC here, and Qimḥi in Ezekiel.

[16]Rashbam's explanation of this passage as referring specifically to *terumah* follows that of Rashi and standard rabbinic exegesis.

The simplest explanation of our verse would be that the restriction against eating "holy things" is a reference to all holy items that lay people may not eat (including both *terumah* [the heave-offering given to the priest] and the parts of various sacrifices that priests may consume but that lay people may not). The standard halakhic exegesis (including Rashi, following Sanh. 83b) claims that our verse is referring only to *terumah*. Rashi already ad vs. 7 argues that our whole section is referring only to *terumah* and not to other holy items. The logic of Rashi's argument here ad vs. 7 is found also in Rashbam's commentary to 12:7. See note 9 there.

See also Rashbam's commentary and notes to Num. 17:27–28 and 18:27.

[17]See note 16.

[18]The syntax of this verse is unclear. Almost all commentators feel that the subject of the verb והשיאו is the priests, and the word means that the priests bring down guilt, either upon themselves or upon the people. The simplest explanation of the word באכלם ("when *they* eat") would then be that it means "when *the priests* eat." While such a reading is syntactically smooth, it is problematic from the conceptual perspective: why should there be any sin involved when "they" [= the priests] eat the *terumah* that was given to them in the first place?

Onq.'s solution is that the verse is referring to priests who eat *terumah* when they are impure. In that case, vs. 16 is best seen as a continuation of vs. 6 or 7. Despite the distance between those verses, Wessely, for one, says that Onq.'s reading should be seen as the *peshaṭ*.

Rashbam, on the other hand, follows the more common rabbinic approach of saying that the "eating" described here is that of lay people who eat *terumah*, a forbidden act. So also Rashi and many others, including some moderns (e.g. NJPSC). Rashbam does not tell us how he would understand the beginning of the verse. Presumably he would explain it as Rashi did—that priests bring guilt upon themselves if they allow lay people to eat of the *terumah*.

[19]See note 16.

22:23 וקלוט: I.e. [an ox or a sheep] with hoofs that are closed (קלוטות).[20] נדבה תעשה YOU MAY MAKE IT A VOLUNTARY DONATION: [to the Temple treasury, so that the proceeds may be used] for the maintenance of the Temple, ולנדר BUT FOR A VOW, i.e. as a sacrifice, [IT SHALL NOT BE ACCEPTED].[21]

23:2 אשר תקראו אותם מקראי קדש WHICH YOU SHALL PROCLAIM AS SACRED OCCASIONS: I.e. which you shall establish as sacred times. Any use of the verb קרא connected with the noun מועד means to establish a time, as in the phrase (Lam. 1:15), "he set a time against me (קרא עלי מועד)."[22]

That is how the Targum also understands [the phrase here, when it translates מקראי קדש as] "מערע קדיש—a solemn occurrence." So also the phrase (Eccl. 2:15), "the destiny (מקרה) of the fool."[23]

---

[20]In other words, this particular animal has the defect of having closed hoofs, even though it is a member of a kosher species, the animals of which generally have split hoofs.

So also Rashi, following Sifra.

[21]So also Rashi, following Sifra.

The interpretation offered here by both Rashi and Rashbam does not accord with the way that the words נדר and נדבה are usually used in rabbinic literature. Usually they are seen as two types of sacrifices. (See also notes 5 and 10 on Rashbam's commentary to Num. 30:2.) But, as Nahm. notes here, such an interpretation would make little sense in this verse. We would have to say that animals with the blemishes described in vss. 22 and 24 are unacceptable as any sacrifice, while animals with the blemishes described in vs. 23 are acceptable as one type of sacrifice, but not as another type. Such an interpretation, according to Nahm., is unthinkable (לא יתכן בשום פנים). Instead, Rashi and Rashbam say that none of these blemished animals is acceptable as any type of sacrifice. When the verse says of some of them, "you may make it a נדבה," it means only that you may donate them to the Temple treasury. (See further discussion of the question of dedicating animals to the Temple treasury in Rashbam's commentary to 27:9, 27:11 and 27:27 below.)

Most moderns (e.g. Noth and Gerstenberg) interpret in the way that Nahm. (and presumably Rashi and Rashbam) considered unthinkable. JBS also offers that interpretation, as one of two possibilities.

[22]This first part of Rashbam's comment is fairly clear. He is opposing Rashi's explanation (ad Ex. 12:16 and Lev. 23:35) of מקרא(י) קודש, which Rashi says means that the celebrants should make the day holy through special clothing or food or in some similar manner. Rashbam says that the phrase simply means that the day has been "set" as a special occasion. See also Rashbam's commentary to Num. 16:2.

[23]This second part of Rashbam's comment is harder to understand. Rashbam apparently connects verbs that mean "to happen" with verbs that mean "to establish" or "to set." See also Rashbam's comment to Ex. 1:10 and to BB 113b, s.v. אורעה.

Just as he does in his commentary to Ex. 1:10, Rashbam here also sees the verbs ק-ר-א and ק-ר-ה as synonymous. See note 9 there.

23:11 ממחרת השבת ON THE MORROW OF THE "SABBATH": I.e. on the morrow of the first day of Passover.[24]

23:16 מנחה חדשה [YOU SHALL OFFER] AN OFFERING OF NEW GRAIN: [This offering is] in order to permit the use of the new grain in the Temple,[25] because that is the season in which the crops have ripened.[26]

23:22 ובקוצרכם WHEN YOU REAP [THE HARVEST OF YOUR LAND]: I.e. after the morrow of Passover, after the *'omer* sacrifice has been made.[27]

23:24 זכרון תרועה REMEMBRANCE THROUGH BLASTING [THE SHOFAR]: Through the blasting [of the shofar] you will be remembered by God. So it is written (Num. 10:9), "You shall blast on the trumpets, that you may be remembered [before the LORD your God]."[28]

---

[24]Rashbam follows the standard rabbanite/Pharisaic interpretation of this phrase. See e.g. Rashi, following Men. 66a. The Karaites, and before them the Sadducees, claimed that "Sabbath" here means Saturday. It is not surprising that Rashbam avoids the *peshaṭ* reading on a verse like this, a focal point of controversy between rabbinic Judaism and its opponents. Classical rabbinic opposition to the "plain" meaning of this phrase was very strident; see e.g. Mishnah Men. 10:3.

[25]The more common *peshaṭ* understanding of the verse is that this phrase is an instruction to "bring an offering of new grain" on the holiday of Shavuot. Rashbam follows the midrashic reading of Men. 83b. There our verse is understood as saying that until Shavuot it is forbidden for anyone to bring a *minḥah* offering using the crops grown in the new year. Beginning with this *minḥah*, it becomes permissible. That is why our verse says, that from Shavuot on, "you may offer offerings of new grain to the LORD." (Outside of the Temple, using the crops of the new season became permitted earlier, on the second day of Passover. See Mishnah Men. 10:6.) So also Rashi.

[26]Rashbam is offering his own explanation of the reason for the distinction (mentioned in note 25) between using new crops for private use and using them in the Temple. According to Rashbam the new crop is not to be used in the Temple until after the holiday of Shavuot, because by then the wheat crop is totally ripe. In Ex. 34:22 Shavuot is called the holiday of "the first fruits of the wheat harvest."

[27]The difficulty of our verse is that it is placed in the middle of a long section about the holidays of the Jewish calendar, but the verse deals with the responsibilities of landowners toward the poor. Rashbam opposes the midrashic explanation offered by Rashi (following Sifra) to explain the juxtaposition—that fulfilling one's obligations to the poor is tantamount to building the Temple and sacrificing therein the sacrifices of this chapter. Rashbam explains more simply that since the theme of harvesting was introduced in the chapter, the text reiterates the need to remember the poor at that time. Different versions of this same explanation can be found in the commentaries of most *peshaṭ*-oriented exegetes, e.g. iE, JBS, Nahm. and Hizq.

[28]Rashbam opposes both midrashic explanations offered here by Rashi: (1) that (following Sifra) the word זכרון alludes to the custom of reciting verses about God's remembrance (זכרונות) as part of the Rosh Hashanah liturgy; or (2) that (following RH 16a) the word זכרון

23:27 אך בעשור HOWEVER ON THE TENTH DAY [. . . IT IS THE DAY OF ATONEMENT . . . (28) YOU SHALL DO NO WORK (מלאכה)]: On other holidays, work that is necessary for the preparation of food is permitted; only "מלאכת עבודה—work at your occupations" is forbidden. However, on the Day of Atonement because it is a day of affliction, "כל מלאכה—all manner of work" is forbidden.[29]

והקרבתם אשה YOU SHALL BRING AN OFFERING BY FIRE TO THE LORD: As outlined in [the Torah portions] *'Aḥare mot* (Lev. 16) and *Pinḥas* (Num. 29:8–11).[30]

23:36 עצרת: means [a day when one is] stopped or prevented from doing work.[31]

23:39 אך בחמישה עשר יום לחודש השביעי הזה HOWEVER, ON THE FIFTEENTH DAY OF THIS SEVENTH MONTH: [The text introduces the holiday of Sukkot using the word "however," because] even though [the previously-mentioned holidays of] Rosh Hashanah and the Day of Atonement are meant [respectively] for "remembrance" and for "atoning," Sukkot, on the other hand,

---

in some way alludes to the binding of Isaac. Rashbam explains more simply that the purpose of blowing the shofar is to "be remembered before God." Rashbam's explanation can be found later in the commentaries of Nahm. and Wessely and many others. See Nahm.'s lengthy arguments against Rashi's comment.

[29]Rashbam reiterates the distinction that he made in his commentary to Exodus 12:16 between the phrase מלאכת עבודה and the phrase כל מלאכה. See note 51, p. 112, there.

Rosin suggests that Rashbam's comment is also meant to explain why our verse begins with the word "אך—however." It is because the contrast concerning rules about work is a major distinction between the Day of Atonement and the other holidays.

[30]Rashbam's comment appears to be a continuation of Rashi's comments on vss. 8 and 25. There Rashi notes that when our chapter says that on Passover (vs. 8) and Rosh Hashanah (vs. 25) an undefined אשה is to be offered, details about that offering are found in Num. (28:16–25 and 29:1–6, respectively). Rashi does not give the parallel details here in our verse when the text says again (this time concerning the Day of Atonement) that an אשה is offered and again the text provides no details. Since Rashi does not comment on the undefined אשה of our verse, Rashbam fills in the gap by telling us where the details of this third undefined אשה are to be found.

[31]Rashbam opposes the explanation offered by Rashi here (following Suk. 55b), which connects עצרת to the idea of "detaining," i.e. God detains the people for one extra day at the end of the holiday. Curiously, ad Num. 29:35 Rashi does not say that; rather he explains עצרת the same way that Rashbam does here. And in Rashi's commentary to Deut. 16:8, he offers two explanations—the one offered here by Rashbam and an entirely new one. Like Rashbam, see also iE (here and ad Joel 1:14) and Wessely.

Most moderns would explain עצרת as connected to the idea of "assembly." See e.g. NJPS "a solemn gathering." See however Noth who disagrees and says that the word means "a day that requires special abstinences."

is meant for rejoicing and for giving thanks for the fact that [God] filled their houses with all good things[32] during the harvest.[33]

23:40 וענף עץ עבות THE BOUGH OF A THICK TREE: [The word עָבֹות is written with a] *qameṣ* [and is to be understood as an adjective, meaning "thick"], just like קָדוֹשׁ—holy, טָהוֹר—pure, עָמוֹק—deep or גָּדוֹל—large. The phrase means "the bough of a tree that is very thick."[34]

23:42 כל האזרח ALL OF THE CITIZENS [IN ISRAEL]: even those who have their own houses, SHALL LIVE IN BOOTHS.[35]

---

[32]Rashbam's wording here alludes to the language of Deut. 6:11, "houses full of good things." He continues his discussion of this aspect of the holiday of Sukkot (again quoting that same phrase from Deut.) below in his commentary to vs. 43, where he uses the phrase "houses filled with all good things" four times in one comment. The phrase appears to be one that Rashbam likes; he uses it also in his commentary to Gen. 1:1 and to Num. 13:19.

[33]Rashbam opposes Rashi's midrashic explanation (following Pes. 76b), that the ostensibly unnecessary word "אך—however" here teaches us a detail concerning the *ḥagigah* sacrifice that is offered on Sukkot. Rashbam explains more simply that the changeover from the solemn Days of Awe to the joyous holiday of Sukkot is the reason for this contrastive word. Minor variations on Rashbam's explanation may be found in iE and JBS.

[34]Rashbam opposes Rashi who understood the word עבות here as meaning "corded" or "intertwined." Rashbam disagrees because the word for cord in the Bible is עֲבֹות, with a *ḥataf pataḥ* under the first letter (e.g. Ex. 28:14). Since our word עָבֹות has a *qameṣ* under the first letter, Rashbam connects it to the Hebrew word עָבָה—thick. As Wessely notes, if that is the meaning, then the text really has not specified at all which type of bough is required as there are many thick trees. Rashbam's interpretation appears to be unique.

In Rosin's text, the last few words of Rashbam's comment read: שהוא מעובת הרבה. I prefer the reading as quoted by Wessely and as quoted (or perhaps paraphrased) in *Qeren Shemuel*: שהוא מעובה הרבה.

[35]The difficulty in this verse is that it seems to imply that only an אזרח is required to live in a *sukkah* (booth) during the holiday of Sukkot. Whatever the word אזרח means, it is usually contrasted or compared with the גר. See e.g. Lev. 17:15, 19:34 and 24:16. Our verse is the only passage in the Torah that says that a certain rule applies to the אזרח without then saying that it also applies to the גר.

The simplest explanation—that only the "citizen" is required to live in a *sukkah* on Sukkot, and the גר is not required to do so—is not attractive to halakhic exegetes. ibn Ezra, who interprets גר as a stranger who has *not* converted to Judaism, might have no difficulty with this explanation. See iE's comment to Lev. 16:29 where he points out that the text requires the גר, for public policy reasons, to refrain from work on the Day Atonement, but it does not require him or her to fast.

But a standard halakhic exegete who interprets גר as convert (see e.g. Rashbam's comment to Ex. 22:20 and notes 52, 56 and 57 there) has to explain why the verse seems to legislate that only the אזרח has to live in a *sukkah*. Rashi follows a forced *midrash halakhah* approach in order to explain how we know that even a convert to Judaism must live in a *sukkah*. Depending on the reading of Rashi's commentary that one chooses here (see

23:43 למען ידעו דורותיכם IN ORDER THAT FUTURE GENERATIONS MAY KNOW [THAT I MADE THE ISRAELITES LIVE IN BOOTHS]: The plain meaning of the verse follows the opinion expressed in Tractate *Sukkah* that the word סוכה ("booth") here should be understood literally.[36] This is the idea behind the text (Deut. 16:13):

> "You shall hold the Feast of Booths . . . after the ingathering from your threshing floor and your vat." [In other words,] when you gather the produce of your land and your houses are full of all good things,[37] grain, wine and oil,[38] [that is the appropriate time for you to celebrate Sukkot,] so that you will remember THAT I MADE THE ISRAELITES LIVE IN BOOTHS for forty years in the wilderness, without any settlements and without owning any land. As a result of [contemplating] this, you will give thanks to the One who allows you to own your land and your houses which are filled with all good things. And do not "say to yourselves, 'My own power and the might of my own hand have won this wealth for me'."[39]

---

discussion in Nahm.), Rashi either sees the word בישראל or the ostensibly unnecessary initial letter of האזרח as teaching that the law applies also to converts. See also Sifra here, BT Suk. 28a and Rashi there, s.v. האזרח.

Rashbam offers an entirely new approach to the question. He says that the text does not mean "*only* the אזרח should live in a *sukkah*," but "*even* the אזרח should live in a *sukkah*." In other words, the more upper-class elements of society might feel that they are above the requirement of living in a primitive structure like a *sukkah*. The text emphasizes that even they must do so. Rashbam's comment may be read as an independent *midrash halakhah* of a phrase in a legal passage. (See also above ad 17:15). Rashbam's explanation then is that the ostensibly unnecessarily long wording here has a rhetorical purpose, but it is not teaching a new rule. For a similar example of this difference between Rashbam's approach and the standard *midrash halakhah* approach, see his commentary to Ex. 34:21, s.v. בחריש, and note 18 there.

Rashbam's interpretation is later adopted and expanded by Hizq. and JBS. See also Hoffmann: "it is specifically the אזרח who owns property in the land who is commanded to leave his home . . . in order to remember that once our forefathers walked through the desert without owning any land . . .." See, however, Wessely who writes that Rashbam's interpretation is unsatisfying (אין נחת בפי' זה).

[36]In Suk. 11b and in Sifra there are two opinions expressed about the meaning of the phrase, "I made the Israelites live *in booths*." One opinion is that the phrase is a metaphor for the safekeeping that God afforded to the Israelites when he surrounded them with His protective clouds of glory. The other opinion is that the phrase should be understood literally—that God made the Israelites live in booths as they wandered through the desert. Rashi offers only the first explanation, the metaphorical one. Rashbam's comment could be paraphrased: "A *peshaṭ*-oriented commentary (which Rashi claims to be writing) ought to follow the legitimate rabbinic opinion expressed in the Talmud that 'booth' means 'booth'." See, on the other hand, Nahm.'s defense of Rashi, where he argues that the metaphorical reading here should be considered the *peshaṭ*. So also Wessely. See notes 40 and 41 below.

[37]On the allusion to the language of Deut. 6:11, see commentary above to vs. 39, and note 32 there.

[38]An allusion to the words of Deut. 28:51.

[39]Deut. 8:17.

This same progression [of thoughts] may be found in the verses (Deut. 8:2–18) in the Torah portion, *'Eqev tishme'un*:

> "Remember the long way that the LORD your God made you travel [in the wilderness] for forty years . . . giving you manna to eat . . .." And why am I commanding you [to remember] that? "For the LORD your God is bringing you into a good land . . . [and,] when you have eaten your full, [perhaps] your heart will grow haughty and you will forget the LORD . . . and you will say to yourself, 'My own power and the might of my own hand have won this wealth for me.' [Rather] remember that it is the LORD your God who gives you the power to get wealth."

That is why at harvest time they [= the Jews] are to leave [their] houses that are full of all good things and live in booths, so that they will remember that in the wilderness they had no land [which they owned] and no houses in which to live.[40]

It is for that reason that God set the holiday of Sukkot at the time of the harvest of the threshing floor and the vat.[41] So that their hearts will not grow

---

[40]Rashbam explains the purpose of the holiday of Sukkot in an innovative manner. The *sukkah*, he argues, is not built *as a sign of* the joy of the season, but rather *to temper* the joy of the season. The Jew remembers the wilderness experience not in order to celebrate God's care of the Israelites there (protecting them in clouds of glory) but rather in order to remember the humble beginnings of the nation when they had no land and no homes. See the useful discussion in N. Leibowitz's *'Iyyunim*, pp. 372–375, where she contrasts Rashbam's explanation of the reason for this holiday with explanations offered by other Jewish thinkers. See also Touitou's discussion of this passage (*Milet* 2, 286–7), where he notes that Rashbam explains the *miṣvah* here as serving an educational purpose—teaching people to be humble and grateful for what they have.

Rashbam offers this same explanation of the holiday of Sukkot in a much shorter manner in his commentary to Ex. 23:16.

[41]Since the holiday of Sukkot in some sense "commemorates" the Exodus from Egypt, halakhists often ask why the Torah scheduled the holiday for the fall, and not for the spring, when the Exodus took place. Both iE and Nahm. say that, even though the Exodus took place in the spring, the Israelites in the wilderness did not require the protection of booths until the colder days of the fall set in. JBS says that at the Passover season Jews are too busy to celebrate the joyous holiday of Sukkot since there is too much agricultural work waiting to be done. Another explanation, apparently first recorded in the *Tur* (OH 625), is that although Sukkot does belong in the spring, were Jews to live in booths in the spring no one would notice, since it is common for people to leave their homes for a more outdoors-oriented lifestyle in the spring. That is why the Torah legislated that Sukkot be celebrated in the fall, so that it would be clear that Jews were going outside of their homes because of the *miṣvah*, not in order to enjoy the fresh air.

Rashbam has a different approach to the question, an approach that goes along with his comments on the purpose of the holiday. The question itself, for Rashbam, is illegitimate, since it is not the case that Sukkot commemorates the Exodus. It celebrates the harvest. Celebrations of the harvest could get out of hand, and remembering the humble beginnings of the people—the booths they lived in after the Exodus—could help keep the harvest festivities from becoming excessive.

haughty[42] about their houses that are full of all good things, lest they say "Our own hands have won this wealth for us."

24:2 ויקחו אליך שמן זית זך [COMMAND THE ISRAELITE PEOPLE] TO BRING YOU CLEAR OLIVE OIL: This portion of text is being repeated here [for the following reason]. Since the lampstand [in the Tabernacle] was placed opposite the table,[43] to light up the table, on which the "bread of display" was arranged, and since the rules about the bread of display [are about to] appear here (in vss. 5–9), [accordingly the rules about the oil for the candelabrum are appropriately repeated. The repetition occurs now since our chapter's theme is the explanation of] all those things [that] are part of the arrangement of the table: the oil that is used to light it up and the bread that is set out on it.[44]

24:11 ויקב: means that he pronounced God's Name; after that he cursed.[45]

---

[42]Rashbam's phrase, לבלתי רום לבבם, alludes to the language of Deut. 17:20.

[43]Rashbam uses the language of Ex. 26:35.

[44]The rules about the oil for the lampstand of the Tabernacle were already outlined in detail in Exodus. In fact, verses 2 and 3 here are virtual recapitulations of Exodus 27:20–21. As NJPSC writes: "The traditional commentators were understandably troubled by the precise repetition."

Rashi suggests that our chapter in Leviticus should be seen as the true source for the laws of the oil for the lampstand. The verses in Exodus appear, he argues, simply as part of the narrative about the Tabernacle.

Rashbam disagrees (and see also Nahm: "ואיננו נכון בעיני—I think that [Rashi's] explanation is not correct"). Rashbam explains that since a central theme of our chapter is the "bread of display" (לחם הפנים), it is appropriate for the Torah to reiterate at this point the way that that bread will be illuminated in the Tabernacle. Like Rashbam, see iE. Other explanations may be found in Nahm., JBS and Hizq.

Rashbam discusses the connection between the lampstand and the table for the Tabernacle in his commentary to Ex. 25:31. See note 59 there. See also Rashbam's commentary below to Numbers 8:2 (and note 2 there) where he discusses yet another repetition of laws concerning the lampstand. Concerning the general theme of explaining why some rules are repeated in the Torah, see Rashbam's commentary to Num. 5:6 and note 4 there.

[45]Many exegetes comment on the two separate verbs here that describe the blasphemer's action(s): "ויקב . . . ויקלל." Rashbam adopts the explanation that appears in Rashi's commentary to this verse: the first verb is from the root *n-q-b* and means to mention or pronounce God's (ineffable) Name; the second verb means to curse. That is the most common explanation among medievals and moderns. Rashi and Rashbam are both opposing the talmudic explanation (Sanh. 56a) that sees the root of ויקב as *q-b-b*, and says then that both ויקב and ויקלל mean to curse. (Like the talmudic explanation, see e.g. the Jerusalem Targum and LT.) The Talmud specifically mentions the explanation later offered by Rashi and Rashbam, and rejects it. Rashi in our verse, perhaps in order to assert the orthodoxy of his explanation, notes that this understanding of ויקב is found already in Onq.

24:15–16 איש איש כי יקלל א-לוהיו ANYONE WHO BLASPHEMES HIS GOD: using a non-specific name for God, i.e. without pronouncing God's true Name, [SHALL BEAR HIS GUILT]. However, (16) if he explicitly says the tetragrammaton, God's blessed Name, and then curses,[46] he SHALL BE PUT TO DEATH. Following the plain meaning of Scripture, this is how the verses should be explained.[47]

Another possibility is that the Rashi text here is corrupt. In the standard printed versions of Rashi's commentary to vs. 16, Rashi says that the word ונקב in that verse means to curse, connecting it to the phrase "מה אקב—how can I curse" (Num. 23:8). In other words, he sees the root as *q-b-b*. If that comment is part of Rashi's original text, then the comment of Rashi on our verse may be a later scribe's addition. In that case, Rashbam should be seen here as opposing Rashi, not following his lead.

[46]If נקב really means "to say explicitly," then verse 16—ונקב שם ה' מות יומת—could be saying that one receives the death penalty simply for pronouncing God's ineffable Name (with or without cursing). In fact, there is one such opinion in rabbinic literature (Rabbi Levi's in *Pesiqta deRav Kehana* 22, cited by Hoffmann, here). However, that is not standard *halakhah*. Rashbam carefully writes here that the felon in this verse committed a two-part infraction: "he explicitly says . . . and then curses." See note 47.

[47]In Sifra here and in two passages in the BT (Sanh. 56a and Shev. 36a), there is a dispute between Rabbi Meir and the Sages about the meaning of vss. 15–16. Rabbi Meir says that according to our verses anyone who curses God, using any one of God's names, would receive the death penalty. The Sages say, though, that vs. 16 restricts the capital penalty to the person who cursed the tetragrammaton, God's ineffable Name. Anyone who curses another name of God would receive the unspecified punishment ("shall bear his guilt") of vs. 15.

Rashbam's comment reaches the same halakhic conclusion as Rashi's—that there is a distinction between cursing God depending on what divine name is used. But Rashbam's comment also disagrees with some of the points that Rashi makes (once again if we can accept the printed text of Rashi as accurate. See below.)

Rashi says in his comment to vs. 15 that the phrase, "ונשא חטאו—he shall bear his guilt," means that the person who cursed God should receive the punishment of "being cut off" (*karet*), if the blasphemer was not warned beforehand (ונשא חטאו: בכרת כשאין התראה). This is a standard halakhic principle—that the capital penalty is applied only when the offender was warned; if the severity of the crime warrants a capital penalty but there was no warning, then the offender is punished by God through *karet*. Rashi's explanation then of vs. 15 is that that verse is describing a crime that *does*, generally speaking, warrant the death penalty. There is only a technical reason why the death penalty is not being applied—the offender was not warned. Rashbam, however, says that vs. 15 is describing a crime that *never* warrants the death penalty. The death penalty is applied only to the person (in vs. 16) who curses God's ineffable Name, not the person (in vs. 15) who curses one of God's other names.

The printed texts of Rashi here seem impossible to sustain. Rashi's first comment on vs. 16 seems inconsistent with his comment to vs. 15. Rashi's second comment to verse 16 contradicts his comment on vs. 11 (as I noted in note 45 above). Until a reliable critical edition of Rashi's Torah commentary appears, it is impossible to know what Rashi really said here or what the relationship is between Rashbam's explanation and that of his grandfather.

24:18 ומכה נפש בהמה: means that the person altogether killed the animal; [however] (vs. 21) ומכה בהמה ישלמנה refers to someone who injured an animal, but did not kill it.[48]

[48]The problem that Rashbam is dealing with is the apparent redundancy: both the beginning of vs. 18 and the beginning of vs. 21 say that a person who "smites—מכה" an animal should pay for the damages. As Noth puts it: "Strangely enough vs. 21 repeats these sentences once more . . .." The solution offered by Rashbam is the same one offered by Rashi—that verse 18 (which mentions the word נפש) is referring to killing an animal, while verse 21 is referring to injuring an animal. In his commentary to Ex. 2:11, Rashbam writes that the verb להכות may mean both to injure and to kill.

Interpreting the verb מכה at the beginning of vs. 21 as referring to injuring an animal is problematic, for that verse describes two cases of "smiting": a person who smites an animal, and then pays damages, and a person who smites a human being, and then receives the death penalty (ומכה אדם יומת). But if "smiting" in both cases means injuring, we arrive at the unacceptable conclusion that injuring a human being could incur the death penalty. Rashi, in the continuation of his commentary on vs. 21, explains at length (based on a midrashic reading taken from Sifra and Sanh. 84b) how verse 21 could be referring to two cases of "smiting" that fall short of murder, and yet the death penalty is appropriately imposed in them. Rashbam, though, does not explain how he deals with the end of the verse.

Other medieval attempts to deal with the redundancy may be found in iE, JBS and Hizq. Most moderns are not troubled by the redundancy (presumably seeing vs. 21 as a summary statement after vss. 17–20). See e.g. NJPS, which translates מכה as "kill" consistently in these verses, including the beginning of vs. 21.

בהר (Leviticus 25:1–26:2)

25:1 בהר סיני [THE LORD SPOKE TO MOSES] ON MOUNT SINAI: Before the Tent of Meeting was erected.[1]

25:2 ושבתה THE LAND SHALL OBSERVE A SABBATH: [The verb ושבתה] implies inactivity.[2]

25:3 ואספתה את תבואתה YOU SHALL GATHER IN THE YIELD [OF THE LAND]: Do not abandon it as ownerless.[3]

25:10 ושבתם איש EACH OF YOU SHALL RETURN: to his holding. As it is explained below (vs. 28), a person who sells a field returns to it without payment in the Jubilee year; ואיש אל משפחתו AND EACH OF YOU SHALL RETURN TO HIS FAMILY: This refers to the Hebrew slave who [as it is written below in vss. 40–41] goes free when the Jubilee year arrives.[4]

---

[1]In his commentary to Num. 1:1, Rashbam says that there is a difference between the Torah saying that a commandment was given "at Mount Sinai" and saying that it was given "in the wilderness of Sinai." "At Mount Sinai" means that the commandment was given during the first year after the exodus from Egypt. "In the wilderness of Sinai" means that it was spoken to Moses at the Tent of Meeting (which was erected a year after the exodus, nine months after the theophany at Mount Sinai), in one of the years of wandering through the desert.

Rashbam is taking issue with Rashi here who argues (following Sifra) that our verse teaches that the details of *all* the commandments were given to Moses at Mount Sinai. According to Rashbam, commandments were taught to Moses either at Mount Sinai (in the first year of the wandering) or in the wilderness (in years 2–39) or in the plains of Moab (in the fortieth year). Our verse tells us that the laws of chapter 25 are from the first category, and says nothing about the laws of the Torah in general.

See also commentary to Ex. 12:1 and note 3 there. See also Rashbam's commentary below to 26:46 and note 37 there.

[2]Perhaps Rashbam feels the need to comment here since the verb "to observe a Sabbath," would generally be applied to a person, not to the land. He explains that the verb *sh-b-t* may mean "to be inactive." See similarly Rashi to Neh. 6:3. (There also the subject of the verb *sh-b-t* is not a person.) See also commentary to Exodus 21:19, s.v. שבתו, and note 55 there.

[3]See commentary to Exodus 23:10 (and see note 20 there), where Rashbam offers the same explanation for the parallel phrase there.

[4]Rashbam, as he often does, explains our verse as an example of a general statement, the details of which will be elaborated below. (See e.g. commentary to Ex. 2:15, and note 29 there, and commentary to Lev. 12:2, and note 1 there.) He writes that the explanation of both

25:11 נזיריה [DO NOT HARVEST] ITS 'NAZIRITE' [VINES]: You are not to harvest [vines] that grew from fallen grapes. The same interpretation should be applied to the word ספיחים in relation to crops.[5]

---

phrases—"each of you shall return to his holding" and "each of you shall return to his family"—will follow below in the biblical text.

This comment is opposed to Rashi's in a subtle manner. Rashi explains that the first of the two phrases says that "the fields return to the owners during the Jubilee year." Like Rashbam, he explains that the phrase here and the similar one in vs. 28 both give the same information. But for the second phrase here, "each of you shall return to his family," Rashi provides a *midrash halakhah* explanation, from Qid. 15a and Sifra. Since below in vss. 40 and 41 it is made clear that Hebrew slaves go free in the Jubilee year, our verse, "each of you shall return to his family," must teach some additional law. (See also Rashi's commentary to Qid., *ibid.*, s.v. הרי כבר and s.v. אי במכרוהו.) The new law that we learn from *this* verse, according to classical rabbinic sources, is that even a Hebrew slave who has had his ear pierced (in the ceremony of Ex. 21:6) goes free in the Jubilee year.

Rashi's comment to this verse is methodologically inconsistent. He accepts that the first phrase, "each of you shall return to his holding," teaches nothing new but simply introduces in a general manner the rules that will be elaborated below about fields. But he feels that the second phrase, "each of you shall return to his family," must be adding some new information, namely that even a slave with a "pierced ear" goes free in the Jubilee year.

Rashbam, is more consistent. He says that both phrases in our verse are general statements—one about fields and one about slaves—that will be elaborated below. There is no need to look for new meaning in either phrase here. Note that Rashbam's comment here is inconsistent with his heterodox explanation of Ex. 21:6, where he wrote that, according to the *peshaṭ*, when the text says that a slave who has undergone the ear-piercing ceremony should be a slave "forever," that really means forever (not, as *halakhah* says, until the Jubilee year). See commentary and notes 22 and 23 there.

[5]Rashbam is offering a unique and unusual interpretation. His wording, too, is difficult and unusual.

There is no unanimity of opinion about the meaning of the words ספיחים and ענבי נזיר here and in vs. 5 above. Many commentators including Rashi (ad vs. 5) say that the terms ספיחים and ענבי נזיר refer to two different and unrelated categories. Rashi says that the first term, ספיחים, refers to crops that (legitimately) grew in fields during the sabbatical year, without human care or intervention. The second term, ענבי נזיר, he sees as grapes that were grown on vines that were (illegitimately) guarded by their owners. During the sabbatical and Jubilee years, owners of fields and vines were supposed to allow all people equal access to the crops, and were not supposed to guard the produce of their own fields.

Rashbam appears to be the first exegete to explain the two terms, ספיחים and ענבי נזיר, in a parallel manner. Both mean the same thing: crops/grapes that grew without being tended. After Rashbam, many exegetes attempt to explain the two concepts in a parallel manner. See e.g. JBS, Hizq and Nahm., all ad vs. 5. Nahm. argues at length that whenever the Torah describes the agricultural laws of the sabbatical year, the rules of vines and of fields are parallel to each other. (See e.g. vss. 3, 4, and Ex. 23:11.) Interestingly, this is the second verse in a row where Rashbam in his commentary addresses two phrases, agrees with Rashi about the meaning of one of the phrases, and implicitly criticizes Rashi for not interpreting the second phrase in a parallel manner. See note 4 above on vs. 10.

25:12 מן השדה תאכלו את תבואתה YOU MAY EAT [ONLY] THE GROWTH OF THE FIELD: And not that which was gathered into the house, for it is forbidden to gather it.[6]

25:16 כי מספר תבואות FOR [HE IS SELLING TO YOU] THE NUMBER OF CROPS: between now and the Jubilee year; he is not selling you the land itself.[7]

The phraseology of Rashbam's interpretation is unusual. Since Rashi writes (ad vs. 5) that ספיחים are crops that grow from seed that falls to the ground accidentally during harvest, Rashbam writes that ענבי נזיר are vines that grow from grapes that fell to the ground. (Later exegetes who interpret the two phrases as parallel see ענבי נזיר as meaning "untended grapes," but say nothing about how those grapes originally grew.) Agriculturally speaking, Wessely argues that Rashbam's explanation is unusual, or perhaps impossible (ותמה אני עליו). According to him, vines do not grow from fallen grapes, and, even if they did, one would not be allowed to eat their product for three or four years in any case (following the law of Lev. 19:23–25).

Rashbam lived in or near the Champagne district of France and may have known more about viticulture than Wessely did. From conversations that I have had with grape growers in Israel I have learned that, although it is unusual, wild vines can and do grow today from fallen grapes. In theory, such a vine could produce fruit for more than four years. Following Rashbam's interpretation, the verse could be saying that it is forbidden, in the sabbatical year, to harvest the product of wild vines in their fifth and subsequent years. Such an interpretation is unusual, but it is possible, and it does reflect a consistent reading of our verse.

6Rashbam's words represent the standard understanding of the *halakhah* concerning crops that grow during sabbatical and Jubilee years. The owner of the field may eat those crops, but so may anyone else. The owner may not assert ownership over the crops in any way, including gathering it all into his home.

Rashbam's interpretation of this verse opposes that of Rashi who (following Sifra) offers a *midrash halakhah* reading of this phrase, and learns from it certain principles about the time of *be'ur*, the point at which, according to *halakhah*, it becomes forbidden during sabbatical and Jubilee years, to eat each individual species of produce at all.

Rashi would accept Rashbam's halakhic statement that owners should not assert ownership over their crops during sabbatical and Jubilee years. In his commentary, however, he makes that point ad vss. 5 and 11 (s.v. ענבי נזיר). So when one combines Rashbam's comments on vss. 11 and 12, one finds that he is saying: "Rashi is wrong about his interpretation both of the last phrase of vs. 11 (ולא תבצרו את נזיריה) and of the last phrase of vs. 12 (מן השדה תאכלו את תבואתה). What Rashi thinks the first phrase means is actually what the second phrase means."

Like Rashbam, see iE, Hizq., Nahm., NJPSC and Noth.

7Rashbam's interpretation is the clear plain meaning of the text. It opposes the *midrash halakhah* reading of the Sifra (quoted in part by Rashi to the previous verse). According to that explanation, the phrase במספר שני תבואות in vs. 15 teaches that a field that has been sold may not be redeemed until **two** years have elapsed; then the phrase, מספר תבואות, in our verse adds that even if those two years included (parts of) three separate harvests, still the sale must stay in force for two years. Even Rashi is troubled by the distance of that *midrash halakhah* from the simple meaning of the text, and he attempts to make it slightly more *peshaṭ*-oriented. Rashbam goes farther and simply reads the verse in its plain sense.

25:21 לשלש השנים [IN THE SIXTH YEAR IT SHALL YIELD A CROP SUFFICIENT] FOR THREE YEARS: Following the plain meaning of Scripture, this means that the seed of the sixth year will feed you during the sixth year and the seventh year. Then, in the eighth year you will sow [with it]. But you will eat the crops of the sixth year until the beginning of the ninth year, when you will begin to eat of the crops that were sown in the eighth year.[8]

25:24 גאולה תתנו לארץ [THROUGHOUT THE LAND THAT YOU HOLD] YOU MUST PROVIDE FOR THE REDEMPTION OF THE LAND: If the seller wishes to redeem it before the Jubilee year.[9]

---

[8]The verse is difficult: if one year of crops is lost because of a sabbatical, why should the crop before the sabbatical have to last for three years? Should two years not be enough?

Rashi says essentially that those crops will last you for only two years. When the verse says "three years," it means parts of three separate years. Crops grown during the year before the sabbatical are used in "three years"—in the second half of the pre-sabbatical year, throughout the sabbatical year and then in the first half of the year after that sabbatical. The problem, though, is that vs. 22 says explicitly that "you will be eating the old until the ninth year." Rashi has a complicated excursus in his commentary to that verse to explain why it says "until the ninth year" when people will actually be eating the new crops in the second half of the eighth year.

Super-commentaries as far back as Nahm. have not been satisfied with Rashi's explanation. Some, like Nahm., have suggested that a crop that lasts for three years is needed only when a sabbatical and a Jubilee year come one after the other and there is no agricultural activity for two years in a row. Actually both of these opinions—that our verse refers to a regular sabbatical year or to one adjacent to a Jubilee year—are found in the Sifra here.

Rashbam's approach appears difficult. As Wessely says, it seems as if Rashbam simply asserts that the explanation found in Rashi is the *peshaṭ*, and does not even address the difficulties of that approach. Rashbam's language in the comment is not clear; Rosin felt the need to emend the wording, but his emendation did not really clarify the meaning.

My understanding of Rashbam's comment is that he does *not* agree with Rashi and that he *does* address the aforementioned difficulty. Rashbam is saying that the crops that grow in the sixth year will be used for three different years: the seeds of those harvested crops will be used for producing the food that is eaten in the sixth, the seventh and the eighth years (since nothing will be planted in the seventh year). Miraculously, there will still be enough seeds left for planting crops in the eighth year. My explanation (of Rashbam's explanation) removes the problem of "three years" by saying that, in a regular year, the seeds of crops are used for two years (to eat in the year they grew and to plant for the next). Seeds of the crops from the year preceding the sabbatical year have to be used for three years.

[9]Rashi provides two explanations for this verse. The first, following Qid. 21a, says that our verse teaches us something new: that the rules of land redemption apply also to houses and to slaves. Rashi's second explanation, which he labels *peshaṭ*, is that our verse teaches no new laws but is an introduction to the laws that follow in verses 25f. As Nahm. rephrases Rashi's explanation (while disagreeing with it):

25:27 והשיב את העודף REFUND THE REMAINDER: [Based on the number] of years left until the Jubilee year, years in which he has not yet had the opportunity to use the field. "THE REMAINDER" means beyond the years that he has already used it.[10]

25:33 ואשר יגאל מן הלוים WHOEVER FROM AMONG THE LEVITES REDEEMS [PROPERTY][11] . . .: As we said above (vs. 32), "Levites shall forever have the right of redemption." [Our phrase, ואשר יגאל מן הלוים, means] when a Levite wishes to redeem a field but does not have [means] to do so, then " ויצא ממכר בית—A HOUSE SOLD SHALL BE RELEASED [THROUGH THE JUBILEE]," i.e. it shall return to him [at the Jubilee year] without payment.[12]

---

(24) "You must provide for the redemption of the land." In what way [is this done]?

(25) "If your kinsman is in straits and has to sell part of his holding, his nearest redeemer shall come . . ."

Rashbam, as is often the case, follows the explanation that Rashi calls *peshaṭ* and does not mention the other possibility. See similarly JBS: "כך מפרש ואזיל—the text continues to explain [in the following verses what it means to provide for the redemption of the land]."

Nahm.'s principal objection to that explanation is that it involves ignoring the "break" found in the Torah between verses 24 and 25. See NJPSC which also ignores that break and explains the verse as Rashbam does seeing verses 1–23 as one unit of text and verse 24 as the first verse of the next unit.

[10]Rashi says that "the remainder" is a reference to the remaining money. Rashbam says that it is a reference to the remaining years (or, perhaps it would be more accurate to say, to the money that it is due because of the remaining years). Ultimately they (and all other exegetes whom I have seen) understand what the verse is saying in the same way—that when a field that was sold is redeemed by the original owner, the redemption price is determined by the number of years left until the Jubilee. The question is only what implicit noun is being modified by the word העודף.

[11]There are a number of possible ways of understanding and translating the Hebrew words, ואשר יגאל מן הלוים. See e.g. NJPS: "Such property as may be redeemed from the Levites." I translated the phrase the way Rashbam understands it. See note 12.

[12]As Noth notes, "Verse 33 is very hard to understand." Rashi offers two separate and very complicated interpretations of our phrase, ואשר יגאל מן הלוים. According to the first interpretation, יגאל means "to buy," not "to redeem." According to the second, מן הלוים is a reference not to the original Levite owner of the property, but to the Levite who bought it from him. A variety of other explanations may be found in Nahm., JBS and Hizq.

The explanation proposed here by Rashbam is that our verse, as Wessely points out, expresses the same idea as vs. 28: "If he lacks sufficient means to recover it, what he sold shall remain with the purchaser until the Jubilee; in the Jubilee year it shall be released." Wessely claims that the words of the verse do not fit smoothly according to Rashbam's explanation, but that same criticism may be leveled against almost any reading of this difficult verse. The translation of the verse in Gerstenberg's commentary closely parallels Rashbam's understanding.

25:34 ושדה מגרש THE UNENCLOSED LAND AROUND THEIR CITIES: The areas described in the Torah portion, *'Elleh mas'e.*[13]

25:39 עבודת עבד DO NOT SUBJECT HIM TO THE TREATMENT OF A SLAVE: I.e. by (vs. 43) "ruling over him ruthlessly,"[14] as [one might do] with a Canaanite slave.[15]

25:47 או לעקר: [An עקר means an *émigré,*] a person who was uprooted (נעקר) from this realm to some far away place.[16] He is [accordingly classified] neither as a resident, nor as a convert, nor as a non-Jew nor as a citizen.[17]

26:1 משכית: The word משכית comes from the root שכה, just as the word מרבית ("increase" or "growth")[18] comes from the root רבה ("to increase" or "to grow"). I am unable to find another [such] use of [words from] this [root] in the Bible[19] other than in the phrase (Ps. 73:7), "עברו משכיות לבב—they have surpassed the

---

[13]See Num. 35:2–4. Rashbam notes quite reasonably that the מגרש of the Levites mentioned here is defined there in Numbers. Wessely copies Rashbam's comment.

[14]As is often the case (see e.g. commentary to vs. 10, and note 4 there), Rashbam interprets a phrase at the beginning of a legal section as serving an introductory purpose. The rules about a Jewish slave begin with the general principle, "do not subject him to the treatment of a slave." The meaning of that phrase, Rashbam argues, will become clear from the continuation of the passage (vs. 43) where we read that he may not be "ruled over ruthlessly."

Rashbam's approach is opposed to that of Rashi who (following Sifra) interprets our verse and vs. 43 as teaching two different laws about the mistreatment of Hebrew slaves. As is often the case, Rashi is not satisfied with seeing a verse as serving the rhetorical purpose of "introducing" the issue. He prefers to find different legal meaning in as many of the words of the text as possible.

[15]That it is permitted to rule over a Canaanite slave ruthlessly (בפרך) appears to be the simple meaning of vs. 46: "but as for your Israelite kinsman, no one shall rule ruthlessly over the other." So also Maimonides (MT *'Avadim* 9:8), who notes that such treatment of a Canaanite slave is permitted, but argues that it is neither the pious nor the wise course of action.

[16]Rashbam's comment is opposed to that of Rashi who (following Sifra) says that being sold to an עקר means being indentured to an idolatrous religion.

Like Rashbam, see Hizq. See also Wessely's arguments against Rashbam's explanation.

[17]Rashbam is explaining why the unique and unusual word, עקר, is used here. It is because our text is talking about an unusual category, rarely discussed in the Torah—the Jew who has left the land (of Israel).

[18]The word מרבית is aptly chosen by Rashbam as an example as it just appeared in the biblical text a few verses before (25:37).

[19]When Rashbam writes איני מוצא לו חבר, the standard phrase used to introduce a *hapax legomenon*, he is overstating his case. See e.g. Ezek. 8:12 and Proverbs 18:11. Perhaps Rashbam means that the verse in Psalms is the only other example he can find of a word from this root being connected to the idea of seeing.

desires of their hearts," where the phrase means "that which his heart envisioned."[20] Here also [אבן משכית means] a "stone of sights," a stone on which there are drawings and images[21] for people to look upon.[22]

---

[20]The verse in Psalms is very difficult and there is no consensus about what it means.

[21]In his commentary to Ex. 20:21, Rashbam uses this same phrase, צלמים וציורין, to describe the decorations found on idolatrous altars.

See also Kalman Bland, *The Artless Jew: Medieval and Modern Affirmations and Denials of the Visual* (Princeton, 2000), p. 123. Bland (referring to the passage in Rashbam's Exodus commentary, but the same would presumably apply to this passage) is certain that Rashbam's language alludes "to the idolatrous Christian practice of surmounting crucifixes on altars that are decorated with all sorts of 'images and sculptured reliefs'."

[22]As NJPSC writes, "Hebrew *'even maskit* is difficult to explain precisely." Rashbam's explanation is opposed to that of Rashi who (following Meg. 22b) says that the phrase means a stone floor. Rashi, like Rashbam, sees the root of משכית as שכה, but he argues that שכה means "to cover."

Like Rashbam, see JBS and iE here and see Qimḥi, *Shorashim*, s.v. שכה. So also Mendelssohn, in the comment that he interpolated into the middle of Wessely's *Be'ur* to this verse.

בחוקותי (Leviticus 26:3–27:34)

26:10 וישן מפני חדש תוציאו IN ORDER TO MAKE ROOM FOR THE NEW, YOU WILL HAVE TO CLEAR THE OLD OUT: of the granaries, to sell it.[1] [The verb תוציאו can mean "to clear out the granaries,"] as in the phrase (Deut. 14:28) "You shall clear out (תוציא) the full tithe of your field . . . [but leave it within your gates]. . . and give it[2] to the Levites."

26:13 מוטות עולכם [I BROKE] THE מוטות OF YOUR YOKE: As it is written (Jer. 27:2), "Make for yourself מוסרות [and מוטות of a yoke." מוסרות is] the name of the straps that are used for tying the wood of the yoke [to the animal. That wooden part] is called the מוטות,[3] because it tilts (מטה) the ox's head and

[1]Rashbam's interpretation is opposed to that of Rashi who (following Sifra) says that the verse means that they will run out of storage areas. The granaries and the storehouses will all be overflowing. Rashbam's explanation, as Krinski points out here (*Qarne 'or* 5), explains the verse in a way that it is truly a blessing. It is not that you will run out of space, but rather that crops that you would normally have had to keep for yourself will now be available for selling. See Wessely who also emphasizes the financial implications of this verse.

[2]I have translated the text as it appears in Rosin's edition, even though I am fairly certain that it contains a copyist's error. First of all, there is no such verse in the Bible. The phrase "ונתתה ללוי—give it to the Levites" does appear once in Deuteronomy (26:12) but not as the continuation of a verse that includes the word תוציא. Secondly, Rashbam's prooftext would be considerably stronger if Deut. 26:12 were correctly quoted. The verse in its accurate form says that one clears out the crops but leaves them within the fields and then the Levite comes and takes them on his own. This seems to show that "to clear out" just means, as Rashbam would have it here, to take the crops out of the granaries.

My estimation is that the text of Rashbam's commentary may have originally read: ". . . as in the phrase (Deut. 14:28) 'You shall clear out (תוציא) the full tithe of your field . . . but leave it within your gates'."

[3]Rashbam's explanation—that מוטות means the wooden part of the yoke and מוסרות means the straps—is also the common understanding among moderns. See e.g. NJPS to Jer. and NJPSC here.

In some versions of Rashi's commentary there is a comment on the word מוטות, that explains the word as meaning the part of the yoke that is on top of the wooden section and is shaped like a "peg." If that comment is original to Rashi (but probably it is not), then Rashbam's commentary should be seen as disagreeing with Rashi's.

makes it bend over.[4] קוממיות [I MADE YOU WALK] ERECT: Once the yoke is removed, he can lift up his head.[5]

26:18 שבע על חטאתיכם [I WILL GO ON TO DISCIPLINE YOU] FOR YOUR SINS SEVENFOLD: I.e. you will receive *many*[6] punishments for your sins. So also [numbers are not to be understood literally in verses such as] (Prov. 24:16) "Seven times the righteous man falls and gets up," or (Is. 30:26) "The light of the sun shall become sevenfold," or (Is. 4:1) "Seven women shall take hold [of one man]."[7]

26:19 ושברתי את גאון עזכם I WILL BREAK YOUR POWERFUL PRIDE: [This refers to causing famine conditions in the land,] as it is written (vs. 26), "I

---

[4]Rashbam's explanation of the derivation of the word מוטות is weak. (Generally מוט is not seen as being from the root נ-ט-ה.) From his commentary to Num. 4:10 (see also note 32 there) it is clear that Rashbam understands the Hebrew word מוט, there, in its more common sense as "a bar." There he does not see any need to explain how the idea of bending might be connected to that bar. Nevertheless, Rashbam's explanation about the מוטות of a yoke achieved a certain popularity in northern France; it is found also in the commentaries of JBS and Hizq. here.

Probably the reason that Rashbam neglects the simplest understanding of the word מוטות (as meaning the wooden bars that constitute the yoke) is that in his days yokes were not made from wooden bars but from one large piece of wood. See the discussion about developments in yokes and harnesses in medieval Europe in *The Cambridge Economic History of Europe*, ed. by Michael M. Posten, vol. 1, p. 144.

[5]Rashbam's explanation of קוממיות is the common one, and appears to be the plain meaning of the text. It goes back as far as the Sifra. Many other commentators follow Rashbam's lead in explaining that the removal of the yoke in the beginning of the verse is what allows people to "walk erect."

[6]I.e. "seven" is not to be taken literally. It simply means "many" times.

See similarly comment below on vs. 26, s.v. עשר, and note 15 there, and commentary to Gen. 31:7 and Num. 14:22.

[7]Rashbam's comment is opposed to that of Rashi (here, and ad vs. 15 above) who (following Sifra) takes the number "seven" in our verse literally and says that, if you look carefully at the previous verses, you find seven sins enumerated there and that is why seven punishments are promised. See also Hizq.'s explanation that the word seven appears here because the primary sin of the Israelites was that they failed to observe the laws of the sabbatical, the *seventh* year.

See iE here who, like Rashbam, argues against the literal explanation of the number "seven." See also JBS who first enumerates, like Rashi, the seven sins and then says, like Rashbam, that, following the plain meaning, the word seven is not to be taken literally (ולפי הפשט שבע לאו דווקא). So also Noth here: "Here, the number seven simply expresses the extensiveness and completeness of the divine chastisement."

Kogut (pp. 195 and 206) argues (for me unconvincingly) that Rashbam's understanding of the verse reflects a syntactical reading that is not in consonance with the cantillation marks.

will break your staff of bread," and it is written (Ezek. 16:49) "She had the pride (גאון) of having plenty of bread."[8]

According to an *'aggadah*, the phrase ["your powerful pride"] means the Temple. [This interpretation is based on the similarity of our verse to the verse in Ezekiel (24:21), where] it is written "I am going to destroy my temple, your powerful pride (מקדשי גאון עזכם)."[9]

However, the plain meaning of Scripture is as I have explained it. The end of [our] verse proves [that the verse is referring to agricultural desolation, not to the destruction of the Temple, for it reads]: "I WILL MAKE YOUR SKIES [LIKE IRON] . . .."[10]

26:20 כחכם YOUR STRENGTH [SHALL BE SPENT TO NO PURPOSE]: Because the land "will no longer yield its strength to you ."[11]

---

[8]Rashbam's first proof of this interpretation—that our phrase is a reference to famine—is based on the fact that both the verb "to break" and the noun "pride" are used in the Bible in contexts relating to having plenty of bread. As Rashbam's comment unfolds, it becomes clear that his major proof is from the immediate context. The verses that he cites here only show that it is possible to use words like this to refer to agricultural desolation.

There are other interpretations of the verse in Ezekiel, but I have translated it in a way that conforms with the interpretation of Rashbam, and of many other Jewish exegetes. See e.g. Qimḥi there.

[9]This is the interpretation that is given by Rashi here (following Sifra).

[10]Rashbam is opposing Rashi's reading of the verse. Both Rashbam and Rashi use the tools of the *peshaṭ*-oriented exegete here in their comments. Rashi looks for a passage with similar wording in another biblical book to help us understand the phrase גאון עזכם here. Rashi is correct that Ezekiel used that phrase as a reference to the Temple. Rashbam, on the other hand, feels that reading a verse in its immediate context must be the paramount consideration in *peshaṭ* exegesis. The rest of vs. 19 and verse 20 do demand, as Rashbam suggests, a reading of our phrase as a reference to agricultural desolation, not to the destruction of the Temple. Like Rashbam, see iE, Wessely, Hoffmann and NJPSC.

[11]An allusion to Gen. 4:12.

It is possible to understand Rashbam's comment here in two ways. Hizq. writes (presumably following his understanding of Rashbam), that the prooftext from Genesis helps us understand the word "strength" here; one sees from there that the word can be applied to agriculture. Hizq.'s version of Rashbam's commentary might have been the same one that Wessely was using (not the one in Rosin's text); it presumably began with the words, כחכם: כח האדמה, instead of our (= Rosin's) reading, כחכם: כי האדמה. Based on the reading that I assume he had, Wessely concludes that Rashbam is trying to prove that "your strength" in our verse *means* "the land's strength," and Wessely argues against that explanation.

The other simpler way of understanding Rashbam (particularly if we accept the reading from Rosin's text) is that he is explaining the idea of the verse, not the meaning of the word. He writes that human "strength" invested in agricultural efforts will be wasted because God will ensure that the land will not cooperate but will withhold its "strength," or produce.

26:21 ואם תלכו עמי קרי AND IF YOU WALK WITH ME קרי: Menaḥem explained [that קרי is related to] the idea of "holding back," as in the phrase (Prov. 25:17) "Hold you foot back (הוקר רגלך) [from your neighbor's house]." This explanation is folly. הוקר is from a root with a weak first letter [i.e. the root י-ק-ר. It follows] the same pattern as [the word הושב in the phrase,] (Gen. 47:6) "settle (הושב) your father," which is from [the root י-ש-ב, the same root as the word ישב, in the phrase] (Gen. 13:12), "Abram settled (ישב)." On the other hand, קרי [in our verse] is from the root ק-ר-ה, the same root as [the word אקרה in the phrase (Num. 23:15), "I will attempt to make Him] happen to appear to me (אקרה)."[12]

The phrase then means, "If you will walk with Me in a haphazard manner," not with consistency, [i.e. if you behave] like a person who is not involved with the Creator in a consistent way.[13]

26:25 נקם ברית VENGEANCE FOR THE COVENANT: which you have broken. Just as it is written above (vs. 15) "Because you broke my covenant (בריתי)."[14]

---

[12]The phrase in Num. 23 is very difficult, but Rashbam accepts the standard Jewish exegetical reading. Balaam knows that God's appearances to him are haphazard and unpredictable, and that is why both he and the narrator use words related to the idea of coincidence (מקרה), to describe those encounters. See e.g. Rashi ad Ex. 3:18 and Nahm. ad Num. 23:4.

[13]Rashi offers two explanations of the word קרי in this verse. The first, which he labels the interpretation of "our rabbis," (see e.g. Sifra here) connects the word קרי to the idea of "coincidence." Then Rashi presents the interpretation of Menaḥem, the one that Rashbam rejects as "folly"; Rashi argues further that Onq. interprets the word the same way that Menaḥem does. So Rashbam's interpretation should be seen as supporting one of the two options offered by Rashi, while rejecting the second one, using strong language.

Rashbam's grammatical argument—that הוקר is from a prima-*yod* root (י-ק-ר) while קרי is not—is strong. Some would disagree with Rashbam and say that the root of קרי is not ק-ר-ה but rather ק-ר-ר (e.g. NJPSC); others, like BDB and Ehrlich, agree with Rashbam and connect the word to the idea of coincidence (ק-ר-ה). In either case, Rashbam's criticism of Menaḥem's position stands.

There is no consensus today about what the word means. As NJPSC notes, the word is difficult and "its meaning remains uncertain."

See also Rashbam's commentary on קרך in Deut. 25:18.

[14]In other words, Rashbam is saying that the word "covenant" should be interpreted the same way that it was interpreted earlier in this chapter—the covenant between Israel and God that obligates the Israelites to observe the Torah.

Rashbam is agreeing with the second of the two interpretations offered by Rashi. (That understanding also seems to be reflected in Shab. 33a.) Rashi's first explanation, which Rashbam rejects, sees the phrase נקם ברית (following Sifra) as meaning "a just vengeance." Rashbam's interpretation might also be directed against JBS who sees here a reference to the "covenant" of circumcision.

26:26 עשר נשים TEN WOMEN: In other words, *many* women. Just like (Job 19:3) "Ten times you humiliated me."[15]

---

[15]Rashbam reiterates the point that he made above (ad vs. 18) that numbers need not be taken literally. See notes 6 and 7 above.

In the Job commentary that appears in Manuscript Jewish Theological Seminary N.Y.L. 778—the commentary that Sara Japhet identifies as Rashbam's Job commentary—that verse in Job is interpreted as follows:

> "'Ten times you humiliated me': There have been ten sections of speeches (פרשיות) [up to this point in the text of Job], if one counts both the speeches of Job and those of his friends. In all of those speeches, Job was humiliated. Job's friends considered him wicked [and thus humiliated him]. And he was also embarrassed [in his own speeches] when he had to defend himself against their accusations." (Japhet's edition, p. 386; my translation)

In other words, the author of that commentary on Job says (following Rashi there) that "ten" means "ten." He does *not* agree with the author of this commentary on Leviticus, who says that "ten" in the verse in Job 19 is not to be taken literally.

Japhet realizes that this comment of Rashbam on Leviticus weakens her argument that the Job commentary is Rashbam's. She offers two possible explanations of the contradiction (p. 67, note 61). First she suggests that the commentary here in Leviticus may have been tampered with; some later hand may have inserted the prooftext from Job. Secondly she suggests that it is possible that Rashbam changed his mind after writing his Torah commentary (assuming, as she does, that the Job commentary was written later) and became convinced that an interpretation of "ten" in a literal manner was fitting in the Job passage.

I find neither of those suggestions appealing. To be sure, the commentary to the Torah that we have has been tampered with and does not represent Rashbam's original text. But if we say that some later hand inserted the prooftext from Job into the Torah commentary here, we also have to say that that same later hand jumped to Num. 14:22 and inserted that same prooftext from Job, to prove the same point, into Rashbam's commentary there.

Moreover, to me it seems that the interpretation of Job 19:3 in the commentary that Japhet attributes to Rashbam is the type of comment that Rashbam of the Torah commentary would relate to derisively. It is also the type of interpretation that contradicts the interpretive methodology clearly spelled out in the work of, ostensibly, the same exegete, in the commentary on Job 5:19–23. (For the text, see Japhet's edition p. 356. See also her discussion on pages 65–67.) There the exegete forcefully claims that the numbers six and seven should not be interpreted literally in Job.

Is it reasonable to think that the same person who wrote the Torah commentary, or that the person who wrote the commentary on Job 5, changed his mind about the number "ten" and chose to explain it literally in his commentary to Job 19? Of course, it is possible that an exegete like Rashbam, who believes in "insights into the plain meaning of Scripture that are newly thought of day by" (commentary to Gen. 37:2) might change his mind about any exegetical question over time. The alternative theory—that that Job commentary contains much material from Rashbam but is not his composition—seems more attractive. See the discussion in my article, "'Rashbam' on Job: a Reconsideration," *Jewish Studies Quarterly* 8 (2001), 80–104.

בתנור אחד [TEN WOMEN SHALL BAKE BREAD] IN A SINGLE OVEN: For one woman will not have enough bread to fill up the oven.[16]

והשיבו לחמכם במשקל AND THEY SHALL COLLECT THEIR BREAD BY WEIGHT: The meaning is that they weigh the bread when they bring it to the oven, and then they weigh it when they take it out, in order to feed the owners [the correct] weighed-out and rationed portions—"meager bread and scant water" (Is. 30:20).

So it is written (Ezek. 4:16) "O mortal, I am going to break the staff of bread in Jerusalem, and they shall eat bread by weight, in anxiety, and drink water by measure." Here [we should] also [understand our verse,] "when I break your staff of bread," [in the same way. It means that] your bread will be both baked by weight and eaten by weight.[17]

ואכלתם ולא תשבעו THOUGH YOU EAT, YOU SHALL NOT BE SATISFIED: Because you will eat it in weighed-out and rationed portions.[18]

---

[16]Rashi interprets this phrase (following Sifra) as a reference to the fact that they will not have enough *wood*, and for that reason many women will have to come together to do their baking. Rashbam says that the reference is still to the lack of *crops*. They will have so little bread to bake that they will get together to assemble a full oven's load of dough. See also the next two comments of Rashbam on the next two phrases of this verse (s.v. והשיבו and s.v. ואכלתם) and notes 17–19.

[17]Rashbam writes at great length to make his opposition to Rashi's explanation clear. Rashi (following Sifra) says that the idea of "collecting the bread by weight" is a further curse: in the oven, the bread will be damaged and the remaining scraps will have to be distributed carefully by weight. Rashbam disagrees. All the phrases here are simply descriptions of one curse: the agriculture will be so devastated that there will be famine conditions. This one disaster leads to all the problems of our verse: that many women will use one oven, that bread will be collected by weight and that that which is eaten will not satisfy. Rashi, on the other hand, sees each of these curses as something added on to the curse of famine. See Wessely who writes that following Rashbam's understanding there are redundant unnecessary phrases in our verse (מקרא שאינו צריך הוא).

In order to prove his interpretation, Rashbam cites the verse in Ezekiel, which uses similar language. There, the connection of "weight" to the bread that is eaten is not something new that happened just when the bread was removed from the oven (as Rashi would have it). Accordingly Rashbam emphasizes, in contradistinction to Rashi, that the verse is describing bread that was both baked by weight and eaten by weight.

See also the following comment and note 18.

[18]Just as in his previous two comments to the verse, Rashbam explains that this phrase, too, is simply a description of another result of the famine. Because there are famine conditions, people will eat and will not be satisfied. This interpretation again is opposed to that of Rashi who says that the text is enumerating here a further problem, beyond the problem of the famine. See the following note.

It is also possible to explain that that bread, even when eaten in large quantities, will not satisfy or satiate the one who eats it, because there will be a curse on it.[19]

26:28 וְיִסַּרְתִּי I WILL DISCIPLINE YOU: From the root י-ס-ר, the same root as that of ייסר, in the phrase (Deut. 8:5), "just as a man disciplines (ייסר) his son." it is appropriate to say [in the *piel* perfect] וְיִסַּרְתִּי [as it says here,] or וְיִסְּרוּ, as in the phrase (Deut. 21 : 18), "they disciplined (וְיִסְּרוּ) him." Just as from the root י-ש-ב, it is appropriate to say [in the *piel* perfect] וְיִשְּׁבוּ, as in the phrase in Ezekiel (25:4) "They will set up (וְיִשְּׁבוּ) their encampments among you."[20]

26:30 על פגרי גלוליכם [I WILL DESTROY YOUR CULT PLACES . . . AND I WILL HEAP YOUR LIFELESS BODIES] UPON THE LIFELESS BODIES OF YOUR FETISHES: For you will be killed in the houses of your cult places, as it says in Jeremiah (7:32), "[A time is coming when men shall no longer speak of Topheth or the Valley of Ben-hinnom,] but of the Valley of Slaughter; and they shall bury in Topheth until no room is left."[21]

26:32 ושממו עליה אויביכם SO THAT YOUR ENEMIES WILL BE APPALLED BY IT: when they come to settle there. So it is written (Jer. 19:8), "Everyone who passes by it will be appalled (ישום) and will hiss over all its wounds."[22]

---

[19]Here Rashbam appears to retreat from the general thrust of his comment to this verse. He suggests that this last phrase, "though you eat, you shall not be satisfied," may be interpreted the same way that Rashi interprets it—as an additional problem beyond that of the agricultural devastation. Rashbam's comment is clearly dependent on Rashi's, even using some of the same wording about there being a "מארה—curse" on the bread.

Perhaps Rashbam really disagrees with Rashi about all the other phrases in this verse but thought that Rashi might be right about this last one. More likely, as I suggested above in note 3 to 21:1, the phrase "it is also possible to explain" is the sign of a copyist's interpolation of a more orthodox explanation into Rashbam's commentary.

[20]Rashbam's grammatical explanation is unobjectionable and clear. It is, in fact, so straightforward that it is hard to understand why the explanation is here at all.

Rashbam's comment would make more sense if it were written in a commentary on Ezekiel. The word וְיִשְּׁבוּ in Ezekiel is the only example in the Bible of a *piel* form from the root י-ש-ב. Perhaps Rashbam is using the unremarkable form, וְיִסַּרְתִּי, here, as an excuse to explain the unusual form וְיִשְּׁבוּ in Ezekiel.

[21]Rashbam's explanation opposes that of Rashi, who (following Sifra) explains the idea of the people dying and falling on their idols in this midrashic way: when the people were dying of starvation, they would pull their idols out of their pockets to pray to them and would fall dead upon their idols. Rashbam's explanation is much simpler. Like Rashbam, see iE.

[22]Rashbam opposes the very common midrashic interpretation (originating in Sifra; see also Rashi, iE and Nahm.) that the phrase ושממו עליה אויביכם means that the land will remain

26:35 כל ימי השמה תשבת THROUGHOUT THE TIME THAT IT IS DESOLATE IT SHALL OBSERVE THE REST [THAT IT DID NOT OBSERVE IN YOUR SABBATH YEARS]: For, as the rabbis explained,[23] the Babylonian exile lasted for seventy years as a *quid pro quo* for the [seventy sabbatical] years [during the First Temple period] in which the land was supposed to have rested but did not.[24]

The word תִּשְׁבֹּת is vocalized with a *ḥolam*[25] [because it appears] at [a pausal cantillation sign, an] *'etnaḥta'*. If it were not at an *'etnaḥta'*, it would be vocalized with a *pataḥ* vowel, as in the phrase (vs. 34), "then the land shall rest (תִּשְׁבַּת)." Similarly verbs like וַיָּמָת or וַיָּנָס all take on a *ḥolam* vowel at an *'etnaḥta'*, and become וַיָּמֹת (e.g. Gen. 9:29) or וַיָּנֹס, as in the phrase (Ps. 114:3), "The sea saw and fled (וַיָּנֹס)."[26]

---

cursed to the extent that the enemies of Israel who settle there will not be able to make it grow. Despite all their efforts, the land will remain desolate (שממה).

Rashbam, on the other hand, says that the reference here is to the enemies who have just arrived at the land (not those who try for years to make it bloom). The first reaction of anyone who sees the land is ושממו, a feeling of being appalled. Our verse then is similar to the description of the shocked reactions of the "foreigners who came from distant lands" in Deut. 29:21f. To prove his explanation Rashbam cites a verse in Jeremiah where a verb from the same root as here (ש-מ-מ) is used, and where it is clear that the verb is describing the reaction of a gentile passer-by, not the fate of an unsuccessful gentile settler.

Like Rashbam, see Hizq.

[23]The explanation may be found in Sifra here, and in Sanh. 39a. As Rashi and Rosin both point out, this is also the simple meaning of the biblical text in II Chr. 36:21.

[24]So also Rashi (at much greater length) and most Jewish exegetes. See also Rashbam's commentary to vs. 46 below.

[25]Rashbam (here and in other passages) refers to a *ḥolam* vowel as a מלא פום. See e.g. his commentary to Gen. 26:35 and see also Rashi's commentary to Ex. 23:27.

[26]Rashbam's point about words like וינס or וימת and the vowel change they undergo at a pause is clear and well taken. See e.g. G.-K. 29p: "All forms of imperfect consecutives, whose final syllable, when not in pause, loses the tone and is pronounced with a short vowel, take, when in pause, the tone on the ultima with a tone-long vowel." Cf. iE, *Shiṭṭah 'aḥeret* to Gen. 9:29, where he writes that whoever says that the reason why the word וימת there has a מלאפום vowel (= *ḥolam*) is because it appears at a pausal cantillation sign (as Rashbam writes explicitly here) is wrong. From the continuation of iE's comment there it appears that the object of his criticism is someone other than Rashbam.

Rashbam's comparison of the וַיָּנֹס/וַיָּנָס alternation with the תִּשְׁבַּת/תִּשְׁבֹּת alternation is not compelling. The imperfect *qal* has two patterns—*yiqtol* and *yiqtal*. The alternation between them is, to the best of my understanding, not a function of stress. See G.-K. 47h-i.

Aside from the aforementioned difficulty, Rashbam also is comparing a *pataḥ/ḥolam* alternation (תִּשְׁבַּת /תִּשְׁבֹּת) with a *qameṣ/ḥolam* alternation (וַיָּנֹס/וַיָּנָס). On Rashbam's use of the word *pataḥ*, see his commentary to Ex. 22:19, and note 49 there.

26:36 מרך [I WILL CAST] A FAINTNESS INTO THEIR HEARTS: The word מֹּרֶךְ is not from [the root *r-k-k*, the same root as the word רך in the phrase] (Deut. 20:8) "soft-hearted (רך הלבב)" or [the word הרך in the phrase] (Job 23:16) "God has made me faint-hearted (הרך)." The letter *mem* in the word מֹּרֶךְ must be part of the root, because the stress is on the *mem*.[27] [It follows the pattern of many segolate nouns,] like אֹהֶל (tent), or [אֹכֶל in the phrase] (Deut. 2:28) "food (אֹכֶל) for money," or [עֹנֶג in the phrase] (Is. 58:13) "If you call the Sabbath a delight (עֹנֶג)."

There is no other example [of the root *m-r-k* in the Bible. Another example of this verb may be found] only in the Talmud, in tractate *Sheḥiṭat ḥullin*,[28] in the chapter *'Elu ṭerefot* [where we find the form]: נתמרך.[29]

26:39 ימקו SHALL BE HEARTSICK: [The word יִמַּקּוּ is] from [the root *n-m-q*, the same root as נָמַקּוּ in the phrase (Ps. 38:6),] "נָמַקּוּ חבורותי—my wounds fester." So also from the root *n-s-'* [one says] יִסְעוּ and [in, the pausal form,] יִסָּעוּ.[30]

---

[27]In other words, the stress is penultimate.

Rashbam's grammatical point is based on the reasonable principle that stress in Hebrew is generally not found on a prefix or some other preformative element of a noun.

[28]The name that Rashbam and many other medieval rabbis use for the tractate that today is commonly called *Ḥullin*.

[29]Hul. 45b. The word נתמרך there is generally understood to mean to become soft, or crushed or liquefied.

Rashbam's comment is directed against Rashi who claims that the root of מרך is *r-k-k* and that the *mem* is a preformative added to the root (in Rashi's language: יסוד נופל הוא) to make this noun. Rashi compares this *mem* to the *mem* of such words as מועד (from the root *y-'-d*) or מוקש (from the root *y-q-sh*). Rashbam then argues that in those examples there is no stress on the preformative element. If the stress in מרך is on the first syllable, Rashbam argues, the *mem* must be one of the letters of the root.

Although Rashbam's arguments are reasonable, most scholars, ancient and modern, connect the word מרך to the root *r-k-k*. See e.g. iE, BDB and NJPSC. The dispute actually predates Rashi and Rashbam. Ḥayyuj argues that the root could not be *r-k-k* while ibn Janaḥ says that it is. See the latter's *Sefer ha-shorashim*, s.v. רך and his *Riqmah*, ed. by M. Wilensky, p. 87. See also Ḥayyuj's *Sefer po'ole ha-kefel*, s.v. רכך, where Ḥayyuj writes that the root of מרך could not be רכך. Ḥayyuj's translator, Moshe Jiqatila, argues at length against Ḥayyuj's position. In part he says that Ḥayyuj is inconsistent, as Ḥayyuj believed that the root of the noun מֶכֶס was כסס (despite the fact that the stress is on the first syllable, the one with the letter *mem*), but opposed seeing מרך as being from the root רכך. It is noteworthy that Rashbam in his commentary to Ex. 12:4 argues, in a consistent manner, that the *mem* in the word מֶכֶס is part of the root. See notes 21 and 32 there.

Wessely here agrees with Rashbam. See also the discussion in Krinski's *Qarne 'or*, here, note 20.

[30]For יִסְעוּ, see e.g. Ex. 40:36; for יִסָּעוּ, see e.g. Num. 2:9.

Apparently Rashbam is offering the dubious explanation that the root of נמקו is *n-m-q*. The root is universally seen as being *m-q-q*. See Rosin's comment in RSBM, p. 137, note 7.

26:42 חכרתי THEN I WILL REMEMBER [MY COVENANT]: If (vs. 41) "their heart humbles itself."[31]

26:43 והארץ תעזב מהם THE LAND SHALL BE FORSAKEN OF THEM [MAKING UP FOR ITS SABBATH YEARS BY BEING DESOLATE]: [to compensate for] the number of sabbatical years that were not observed. Then, their sin will be expiated and forgiven. And then (vs. 45), "I WILL REMEMBER . . . ."[32]

וְתִרֶץ MAKING UP: The word וְתִרֶץ is from the root *r-ṣ-h,* just as וַיִּבֶן ("he built" e.g. Gen. 2:22) is from the root *b-n-h.*[33]

יען וביען במשפטי מאסו ואת חקותי געלה נפשם.[34]

---

[31]See note 32.

[32]Rashbam is reacting to the ostensibly redundant doubling of the phrase "I will remember." This chapter of chastisements has a double ending. God promises twice, both in vs. 42 and in vs. 45, to remember the covenant with the ancients. In between there appears a further description of the desolate land.

Rashbam offers a well-grounded explanation of the text. God will remember His people and cease to punish them for one of two reasons. Either, as described in vs. 42, because they repented (in vs. 41). And if they did not repent, then (vs. 45) God will remember His people once the Jews have served all the years of their sentence (vs. 43). Contrast Rashbam's explanation with that of Hoffmann, who argues that vss. 43–45 qualify and restrict the promise of vs. 42. God will remember His people, but only after the full sentence for their sin has been served. Like Rashbam, see Nahm. ad vs. 41 ("I will bring them into the land of their enemies, either until their obdurate heart will humble itself, or until they do [full] expiation for their sin through a lengthy exile") and JBS ad vs. 43. Rashbam's idea—that the Jews' redemption will come either quickly, through repentance, or more slowly, after they have been punished for the appropriate amount of time—may be compared to the rabbinic explanation of the phrase in Isaiah 60:22, "I, the LORD, will bring it speedily in its due time." See e.g. Song Rabba 8 and Rashi's commentary to Is., *ad loc.*

Rashbam's explanation is premised on understanding the words in vs. 41, או אז יכנע, as meaning "*perhaps* then their heart will humble itself," not (like NJPS) as "then at last shall their obdurate heart humble itself." Rashi offers two explanations of the word או; Rashbam agrees with the first explanation, but not with the second. (Rashi, though, does not address the question of why there are two verses that describe God's remembering.)

The idea that the years of punishment are equal to the years of non-observance of the sabbatical laws is the simple meaning of vs. 35. See Rashbam's comment there and his comment to vs. 46.

[33]Rashbam often comments on this grammatical form: *vav*-consecutive imperfects of final-*heh* verbs. See e.g. commentary to Ex. 4:26 and to Gen. 1:22.

[34]Rosin writes that in the ms. of Rashbam's commentary that he used, these eight Hebrew words from the verse (translated by NJPS as "For the abundant reason that they rejected My rules and spurned My laws") appear without any commentary on them. Rosin, following the suggestion of Heidenheim, suggests adding a commentary to these words that would have

26:45 ברית ראשונים [I WILL REMEMBER IN THEIR FAVOR] THE COVENANT WITH THE ANCIENTS: for the sake of whom I FREED THEM [= the later generations, FROM THE LAND OF EGYPT].[35]

26:46 בהר סיני ביד משה [THESE ARE THE LAWS ESTABLISHED] THROUGH MOSES ON MOUNT SINAI: [This unit of text, chapters 25 and 26, concludes with a reference to Mount Sinai,] just as the unit about the sabbatical year began with the words (25:1) "The LORD spoke to Moses on Mount Sinai."[36]

[Chapters 25 and 26 should be seen as one unit of text;] the "chastisements" [of 26:14–43] at the end [of the unit] are for [failure to observe] the laws of the sabbatical. So it is written (26:35), "Throughout the time that it is desolate

---

Rashbam interpreting the verse the same way that his older contemporary, Joseph Qara, did. (See *Peleṭat soferim*, p. 20). If we follow Rosin's suggestion, Rashbam is commenting on the doubled form here, "יען וביען—because and because"; Rosin's proposed emended text of Rashbam's comment would read: "יען במשפטי מאסו וביען את חקותי געלה נפשם—because they rejected My rules and because they spurned My laws."

I am more attracted to the explanation suggested by Ashkenazi in *Qeren Shemuel* here. If we bracket Rashbam's grammatical comment on the form ותרץ, the rest of his commentary on vss. 42–45 can be read as expressing one idea with two parts: if the Jews repent, the exile will finish more quickly, and if they do not repent, the exile will last longer. Rashbam's comment on vss. 42–45 (without the grammatical aside about ותרץ) would read as follows:

> THEN I WILL REMEMBER [MY COVENANT]: [And redeem them quickly, if (vs. 41) "their heart humbles itself." [Alternatively] THE LAND SHALL BE FORSAKEN OF THEM [MAKING UP FOR ITS SABBATH YEARS BY BEING DESOLATE]: [For a long time, to compensate for] the number of sabbatical years that were not observed. Then their sin will be expiated and forgiven. And then (vs. 45), "I WILL REMEMBER . . .." [This alternative, a much longer exile, would happen] FOR THE ABUNDANT REASON THAT THEY REJECTED MY RULES AND SPURNED MY LAWS.

[35]The simplest translation of the verse is: "I will remember in their favor the covenant with the ancients (ראשונים) whom I freed from the land of Egypt." This translation requires understanding that the "ancients" are, as NJPSC writes, "the Israelites . . . who left Egypt." iE, who also agrees with this understanding, writes that the covenant referred to in the verse is the covenant at Sinai.

Rashbam rejects that simple understanding, perhaps because he does not like the idea that the generation that left Egypt would be referred to as "the ancients." Instead he offers a complicated syntactical reading that allows him to say that the "ancients" referred to here are the forefathers, Abraham, Isaac and Jacob, and the covenant referred to is the same one mentioned in verse 42. Wessely argues against Rashbam.

Rashi's comment on the verse is short and difficult to understand ("ברית ראשונים של שבטים—'the covenant with the ancients': with the tribes"). Whatever that comment might mean, Wessely argues reasonably that Rashbam and Rashi do not agree about what our verse means.

[36]Another example of Rashbam's sensitivity to the fact that a unit of text may open and close with similar phrases may be found in his commentary to Deut. 8:20.

it shall observe the rest [that it did not observe in your sabbath years]." And all of the commandments of the Torah portion *Behar Sinai* (25:1–26:2) are concerned with the laws of the sabbatical year and the Jubilee, and [the related issues of] setting slaves free and returning land [to its original owners in the Jubilee]. That is why the chastisements for transgressions of the sabbatical laws were delivered here "at Mount Sinai" [just as the laws about the sabbatical were delivered "at Mount Sinai" (25:1); the laws and the chastisements were delivered] all at once.[37]

27:2 כי יפלא ANYONE WHO EXPLICITLY VOWS: The word יפלא means to separate.[38] It is related to the idea of making something explicit. A person who vows has to make explicit the matter about which he is vowing and how much he is vowing.[39]

27:3 ערכך: The two letters *kaf* [in that word] are a doubling. Just as from the word אודם (redness) one says אדמומית and from the word לבן (white) one says לבנונית.[40]

---

[37]Rashbam points out that chapters 25 and 26 are one congruent unit of text that is bracketed, in the first and last verses of the unit, by verses that say that this unit was delivered at Mount Sinai. Above in note 1 to 25:1, I pointed out that Rashbam's approach opposes that of Rashi who learns from 25:1 that *all* the laws of the Torah originated at Mount Sinai. Rashi goes one step further in his commentary to our verse. Not only do all the laws of the written Torah originate at Sinai (as he says ad 25:1); the word והתורות in our verse teaches us that both "Torahs," the Written *and* the Oral Torah, originate at Mount Sinai.

Rashbam's comment here should be seen as a continuation of his argument there. Some laws of the Torah were given at Sinai; others were given later, when the Jews were wandering in the wilderness. Our verse does not expand but rather limits the amount of Sinaitic material; it teaches that a unit of text that originated at Mount Sinai has now concluded.

[38]Rashbam often comments on verbs that he sees as implying the idea of "separation." See his comments to Gen. 31:9 and to Ex. 8:18 and 8:19. Ad Ex. 8:18 Rashbam says that the Hebrew root *p-l-h* refers to the idea of separation; here he adds that the perhaps related root *p-l-'* also does. See similarly NJPSC here: "The verb *hipli'*, with a final *alef*, is a variant of the verb *palah*, with a final *heh*, a verb whose meaning is clearly known: 'to set apart'."

[39]Rashi's comment here is very short (יפליא: יפריש בפיו) and it is difficult to tell what he is saying. (Should the word יפריש in his comment be understood as meaning "set aside" or "explain" or are both ideas intended?) Accordingly it is hard to say whether Rashbam is agreeing with, disagreeing with, or explaining Rashi's comment.

In any case, Rashbam is saying that just as forms of the verb *p-r-sh* can mean "to separate" or "to explain," so also forms of the verb *p-l-'*.

[40]In his comment here, Rashi writes that he does not know the reason for the doubling of the *kaf* in the word ערכך. While Rashbam does not really explain why the doubling occurs, he notes other instances of doubling of a root letter in biblical Hebrew. Wessely here criticizes

27:9 כל אשר יתן ממנו לה׳ ANY SUCH THAT MAY BE GIVEN TO THE LORD SHALL: if it was consecrated without any express condition, BE considered HOLY as a sacrifice. It shall not be [simply] assigned to the Temple treasury.[41]

27:11 ואם כל בהמה IF ANY ANIMAL: that is holy, because it was consecrated as a sacrifice, then became "טמאה—IMPURE," i.e. blemished, THEN THE ANIMAL SHALL BE PRESENTED BEFORE THE PRIEST. [After the priest assesses it,] he [= the person who consecrated it] shall bring an[other] animal of similar value as a sacrifice [in its stead].[42]

Rashbam and argues that the proofs Rashbam cites are not legitimately comparable to the form ערכך.

[41]Following standard *halakhah*, there are two possible ways of interpreting what a person means when he or she consecrates an item. It could be that the item itself is to be used as a sacrifice in the Temple (or the Tabernacle). It could also mean that ownership of the item has been ceded to the Temple treasury, which will use the item as it sees fit. If an animal were consecrated in the latter manner, it would, theoretically, be possible for the animal to be redeemed from the Temple treasury and then again be used for secular purposes by the one who redeemed it

Rashbam interprets our verse as saying that any item that could, potentially, be used as a sacrifice, and that was consecrated without further explanation of the wishes of the person consecrating it, shall be considered to have been consecrated as a sacrifice, not as a donation to the Temple treasury. (Cf. Rashbam's comment to 22:23 above and note 21 there.)

As Wessely points out, this position is not entirely in consonance with the accepted halakhic position. Maimonides rules (*'Arakhin va-ḥaramin* 5:7) that an animal consecrated without further explanation of the wishes of the person consecrating it is not to be considered a sacrifice but is considered property of the Temple treasury. However, such an animal may be redeemed only by someone who will then use that animal for a sacrifice. Rashbam's sweeping language here, "ולא לבדק הבית—it shall not be assigned to the Temple treasury," is not in consonance with any talmudic opinion on the issue.

Rashbam's explanation opposes that of Rashi who (following Sifra) explains the verse in a more midrashic manner, as referring to a person who consecrated only part of an animal (e.g. one of the animal's limbs). See Luzzatto's comment here that, following the *peshaṭ*, our verse could not be referring to the consecration of a limb of an animal.

[42]Here Rashbam departs sharply from the simple meaning of the text and offers the standard *midrash halakhah* reading of our verse. Tem. 32b-33a explains that our verse, that appears to be discussing an impure animal ("בהמה טמאה") that was consecrated, could not be doing so, since there is another verse about impure animals that were consecrated (vs. 27, below, following the rabbinic explanation; see Rashbam's commentary and notes 50 and 51 there). So also Rashi here. Wessely writes at length trying to provide reasons why the verse could not be read in its simple sense. On this occasion it is Nahm. who advocates the simple *peshaṭ* reading of the text. See his commentary to vs. 27 where he discusses our verse.

27:20–21 ואם מכר [IF HE (= the owner) DOES NOT REDEEM THE FIELD] AND IF HE: the treasurer,[43] SOLD[44] [THE FIELD] TO ANOTHER PERSON, then the [original] owner is no longer allowed to redeem the field. When the Jubilee year arrives, the field becomes the property of the priests, i.e. it is divided up among the priests of the "watch"[45] [which happens to be on duty at the moment when the Jubilee year begins].[46]

תהיה אחוזתו HIS HOLDING: i.e. the holding of the person who consecrated the field, SHALL BECOME [THE PRIEST'S property].[47]

27:24 לאשר קנהו מאתו [IN THE JUBILEE YEAR THE LAND SHALL REVERT] TO HIM FROM WHOM IT WAS BOUGHT: Because the person who purchased the field [and then later consecrated it] was unable to consecrate it [since he did not really own the field; the] only [part that he really owned and

---

[43]So also Rashi, verbatim, following Sifra. Again Rashbam is offering the standard halakhic understanding of the verse, even if it is far from the plain meaning of the text. See Luzzatto who attempts to find an explanation that is better grounded in the text, and who criticizes the traditional understanding as not reflecting the *peshaṭ* ("where did the verse mention a 'treasurer'?")

[44]The reference is to the type of "sale" of fields envisioned in chapter 25: the purchaser receives title to the field in the form of a long-term lease until the next Jubilee year. Normally ownership of the field would then revert to the original owner when the sabbatical began. But since this original owner ceded his rights when he consecrated the field, ownership reverts to the priests of the Temple when the Jubilee year begins.

[45]Duties in the Temple were allocated among the priests in a rotation. The priests were divided into twenty-four משמרות, or "watches"; each watch served for a week at a time. See e.g. I Chron. 24, and Maimonides, *Kele ha-miqdash* 4:3.

[46]So also Rashi and most Jewish exegetes, following Sifra and BT Arakh. 25b.

[47]Rashbam offers a novel syntactical reading of the last three words of the verse: לכהן תהיה אחוזתו. Generally the word, "אחוזתו—*his* holding," is seen as meaning *the priest's* holding. The final words of the verse are then translated as "it becomes the priest's holding" (NJPS). Rashbam understands the word, "אחוזתו—*his* holding," as meaning the holding of the person who consecrated the field. This would yield a translation "his holding shall then revert to the priest."

Grammatical analysis supports Rashbam. According to the NJPS understanding, the subject of the feminine verb תהיה would have to be the masculine noun, השדה, mentioned at the beginning of the verse. According to Rashbam, the feminine noun, אחוזתו, is the subject of the feminine verb.

See Wessely who follows Rashbam. See also Hoffmann who recognizes the grammatical argument in favor of Rashbam's reading and still prefers the other syntactical understanding.

that he was able to consecrate was] the produce that the field would yield [from the time of consecration] until the Jubilee year.[48]

27:26 לא יקדיש איש אותו [A FIRSTLING OF ANIMALS] CANNOT BE CONSECRATED BY ANYONE: for the sake of some other sacrifice, since it is already considered consecrated as a "firstling sacrifice."[49]

27:27 ואם בבהמה הטמאה IF IT IS AN ANIMAL THAT IS IMPURE: literally, and a person consecrated it, in such a case the animal is to be ransomed, as I explained.[50] The rabbis said that this verse refers to an animal that is literally impure; the rules [for the ransoming of such animals] are the same whether the animal is whole or blemished.[51]

27:29 יחרם מן האדם ANY HUMAN BEING WHO HAS BEEN PROSCRIBED [SHALL NOT BE RANSOMED]: A person who was found guilty of a capital crime by a Jewish court may not be ransomed.[52]

---

[48]Rashbam's analysis conforms to the general halakhic understanding of the verse. See e.g. Arakh. 26a and Rashi's long comment to vs. 22. JBS and Hizq. closely follow the language of Rashbam's comment.

[49]Again Rashbam follows the standard halakhic explanation (e.g. Bekh. 15b) and reworks only slightly the language of Rashi's comment to this verse. Cf. Nahm. who says that the verse means that it is not necessary to consecrate a firstling since its birth automatically consecrates it.

[50]Above in his commentary to vs. 11 Rashbam says that the reference *there* to an "impure animal—בהמה טמאה," is not to be understood literally. There the word טמאה means an animal that has a blemish. Accordingly he tells us that in this verse the word טמאה is to be understood literally. See note 42 there.

Again Rashbam's explanation conforms to the standard halakhic position (e.g. Tem. 32b) which is significantly different from the *peshaṭ*. On the *peshaṭ* level, our verse is a continuation of the previous verse, which dealt with issues of firstling animals. The "בהמה טמאה—impure animal" of our verse would then be a reference to a firstling from some non-kosher species.

Rashi in his commentary to this verse explains why such a position is unacceptable to the halakhist. Rashbam tacitly accepts those arguments and says that our verse is about an impure animal, which some person consecrated to the Temple, and not about an impure animal whose holiness is a result of its firstling status.

[51]In other words, as opposed to the rules of the ransoming of consecrated animals that are from kosher species—where different rules apply depending on whether the animal is whole or blemished—the rules for the ransoming of animals from non-kosher species are the same whether the animal is blemished or not.

[52]Our verse is very difficult on the *peshaṭ* level. Traditional Jewish exegetes must avoid at all costs explaining the word "יחרם—to be proscribed," in this verse, the same way that they understand it in the previous verse. There חרם is generally understood by halakhists as some item concerning which the owner said, "This item is *ḥerem* for the priests," or some other

27:30 מעשר הארץ TITHES FROM THE LAND: Second tithes [ARE THE LORD'S].[53]

similar formulation. (See Rashi vs. 28.) Naturally halakhists do *not* want to say that our verse—"any human being who is *ḥerem* must die and may not be ransomed"—refers to a human being who became *ḥerem* through another human being's declaration. See e.g. Luzzatto's impassioned argument against critics who suggest that this verse implies that a man might have the right to declare his sons or his slaves *ḥerem* and they would then be killed. ("This contradicts the ways of the Torah of Moses . . .. Blessed be He who separated us from those who err and gave us His Torah, a Torah of truth, whose ways are ways of pleasantness and all of whose paths are peace.")

Rashi offers a much more complicated halakhic understanding of our verse, which says that the monetary "valuation" (ערך) of a person who has been sentenced to die is zero. Rashi's explanation is one of the two explanations of this phrase found in Arakh. 6b. Rashbam's explanation here is the other one, the explanation offered by Rabbi Yishmael, the son of Rabbi Yoḥanan b. Beroqa. Variations on Rashbam's understanding of the verse may be found in JBS, Wessely and Luzzatto.

[53]Rashbam's explanation is the standard halakhic explanation, found in Rashi here (following Sifra). The logic of the comment is that first tithe would not be called "the LORD's" since it is given to the Levites and they are allowed to use it for whatever purpose they wish. Second tithe food which must be eaten "before the LORD" (Deut. 14:23) is then more appropriately called "the LORD's."

COMMENTARY ON NUMBERS
פירוש לספר במדבר

במדבר (Numbers 1:1–4:20)

1:1 במדבר סיני באוהל מועד באחד לחודש השני [THE LORD SPOKE TO MOSES] IN THE WILDERNESS OF SINAI IN THE TENT OF MEETING ON THE FIRST DAY OF THE SECOND MONTH [IN THE SECOND YEAR FOLLOWING THE EXODUS]: Whenever divine communication occurred in the first year [following the exodus], before the erection of the Tabernacle, the text writes that it took place "at Mount Sinai."[1] But after the Tabernacle was erected—on the first day of the [first] month in the second year after the Exodus[2]—the text does not say [that divine communication occurred] "at Mount Sinai," but rather "in the wilderness of Sinai in the Tent of Meeting."

This [distinction—between the implications of the two phrases "at Mount Sinai" and "in the wilderness of Sinai"—] is proven below. It is written (3:1) "These are the descendants of Aaron and Moses on the day that the LORD spoke to Moses *at Mount Sinai*." The time when Aaron had four sons was *before* the Tabernacle was erected,[3] [as the next verse there (3:2) says,] "These were the names of Aaron's sons: Nadab, the first-born, and Abihu, Eleazer and Ithamar." But later, once the Tabernacle was erected in the second year, he had only two sons. For later, once the Tabernacle was erected in the second year,[4] it is written that (3:4) "Nadab and Abihu died before the LORD *in the wilderness of Sinai*."

---

[1]E.g. Lev. 25:1.

[2]See Exodus 40:17.

[3]Here Rashbam is taking issue with Rashi's comment to 3:1, s.v. ביום דבר. There Rashi argues that the ostensibly unnecessary phrase, "on the day that the LORD spoke to Moses at Mount Sinai," was written because it was as a result of that day, the day that Moses learned the Torah, that Moses taught Aaron's children, who thereby should, according to Rashbam, be considered in some sense Moses' children. Rashbam explains more simply that "on the day that the LORD spoke to Moses at Mount Sinai" is emphasized because on that day Aaron had four children, although later he did not. See also commentary to 3:1, and note 20 there, and commentary to 10:33, and note 21 there.

[4]It appears that the text of Rashbam contains a dittography: the phrase לסוף בשנה שניה שהוקם המשכן appears twice, for no apparent reason, within two lines with tiny variations. I translated without emending; the suspected dittography does not change the meaning, but merely makes the style inelegant.

At Mount Sinai[5] they [= Aaron's children] numbered four. Later there were only two, because Nadab and Abihu died on the very day that the Tabernacle was erected.[6]

1:2 שאו את ראש כל עדת TAKE A CENSUS OF THE WHOLE COMMUNITY: [A census of males above the age of twenty should be conducted on the first day of the second month] since they now have to go to the land of Israel and [males] over the age of twenty are suitable to make up the fighting force.[7]

For, as it is written in the Torah portion *Beha'alotekha* (Num. 10:11), on the twentieth day of the second month "the cloud lifted [from the Tabernacle]." [Immediately] after that, it is written (10:29) [that Moses told the people,] "We are setting out for the place [which the LORD has said . . .," in order to capture that land.] That is why God ordered a census at the beginning of that same month.[8]

---

[5]Here I have based my translation on my conjectural emendation of the text of Rashbam's commentary. The text reads: במדבר סיני היו ארבעה. I think that the text would read much more smoothly as: בהר סיני היו ארבעה.

A possible translation of the unemended text would read: "[At the beginning of their stay] in the wilderness of Sinai, they [= Aaron's children] numbered four. Later there were only two, because Nadab and Abihu died on the very day that the Tabernacle was erected."

[6]Rashbam reiterates the point that he made in his commentary to Ex. 12:1, to Lev. 25:1 and to 26:46—that in the first year following the Exodus God spoke to Moses at Mount Sinai, and, in subsequent years, God spoke to him at the Tent of Meeting, which the text calls "in the wilderness of Sinai." Rashbam implies that not all the laws given to Moses originate with the theophany at Mount Sinai. Many come later. In this, he opposes the contention of Rashi (and of many rabbis) that all the laws originate at Mount Sinai. See e.g. Rashi ad Lev. 25:1 and 26:46. See also Rashbam's commentary to 1:19 below, and note 10 there.

Like Rashbam, see also iE, Nahm. (here and ad 3:1) and Hizq.

[7]The phrase לצאת בצבא המלחמה is an allusion to I Chr. 7:11, translated here following NJPS there.

[8]Rashbam's comment is directed against Rashi, who says (in his opening comment to the book of Numbers, following Tanh. *Bemidbar* 4 and Tanh. B *Shemot* 2) that the census is taking place at this point because the Tabernacle was just built and God wants to count the Jews people before making His Presence descend on them. Rashi offers this explanation as part of a didactic point—that God loves the Jewish people so much that he constantly counts them. Rashbam says that the count here has a much more practical purpose—to determine the number of soldiers available for the military campaign that was supposed to begin now (and that was later delayed because of the sin of the spies).

Like Rashbam, see JBS and Hizq. See also Nahm. ad vs. 45 who offers three reasons for the census here, the third of which is the same as Rashbam's. See also a similar dispute between Rashi and Rashbam concerning the count of the "sons of Israel" at the beginning of the book of Exodus.

1:19 ויפקדם במדבר סיני HE COUNTED THEM IN THE WILDERNESS OF SINAI: It is written here that this first count[9] took place "in the wilderness of Sinai," because concerning the second count, [the one recorded] in [the Torah portion] *Pinḥas*, it is written (26:1–3), "[The LORD said . . . 'Take a census . . ..'] So Moses and Eleazar [the priest] gave instructions to them *on the steppes of Moab*."[10]

1:47 והלוים למטה אבותם לא התפקדו בתוכם THE LEVITES, HOWEVER, BY THEIR ANCESTRAL TRIBE, WERE NOT RECORDED: As the text continues to explain: God [had] said to Moses (vs. 49), "But do not count the Levites."[11] Then the text explains the reason [why the Levites are not counted]: the Levites are not part of the fighting forces. [Moses was rather commanded (vs. 50),] "Put the Levites in charge of the Tabernacle of the Pact."[12]

---

[9]Rashbam's claim here that this is the "first count" seems to be at odds with what he writes ad Ex. 30:12, namely that Moses counted the Israelites at the time that he collected donations from them for the Tabernacle. (As Rashbam himself points out ad vs. 1, the count of this chapter occurs *after* the Tabernacle was erected.) Perhaps Rashbam's reference here to the "first count" means the first of the two counts in the book of Numbers.

See however JBS who writes that this was the first time that a census took place and that the count here and the count from the end of the book of Exodus are one and the same event (וזהו זה מנין שבכאן). See also JBS to Ex. 38:28 and Rashi to Ex. 30:15.

[10]Since the beginning of the chapter (v. 1) already recorded the fact that the events were taking place "in the wilderness of Sinai," the repetition of the phrase in our verse requires explanation. Rashbam explains that the phrase is repeated as it serves two purposes. In vs. 1, "in the wilderness of Sinai," means "not at Mount Sinai." See commentary there. Here he explains that "in the wilderness of Sinai" in our verse means, "not on the steppes of Moab."

[11]Rashbam is explaining the troubling order of vss. 47–50. Vs. 47 tells us that the Levites were not counted, but it is only in vs. 49 that Moses is given *the instruction* not to count the Levites. A number of midrashic sources suggest that Moses acted on his own initiative in not counting the Levites, and that only later did God support that decision. See e.g. NR 1:11. Later, Nahm. also explains the verse in that way.

Rashbam explains more simply that the text makes a general statement—that the Levites were not counted—and then provides the details of how that came about. It was because God *had spoken* to Moses saying . . .. See NJPS which translates the phrase וידבר ה' in the same way that Rashbam explained it: "for the LORD *had* spoken . . .." So also iE here.

Rashbam often explains biblical narratives in this manner. See e.g. his commentary to Gen. 18:1 or Exodus 2:15.

[12]Rashbam now opposes Rashi's two explanations (in his commentary to vs. 49) of why the Levites were not counted. Rashi suggests that (1) either the "royal legion" of Levites deserves to be counted separately, or (2) that God protected the Levites from the count which was later to determine who would be barred from entering the Land of Israel.

Rashbam explains more simply and contextually: the count (as he had explained ad vs. 2) is for military purposes. When vs. 50 tells us that the Levites have different, non-military duties, it is effectively explaining why God said (in vs. 49) that the Levites should not be part of the count. So also iE.

2:2 באותות [THE ISRAELITES SHALL CAMP IN THEIR THREE-TRIBE UNITS,[13]] UNDER THE SIGN [OF THEIR ANCESTRAL HOUSES]: On the flag of each three-tribe unit there was an insignia: for example on Judah's [flag] there was a lion and on Joseph's there was an ox.[14]

מנגד: means far away.[15]

2:17 בתוך המחנות [THEN THE TENT OF MEETING SHALL MOVE] BETWEEN THE DIVISIONS: First two three-tribe units would travel, followed by the Tabernacle and the Levites. Then the last two three-tribe units would travel.[16]

כאשר יחנו כן יסעו AS THEY CAMP, SO SHALL THEY MARCH [EACH IN POSITION]: The position of the four three-tribe units around the Tabernacle

---

[13]The word דגל in Rashbam's commentary should be understood in the same way that it is used in vss. 3, 10, 18 and 25, where it refers to a unit of three tribes.

[14]Rashbam opposes both explanations offered in Rashi of what the אות, or sign was on each flag. Rashi suggests that the phrase איש על דגלו באותות either means that each flag had its own color, or that each tribe would travel through the wilderness in a formation that Jacob had foretold. Rashbam, on the other hand, says that the word אותות means that there was an appropriate emblem on each flag. For Judah a lion is fitting, following Gen. 49:9. An ox is the symbol of Joseph, following Deut. 33:17. The reference to Joseph's flag is presumably a reference to the unit consisting of Ephraim, Menasseh and Benjamin (vss. 18–24). In Rashbam's commentary to 7:13, he refers to this grouping as "the three-tribe unit of Ephraim."

Both the explanation that the אות refers to the color of the flag (Rashi) and the explanation that it refers to the emblem on the flag (Rashbam) may be found in NR 2:7. Like Rashbam, see also LT and iE.

[15]Rashbam offers a *peshat*-like reworking of Rashi's comment. Rashi, too, says that the word מנגד means far away, but Rashi also tries to define the term more exactly; (following Tanh. *Bemidbar* 9) he writes a precise description of just how far away from the Tabernacle the tribes stood. Rashbam simply says that מנגד means far away. Ad Deut. 32:52 Rashi interprets מנגד the same way that Rashbam does here.

Most moderns would agree that מנגד means far away. See e.g. NJPSC here.

[16]Rashbam's language and Rashi's language here seem very similar but there is a subtle difference between them. Rashi suggests that the two three-tribe units mentioned before vs. 17, the one led by Judah and the one led by Reuben, would always travel first, followed by the Levites and then followed by the other two three-tribe units. Note Rashi's language: ונסע אוהל מועד: לאחר שני דגלים *הללו*. Rashi's position seems to be the simple meaning of the phrases at the end of vss. 9 and 16: "These shall march first" and "these shall march second."

Rashbam, on the other hand, says that the order was always: two unspecified three-tribe units would travel first, followed by the Levites and then followed by the last two three-tribe units. As Rashbam's comment continues, the logic of his position and the importance of the distinction become clearer. See note 17.

when they are marching should be in every way like their position around the Tabernacle [when they are encamped].[17]

The order in which the three-tribe units were enumerated is the order used when turning to the right: east, then south, then west, then north.[18]

3:1 ואלה תולדות אהרן ומשה THESE ARE THE DESCENDANTS OF AARON AND MOSES: First the text counted the descendants of the Israelites (in chapter 2), then the descendants of the priests (in 3:2–4) and then the descendants of the Levites (in 3:14–39).

---

[17]In other words, the three-tribe unit that was to the east when the Tabernacle was encamped would always be to the east when they were traveling. So also for all the other three-tribe units.

See P.T. Eruv. 5:1 (cited by Rashi ad 10:25, below) where there are two opinions about the pattern of the placement of the tribes when they were traveling. One opinion says that they traveled in formation, with Judah always in the east and Reuben always in the south and so forth. Our verse "as they camp so shall they march," is the prooftext used to establish that opinion. Rashbam clearly follows that understanding, not the opinion in P.T. there that the tribes traveled in a straight line. (Cf. e.g. Luzzatto ad 10:14, who is certain that the tribes must have traveled in a straight line, not in formation.)

Now the logic of Rashbam's previous comment becomes clear. The "Judah" unit, he argues, always has to be to the east (vs. 3) and the "Reuben" unit always has to be the south (vs. 10). Then Rashi's claim—that those two units were always the ones that traveled first—does not make sense (unless the tribes always traveled in a south-easterly direction). Rashbam says instead that, depending on the direction that the Israelites were to move, whatever two three-tribe units ought to be traveling first, did so. This was done in such a way that the unit to the east always stayed in the east, and so forth.

Rashbam does not tell us how he would explain the phrases "These shall march first" and "These shall march second" at the end of vss. 9 and 16. Nor does he comment on 10:5–6 or 10:11–25 where again the simplest explanation is that there is a set order of travel for the tribes, rather than a set position for each tribe in the camp as it moved. One can only speculate that he understands these phrases as the instructions for the first time that the camps moved. In future travels, the order would be determined by the direction traveled.

[18]Rashbam continues to dispute Rashi's claim that the order in which the three-tribe units were listed is the order in which they always traveled. Rashbam says that the order is simply the natural order that one would expect from a biblical text: the narrator begins by facing east and then turns clockwise ("to the right").

The Talmud often suggests that the "normal" order in the Temple is that one begins by facing east and then moves to the right. See e.g. *Yoma'* 15b.

The dispute between Rashbam and Rashi here (does the order of listing reflect the required order of travel?) follows the same pattern as the dispute between them in explaining the phrase (Gen. 28:12), "angels of God were going up and coming down on it." Rashi feels that the order—first going up and then coming down—must say something about the order in which the events occurred. Rashbam, on the other hand, says that standard style dictates writing "going up" before "coming down."

[Despite the fact that the text now says that it is counting "the descendants of Aaron and Moses," that is just a general introductory statement.] Now [i.e. in vss. 2–4, only] Aaron's descendants are listed. Moses' descendants will be listed below among the Levites, in the verse (27), "To Kohath belonged the clan of the Amramites." This [phrase, "clan of the Amramites,"] means Moses and his sons[19] who are considered part of the tribe of the Levites. [The phrase "clan of the Amramites" in verse 27, in the middle of this enumeration of Levites, could only be a reference to Moses' children,] since Amram had only two sons, Moses and Aaron, and (I Chr. 23:13–14) "Aaron was set apart [he and his sons] to be consecrated . . . but as for Moses . . . his sons were named after the tribe of Levi."[20]

ביום דבר AT THE TIME THAT THE LORD SPOKE WITH MOSES AT MOUNT SINAI: In other words, before the Tabernacle was erected Aaron had four sons. But, once the Tabernacle was erected in the wilderness of Sinai in the second year, only Eleazar and Ithamar remained [alive], as I explained above in the beginning of the Torah portion. For whenever the text says [that God spoke to Moses] "at Mount Sinai" it means before the Tabernacle was erected. Once the Tent of Meeting was built, the text always says [that God spoke to Moses] "in the wilderness of Sinai."[21]

3:9 נתונים נתונים THEY ARE FORMALLY ASSIGNED: [The repetition of the word נתונים] is [simply] a doubling, just like נתון תתן in the phrase (Num. 27:7)

---

[19]I have translated based on my conjectural emendation: זהו משה ובניו, instead of Rosin's text: זהו משה ואהרן ובניו. My proposed reading is supported by the continuation of the comment where Rashbam clearly distinguishes between Aaron's children, who are listed under the category of priests, and Moses' children, who alone are considered among the Levites. See also Rashbam's comment to vs. 27: "משפחת העמרמי' משה ובניו"—'the clan of the Amramites' [means] Moses and his sons."

Without the emendation, Rashbam's comment as it stands משה ואהרן ובניו goes against the rules of grammar. At a minimum, one would have to emend בניו to בניהם.

[20]Rashbam is opposing Rashi's midrashic explanation of the phrase "the descendants of Aaron and Moses." Rashi, like Rashbam, addresses the difficulty that the phrase here in vs. 1 is followed immediately by an enumeration of Aaron's children alone. Rashi's midrashic solution (following Sanh. 19b) is that the children of Aaron are legitimately considered also to be Moses' children, since Moses was the one who taught them Torah.

Rashbam suggests more simply that the phrase "children of Moses and Aaron" in vs. 1 does not refer only to the children enumerated in vss. 2–4 but also to the "clan of the Amramites" referred to later in the chapter. So also Nahm., JBS and *Be'ur*.

[21]Rashbam repeats here the point that he made in his commentary to 1:1. As I noted there (in note 3), that point serves to oppose the explanation that Rashi offered here in his commentary, s.v. ביום דבר.

"you should give (נתון תתן) them a hereditary holding."[22] In the vernacular one would say *donnant donnez.*[23]

3:10 ואת אהרן ואת בניו תפקד YOU SHOULD תפקד AARON AND HIS SONS: You should appoint him to be in charge of them [i.e. of the Levites]. [The verb is to be understood] like [the verb ויפקד in the phrase (Gen. 40:4),] "The chief steward appointed (ויפקד) Joseph."[24]

3:15 כל זכר מבן חדש ומעלה תפקדם COUNT EVERY MALE FROM THE AGE OF ONE MONTH UP: Since the Levites were to replace the first-borns and the first-borns are liable for redemption once they are one month old. For that reason, [all] the Levites [even] from the age of one month up were to be counted.[25]

---

[22]Rashbam simply notes the doubling of the word נתונים in the verse. He does so, as is usual with him, without attributing any particular significance to the stylistic phenomenon that he identifies. כפל, according to Rashbam, is common biblical style. While he most often uses the word in discussions of poetic parallelism (e.g. in his commentary to Gen. 18:23 or 49:3), he does sometimes use it when commenting on other examples of doubling in the Bible where, to his mind, the doubling does not change the meaning of the text. See e.g. commentary to Ex. 14:11 or Lev. 27:3 and see RSBM, p. 143.

Rashbam's explanation may be seen as opposing the midrashic explanations of the doubling found in various sources—for example LT's claim that the Levites are "assigned to the Tabernacle and assigned to the Temple."

[23]Rashbam is saying that the same phenomenon of doubling may occur in Old French.

It is hard to know precisely what Old French phrase he is reproducing here. See RSBM, pp. 95–96.

[24] *Hifil* forms of the root *p-q-d* usually mean "to appoint." *Qal* forms generally mean "to count" (e.g. 1:49) or "to remember" (e.g. Gen. 21:1).

Both here and ad Gen. 40:4 Rashbam interprets a *qal* form of *p-q-d* as meaning "to appoint." In note 1 to the commentary there, I pointed out that Rashbam's interpretation there opposes Rashi's understanding of that verse. Here Rashi and Rashbam concur. It may be that the reason that Rashbam comments on our verse, despite the fact that he is just reiterating what Rashi writes, is that he wishes to suggest that just as Rashi is willing to interpret the *qal* of *p-q-d* here as meaning "to appoint," so Rashi ought to be willing to interpret the verb the same way in Genesis.

[25]Rashbam is explaining why the Levites were counted from the age of one month, if the rest of the people were counted only from age twenty years and above (1:3). His explanation is opposed to Rashi who says that the Levites receive special treatment because their holiness really is from birth. They are counted from age one month and above, because only at age one month do we assume that a baby will survive. Like Rashbam, see Hizq. So also Levine.

3:27 ולקהת משפחת העמרמי TO KOHATH BELONGED THE CLAN OF THE AMRAMITES: I.e. Moses and his sons. Now the text is explaining what was written above (3:1) "These are the descendants of Aaron and Moses."[26]

3:49 הפדיום THE REDEMPTION: The *mem* of הפדיום is extra, just like the *mem* of the words ריקם ("empty-handed"; Gen. 31:42) and הכנם ("lice"; Ex. 8:13) and שלשום ("the day before yesterday"; Gen. 31:2).[27]

The three hundred Levites beyond the 22,000 enumerated (in vs. 39) were first-borns and [they were not tallied in that grand total since] a first-born [Levite] cannot serve as ransom for a first-born [Israelite]. That is what our rabbis explained.[28]

4:5 אהרן ובניו בנסוע המחנה AARON AND HIS SONS SHALL COME [TO TAKE DOWN THE CURTAIN] WHEN THE DIVISION MARCHES: I.e. [Aaron and his sons will come to dismantle the holy items] after the first two three-tribe units march, before the Levites and the Tabernacle march.[29]

---

[26]Rashbam is reiterating what he wrote in his commentary to 3:1. (See commentary and note 20 there.) There he noted the difficulty that the text announces that it will list "the descendants of Aaron and Moses" but, in the verses that follow immediately, only Aaron's descendants are listed. He explains, there and here, that verse 27 actually fulfils the promise of mentioning the names of Moses' descendants.

[27]In other words, in each of those words the *mem* is not the sign of a plural ending. See my Exodus volume, p. 78, note 8, for more sources and further discussion.

It is possible that Rashbam comments specifically here because he wishes to highlight the difference between the word הַפְּדְיוֹם here, where the *mem* is *not* the sign of a plural form, and the very similar word הַפְּדֻיִם in vs. 51, where the *mem is* the sign of a plural form.

[28]In Bekh. 5a. So also Rashi ad vs. 39.

Rashbam's free-standing comment here—unattached to any quotation from the biblical text—centers around vs. 39. When one adds up the three figures (in vss. 22, 28 and 34) for the numbers of Levites in the three branches of the family, the total is 22,300. But vs. 39 tells us that the total of Levites is 22,000. The solution proposed here by the Talmud and adopted by Rashbam and Rashi is that there is a reason why the three hundred were excluded from the grand total. The purpose of counting up the Levites is so that they can "redeem" the first-born Israelites who should have been serving in "levitical" roles. To that end it was necessary to know how many non-first-born Levites there were. That is why the total presented in verse 39 is not the sum of the three sub-totals. The sub-totals include first-born Levites; the total excludes them. So also iE, who considers and dismisses the possibility that the number in vs. 39 should be seen as an approximation.

[29]See commentary to 2:17.

Rashbam explains that when the text says that Aaron shall do these things "when the division (המחנה) marches," what it means is after two three-tribe units have begun their march. (Those units are sometimes referred to as מחנות; see 2:17 and Rashbam's commentary.) Rashbam is opposing Rashi who says that "when the division marches" means when the

4:10 ונתנו על המוט AND THEY SHALL PLACE IT ON THE BAR (המוט): Rabbi Joseph Qara used to interpret[30] this verse incorrectly. [His mistaken understanding was] based on the fact that the verse [reads "על המוט—*on* the bar," and] does not read ["במוט—*with* the bar,"] as in the phrase (13:23) "Two of them carried it with a bar (במוט)." He wanted to argue that "*on* the bar" means that the entire bar[31] was under the vessels [that were being carried].

I answered him that the מוטות [of this verse] were [bars that were] attached at the side of the vessels.[32] [This was done the same way] as was customary for any item that was being carried. Bars (מוטות) were put in rings [that were attached to] the sides of the items being carried, as it is written in the portion of the Torah that describes the Tabernacle.[33]

However, [the distinction between "*on* the bar" and "*with* a bar" may be explained as follows:] when the verb "to place" (ונתנו) is used, it is appropriate that it be followed by [the preposition,] "*on*." When the verb "to carry" is used, it is followed by [the preposition] "*with*," as in the verse (13:23) "they carried it with a rod (במוט)," or (Ex. 25:28) "they carried the table with them (בם)."

And similarly [one sees that when using the noun "shoulder (כתף)," the prepositions ב and על do not imply two different ways of carrying an item. One

---

divine signal—the rising cloud (9:17f.)—is given that a march is about to begin. Still, one see from Rashi's commentary to 10:17 that he and Rashbam understand the order of the travel of the Israelite camps similarly. They differ only concerning the exegesis of "when the division marches" in this verse. See also Nahm. ad 10:17.

[30]Rashbam's phrase, "*used to* interpret incorrectly (טועה היה בזה)" might imply that Qara changed his mind after Rashbam explained to him his "error." I think it more likely that the use of the past tense here implies that Qara was no longer alive when Rashbam wrote his Bible commentary. On this point I take issue with Avraham Grossman, *Ḥakhme Ṣorfat*, p. 28, who argues that Rashbam's Torah commentary was written while Qara was still alive. (In a personal communication to me, Professor Grossman wrote that his estimation is that Qara died around the year 1130 and that Rashbam's commentary was written in the 1120s.) I have argued in my "The Connection Between Rabbi Samuel ben Meir's Torah Commentary and Midrash Sekhel Ṭov" that Rashbam's Torah commentary was written at least twenty years later, well after Qara's death. On this point see further note 24 on 31:49–50 below.

[31]It is possible that Joseph Qara does not understand מוט as meaning a pole or a bar, but rather, as NJPS would have it, "a carrying tray." See note 32.

[32]The most crucial difference between the approach of Rashbam and the explanation that he heard from and reports in the name of Qara is that Rashbam feels that the מוט of our verse is a bar, and is synonymous with the בדים described in Exodus for carrying the Tabernacle's vessels. We have no further knowledge of what Qara said (since his Torah commentary is not extant, except in fragments), other than what Rashbam writes here. Accordingly it is difficult to know how he interpreted מוט, except to say that he thought that the מוט went under the item being carried. See also iE and Luzzatto here, who do not think that מוטות and בדים are synonymous.

[33]See e.g. Ex. 25:14 and 25:27.

verse reads] (Is. 46:7) "they must support it on their shoulders (על כתף)" and [another verse reads] (II Chron. 35:3) "you shall no longer carry it on your shoulders (בכתף)." [The preposition ב in that last phrase could not imply that the item is carried *alongside of* the shoulder; it is rather the instrumental use of the letter ב,[34]] i.e. by means of (ב) this, some item is carried.[35]

4:15 ואחרי כן יבואו בני קהת ONLY THEN SHALL THE KOHATHITES COME: After you cover up the Ark and the other vessels [of the Tabernacle].[36]

4:20 כבלע את הקודש [THEY SHALL NOT GO INSIDE TO SEE] WHEN THE TABERNACLE IS DISMANTLED: When they dismantle the Tabernacle, [God][37] is revealed and if they see [Him] they would die. So we see also concerning the men of Beth-shemesh, [that God put some of them to death] (I Sam. 6:19), "because they looked into the Ark of the LORD."

[The root *b-l-'* appears, as it does here, in other biblical passages in the *piel,*] e.g. the phrase (Lam. 2:2) "The Lord has swallowed up (בִּלַּע) or (Is. 3:12)

---

[34]See G.-K. 119o.

[35]In other words, Rashbam believes that the variation in the use of prepositions על and ב in verses that describe carrying should not be seen as reflecting different ways of carrying. Surely the only way of using one's shoulder to carry an item is to put the item *on* one's shoulder; the preposition ב could not be seen as implying anything else.

My translation above is based on Rosin's speculative emendation of the text he found in the manuscript (to על כתף יסבלוהו). In the now lost ms., Rashbam's second to the last proof text is (according to Ashkenazi's report) "בכתף יסבלוהו" (or, as Rosin reports "בכסף [!] יסבלוהו," although I am inclined to think that the word בכסף is simply a typo for בכתף). In any case, the text requires emendation since neither of those phrases appears in the Bible.

Ashkenazi emended in a more cavalier manner to "בכתף ישאו"; that reading yields a much simpler text. If we follow Ashkenazi's emendation, then we find that Rashbam concludes his comment by citing four verses, all of which prove the same point—that the preposition ב is the one that is used after the verb "to carry (נשא)."

[36]Rashbam explains here that the Kohathites should absent themselves until after the Ark and the other vessels are covered up. This is the simple meaning of the text. In his next comment to vs. 20 he will explain that it is not actually the act of covering the vessels that is the source of the Torah's concern. See notes 37 and 39.

[37]On Rashbam's attitude to seeing God, see also his commentary to Gen. 48:8 (and note 3 there), to Ex. 24:11 (and note 17 there), to Ex. 33:18 (and note 20 there), to Lev. 16:2 (and note 4 there) and to Num. 15:39 (and note 94 there).

In my notes to Exodus (p. 301), I take issue with Rosin's reading and understanding of this text. Rosin claims that the comment means, "When they dismantle the Tabernacle, [the Tabernacle] is revealed and if they see [it] they would die." I feel that the context of the comments here and in Leviticus and in Exodus demonstrate that Rashbam is referring to the problem of seeing God or at least seeing God's Presence hovering over the Ark. As I argued in Exodus, Rosin is much more concerned about the anthropomorphism problem ("How can one see God?") than Rashbam was.

"They have confused (בִּלְּעוּ) the course of your paths," or (Lam. 2:5) "laid waste (בִּלַּע) all her citadels," or (Is. 9:15) "they that are led have been confused (מְבֻלָּעִים)."[38]

So it is written above that when [the priests] started to dismantle the Tabernacle, the Kohathites would move far away. As it is written (vs. 5f.) "At the breaking of camp, Aaron and his sons shall go in and take down the screening curtain . . .," and [shall do] all [the things that are listed in] the continuation of that portion [of the text] up to (vs. 15a), "When Aaron and his sons have finished covering [the sacred objects . . .], only then shall the Kohathites come."[39]

---

[38]Rashbam does not explain what the difficult verb *b-l-'* really means in our verse. He merely points out that, although that verb generally appears in the *qal*, we should not be surprised that it appears here in the *piel*. He cites four other examples of *b-l-'* in the *piel* (or, in the *pual*, *piel*'s partner).

[39]While, as mentioned in the previous note, it is not certain how Rashbam understood the word כבלע, it is clear that he is disagreeing with Rashi's explanation of it. Rashi explains that the verse means that the Kohathites should not watch while the vessels of the Tabernacle are being *covered up*. He explains that the verb *b-l-'* has its standard meaning of "swallowing up" here; when vessels are covered up the Torah describes them as being "swallowed." Rashbam disagrees. It is the *dismantling* of the Tabernacle that the Kohathites are not allowed to see. For that reason, Rashbam explains that the Kohathites are to absent themselves from the vicinity during all the events that are described in vss. 5–15.

iE first offers the explanation found here in Rashbam. Then he offers Rashi's interpretation and writes that that is the better explanation. Nahm., on the other hand, praises iE's first explanation (= Rashbam's). Like Rashbam, see NR 5:9. Some moderns agree with Rashbam. See e.g. NJPS and NJPSC. Many other moderns say that כבלע means "even for a moment." See e.g. Luzzatto, Noth and Levine.

נשא (Numbers 4:21–7:89)

4:22 גם הם [TAKE A CENSUS OF THE GERSHONITES] ALSO: [The text says "also,"] because above it says (4:2) "Take a census of the Kohathites."[1]

5:1–4: Now that the order of the tribes and the way in which they would encamp has been established and set, it is necessary to write about the removal of all the impure people from the camp.[2]

5:6 חטאות האדם [WHEN A MAN OR A WOMAN COMMITS ANY] WRONG TOWARD A FELLOW: [This refers to the type of wrongs] that are recorded in the section at the end of the Torah portion *Va-yiqra'*, which describes the *'asham gezelot* offering (Lev. 5:21): "dealing deceitfully with a fellow in the matter of a deposit [or a pledge] . . .."[3] [The procedures of that sacrifice] are repeated here in order to add [the rule about what happens] (vs. 8) if one steals from a convert who has no kinsman and that convert dies [before restitution was made].[4]

---

[1]So also Rashi and iE. See Mizraḥi's super-commentary on Rashi where he argues, I think unconvincingly, that Rashi and iE are actually disputing whether the *count* of the Kohathites had already taken place, or whether there had simply been a previous *command* to count them, and that command had not yet been fulfilled. If Mizraḥi is right, then Rashbam might be seen as siding with Rashi. "Also count the Gershonites," according to Rashbam, does not mean "as you have already counted the Kohathites"; it means "as I have already *asked you* to count the Kohathites."

[2]Minor variations on Rashbam's reasonable explanation of the juxtaposition of 5:1–4 with the previous chapters may be found in iE and Nahm. See similarly NJPSC.

[3]See commentary to Leviticus there.

[4]Rashbam's explanation is essentially the same as Rashi's (following Sifre 2 and 4, and LT). See also Rashbam's commentary to 18:9 below. The interpretation of verse 8 here as referring to a convert is based on the Sifre's argument that the only Jew who does not have a redeeming kinsman is a convert who had no children after converting.

This is one of only two times in Rashbam's commentary that he explicitly addresses the question of why a law is repeated. (See also commentary to Lev. 24:2.) On this passage, but not on Lev. 24:2, Rashbam's answer conforms to the old rabbinic principle of the school of Rabbi Yishmael that a portion of the Torah is repeated only when some new rule is included in the repeated version (כל פרשה שנאמרה ונשנית, לא נשנית אלא לדבר שנתחדש בה; see e.g. BQ 64b). Rashi here in fact finds *two* new rules in the Numbers version that one could not have learned from the Leviticus version. Rashbam makes due with one, as do the older rabbinic sources.

5:7 והשיב את אשמו HE SHALL MAKE RESTITUTION OF THE *'asham*: I.e. of the principal.[5]

5:8 מלבד איל IN ADDITION TO THE RAM: that is called an *'asham* offering in Leviticus (5:25). [But here, the word *'asham* has a different meaning;] האשם המושב, "THE *'ASHAM* THAT IS BEING RETURNED" [means] "the principal."[6] [That is] returned to the priests.[7]

5:9 וכל תרומה ANY *TERUMAH:* [The text says *any terumah* because the reference is to more than one kind:] either the *terumat reshit*[8]—the *terumah* that an Israelite gives [to the priest], or the *terumah* which the Levite gives [to the priest from the *ma'aser* that he, the Levite, receives].[9] Both of these are described below in the Torah portion *Shelaḥ lekha.*[10]

---

[5]So also Rashi (following BQ 110a).

Rashbam in this comment and in his comment to the next verse is dealing with the problem of the word *'asham,* which is used in two different ways in the two related texts—Leviticus 5 and Numbers 5. In Leviticus, *'asham* is the name of the sacrifice offered; here in Numbers, *'asham* means "principal." Note that in Rashbam's own language (commentary ad vs. 6 and vs. 8), the word *'asham* is the name of a type of sacrifice. In that he follows standard halakhic usage. See e.g. Zev. 5:5.

[6]See note 15.

Rashbam's commentary is at odds with that of Rashi and the earlier halakhic sources on one point. The Talmud in BQ (*ibid.*) reads into the phrase "האשם המושב—the *'asham* that is being returned" the meaning "the principal plus one 'fifth'." (The "fifth" is reinterpreted in halakhic literature to be a quarter; see e.g. BM 54a and Sifra on Lev. 5:24). The Talmud reads the phrase in our verse mechanistically: "אשם - זה קרן, המושב - זה חומש—the word *'asham* means 'principal'; the word 'returned' means 'a fifth'." Rashi in his commentary here interprets the phrase האשם המושב as a unit, meaning "principal plus one fifth." Rashbam, in a more *peshaṭ*-like manner, says that האשם המושב just means "the principal."

[7]The verse describes the problem of the person who wishes to make restitution to someone who died without heirs. The text says that restitution is made "to God." Rashbam explains, in the standard halakhic manner, that that means "to the priests." See similarly Rashi (following BQ 109b).

[8] The phrase תרומה ראשית is a phrase found in rabbinic literature for the "standard" *terumah* ("heave-offering") given to the priest. (See e.g. Sifre, paragraph 165.) It is called "ראשית—first," because of the phrase in Deut. 18:4, "ראשית דגנך—[You shall give him (= the priest)] the first fruits of the new grain," a phrase which is interpreted in rabbinic literature as referring to *terumah.* See e.g. Sifre and Rashi there. See also Num. 18:12 and Rashi there, and Rashbam's commentary to 15:20 below.

[9]That which the rabbis call תרומת מעשר and the Bible calls מעשר מן המעשר. See Num. 18:26.

[10]As noted by Rosin, there is an error here. The rules of *terumah* are not found in the Torah portion *Shelaḥ lekha* but in the Torah portion *Qoraḥ* (Num. 18).

Rashbam's interpretation is opposed to that of Rashi who says (following the opinion of Rabbi Yishmael in the Sifre, here) that the *terumah* referred to in this verse is *not* what we

5:10 איש אשר יתן לכהן WHEN A PERSON GIVES SOMETHING TO A PRIEST [IT BECOMES HIS]: When a person gives a donation of something that is fitting to become a priest's property[11]—e.g. if it is a *ḥerem*[12]—then לו יהיה IT SHALL BE HIS [= the priest's], i.e. he should give it to a priest.[13] But there is a *midrash 'aggadah* that interprets our verse as meaning: איש אשר יתן לכהן A PERSON WHO [piously] GIVES TO THE PRIEST everything that he should give [to the priest], then לו יהיה i.e. *he* [= the person who gives] will have much money.[14] They offered that interpretation since the words of the phrase are superfluous.[15]

5:12 כי תשטה IF [A MAN'S WIFE] HAS DEVIATED: תשטה means to go astray,[16] as in the phrase (Prov. 4:15), "Turn away (שטה) from it," or (Hos. 5:2)

---

standardly call *terumah* but a reference to *bikkurim*—the "first fruits" that are given to the priest according to the procedure described in Deut. 26:1–11. Rashbam explains more simply that *terumah* means *terumah*. See Nahm. here who also takes issue with Rashi's explanation. Nahm. notes that the explanation that *terumah* really does mean *terumah* here (= Rashbam) is both the simple meaning of the text and is also a common explanation in classical rabbinic literature. For that reason Rashi's decision to interpret according to Rabbi Yishmael's idiosyncratic midrash is puzzling.

[11]See commentary to Lev. 27:9, and note 41 there. There Rashbam explains that an animal that is worthy to be used as a sacrifice would, if donated, be considered a sacrifice, and not the property of the priest or of the Temple treasury. Accordingly Rashbam specifies here that our text is describing the type of donation that could appropriately be assigned to a priest.

[12]See Num. 18:14, "Any *ḥerem* in Israel shall be yours (= the priest's)."

[13]Rashbam's explanation is not clearly worded. But it appears that he is explaining our verse as saying that if a person donates some item, e.g. by declaring it *ḥerem,* and explains his intentions no further, then, if the item is not worthy to be a sacrifice, it should be given to a priest.

[14]So Rashi, following Ber. 63a.

[15]This type of comment is rare in Rashbam; he explains the way in which superfluous wording in the verse serves as the basis for a midrashic explanation. Rashbam does clearly say more than once that that is his understanding of the *theory* of midrashic exegesis. See e.g. his commentary to Gen. 1:1 and Gen. 37:2. But rarely does he provide an example of the way that midrash works, as he does here. (For other examples, see his commentary below to 11:35 [and notes 67 and 71 there] and to 34:6 [and notes 18–20 there]. See also his commentary to Gen. 37:35.)

It is possible that Rashbam does this here because he wishes to emphasize that Rashi's explanation is *not* the *peshaṭ*. The verse, according to Rashbam, has a simple explanation. The antecedent of the word "לו—his" is, if one uses *peshaṭ* analysis, "the priest." The explanation offered by the Talmud and Rashi—according to which the antecedent of "his" is "the person who gives the item,"—is not based on *peshaṭ* analysis but, like most *midrashim*, on the superfluity of the phrase.

[16]Rashbam's explanation is the simple meaning of the Hebrew text. He is opposing a homiletical explanation found in Tanh. *Naso'* 5, according to which the word תשטה is related to

"Those who stray (שטים) went so low as to murder."[17]

5:13 ועד אין בה THERE IS NO WITNESS AGAINST HER: [testifying] that she committed adultery.[18]

והיא לא נתפשה BUT SHE WAS NOT 'GRABBED': i.e. she was not forced. For if she was forced to be alone with a man, she is exempt [from the ceremony].[19]

---

the word "foolishness" (שטות); the midrash is saying that people would not commit adultery unless a spirit of foolishness overpowered them.

It is difficult to say what the relationship is between Rashbam's comment on this verse and Rashi's, because it is difficult to know what Rashi's comment on this verse really was. If we accept the version that is in our printed texts, then Rashbam is agreeing with the second explanation offered by Rashi, the one Rashi labels the plain meaning of Scripture (פשוטו של מקרא), and disagreeing with Rashi's first explanation (= Tanh.). But in a number of editions and manuscripts, Rashi does not offer any midrashic explanation of the verse. If that is the correct version of Rashi's commentary, then Rashi and Rashbam are in total agreement.

[17]The verse in Hosea is extremely difficult and it is impossible to know how Rashbam understands it. But he does see the word שטים there as meaning "to stray." See also Qimḥi in Hos., who uses our verse in Numbers to explain the much more difficult verse there.

[18]Rashbam follows the halakhic line in his explanation. Standard halakhic exegesis says no man may subject his wife to the *soṭah* ceremony if he has no witnesses to testify against her. He must have witnesses that she was alone in a closed room with another man. When the text says that "there is no witness against her," it means only that there is no witness who can testify to the act of adultery itself. So also Rashi, following Sot. 2b.

[19]Rashbam's explanation is very similar to that of Rashi but not identical. Both of them are in general agreement with the older halakhic literature. See e.g. Yev. 56b. Both of them say that the word נתפשה means נאנסה, which is the common word used in the old halakhic sources. But the word נאנסה appears to mean two different things in Rashi and in Rashbam.

In the halakhic understanding, the *soṭah* ceremony is done only if: (1) the husband warned his wife beforehand not to be alone with a man; (2) there are witnesses that the wife was alone with that man; (3) there are no witnesses about an act of adultery; and (4) the wife denies that an act of adultery has taken place.

In this understanding, which both Rashi and Rashbam accept, when the ceremony is taking place it is not at all an established fact that *any* sexual act has taken place. So Rashi, following the rabbis, has a problem with the phrase והיא לא נתפשה, which he interprets in the usual way as meaning "she was not raped." If we do not even know whether any sexual act has taken place, then how can we add the condition "she was not raped"?

The rabbis, and Rashi, answer that the phrase is not to be seen as yet another precondition for the *soṭah* ceremony. Instead, this phrase indicates which sexual indiscretions would and would not cause a husband and wife to terminate their relationship. When the woman is involved in a consensual adulterous relationship, the marriage is to be terminated; if she was raped, then the marriage is not terminated (except in the case of the wife of a priest).

Rashbam, however, solves the problem of והיא לא נתפשה in a different way. Instead of interpreting it as "she was not raped," he interprets it as "she was not forced to be alone with a man other than her husband." This is what Rashbam means by the phrase הסתירה באונס.

5:17 מים קדושים SACRAL WATER: Water from the laver.[20]

5:21 לאלה ולשבועה AS A CURSE AND AN OATH: A person who makes someone else swear will say: "I am making you swear about this matter in God's Name that if you are lying to me, you will be [cursed] like that certain woman whose thigh sagged and whose belly distended."[21]

5:28 ונזרעה זרע SHE SHALL RETAIN SEED: I.e. she shall become pregnant.[22]

Thus Rashbam can read the verse as dealing with one consistent theme: the pre-conditions for the *soṭah* ceremony. In addition to all the other pre-conditions mentioned (explicitly or through *midrash halakhah*) in these verses—the husband warned the wife beforehand, witnesses say that the wife was alone with a man, and so forth—there is one more condition. Even if it is established that she *had been* alone with another man, if she had been *forced* to be alone with him the ceremony again would not take place.

To the best of my knowledge, Rashbam was the first to offer this explanation. It is later adopted by the *Be'ur*. JBS offers both Rashi and Rashbam's explanations. Many commentators, ancient and modern, understand the word נתפשה in an entirely different manner—simply, "she was not caught in the act." See e.g. iE, Luzzatto and Levine.

[20]The laver (כיור) is described in Ex. 30:18–21.

Rashbam's explanation agrees with Rashi (following Sifre) who gives a homiletical reason why water from the laver was particularly appropriate for the *soṭah* ceremony.

[21]It is not possible to know how Rashbam understands the difficult phrase צבתה בטנה ונפלה ירכה. I have simply translated according to NJPS.

Rashbam's explanation of the phrase לאלה ולשבועה is very similar to that of Rashi, but not identical. Both say that the phrase "as a curse and as an oath" means that the guilty woman will be held up as an example of what happens to an evildoer.

Rashi says, following Sifre 18, that there are two separate thoughts expressed by this phrase, "as a curse and as an oath." A person who wishes to curse someone will say, "May you be like that adulterous woman." That is the meaning of "as a curse (לאלה)." A person who wishes to make someone swear will say, "May the fate of that adulterous woman befall you if you are not swearing truthfully." That is the meaning of "as an oath (לשבועה)," according to Rashi. But Rashbam says that both words express one idea—the curse that has befallen that woman will be used in oaths.

Rashbam's understanding of the verse is somewhat poetic. The verse says that when the suspected adulteress is asked to take an oath, she is threatened that, if she has spoken falsely, a terrible fate will befall her. Part of that terrible fate is that, in the future, in a parallel situation where one person forces another to take an oath, this woman will be cited as an example of what happens to someone who swears falsely.

[22]Rashbam's explanation is close to the opinion of R. Aqiva in Sifre 19, "if she had been barren, she would conceive." Rashbam takes issue with the explanation of Rashi, who follows the opinion of R. Yishmael there. According to R. Yishmael and Rashi, the text is referring to a woman who already has children. It is saying that that such a woman will now have easier pregnancies or more preferred outcomes ("light-complexioned babies instead of dark-complexioned"). Rashbam and R. Aqiva are clearly closer to the simple meaning of the text.

R. Aqiva's formulation, "if she had been barren, she would conceive," actually limits the promise of reward in this verse to barren women. Rashbam says more generally that any

5:31 ונקה האיש מעון THE MAN SHALL BE CLEAR OF GUILT: even though he is the one who brought this calamity upon her, through the warning that he gave her.[23]

[That is one interpretation;] but I think that the verse means that "the man shall be clear of guilt" *because* he did not tolerate his wife's infidelity. If he had held his peace [and continued to have intercourse with his unfaithful wife], then he would *not* be clear of guilt, for it is forbidden for him to do so.[24]

Rather she תשא את עונה, BEARS RESPONSIBILITY FOR HER OWN PUNISHMENT. The disaster befell her because of her infidelity.[25]

---

woman who was unjustly subjected to this ordeal would be rewarded by being granted pregnancy. Like Rashbam, see Luzzatto: "'she shall retain seed' . . . she shall become pregnant just as she became pregnant in the past; the text describes the normal case and most women are *not* barren." See also Andrew of St. Victor here (p. 182), who says simply that the phrase means that she will successfully conceive and give birth.

Many commentators point out that the woman's punishment if guilty, "a sagging thigh and a distended belly," means that she will become infertile. Logically enough, then, the reward that she will get if she is innocent (and was falsely accused) is that she *will* conceive (ונזרעה זרע). See e.g. NJPSC, and see also Josephus, *Antiquities* 3:271.

See also commentary to Lev. 12:2, s.v. אשה כי תזריע, where Rashbam interprets the word תזריע as meaning "to conceive." See note 1 there.

[23]Rashbam's phrase, על ידי קינוי שקינא בה, refers to the halakhic principle that the *soṭah* ceremony takes place only in a case where, before the suspected indiscretion took place, the husband had warned his wife, in front of witnesses, that she should stay away from a certain man. The noun used for that warning is קינוי, and the verb used to describe the husband's action is מקנא. (See e.g. M. Sot. 1:1 and BT Sot. 2a.) The rabbinic understanding of the phrase in vs. 14, וקינא את אשתו, is not "he is wrought up about his wife," but rather "he warned his wife."

[24]Rashbam's explanation in this paragraph is similar to the comment of iE and to the second explanation that Rashi offers to this phrase. See note 25.

[25]M. Katenellenbogen, the author of the notes to Rashbam's commentary in the *Torat ḥayyim* Pentateuch, points out astutely that this last part of Rashbam's comment—his explanation of the phrase "תשא את עונה, she bears responsibility for her own punishment"—is actually a continuation of his first comment to the verse, not a continuation of what appears above in the second paragraph, "But I think that the verse means (ולי נראה) . . ." The first and the third paragraphs of Rashbam's comment to this verse say: the man should feel no responsibility for the calamity that his "warning" ultimately brought upon his wife. That calamity is more appropriately attributed to her infidelity, not to his jealous warning. (See similarly Licht here.)

Based on that insight into the structure of Rashbam's comment here I feel that it is likely that the second paragraph of the comment, the section that begins with the words, "But I think that the verse means (ולי נראה)," represents a later interpolation of an alternate interpretation. It is hard to imagine that Rashbam himself would interrupt the natural flow of ideas between part one and part three of this comment. See similarly note 3 to Lev. 21:1 and note 19 to Lev. 26:26 where I suggest that the phrases, "גם יש לפרש—it is also possible to interpret," and "גם יש לומר—it is also possible to say," may also be signs of interpolations into Rashbam's commentary. See also note 52 below on 7:3, s.v. צב.

6:3 משרת ענבים IN WHICH GRAPES HAVE BEEN STEEPED: Menaḥem explained[26] that the word משרת comes from [the root *sh-r-t*, the same root as in the phrase] (8:26) "he shall serve (ושרת) with his brothers." [According to that explanation,] the *mem* [at the beginning of the word משרת] is like the *mem* at the beginning of the word מרמס ("a trampled thing"; Is. 10:6) or משמר ("custody"; Gen. 40:3) or משמן ("fatness"), in [the phrase] (Is. 17:4) "the fatness (משמן) of his body will become lean."[27]

But [that explanation is incorrect;] words [from the root *sh-r-t* are] connected to the idea of "service" and are used only in the context of human beings serving their masters.

Accordingly I say that the word משרת is from a root with a final weak letter, the root *sh-r-h*.[28] It is like the word מקנת ("purchase") from the root *q-n-h*, as in the phrase (Ex. 12:44), "a monetary purchase (מקנת)."[29]

Even if its explanation[30] may not be found in the Bible, one may find it in talmudic Hebrew, as in the phrase (Naz. 36a) "a Nazirite who soaked (שרה) his bread in wine."[31] And if [one insists on finding an example] in the Bible, one could cite Jeremiah (15:11), "I release you (שריתיך) for a better fate." [The Hebrew word שריתיך in that phrase] was interpreted[32] as meaning the same thing as [the Aramaic word משרא, in the phrase] (Dan. 5:12) "to untie (משרא) knots." In other words, [in the phrase in Jeremiah, God is saying to Jeremiah] "I untie your chains," which is what actually happened [to him].[33] [The vocalization of the

---

[26]See *Maḥberet*, s.v. *sh-r-t*.

[27]In other words, Rashbam is writing that the preformative *mem* makes sense not just according to his own explanation, which follows, in which the root of משרת is seen as *sh-r*-h. Following Menaḥem's explanation it also makes sense to see the *mem* as a preformative element added to the root *sh-r-t*.

[28]Rashbam's explanation of the root of the word would be accepted by all modern grammarians. See e.g. BDB, *sh-r-h* II.

[29]In other words, the final *tav* in משרת is not one of the letters of the root. The root is *sh-r-h*. The final *heh* of the noun משרה becomes a *tav* for the same reason that the final *heh* of the noun מקנה becomes a *tav* in the word מקנת—because it is in the construct state.

[30]The Hebrew here reads *ופרשתו* אם לא נמצא במקרא נמצא בלשון התלמוד. The word ופרשתו is very unusual. Rosin, in RSBM (p. 158) argues that the word simply means explanation (פירוש). He cites Rashi and iE's commentaries to Est. 4:7 as proof.

I would hesitatingly suggest that ופרשתו may be a corruption of the word ודוגמתו or וחבירו. In any case, the meaning of Rashbam's comment is clear.

[31]This example is also cited by Rashi in his commentary here. Still Rashi's explanation of the meaning of the root *sh-r-h* differs somewhat from that of Rashbam. Rashi feels that the word connotes soaking for the sake of coloring an item.

[32]See Rashi there, following Dunash, *Teshuvot*, p. 36.

[33]See Dunash, *ibid.*, who cites Jer. 40:4 and 42:2 as proof that God's words in Jer. 15 were fulfilled. See the criticism of that explanation by Rashbam's brother, Rabbenu (Jacob) Tam, in his comments on Dunash, *ibid.*

word] שְׁרִיתִךָ [is standard; it] is like [the vocalization of the word] זֵרִיתִי in the phrase (Mal. 2:3) "I will throw (זֵרִיתִי) dung upon your faces," which is [from the root *z-r-h*,] like זְרֵה in the phrase (Num. 17:2) "Throw (זְרֵה) far away."[34]

So here also the phrase משרת ענבים means that which was detached and exuded from the grapes, like a person who is detached and untied from the knots of the chains and shackles in which he had been tied up.[35]

6:13 יביא אותו HE SHALL BRING IT: The sacrifice itself, as the text explains further along.[36]

6:21 מלבד אשר תשיג ידו [HE WHO VOWS AN OFFERING TO THE LORD] OF WHAT HE CAN AFFORD BEYOND [HIS NAZIRITE REQUIREMENTS]: If he vowed more sacrifices to God, he should bring them in addition to the obligatory [Nazirite] sacrifices. This phrase should be understood like the phrase (Lev. 23:38) "beyond (מלבד) your gifts and your votive offerings."[37]

6:23–27 כה תברכו את בני ישראל THIS IS HOW YOU SHOULD BLESS THE PEOPLE OF ISRAEL: In other words, [God is saying,] "Do not bless them using your own words, as someone might say 'May it befall so-and-so that . . ..' Rather pray to Me that I should bless them.[38] (As the text explains further, [the

---

[34]The comparison of the verbs *sh-r-h* and *z-r-h* is also taken from Dunash, *ibid.*

[35]Rashbam and Dunash are correct that the root *sh-r-h* can mean to untie, at least in Aramaic and in later Hebrew. Their explanation of the difficult phrase in Jer. 15 is distinctly possible. Rashbam is also correct that the root of משרת here is *sh-r-h*. But most moderns would take issue with his claim that the root *sh-r-h* here means the same thing that it means in Jer. See e.g. BDB who argues that there are two separate roots *sh-r-h* in Hebrew—one meaning "to soak" and the other meaning "to untie."

[36]In vss. 14 and 15.

Rashbam's explanation opposes that of Rashi who explains, following Sifre Num. 32, that the phrase יביא אותו means that the Nazirite should "bring himself" (to the Temple or the Tabernacle). The phrase יביא אותו is difficult. Furthermore, the precise meaning of the wording of Rashbam's comment ("את עיקר קרבנו") is also unclear. Rosin writes (RSBM, p. 158) that Rashbam's phrase means "his entire sacrifice."

[37]The syntax of this verse is very difficult. iE suggests that the phrase מלבד אשר תשיג ידו implies that the Nazirite has an *obligation* to offer additional sacrifices beyond the legislated ones, if he can afford them. Nahm. also offers that explanation as one alternative. Rashbam here agrees with Rashi's reading that the text is simply saying that the wealthy Nazirite who vows extra sacrifices is obligated to fulfil that vow, in addition to the standard obligatory Nazirite sacrifices. So also Andrew of St. Victor (p. 182).

[38]Rashbam's explanation opposes the different attempts of the Sifre here to derive various laws concerning the priestly blessing from the phrase "כה תברכו—this is how you should bless." (Different suggestions in Sifre of what one learns from this phrase include: that priests must stand when blessing the people, that they must stretch out their hands and that the

priest should use the wording], 'May the LORD bless you . . ..') I will hear your voices when you say those words, and then I will bless the Israelites."

That is the meaning of the continuation (vs. 27), ושמו את שמי על בני ישראל: When the priests bless the Israelites in My Name, not in their own name, then ואני אברכם—I will give the Israelites the blessing[39] that the priests prayed for when they said "May the LORD bless you."[40]

6:26 ישא ה' פניו אליך MAY THE LORD LIFT HIS FACE TOWARDS YOU: As it is written (Lev. 26:9) "I will turn to face you [with favor]," which means that He will not hide His face from you.[41]

And as for the verse (Deut. 10:17) [that says that God] "לא ישא פנים—does *not* lift up the face,"[42] [that means] that God does not lift up the face of a person to wipe away all of that person's sins. But God does lift up His *own* face towards a person whom He loves. He will turn to face such a person to show

---

blessing must be in Hebrew.) Rashbam says more simply that כה תברכו means "this is the proper formulation for a blessing." Like Rashbam, see NJPSC "'Thus [shall you bless]' That is when you bless, use this formula, not one of your own devising."

[39]Many commentators note the ambiguity of the phrase "ואני אברכם—I will bless *them*." At least in theory, "*them*" could be a reference either to the Israelites or to the priests. Rashi, iE and Sifre all offer both possibilities. Rashbam says that the context makes it clear that the reference is to the Israelites.

[40]Again Rashbam opposes one explanation found in the Sifre (and cited also by Rashi) according to which one may learn from the phrase ושמו את שמי the law that the priests are supposed to use the tetragrammaton when blessing the people. Rashbam says more simply that this phrase reiterates the idea that Rashbam sees in verse 23, that the blessing must be God's, not the priest's. One explanation found in the Sifre expresses the same idea: "שלא יהיו הכהנים אומרים אנו נברך את ישראל ת"ל ואני אברכם אני אברך את עמי ישראל—The priests should not say that they are the ones who are blessing the Israelites. That is why the verse says 'I shall bless them' i.e. 'I am the one who blesses My people Israel'." Like Rashbam, see also NJPSC: "Hebrew *va-ani* is emphatic, thrusting home the point that not the priests but the Lord is the sole author of the blessing."

[41]Rashbam is suggesting that comparing this blessing to a similar one in Lev. 26 teaches us that the blessing "I will look upon you" is the opposite of the curse of God hiding His face from the Israelites.

[42]Rosin reports that the ms. here reads "אשר לא ישא פני איש," which is not a verse in the Bible. In RSBM (p. 59, note 1), Rosin suggests emending to אשר לא נשא פני שרים, a phrase from Job 34:19 (" he does not lift up the faces of princes"). Later, in his edition of the commentary, Rosin changes his mind and suggests the emendation "אשר לא ישא פנים." I translated according to that second proposed emendation.

Hizq. (whose commentary is so often dependent on Rashbam's) quotes the same non-verse אשר לא ישא פני איש and poses the same question that Rashbam does. Hizq. then offers a slightly different solution to the problem.

grace to him, as it is written (Lev. 26:9), "I will turn to face you . . . and I will multiply you."[43]

7:2 הם העומדים על הפקודים [THE CHIEFTAINS OF ISRAEL,] THE ONES WHO ARE OVER THOSE WHO ARE NUMBERED: I.e. the ones who were "designated by name"[44] (1:17) in [the Torah portion] *Bemidbar Sinai.*[45]

7:3 עגלות WAGONS: [The vocalization of this word is] עֶגְלוֹת because the word is a construct form; [the phrase means] "wagons *of* צב."[46] Just as the word עֲשָׂרָה (ten) becomes [in the construct plural] עֶשְׂרוֹת,[47] so also from the word עֲגָלָה (wagon)—as in the phrase [in this verse] "a wagon (עֲגָלָה) for each two chieftains"—becomes [in the construct plural] עֶגְלוֹת.[48] From the noun עֲנָוָה (meekness)[49] one says [in the construct plural] (Ps. 76:10) "the meek (עַנְוֵי) of

---

[43]As Rosin notes, the question Rashbam poses here is the same one posed in the Talmud in three places (RH 17b, Nid. 70b and Ber. 20b): why does one verse say that God "does not lift up the face" while our verse promises that God will lift up His face? The Talmud offers more than one midrashic answer. Rashbam suggests that the distinction is between God lifting up *His own* face and God lifting up *a person's* face. Lifting up His own face (something that God *will* do) means turning to a loved one in a gracious manner. Lifting up some person's face (something that God *will not* do) means showing favoritism and thus wiping away all of the person's sins.

Aside from solving what the Talmud considers an exegetical problem, perhaps Rashbam is belittling Christian theology, which often claims that God *does* wipe the slate of a sinner clean. Rashbam writes that God does "show grace" to those whom He loves, but He does not wipe away the sins of any sinner.

[44]See Rashbam's commentary to 13:2.

[45]Those listed in Num. 1:5–15. On the phrase, see also commentary to 13:2.

Rashbam's explanation agrees with the end of Rashi's comment to this verse. Rashi also offers a midrashic reading of the beginning of this verse—that the phrase "chieftains of Israel" teaches us that the people named in this verse were the very same "foremen of the Israelites" who were beaten by their Egyptian taskmasters (Ex. 5:14). Rashbam's explanation is more oriented to the *peshaṭ*.

[46]On צב, see Rashbam's next comment and notes 51–53.

[47]The form עֶשְׂרוֹת is not found anywhere in the Bible, but it is without doubt the correct form for the construct plural of עֲשָׂרָה. See e.g. *The Concise Sapphire Dictionary* (1997), p. 851.

[48]Rosin vocalized this last word עֲגָלוֹת. Rashbam would then be saying that the *context* plural form of עֲגָלָה is עֲגָלוֹת. However, in this comment Rashbam is discussing construct plurals, not context plurals. Here he is pointing out that in the plural construct, the vowel under the second letter of the root in such nouns changes to a quiescent *sheva* (and also the vowel under the first letter of the root changes from a *ḥaṭaf* vowel to a full vowel). As such, the form that proves Rashbam's point is עֶגְלוֹת, not עֲגָלוֹת.

[49]The formulation of Rashbam's comment here is somewhat inaccurate. The form עַנְוֵי is *not* derived from the noun עֲנָוָה (meekness), but from the noun עָנָו (a meek person). Rashbam's

the land," and from the noun עֲרָבָה (willow) one says [in the construct plural] (Lev. 23:40) "willows (עַרְבֵי) of the brook."[50]

צב: The word צב [in the phrase "wagons of צב"] should be understood [as a type of beast of burden that might pull a wagon], like the word צבים in the phrase (Is. 66:20), "on צבים or mules." The word [צבים in that verse] should be interpreted according to the context.[51]

To me it seems[52] that the phrase, "wagons of צב," should be understood to mean wagons that are built in such a way that they could be used for travel for military purposes (צבא) or for long journeys.[53]

7:13 וקרבנו AND HIS SACRIFICE: [The reason that this verse says "*and* his sacrifice," even though the sacrifice of each of the other chieftains is introduced

---

argument could be reformulated more accurately as saying that one sees that from the root ʿ-*n*-*v* one may derive nouns both on the pattern of עֲנָוָה and on the pattern of עֲנָוֵי.

[50]Perhaps Rashbam discusses the form עֲגָלוֹת at such length in order to distinguish between the meaning of this word and the meaning of the identical word עֲגָלוֹת meaning "calves." (See e.g. Hos. 10:5.) In other words, his comment could be saying that one should not think that the word עֲגָלוֹת in our verse is derived from the noun עֶגְלָה (calf), despite the fact that, from the vocalization of עֲגָלוֹת makes it look most similar to the noun עֶגְלָה. The contextually more reasonable solution—that עֲגָלוֹת here is derived from the noun עֲגָלָה (wagon)—is, Rashbam argues, in conformity with the rules of grammar.

[51]The word צב here and the word צבים in Isaiah are both difficult, so when Rashbam says here that צב should be understood like צבים and that the verse (one of them?) should be interpreted according to the context, it is hard to know what he means. It appears that he is explaining the verse in the same way that ibn Ezra does—that צב in our verse is a type of beast of burden. He is then opposing the interpretation of Rashi (and of many medieval and modern commentators) that עגלות צב means covered wagons.

A number of other sources (e.g. NR here) compare the two verses, but offer other explanations. See also Menaḥem, *Maḥberet*, s.v. צב, who says that the word צב(ים) in our verse and in the verse in Isaiah has a different meaning than the normal one, but he does not tell us what that meaning is.

See also the commentary of Eliezer of Beaugency to Isaiah, *ad loc.* There, Eliezer cites our verse in Numbers to explain the word in Isaiah. Harris (p. 88) lists that comment of Eliezer's among those that, to his mind, show that Eliezer was a student of Rashbam.

[52]Rashbam is now offering a second explanation of the phrase עגלות צב, introduced by the words, "ונראה בעיני—(lit.) it appears to my eyes." I consider it likely that this explanation has been added by some second hand. See note 25 above on 5:31, where the printed text of the commentary has a second interpretation introduced by the similar phrase, "ולי נראה." Also see note 3 to Lev. 21:1 and note 19 to Lev. 26:26.

[53]As far as I can tell, this is the first time that this precise interpretation of צב appears in a normative Jewish text, although a somewhat similar explanation is found in Song Rabba 6:4: "צב שצבא הלוים עומדים עליהם—the word צב means that the troops (צבא) of the Levites are in charge [of those wagons]." As NJPSC notes, the interpretation of צב as meaning "military" is found also in Symmachus.

by the words "his sacrifice," without the word "*and*," is that this verse] is a continuation of the previous verse. [Verses 12 and 13 should be understood thus:] "The person who sacrificed on the first day was Nahshon . . . *and* his sacrifice was the following."[54]

They [=the chieftains of the tribes] brought their sacrifices in the same order as [the listing of the tribes in the text (2:3–29) about] the four three-tribe units:[55] the three-tribe unit of Judah, followed by the three-tribe unit of Reuben, followed by the three-tribe unit of Ephraim, followed by the three-tribe unit of Dan.[56]

7:84–88 ביום המשח אותו [Verse 84 says, "THIS WAS THE DEDICATION OFFERING OF THE ALTAR] *ON THE DAY* ON WHICH IT WAS ANOINTED": [because it is saying, concerning the day of anointing, that] that is the day on which the dedication [sacrifices] *began* [to be offered], as it says in this portion (above, vss. 1 and 12). [However, below in vs. 88 the formulation is, "THIS

---

[54]Rashbam opposes the midrashic explanations of the ostensible "difficulty": our verse begins "*and* his sacrifice," while the parallel verses (25, 31, 37 etc.) are absolutely identical to ours except that they do not have the initial letter *vav* ("*and*"). See Genesis Rabba 87 (which sees the "extra" *vav* as alluding to extra blessings which the tribe of Judah received) or NR here (which sees the *vav* as a signal to Judah that he should not be too self-important because he went first).

Rashbam explains more simply: the reason that our verse, verse 13, uses a different formulation is because it is a continuation of vs. 12, which is also phrased differently. Generally, the sacrifice of each chieftain (e.g. vss. 24, 30, 36 etc.) is introduced by *a sentence fragment* ("On the *xth* day, the chieftain of tribe *y*, *a* son of *b*") which is followed by a statement—"his sacrifice [was]." However, the first sacrifice, Nahshon's, is introduced in vs. 12 by *a sentence*: "The person who sacrificed on the first day *was* (ויהי) Nahshon the son of Aminadab from the tribe of Judah." That sentence is naturally followed by the statement, "*And* his sacrifice was . . .."

Once Rashbam explains that the non-standard formulation of vs. 13 is a function of the non-standard formulation of vs. 12, the question might arise, "Why then is verse 12 formulated in a non-standard manner?" Rashbam does not concern himself with that question. I presume that his real concern is not so much to explain the anomalies but to show that, on the *peshaṭ* level, there is no justification for the midrashic explanations of the Midrash Rabba. Cf. the comment of Qara to this verse (in Berliner's *Peleṭat Soferim,* p. 21). Qara explains the verse just as Rashbam does, but he also tries to explain why the opening sentence is different for the first chieftain's offering. See also Hizq. who offers both Rashbam's explanation and a midrashic one (the one from Numbers Rabba).

[55]On דגל as a "three-tribe unit," see note 13 to 2:2 above.

[56]Rashbam notes that the twelve tribes here are listed in the same order as in chapter 2. Many commentators make this same comment; it can be traced back as far as Sifre (47). Rashi (in his commentary to vss. 18–19) presents this idea as part of a midrashic explanation (about Reuben's anger that his birthright was usurped not just by Judah, but even by Issachar and Zebulun). Rashbam offers the comment without the midrashic explanation.

WAS THE DEDICATION OFFERING FOR THE ALTAR] אחרי המשח אותו *AFTER* ITS ANOINTING," [because] it is saying that *at the end of* the twelve days, once the dedication was completed, the total [of sacrifices] amounted to this.[57]

---

[57]Rashbam is opposing the comment of Rashi (to vs. 84) who writes (following Sifre 53) that the combination of these two formulations—"*on the day of* the anointing," and "*after* the anointing"—teaches us that the sacrifices took place on the same day as the anointing, but later on that day, *after* the anointing.

בהעלותך (Numbers 8–12)

8:2 בהעלותך WHEN YOU KINDLE THE LAMPS: Since this is a task that is ongoing [in the Tabernacle and the Temple,] it is mentioned here [yet again].[1] Even though all the other tasks associated with the [construction and furnishing of the] Tabernacle have already been completed, the task of the lighting of the lampstand has not been completed, as it is an ongoing duty.[2]

אל מול פני המנורה [LET THE SEVEN LAMPS] GIVE LIGHT AT THE FRONT OF THE LAMPSTAND: He [= Aaron] would tilt the tops of the wicks of the seven lamps in such a way that they would cast light on the table.[3]

8:7 וְהֶעֱבִירוּ THEY SHALL PASS: [וְהֶעֱבִירוּ is a third-person plural *vav*-consecutive form and should be understood as though it were written in future tense, having the force of a future, with the same meaning as the form] וְיַעֲבִירוּ.

---

[1]In Exodus 25–28 the laws of the Tabernacle—including all the laws of the lampstand—are found in detail. Most of the Tabernacle-related laws are not repeated in the Torah. Rashbam comments on why the laws of the lampstand were repeated.

[2]Rashbam's interpretation opposes the midrashic suggestion that the laws of the lampstand were repeated at this point in order to comfort Aaron who had become jealous since so much honor had been given to the chieftains of the tribes. See e.g. Tanh. *Beha'alotekha* 5. In some versions of Rashi's commentary to this verse Rashi also offers that interpretation. Rashbam says more simply that the laws related to the lampstand are constant duties of the priests and as such are repeated here. See also Rashbam's commentary to Lev. 24:2 and note 44 there. There too Rashbam comments on the repetition of laws concerning the lampstand.

Rashbam's explanation of this verse may be seen as a *peshaṭ*-like reworking of an idea found in Tanh. here. According to Tanh., Aaron was told that the laws of the lampstand were much more long-lasting than any of the other laws concerning the Tabernacle. Sacrifices would cease once the Temple no longer stood, but Jews would continue to light lampstands (in synagogues?) for all time ("הקרבנות כל זמן שבהמ"ק קיים הן נוהגין אבל הנרות לעולם"). Rashbam says that in the days of the Tabernacle itself the lampstand laws differed from other Tabernacle laws. Other items of the Tabernacle are worked on only once, but the lampstand must be cared for constantly.

[3]Rashbam opposes Rashi's explanation (both here and ad Ex. 25:37) that the phrase אל מול פני המנורה means that the wicks of the six exterior branches of the lampstand were to cast light towards the central branch of the lampstand. For an explanation of his opposition, see note 78, on p. 323 of my Exodus volume.

However the form וְהַעֲבִירוּ would be an imperative; it is similar to the form (Ex. 10:17) "וְהַעְתִּירוּ—and pray [to the LORD, your God]."[4]

8:13 והנפת אותם [YOU SHALL PLACE THE LEVITES BEFORE AARON] AND YOU SHALL LIFT THEM UP: First Aaron lifted up the Levites (in vs. 11) and then Moses did [in this verse].[5]

8:21 ויתחטאו THEY PURIFIED THEMSELVES: [The unusual form ויתחטאו is used here because it refers to the instruction above, where] it is written (8:7) "sprinkle upon them water of purification (חטאת)."[6]

8:24 זאת אשר ללוים THIS IS THE RULE FOR THE LEVITES: [This phrase introduces] a new rule that was not mentioned previously [in the Torah].[7] In the Torah portion *Bemidbar Sinai*[8] and in the Torah portion *Naso'*,[9] God commanded that there should be a count of the Levites between the ages of thirty

---

[4]Rashbam often provides minimal pairs like this (וְהַעֲבִירוּ/וְהֶעֱבִירוּ) to demonstrate the difference between an imperative form and an indicative form. See e.g. his commentary to Gen. 1:28 or Gen. 27:19. See also Rashbam's *Dayyaqut* (Merdler's edition, p. 45).

[5]In his commentary to vs. 11, Rashi notes that there are three references in this chapter to "lifting up" the Levites—in vss. 11, 13 and 15. Rashi writes that that is because the text wishes to say that all three groups of Levites—the Gershonites, the Kohathites and the Merarites—must be "lifted up."

Rashbam does not deal with the issue of the three references, but he solves part of the problem when he correctly notes that the first reference (vs. 11) is explicitly about Aaron "lifting up" the Levites, while the command in the second text (vs. 13), "lift them up," is addressed to Moses. Perhaps Rashbam understands the third verse (vs. 15) as a summarizing statement and sees it (as NJPS does) as meaning, "The Levites shall be qualified for service . . . once you have cleansed them and lifted them up." See the defense of that understanding in note 27 on page 306 of the NJPSC.

[6]This is the first use of a *hitpael* form of the verb *ḥ-ṭ-'* in the Bible. Other forms of this verb in *hitpael* appear only in Numbers 19 and 31, and once in Job. Rashbam notes that the unusual verb makes sense in this context and means "to become pure using the water of purification (חטאת)." The preparation of the water of purification is described below in Numbers 19.

Many exegetes explain the verb in the way that Rashbam does. See e.g. the *Be'ur* and NJPSC. See also Rashi ad Num. 19:12 and 31:19.

[7]Rashbam introduces his lengthy explanation in this way as he wishes to clarify that he rejects the question that Rashi poses in his commentary here. Rashi (following Hul. 24a) sees a contradiction between this verse and previous verses about the Levites. Rashbam therefore emphasizes that there is no contradiction since our text is talking about a new law on a topic not yet discussed. See note 12 below for further explanation.

[8]4:1f.

[9]4:21f.

and fifty, [the ones whose tasks would be] "for labor and hauling"[10] and "to carry the Tabernacle."[11] Now, in this Torah portion, the text explains the rules about "standing guard" at the Tabernacle. For five years before age thirty—[years] when the Levite is not yet fit for hauling—he is fit already to guard the Tabernacle and its vessels, and is [therefore] required [to do so]. Also, after age fifty, when the Levite is no longer fit for the task of hauling, he is still required to perform the task of guarding.

Our text goes on to explain: FROM TWENTY-FIVE YEARS ON THEY SHALL PARTICIPATE IN THE WORK FORCE IN THE SERVICE OF THE TENT OF MEETING. [This refers to] the task of guarding, as the text explains below (vs. 26) "THEY ASSIST THEIR BROTHER LEVITES BY STANDING GUARD." [And when vs. 25 says,] "AT THE AGE OF FIFTY THEY SHALL RETIRE FROM THE WORK FORCE," [that means from the work force] of "hauling," the task that was [elaborated] in the previous Torah portions for [Levites] aged thirty to fifty. [Once a Levite reaches age fifty, the text says] "THEY SHALL WORK NO MORE," [but that means only that he shall work no more] at hauling; rather (vs. 26) "THEY SHALL ASSIST THEIR BROTHER LEVITES."

[This last phrase, "they shall assist their brother Levites,"] refers to both [categories,] to Levites aged twenty-five to thirty and to Levites above the age of fifty. Both are disqualified from hauling duties. So what should they do? THEY, i.e. members of both categories, SHALL ASSIST THEIR BROTHER LEVITES BY STANDING GUARD, BUT THEY SHALL DO NO MORE WORK, i.e. work of hauling.[12]

---

[10]The phrase is from Num. 4:24.

[11]An allusion to the language of Num. 1:50.

[12]Rashbam takes issue with Rashi's reading of the same passages.

The difficulty in vss. 24–26 is that we know from previous passages, e.g. 4:47, that:

(1) A Levite should "work" in the Tabernacle between the ages of 30 and 50.

Our verses teach us three further rules:

(2) Each Levite should come to the Tabernacle at age 25 (vs. 24);

(3) Each Levite should stop working at age 50 (vs. 25); and

(4) ***He*** should serve his brother Levites by standing guard, even though he is to do no "work" (vs. 26).

Rashi understands that ***He*** in vs. 26 is a reference only to the retired Levite who is over 50 years old. Accordingly Rashi has to explain why vs. 24 says that a Levite should come to the Temple at age 25. To what end? We know from point (1) that he will not be able to do "work" until age 30.

Rashi suggests (following Sifre and Hul. 24a) that the Levite comes to the Tabernacle at age 25 in order to train for five years for the service that he will undertake at age 30. However Rashbam offers a more contextually grounded explanation. He says that vs. 26 refers back both to the retired Levite of vs. 25 and to the underage Levite of vs. 24. "***He*** shall serve

8:26 ככה תעשה ללוים במשמרותם THIS IS WHAT YOU SHOULD DO FOR THE LEVITES REGARDING THEIR GUARDING DUTIES: [The plural form, "משמרותם—guarding duties" is used because the reference is to two different periods of guard duty:] they shall be in the guard of the Tabernacle [both] for the five years before age thirty and [again] after the age of fifty.[13]

9:2 ויעשו בני ישראל LET THE ISRAELITES OFFER [THE PASSOVER SACRIFICE AT ITS SET TIME]: "Passover" in Egypt was only a one-day celebration and its sacrifice was not like other sacrifices. Accordingly now that the Tabernacle was built, He [= God] had to command that it [= Passover] be performed in the proper manner of the commandment, not the way it was performed in Egypt.[14]

10:2 והיו לך למקרא העדה THEY [= THE TRUMPETS] SHALL SERVE YOU TO SUMMON THE COMMUNITY [AND SHALL SERVE THE DIVISIONS FOR TRAVEL]: For you, the trumpets will be used for summoning; for the divisions, the trumpets will be needed for travel. (The word מסע is a noun [meaning "travel,"] just like the noun נסיעה).[15] The words את המחנות should be understood as if למחנות were written (i.e. *for* the divisions).[16]

---

his brother Levites" means that both the Levites between ages 25 and 30 and those over the age of 50 have duties of guarding in the Tabernacle.

Like Rashbam, see iE. See Nahm.'s criticism of this explanation.

[13]Rashbam reiterates the point that he made in his commentary to vs. 24. See note 12.

[14]Rashbam's explanation opposes that of Rashi, who says (following Sifre Numbers 57) that this passage appears here to teach that the Israelites (illegitimately) observed Passover only once, during the second of the forty years during which they were wandering through the wilderness. Rashbam, on the other hand, says that this is the appropriate time for instructions about how Passover is to be observed, from this point on, in a manner that differs from the way that the celebration took place in Egypt, on the night before the exodus. These instructions could not be given in the first year of the wandering, since the Tabernacle had not yet been built. Rashbam calls it a "proper" Passover because many of the rules given here apply only when the Tabernacle or the Temple is standing.

[15]Rashbam paraphrases the biblical word, מסע, by using the rabbinic word, נסיעה.

[16]As Touitou notes ("*'Al shiṭato ha-parshanit shel Rashbam beferusho la-Torah*," p. 273, note 142), Rashbam is explaining our verse as having a chiastic structure:

(a) they shall serve you
(b) to summon the community;
(b[1]) and for travel
(a[1]) [they shall serve] the divisions.

This explanation goes against the standard understanding (reflected in Rashi, here) that Moses is told that the trumpets shall serve him (לך) for two purposes: (1) for summoning the community, and (2) for moving the divisions. In order to distance himself from that explanation, Rashbam points out that the words את המחנות should not be read as the object of the verbal

10:3 ותקעו בהן WHEN THEY ARE BLOWN: I.e. when the two of them are blown.[17]

10:29 לחובב TO HOBAB: I.e. to Jethro. [Hobab and Jethro are the same person, for Jethro is described as being Moses' "חותן—father-in-law," and] it is written (Jud. 4:11), "From the descendants of Hobab, Moses' father-in-law (חותן)."[18]

10:31 כי על כן INASMUCH AS[19] YOU HAVE KNOWN: and have paid attention to our needs when we have been ENCAMPED IN THE DESERT AND YOU HAVE SERVED FOR US A GUIDE: when you gave us good advice, as recorded in [the Torah portion,] *Va-yishma' Yitro* (Ex. 18:13–26). [The phrase והיית לנו לעיניים (lit. "you were eyes for us" should be understood figuratively,] as in (Job 29:15) "I was eyes to the blind."[20]

---

noun "moving" (i.e. "for moving the divisions"). Rather את המחנות serves, in the second half of the sentence, the same role served by לך in the first half of the sentence.

Rashbam is also opposing the midrashic explanations (which appear in some printed versions of Rashi) that these trumpets are promised to Moses as a bonus of sorts: they shall be "לך—for you." See e.g. Tanh. *Beha'alotekha* 10 which explains that the trumpets are described as being "for Moses" (לך) because their use was restricted to him and did not continue in future generations. According to Rashbam there is nothing specifically "for Moses" connected with the trumpets. The verse says that for Moses they have one purpose, and for the divisions they have another purpose.

For further discussion of Rashbam's sensitivity to chiasm, see note 21 on p. 24 of my Exodus volume.

[17]So also Rashi. This explanation is the simple meaning of the text. Our verse reads, "If *they* are blown," contrasting with vs. 4, which reads, "If *one of them* is blown."

[18]The phrase in our verse, "Hobab the son of Reuel, Moses' חותן," is, in theory, ambiguous: either Hobab or Reuel could be the person who is described as Moses' חותן. (Furthermore, חותן might not mean father-in-law; see e.g. iE here.) Rashbam cites the verse in Judges 4 to show that it is Hobab who is described here as Moses' חותן. In his commentary to Ex. 2:18, Rashbam makes this same point, as part of a longer excursus, in which Rashbam is arguing against various other attempts to account for all the different names of Moses' father-in-law in the Bible. See notes 31 and 32 on pages 27 and 28 there.

[19]Rashbam paraphrases the words כי על כן ידעת as כי על כן אשר ידעת. See similarly Rashi here. See also Rashbam's commentary to Gen. 18:5 and note 2 there, and Rashbam's commentary below ad 14:43.

[20]The verb והיית is more commonly seen as a *vav*-consecutive form, with a future meaning. Moses is then saying to Hobab, "Stay with us and be (והיית) our guide."

Rashbam's grammatical understanding of והיית—as a perfect ("past-tense") verb—also appears in the works of other classical exegetes. See e.g. Onq. Rashi offers both explanations. But Rashbam's explanation of the *idea* here differs from Onq.'s. For Onq. (and for Rashi who says simply that the phrase may be understood as being in the past tense, " כתרגומו—as [it is explained] in Onq."), seeing והיית as a past-tense verb means understanding the phrase as saying "because you have seen all the great miracles that God performed on our behalf." Rashbam, on the other hand, connects this speech of Moses with

10:33 מהר ה' [THEY MARCHED] FROM THE MOUNTAIN OF THE LORD: [Even though whenever God spoke to Moses in the second year, the speech is introduced as being "in the Sinai wilderness," not "at Mount Sinai," still it is appropriate to say here that they marched away from Mount Sinai/Horeb,][21] since they had not really gone away from the vicinity of Mount Horeb, which is in the wilderness of Sinai. This all occurred after the Tabernacle was erected, as I wrote above. In any case they were still near Mount Sinai until this time.

דרך שלשת ימים A THREE-DAY JOURNEY: I.e. they marched [continuously] for three days; they did not encamp until the end of the third day.[22] And as a result of this difficult trip,[23] "the people took to complaining bitterly" (11:1).

Jethro's advice to the Israelites in Ex. 18. It is not a reference to what Jethro saw, in the past, but to the help that he gave to the Israelites. The same explanation can be found attributed to Joseph Qara (in Berliner's *Peleṭat Soferim,* p. 21).

See Rosin here, who says that Rashbam's interpretation is a mistake (שגגה). On the other hand, see Luzzatto here who vigorously promotes his own interpretation of the verse. He then says that, after coming to that conclusion independently, he discovered that Rashbam had already explained the verse that way. See also iE who cites (without comment) the interpretation found here in Rashbam as an interpretation that many exegetes offer ("ורבים אמרו").

[21]Some of the words in the brackets here were added by Rosin to the text of the commentary in order to make Rashbam's thoughts clearer.

Above (ad 1:1 and ad 3:1) Rashbam writes that the text distinguishes between speeches of God that took place in the first year in the wilderness—which the text says were "at Mount Sinai"—and speeches of God in the second year, after the erection of the Tabernacle—which the text says occurred "in the wilderness of Sinai." That explanation implies that in the second year the Israelites were no longer at Mount Sinai. So why does the text here say that now, in the second year, the Israelites were leaving "the mountain of God"? Rashbam's answer is that even in the second year they were still *in the vicinity of* Mount Sinai. So also Hizq.

Rashbam's comment may be opposed to the midrashic explanations that the phrase ויסעו מהר ה' has negative connotations, implying that the Israelites had deserted God. See e.g. Taan. 29a and Rashi there, s.v. ואמר רבי חמא. See also Shab. 116a.

[22]Rashbam's explanation is opposed to the midrashic explanation of Rashi (following Sifre) who says that in one day the people miraculously traversed a "three-day journey," i.e. an amount of marching that *should have taken* three days. Rashbam understands the verse more simply: they marched for three days. The fact is important for us to know so that we will understand the people's complaints below in 11:1, as Rashbam explains further.

See a similar dispute between Rashi and Rashbam ad Deut. 1:2.

See also JBS here, who writes that it is impossible to say that they marched for three days in a row; they must, he writes, have rested every night. Presumably his comment is meant to modify Rashbam's position. See also Nahm. here, who explains the verse essentially as Rashbam does, although Nahm. adds that the text does not make it clear whether or not they traveled even at night.

[23]Rashbam's phrase, מפני טורח הדרך, may be borrowed from Rashi's commentary to 21:4, s.v. ותקצר. See note 25.

We find [the same pattern of events] in the Torah portion, *Parah*,[24] (Num. 21:4–5) "the people grew restive because of [the hardships of] the journey. [Then] the people spoke against God and against Moses . . . ."[25]

וארון ברית ה׳ נוסע לפניהם THE ARK OF THE COVENANT OF THE LORD TRAVELED IN FRONT OF THEM: for all of those[26] THREE DAYS, TO SEEK OUT A RESTING PLACE FOR THEM. For the cloud traveled over the Ark.[27]

---

[24]I.e. in the Torah portion that is commonly called *Ḥuqqat* (Num. 19:1–22:1).

[25]Rashbam explains the juxtaposition of the narrative here about the people's travels with the narrative about the "complainers" in chapter 11. See also Rashbam below ad 11:1.

Rashbam's comment may be seen as being opposed to that of Rashi, ad 11:1, who writes that the complainers were evil people; they used the journey simply as an excuse to complain. Rashi says below, ad 21:4, that verses 21:4–5 mean that the people became worn out from the travel and that is why they complained. Rashbam is saying that the same explanation that Rashi applies to 21:4–5 applies here too. The people were subjected to a difficult march—three days without rest—and that explains their complaints about the "hardships of travel."

See note 53 to 17:27 for a discussion of Rashbam's tendency to minimize the sins of the Israelites in the wilderness.

[26]There is a redundancy in the verse. The verse says that the people marched "דרך שלושת ימים—for three days," and it says further that the Ark of the Covenant traveled in front of them "דרך שלושת ימים." Rashi understands this second phrase to mean that the Ark was "a three-day distance" in front of the Israelites. As NJPSC notes, such an explanation is very difficult, for "the Ark had to be visible in order to serve as a guide."

Rashbam simply understands the verse as being repetitive. He says that the second phrase, דרך שלושת ימים, means the same thing as the first phrase here: "*for* the aforementioned three days, the Ark traveled in front of the Israelites." Note Rashbam's careful language: "כל אותן שלושה ימים—for all those three days," emphasizing that there is no new information conveyed in that second phrase. So also iE. And see similarly Mendelssohn's translation (אויף דיזן דרייאן טאגרייזן). See the *Be'ur*, who writes that such an understanding would be better supported had the text included the definite article (דרך שלושת הימים) the second time the phrase appears. See also note 27.

[27]Many exegetes feel the need to harmonize our verse—which says that the Ark traveled *in front of* the Israelites to lead them on their way—with the verses that imply that the Ark traveled *in the middle* of the camp, preceded by six tribes. (See e.g. 2:17 and 10:21.) A number of ancient midrashic sources attempt to resolve the problem by saying that there were two Arks. See e.g. *Beraita' di-melekhet ha-mishkan* 6, where Rabbi Judah ben Laqish is quoted as saying that there was one Ark that was positioned inside the camp and a second one "שהיה יוצא עמהם למלחמה והיו בו שברי לוחות—that went before them to battle and in which the broken tablets were placed." (See also similarly PT Sheq. 6:1 [49c] and LT here.) Rashi here quotes that midrash. The Ark here, Rashi argues, is not the same one which was usually in the middle of the Israelites' camp and which contained the whole tablets. See also Rashi's commentary to Deut. 10:1, where he makes it even clearer that he subscribes to the "two Ark" theory, and see also Nahm.'s detailed criticism (in his commentary to Deut. there) of Rashi's position.

10:35 קומה ה' [WHEN THE ARK WAS TO SET OUT, MOSES WOULD SAY,] "ARISE, O LORD": Because then the divine Presence would depart from [its normal place] on top of the cover [of the Ark].[28]

11:1 כמתאוננים [THE PEOPLE TOOK TO] COMPLAINING: They were suffering from the hardships of their traveling.[29]

11:7–10 והמן כזרע גד הוא THE MANNA WAS LIKE CORIANDER SEED: and its color[30] was like the color OF BDELLIUM. In other words, it looked dry and

---

It is hard to know how Rashbam resolves this problem. Nowhere in his commentary does he hint at a "two Ark" solution (and it would be difficult to imagine that he would subscribe to such a theory). Perhaps Rashbam's resolution is the same as that of iE: The phrase, "for all those three days . . . the cloud traveled over the Ark," means that something unusual happened during that specific journey. On those three days, and only then, the Ark and the cloud together led the Israelite camp; on later trips the cloud alone preceded the Israelites, while the Ark traveled in the middle of the camp. See similarly Abarbanel and see Luzzatto's criticism of that position.

On the idea of the cloud being on top of the Ark, see also Rashbam ad Ex. 40:35 and ad Lev. 16:2. On the idea of the cloud leading the Israelites in their travels, see Ex. 13:21, Num. 9:15–23 and Deut. 1:33.

[28]In other words, Moses addressed the divine Presence and told it to arise from its normal resting place, on top of the cover of the Ark, because the Ark was about to be moved. On the idea of the divine Presence (שכינה) resting on top of the Ark, see Rashbam's commentary to Exodus 26:1 and 40:35 and to Lev. 16:2. If we assume that, for Rashbam, the divine Presence is manifested in the cloud on the Ark (as the last two Rashbam comments mentioned imply; see also Hizq. here) then this comment might be a continuation of Rashbam's last one. Rashbam would be saying that, during the three-day journey described in verse 33, the cloud remained on top of the Ark. However, on other journeys Moses would address the cloud and suggest that it depart, as the Ark was about to be moved.

Rashbam's explanation of this verse opposes that of Rashi who says (following Tanh. *Va-yaqhel* 7) that the meaning of קומה ה' is really "Stand still, O Lord." Moses had to ask God not to travel so far ahead of the Israelite camp since, as Rashi said in his commentary to vs. 33, the divine Presence had removed itself to the distance of "a three-day journey" in front of the Israelites.

[29]Rashbam reiterates the explanation that he offered above, ad 10:33, s.v. דרך. (See note 25 there.) The Israelites' complaints here are to be seen as a result of the difficult traveling that they had had to do (described in 10:33). See similarly Nahm. here, who says that the phrase means that the people were in pain and felt sorry for themselves after the last journey.

Rashbam's explanation is opposed to that of Rashi, as I noted above ad 10:33, in note 25.

[30]Or perhaps, "its appearance was like the appearance of bdellium." Rashbam (as reported in Rosin's text) paraphrases the verse's wording ועינו כעין הבדולח as ומראהו כמראה הבדולח. (In some of the printed versions of Rashbam's commentary this text has been hypercorrected, as if Rashbam were simply quoting the biblical verse and not paraphrasing it.) In note 3 to Lev. 14:37, I argued that Rashbam at times uses the word מראה to mean color. From Rashbam's

hard.[31] That is why they said (vs. 6), "Our strength is dried up. [There is nothing at all! Nothing to look at but this manna!]" [They felt] like people who [had to] eat dry wheat.

If so [i.e. if their complaints about the manna had grounds], why did God get angry with them for complaining], as it says below (vs. 10)? The text now [in vs. 8f.] explains the reason for God's anger. For when THEY WOULD GRIND IT BETWEEN MILLSTONES OR POUND IT IN A MORTAR, then והיה טעמו כטעם לשד השמן, ITS TASTE WOULD BECOME LIKE MOIST OIL— i.e. its taste would change.[32]

In the beginning [i.e. in its unprocessed state,] it would be as sweet as (Ex. 16:31) "a wafer in honey,"[33] just as olives and nuts[34] [taste sweet] before they are ground. But after it was ground up or pounded in a mortar,[35] then והיה טעמו—its taste became moist like oil or fatty meat,[36] just like the oil from olives and nuts, whose taste changes after they are ground up.

---

commentary to Ex. 16:31, s.v. לבן, it is clear that he understands our verse as referring to the *color* of the manna. See note 30 there. Either interpretation—color or appearance—would be appropriate in this passage. Like Rashbam, see also Andrew of St. Victor here (p. 184) who writes that the manna was like coriander seed in shape, but like "bdellium" in color. See also commentary below ad 21:5, and note 31 there.

[31]Rashbam's interpretation of this verse appears to be unique. Most commentators follow the approach of Rashi and iE, who both comment that verse 7 contains a *positive* description of the manna. This explains why the reaction of the people was, from the narrator's perspective, inappropriate. The people complained, but they should not have done so, because "The manna was like coriander seed . . .." See also NJPSC: "This . . . description of the manna was deliberately inserted here to refute each point in the people's complaint." Rashbam, on the other hand, says that verse 7 expands on vs. 6. It explains the *unpleasant* characteristics of the manna that caused the Israelites to complain.

Note that once again (just as in his comment to 11:1 and 10:33) Rashbam explains the basis of a complaint of the Israelites. The explanation does not necessarily justify the complaint, but it does make it seem less objectionable.

[32]In his comment to Ex. 16:31, Rashbam clarifies that this explanation is opposed to the midrashic harmonization that the manna tasted like honey to children and like oil to adults. See commentary and note 53 there.

[33]As I pointed out in my notes to Exodus, Rashbam comments on the phrase כצפיחית בדבש in order to take issue with an interpretation that he finds lacking. But he does not write what he himself thinks that the phrase means. I have simply followed the NJPS translation, "like wafers in honey." But judging from the context here, Rashbam perhaps thinks that צפיחית means something harder than a wafer.

[34]Perhaps "walnuts."

[35]Rashbam paraphrases the biblical Hebrew word מדוכה by using the rabbinic Hebrew word מכתשת.

[36]Both Rashi and Dunash (*Teshuvot*, p. 14) argue that the word השמן in our verse is related to the Hebrew word for oil and not the Hebrew word for fat. Rashbam's comment is also

That is why (vs. 10), וישמע ה׳ ויחר אפו THE LORD HEARD[37] AND WAXED ANGRY: because whenever they wanted to, they could grind the manna up and it would be oily, and then their food would not be dry.

In this verse it says that *והיה* טעמו ITS TASTE *WOULD BECOME*, i.e. its original taste would change. However, in the Torah portion *Beshalaḥ*, the phrase is (Ex. 16:31) "*וטעמו* כצפיחית בדבש—ITS TASTE *WAS* LIKE WAFERS IN HONEY," since there the reference is to its taste [in its unprocessed state,] before it had an oily taste.[38]

לשד: All the letters of the word לשד ("moisture") are root letters. It is like the word לשדי in the phrase (Ps. 32:4), "My vigor (לשדי) waned like dried-up summer fruit," i.e. my moisture became like the dryness of dried figs.[39]

---

dependent on Dunash here (see note 39 below re לשד, in vs. 8) and yet he is willing to connect the word here both to the meaning of oil and the meaning of "fatty meat."

See, however, Berzinsky, who emends our text of Rashbam's commentary and removes the words "or fatty meat" (ובשר שמן).

[37]Rashbam misquotes (or perhaps paraphrases) our verse which reads: "Moses heard . . . and the LORD waxed angry."

[38]Again this distinction is found in the Exodus commentary. See my Exodus volume, pp. 180–1, and note 54 there.

[39]Rashbam's comment follows Rashi, both here and in Psalms, and Dunash (*Teshuvot*, p. 14). Rashbam is opposed to Menaḥem's explanation that connects לשד, in Ps., with the root *sh-d-d*. (Both Dunash's explanation and Menaḥem's may be found in Midrash Tehillim 32.) It is also opposed to those *midrashim* (e.g. Sifre Numbers 69) that connect לשד, here, to the word שד, meaning "breast." See Rashi here. There is also a midrashic tradition of unknown origin, cited approvingly by Hizq. here, according to which righteous people ate the manna in an unprocessed state, while only the less righteous felt the need to grind it or cook it. (So also Zohar 2:62b-63a.) This explanation would also be rejected by Rashbam.

Rashi first offers the same grammar-based analysis as Rashbam, and then adds an alternative midrashic reading, based on the *noṭariqon* method of using the letters of the word לשד as an acronym. Rashbam, as is his custom, offers the *peshaṭ*-oriented analysis, but does not offer the midrashic alternative.

Rashbam's reading of the word לשדי in the verse in Psalms is more or less the same as that of Dunash and Rashi. But Rashbam is the only one who says that קיץ means "summer *fruit*" in that verse. (קיץ means either "summer" or "summer fruit" in the Bible. See BDB.) It is possible that Rashbam offers that explanation of the verse in Psalms here because it fits nicely with his explanation of our verse. According to Rashbam, our verse says that grinding the manna turned it from being something hard like a hard fruit, a nut or an olive, into being something soft and oily, something which might be called לשד. Conversely, he says that the verse in Psalms describes the complaint of a person who feels that his vigor and moisture (לשד) are turning into something hard, like a hard dried fig.

11:8 שטו [THE PEOPLE] WOULD GO ABOUT: [The verb שטו should be understood] as in (Job 1:7), "from roaming (משוט) over the earth, or as in (Jer. 5:1) "roam (שוטטו) the streets of Jerusalem [search its squares]."[40]

11:12 יְלִדְתִּיהוּ [DID I (MOSES)] GIVE BIRTH TO [THIS PEOPLE]: [Even though the *qal* form of the verb *y-l-d* is usually used for a woman, and the *hifil* form is usually used for a man, here a *qal* form is used to describe a man "giving birth,"] just as in (Gen. 10:26), "Joktan begot (ילד) Almodad." [The verb has the force of a causative, and means] "caused another person to give birth."[41] That is the reason that both the verb וִירִשְׁתֶּם, in the phrase "you shall dispossess (וִירִשְׁתֶּם) them,"[42] and the verb יְלִדְתִּיהוּ (here) have a *ḥiriq* vowel [between the second and the third letters of the root]. It is because their *qal* forms[43] have a certain connection to *hifil*.[44]

---

[40]Rashi says that the verb שטו here implies effortless strolling. Rashbam's explanation would imply that some effort was involved. As iE writes, the verb שטו implies that the manna did not fall in a concentrated area; it was scattered about and one had to go look for it. See also Hizq.

Curiously it is Rashi here, not Rashbam, who appears to be rejecting the midrashic tradition. The Talmud in *Yoma'* 75a also understands the word שטו as implying a laborious search for the manna and says that it was only the less righteous among the Jews who were required לשוט, to go *searching* for manna. Righteous Jews found it on their doorsteps. Presumably Rashi rejects that explanation because of his desire to accept another midrashic interpretation—one that emphasizes and aggrandizes the manna as an unprecedented boon for the Israelites. See similarly note 31 above where I pointed out that Rashi sees vs. 7 as saying only positive things about the manna, while Rashbam does not.

Here, while iE and Rashbam do not accept the part of the midrash that connects שטו only to evil Jews, they do accept the suggestion that the verb implies extending some effort.

[41]Rashbam's comment to this verse is based on the assumption that Moses, as a man, ought to be asking "did I *father* this people." But he is using a verb, יְלִדְתִּיהוּ, which more often means "did I *mother*"? So also iE and Hizq.

Cf. Nahm., who suggests that Moses could well have been saying, "did I mother this people?"

[42]As noted already by both Qeren Shemuel and by Rosin, there is no verse in the Bible with the phrase וִירִשְׁתֶּם אותם. Rosin suggests that the reference intended might be the phrase וִירִשְׁתֶּם אותה, which appears twice in the Bible. My feeling is that Rashbam's argument would be a little stronger if the reference were to the word וִירִשְׁתָּם (e.g. Deut. 19:1), a word which means the same thing as the phrase וִירִשְׁתֶּם אותם. See note 44.

[43]Rashbam refers to a *qal* form here as לשון מפעל, in contrast with לשון מפעיל. The latter term could either mean *hifil*, or it could mean "causative." The term לשון מפעל is unique in Rashbam's work and unusual. From the context its meaning is clear enough. See the discussion of the term by Ronela Merdler, *Dayyaqut me-rabbenu Shemuel: Diyyun be-sefer ha-diqduq umasqanot* (Master's Dissertation: Hebrew University of Jerusalem, 1995), p. 140, note 11.

[44]Rashbam's unusual grammatical argument goes as follows. Generally when a man "begets" a child, i.e. causes a woman to give birth to a child, the causative *hifil* form of the verb

But [in other prima-*yod* roots, that is not the case.] From the root *y-sh-b* (to sit) which is intransitive,[45] one says (e.g. Lev. 25:18) וִישַׁבְתֶּם; from the root *y-sh-n* (to sleep), one says וִישַׁנְתֶּם.[46] All such verbs have a *pataḥ* [vowel between the second and third letters of the root]. So also from the root *y-r-d*, one says וִירַדְתֶּם.[47]

11:20 עד אשר יצא מאפכם UNTIL IT COMES OUT OF YOUR NOSE: [The phrase is to be understood] as the Targum explained.[48]

למה זה יצאנו ממצרים [God said, "You will be punished because you said,] 'OH, WHY DID WE LEAVE EGYPT?' [This is a reference to] when you said (vs. 5), 'We remember the fish that we used to eat in Egypt for free.'[49] You will be

---

*y-l-*d is used; more rarely, the *qal* form is used. So also, the verb to dispossess (i.e. to cause someone else to cease to possess) is usually conveyed by the *hifil* form of the verb *y-r-sh*; more rarely, the *qal* form of *y-r-sh* has that meaning. Rashbam argues then that these specific *qal* forms of *y-l-*d and *y-r-sh* have a certain affinity with the *hifil*; that is why the vowel between the second and third letters of the root is a *ḥiriq*, the standard vowel of the *hifil* in that position. See also Rosin, RSBM, p. 132, note 15, who writes that Rashbam erroneously sees יְלִדְתִּיהוּ as a form that has some characteristics of *qal* and some of *hifil* ("*eine Art von Zwischenform zwischen Kal u. Hiphil*").

For other explanations of the *ḥiriq* vowel here, see G.-K. 44d and 69s.

[45]Rashbam writes שהוא בגוף האדם. He uses the same phrase in his commentary to Ex. 7:14: "מתיבות התלויים בגוף האדם יאמר וישמן . . .," which I translated in my Exodus volume (p. 70) as: "intransitive verbs." In his review of my Exodus volume (JBL, 1999), Robert Goldenberg contends that my translation there was mistaken and that Rashbam is referring to "*stative* verbs, not intransitive verbs."

I am unconvinced. Rashbam uses the same phrase here to describe the verb *y-sh-b* (to sit), an intransitive verb that surely is not stative. He uses the phrase one more time in his commentary (ad Deut. 7:23: לשון המיון נתלה בגוף האדם), and there too the reference is to an intransitive verb, not a stative one. Other scholars also have understood בגוף האדם as Rashbam's technical term for an intransitive verb. See e.g. Rosin in his notes to the passage here and in Exodus, and in his RSBM, p. 134, note 9. See also Ronela Merdler, *ibid.* ("בגוף האדם" כלומר פועל עומד).

[46]The form does not appear in the Bible, but it would be the correct form of the root *y-sh-n* in the *vav*-consecutive *qal*.

[47]This form also does not appear in the Bible, but is grammatically correct.

[48]Rashbam and Rashi both refer to Onq., who explains that the metaphor means "until you get sick of it" (עד דתקוצון ביה). Rashi adds an explanation of *why* the phrase "until it comes it of your nose" fits the meaning of "getting sick of something."

[49]Rashbam is asking: the text blames the people here for having said, "Oh why did we leave Egypt?" But when did they ever say that?

This is the type of question that Rashi often asks, usually introduced by the phrase, "והיכן דיבר/אמר—where did he/they say this?" (See e.g. ad Gen. 32:13 or Ex. 8:11.) Curiously Rashi does not ask the question here, and perhaps for that reason Rashbam (who sees his commentary as improving and supplementing that of Rashi) does.

punished for your ingratitude. If you had lusted after meat without complaining about the Exodus from Egypt, you would not have been punished so much." For [we see that] there were some complaints for which they were not punished.[50]

11:21 ויאמר משה שש מאות אלף רגלי MOSES SAID "THE PEOPLE NUMBER SIX HUNDRED THOUSAND": This verse must be explained the same way that I explained the verse (Ex. 19:23), "The people cannot come up to Mount Sinai."[51] Here too Moses was fearful after what God had said to him, that [they would eat meat] (vs. 20) "for thirty days" and He also had said that [there would be so much meat that] (*ibid.*) "it will become loathsome to you." So he asked God:

> You said that they would eat [meat] for thirty days. But "the people number six hundred thousand men," aside from the women and children. [Slaughtering] all of their sheep and cattle would not suffice for a month [of eating meat]. How do You plan to bring Your plan to fruition? Are You planning on destroying [most of] them so that only enough of them remain so that they will have [more than] enough [meat] for thirty days? (For You did say that [there would be so much meat left over that] "it will become loathsome for you.") Or are You planning on miraculously bringing them meat from another source [so that you will be able to have more than enough meat for the people without destroying large numbers of people]?[52]

---

[50]A similar idea to Rashbam's may be found in Nahm.'s commentary to Num. 20:3: "In all the trials in the wilderness, the greatest sin they committed was when they said 'why did you take us out of Egypt' (ובכל הנסיונות במדבר חטאם הגדול כשיאמרו למה העליתנו ממצרים)." To prove his contention there—that the people were punished most severely for questioning whether the exodus was to their benefit—Nahm. cites our verse.

Cf. the *Be'ur* here who raises doubts about this pattern. He surveys the various passages in the Torah where the Israelites complain about the fact that they were taken out of Egypt and notes that such complaints do *not* consistently lead to punishment.

[51]See Rashbam's commentary there (in my Exodus volume, pp. 210–212).

In both passages, Moses may be seen as not trusting God, or at least as sharply criticizing God. Instead, Rashbam explains that, in both places, Moses' questions were meant to elicit information.

[52]Moses' strident and apparently unbelieving attitude in this quotation has troubled religious commentators throughout the ages. Rashi gives an uncharacteristically long explanation of this verse, in which he cites three separate lengthy tannaitic explanations (all of them from Tosefta Sot. 6:4) of how to interpret Moses' words. The first such explanation, Rabbi Aqiva's, says that Moses really did speak inappropriately. The second two explanations, those of Rabbis Simeon and Gamaliel III, say that Moses had no doubts at all about God's abilities. They each assume that Moses knew that God could and would give the Israelites what He said He would. They reinterpret Moses' questions as being about whether the miraculous delivery of the meat would actually accomplish its purpose.

Rashbam, like Rabbis Simeon and Gamaliel III, must have been too uncomfortable with the image of Moses challenging God in the blatant manner that the simple meaning of the text would imply. When compared to other explanations that reinterpret Moses' words, Rashbam's innovative suggestion seems closer to the simple meaning of the text than the

11:26 והמה בכתובים THEY WERE AMONG THOSE RECORDED: They were on the list of [those who would] "go out to the tent." Due to their modesty, they did not go out. So it is explained in *Sanhedrin*.[53]

11:28 מִבְּחֻרָיו [JOSHUA THE SON OF NUN, MOSES' ATTENDANT] FROM HIS YOUTH: [The word בְּחֻרָיו is an abstract noun; it] means "from his youth," just like [the word בְּחוּרוֹתֶיךָ, in the phrase] (Eccl. 11:9) "the days of your youth (בְּחוּרוֹתֶיךָ)." However, the word בַּחוּרָיו [is a concrete noun; it] means "the

---

latter two explanations offered by Rashi. See Nahm.'s comment here where he says that the last two explanations of Rashi do not fit into the language of the verses (אין . . . נאותין ללשון הכתוב) and that Rabbi Aqiva's explanation is the true simple meaning of the words of the verse (משמעות הכתוב באמת) but presents a theologically unacceptable image of Moses. For other attempts, see iE and Nahm. and virtually every other traditional commentator.

[53]In Sanh. 17a (and in Sifre here), there are two explanations of what it means when the text says that Eldad and Medad were "among those recorded" but "they remained in the camp." Rashbam follows the second, less famous, explanation, attributed by the Talmud to R. Simeon. Rashbam emphasizes that his explanation is talmudic, presumably in order to say that his opposition to the more famous midrash should not be seen as heterodox.

The first explanation found in the Talmud says that in order to create a group of 70 elders, the first step was getting 6 names from each tribe. That yielded a short list of 72 names. So a lottery system was used to reduce the 72 names to the desired 70. Eldad and Medad were the odd men out. They had originally been "recorded" on the temporary list of 72, but they "remained in the camp" since they were not on the final list of 70.

Rashbam prefers Rabbi Simeon's explanation, which seems closer to the *peshaṭ* since it does not require postulating the existence of a provisional list of 72 names (a fact found nowhere in the text). Eldad and Medad were among those "recorded" as part of the select group. They stayed in the camp because of their humility.

The first explanation is offered here by iE. JBS offers both possibilities. It is hard to say what Rashi's position is on the question. He explains the lottery system used to reduce 72 names to 70, which makes it appear that he follows the first talmudic explanation. However, a careful reading of Rashi shows that he really thinks that Eldad and Medad *were* part of the final group of 70 elders, not just the group of 72 nominees. Despite winning the competition, they did not "come out to the tent" because of their modesty. (Explanations of Rashi as accepting Rabbi Simeon's position may be found here in Mizraḥi and in the *Be'ur*.) If that understanding of Rashi is correct, then Rashbam is essentially following Rashi's lead—explaining the text according to Rabbi Simeon's understanding. But Rashi includes the midrash about the lottery, although Rabbi Simeon's explanation does not require such an addition to the text. Rashbam, as is his custom, leaves the midrash out.

Like Rashbam (and Rashi and Rabbi Simeon), see Andrew of St. Victor (p. 185) who says here that Eldad and Medad remained in the camp and refrained from going out to the tent because of their modesty (*remanserunt in castris non contemptus . . . sed humilitatis causa*).

people that are young," as in the verse (Is. 9:16), "That is why my Lord will not be happy with His young people (בַּחוּרָיו)."[54]

כלאם RESTRAIN THEM: [The word is an imperative *qal* form with a suffix, from the root *k-l-'* ,] as in (Gen. 8:2), "the rain was held back (ויכלא)." It means "restrain them," or "stop them" from going out freely, by putting them in jail. The letters *'alef, ḥet, heh* and *'ayin* cause[55] [the vowel changes which require the word] to be pronounced כְּלָאֵם,[56] similarly to [other verbs where the third letter of the root is a guttural, e.g. שְׁמָעֵנוּ in the phrase] (Gen. 23:6), "Listen to us (שְׁמָעֵנוּ), my lord,"[57] or [יִמְצָאֵהוּ in the phrase] (Deut. 32:10), "He found him (יִמְצָאֵהוּ) in a desert region."[58]

---

[54]Rashbam writes that the distinction between the word בְּחוּרָיו, with a *sheva*, and בַּחוּרָיו, with a *pataḥ*, is that the former is an abstract noun meaning youth, while the latter is a concrete noun, meaning youngster.

Cf. iE who seems to be arguing here with Rashbam (or with another commentary similar to Rashbam's). iE disagrees with Rashbam's explanation on two points. First, iE claims that the word מבחוריו in our verse has nothing to do with the idea—concrete or abstract—of being young. Rather, he says that the word means "from his chosen ones." iE furthermore writes that the noun בחור, meaning young person, could take either a *sheva* or a *pataḥ* vowel in its plural forms, thus rejecting Rashbam's claim that the *sheva* here is necessarily a sign of the abstract noun.

Like Rashbam, see Onq. and NJPS. The *Be'ur* argues that the cantillation signs support Rashbam's reading. See also NJPSC (p. 309, note 66): "*mi-beḥurav* is an abstract plural." Levine offers both explanations, Rashbam's and iE's.

[55]Rashbam often discusses the changes that guttural letters make in the vocalization—and almost always uses some form of the verb "to cause (*g-r-m*)" to describe those changes. See e.g. commentary to Gen. 34:10, Ex. 8:25 and14:16; Lev. 14:56 and Deut. 3:23. See my Exodus volume, p. 83, note 26.

[56]Rashbam comments correctly that, while the standard form for a *qal* imperative with a suffix is שָׁמְרֵם ("guard them"), one does not say כְּלְאֵם from the root *k-l-'*. The fact that the last letter of the root is an *'alef* causes the vowel pattern to become כְּלָאֵם. See similarly iE here, and G.-K. 60c, 65b and 74b.

[57]I have corrected the reading in Rosin's edition שמעני אדוני (not a precise quote from any verse) to שמענו אדוני. In a similar context in his commentary to Ex. 14:16, Rashbam (in Rosin's edition) cites the verse correctly as שמענו אדוני.

[58]Here Rashbam's grammatical comment may have a purpose beyond accounting for the *qameṣ* vowel under the *lamed* of כלאם. Perhaps he is also taking issue with Rashi's first explanation of the word, in which Rashi (following Sanh. 17a, and presumably influenced by the grammar of rabbinic Hebrew) connects the word to the root *k-l-h* ("to destroy"). Rashbam agrees with Rashi's second explanation—that כלאם means "incarcerate them." Rashbam then explains how the vocalization of the verb is fitting in biblical Hebrew for a final-*aleph* verb (but not for a final-*heh* verb). Perhaps for the same reason—to show his disagreement with the first explanation in Rashi—Rashbam provides in the beginning of this comment an example of another use of the root *k-l-'* with a meaning similar to the idea of incarceration.

11:35 מקברות התאוה נסעו העם חצרות THE PEOPLE TRAVELED FROM KIBROTH-HATTAAVAH TO HAZEROTH [AND THEY WERE IN HAZEROTH]: According to the plain meaning of Scripture, [the doubling here,] "the people traveled from Kibroth-hattaavah *to Hazeroth* and they were *in Hazeroth*," means that they were delayed [in Hazeroth] "until Miriam was re-admitted" (12:15). That is the reason for the lengthier formulation here, "and they were in Hazeroth."

The *midrash 'aggadah* in the Sifre, at the end of this Torah portion[59] [which is connected to verse 12:16] says:

> "Then the people traveled from Hazeroth and encamped in the wilderness of Paran." But are there two places named Hazeroth that they traveled from the first and encamped at the second and then they traveled from the second and encamped at the first?

My teachers were not sure how to explain this text. I was asked about it in Paris and I explained it in a sermon.

The midrash derived this idea [that the text implies more than one arrival at Hazeroth] from the beginning of this section[60] [i.e. from our verse], "the people traveled from Kibroth-hattaavah *to Hazeroth* and they were *in Hazeroth*." On this verse the Sifre wrote: "This was when Miriam was smitten with *ṣara'at* ('leprosy')." The Sifre ultimately returned to and completed this theme when it dealt with the last verse of this section—"'Then the people traveled from Hazeroth . . ..' But are there two places named Hazeroth . . .?"

A midrashic explanation of our verse is offered [by Sifre] because the verse does *not* say "the people traveled from Kibroth-hattaavah and *they encamped* at Hazeroth." That is the way most of the travels and the encampments of the Israelites are described: "they traveled [from X] and they encamped [at Y]."[61] Rather the wording "the people traveled from Kibroth-hattaavah to Hazeroth" [without saying "and *they encamped* at Hazeroth"] implies that the people [reached Hazeroth and did not stop; they] also traveled *beyond* Hazeroth. But after that [it says] "and they were *in* Hazeroth." [That means] that they did an about-face while they were in Hazeroth.

---

[59]Or "at the end of this section." See note 60.

[60]Rashbam calls 11:35 תחילת הפרשה. He relates to the end of chapter 11 (the account of the arrival at Hazeroth) and all of chapter 12 (the story of Miriam) as one section or unit of text ("פרשה").

[61]This pattern, "they traveled from X and they encamped at Y," is most common in Numbers 33 but is found in other biblical verses too. Numbers 33:17 is most relevant to our verse: "They traveled from Kibroth-hattaavah and they encamped at Hazeroth."

[In other words, our verse tells us that the events of chapter 12 took place as the Israelites were leaving Hazeroth,[62]] when the first three-tribe unit[63] had already traveled beyond Hazeroth. [At that point,] when the Tabernacle had not yet been dismantled[64] [and the Levites had, accordingly, not yet begun traveling,[65]] Moses and Aaron and Miriam were still [in Hazeroth,] in the camp of the Levites. [That is when] God called to them suddenly (12:4) and Miriam was stricken with *ṣara'at* (12:10). Then they [i.e. the lead tribes who had already left Hazeroth] returned to Hazeroth. After seven days, Miriam was cured[66] of her leprosy. [At that point the text says (12:16),] "After that the people traveled from Hazeroth and encamped in the wilderness of Paran."[67]

I found all of this midrashic explanation in the Mekhilta on the Torah portion *Beshalaḥ*; there the explanation was connected entirely to the first

---

[62]In Rashbam's understanding, the midrashic meaning is premised on the assumption that the last phrase in chapter 11, "and they were in Hazeroth," leads into chapter 12, where the story of Miriam begins.

[63]On דגל as a three-tribe unit, see Rashbam's commentary ad 2:2, and note 13 there.

[64]Rashbam's language here, describing one three-tribe unit traveling and then the Tabernacle being dismantled, is an allusion to 10:14–17. See also 4:5 and Rashbam's commentary and note 29 there. See also the commentaries of Rashi and Nahm. to 10:17.

[65]The words here in square brackets are a translation of a speculative addition to the text proposed by Rosin, who reports that he found a blank space in the ms. at this point.

[66]Rashbam's phrase here—נאספה מצרעתה—might mean "was readmitted to the camp after her leprosy." I prefer to interpret it similarly to the phrase (II Kings 5:6) ואספתו מצרעתו, which is understood by NJPS (and many others) to mean "cure him of his leprosy."

[67]Rashbam offers an uncharacteristically long comment here and for an unusual purpose—to explain how a midrash works. As I noted ad 5:10 (note 15), Rashbam often tells us that, in theory, midrash is based on real exegesis of biblical verses. As he writes in his commentary to Gen. 1:1, midrash is based on superfluities in the text (יתור המקראות), or stylistic variations (שינוי הלשון) or, as he says in his commentary to Gen. 37:2, unnecessarily lengthy language (אריכות הלשון). Rashbam's comments to Num. 5:10 and to Gen. 37:35 give examples of how *midrashim* can be based on superfluities. Here he explains how a midrash can be based on either unnecessarily lengthy language or on a stylistic variation. (Normally travels of the Israelites are recorded using the style, "They traveled from X and encamped at Y." This time a different style was used. What do we learn from that?)

In all three of these examples (here, ad Num. 5:10 and ad Gen. 37:35), Rashbam explains how unusual language led to a midrash, but he also explains how that unusual language is easily explained in a *peshaṭ*-like manner. (Here he begins his comment by saying that the non-standard phrase "and they were in Hazeroth," simply means that they stayed there for a long time.)

In Rashbam's commentary to Deut. 10:6 he refers back to his commentary on our verse. There he explains the verse using the same midrashic methodology that he outlines here. But curiously there he says of this exegetical methodology "וזהו דרך פשוטו—this is the *peshaṭ* way of understanding the text." See notes there in Deut.

verse.[68] Then I found that Rabbi Kalonymus of Rome also explained [this text] in his *teshuvot* as I did.[69]

Furthermore [I would explain in the same manner the midrash found] on the verse (Ex. 12:37) "The Israelites traveled from Raamses to Succoth." In the Mekhilta[70] [commenting on that verse] it says, "Concerning this verse it is written (Ex. 19:4), 'I bore you on the wings of eagles'." I explained to those who asked me [what the basis of that midrash is.[71] The midrash is based on the non-standard style of the verse,] that it does *not* say there, "They traveled from Raamses and *they encamped* at Succoth." This teaches us that the verse [is not simply telling us the order of their travels; rather it] is telling us that the people traveled from Raamses to Succoth in negligible time. [Essentially] at the same time that they left Raamses, they left Succoth too. That is an example of [the Israelites being treated by God in a miraculous manner, traveling] "on the wings of eagles."[72]

---

[68]See Mekhilta *Va-yassa'* 3, commenting on the vs. Ex. 16:13.

Rashbam is saying that the Mekhilta related the midrashic comment—that it appears that there is more than one place called Hazeroth—to the verse Num. 11:35. This confirms Rashbam's point—that even though the Sifre presents this explanation as a midrash on 12:15, the real textual "difficulty" that led to the midrash is found in our verse, 11:35.

See the notes on Rashbam in the *Torat Ḥayyim* Pentateuch that astutely explain Rashbam's difficult comment in this manner. Cf. Rosin, note 2.

[69]The term *teshuvot* generally refers to responsa on issues of Jewish law.

Rabbi Kalonymos moved from Rome to Worms, some time before the year 1080. He is reputed to have been killed there in the Crusader massacres of 1096 (in other words when Rashbam was a youngster). He was an accomplished exegete and halakhist. His *teshuvot* are not extant but they are mentioned in several places. See Avraham Grossman's *Ḥakhme Ashkenaz ha-rishonim* (Jerusalem, 1981), pp. 348–354.

[70]*Pisḥa'* 14.

[71]This explanation and the previous part of Rashbam's comment—the explanation of the midrash on our verse in Numbers—both prove that, despite the radically *peshaṭ*-oriented nature of Rashbam's Torah commentary, Rashbam was not an anti-midrash crusader, interested only in *peshaṭ*. His contemporaries saw him as an authority concerning midrashic method and asked him to explain difficult *midrashim* to them. His reputation as an expert on the meaning of midrash seems to have spread widely; even when he was visiting Paris, people asked him to explain a troubling text in the Sifre.

[72]In Rashi's commentary to Ex. 12:37, the verse is explained in this same manner. There Rashi (following the Mekhilta text quoted here by Rashbam) explains that the Israelites traveled from Raamses to Succoth as if on eagles' wings and they arrived there "לפי שעה—in negligible time." Rashbam here uses that identical phrase and may be alluding to Rashi's commentary there.

In their commentaries on Ex. 19:4, neither Rashbam nor Rashi writes that to "travel on eagles' wings" is a metaphor for speed.

12:1 הכושית THE CUSHITE WOMAN: From the descendants of Ham.[73]

כי אשה כושית לקח FOR HE HAD MARRIED A CUSHITE WOMAN: As it is written in *Divre ha-yamim de-Moshe rabbenu.* Moses reigned in the land of Cush for forty years and married a certain queen [from there]. He never had intercourse with her. So it is written there [in that midrashic work].[74] When they [Miriam and Aaron] spoke against him, they did not realize that he had never had intercourse with her.[75] This is the true plain meaning of Scripture.

For if they slandered Moses concerning [his marrying] Zipporah, why would the text have to[76] add "for he had married a Cushite woman"?[77] Did we

---

[73]See Gen. 10:6. The significance of this genealogical fact becomes clear in Rashbam's next comment. See note 78.

[74]See my Exodus volume, pp. 44–45, note 6. There I discussed the problematic nature of Rashbam's comment here. In his Exodus commentary Rashbam dismisses *Divre ha-yamim de-Moshe rabbenu* as an unreliable, unauthoritative, non-canonical work. Here Rashbam cites it approvingly, and even pays it a rare compliment, calling its interpretation of our verse: עיקר פשוטו—the true *peshat*.

While the legend cited here by Rashbam originates in *Divre ha-yamim de-Moshe rabbenu,* it is found in a number of other, more "kosher" sources, too. See e.g. *Yalqut Shimoni* Exodus, number 168.

[75]The claim that Moses never had intercourse with this Cushite wife is the strangest part of this difficult comment of Rashbam. In notes 78 and 79 I will present Kamin's explanation. Beyond that, perhaps Rashbam's religious principles were offended by the idea that Moses had yet another non-Israelite wife. Rashbam felt, as I argue below, that he had no choice but to say that Moses had taken another wife, in addition to Zipporah. But he did not want to claim that Moses actually had intercourse with her. The implication of Rashbam's comment seems to be that Aaron and Miriam's "slander" about him might have been justified if Moses really had had intercourse with this wife. Their sin was that they incorrectly *assumed* that he had had intercourse with her.

[76]The phrase מה צורך is common in Rashbam's writings when dealing with the question of ostensibly redundant words in a biblical text. See e.g. his commentary to Gen. 18:1, s.v. כחם היום.

[77]In Appendix I of my Genesis volume I discussed Rashbam's attitude to literary anticipation. On pp. 420–421 there, I discussed Rashbam's attitude to our passage. I suggested that Rashbam, like ibn Kaspi (whom I cited there) saw the repetition here of the phrase "For he married a Cushite woman," as a form of "anticipation after the fact." In other words, the text knows that it is introducing new and startling information about another wife of Moses. Accordingly it repeats the fact in order to emphasize that this startling information is true. So also JBS here (לפי שלא מצינו במקום אחר שמשה לקח אשה כושית הגיד לך הכתוב כי בודאי אשה כושית לקח).

Rashbam rejects other interpretations of this phrase, according to which nothing new or startling is being said. As he puts it, "did we not know until now . . .." If the marriage described here was one that we already knew about, what would justify the repetition in our verse, "concerning the Cushite woman whom he married, for he married a Cushite woman"?

not know already that Zipporah was a Midianite? And another argument [against seeing a reference to Zipporah here]: Zipporah was *not* a Cushite. For Cush was a descendant of Ham (Gen. 10:6), while Midian was [not a Hamite but a Semite,] a descendant of Keturah who had borne him to Abraham[78] (Gen. 25:2).

Cf. Robert Harris (*The Literary Hermeneutic of Rabbi Eliezer of Beaugency*, note 68 on pp. 188–189) who correctly points out that Rashbam does not specifically write here that he has recognized the phenomenon of analepsis, or anticipation after the fact, in the biblical text. I still feel that such an understanding is implicit in Rashbam's comment.

[78]Rashbam is opposing the interpretation offered by Rashi and Sifre (and many other Jewish commentators) according to which the slander of Aaron and Miriam was directed against Moses' wife, Zipporah. Rashbam offers two arguments. First, as I explained in the previous note, such an explanation does nothing to justify the redundant language of vs. 1. Secondly, Zipporah is not a Cushite.

Rashbam's comment to this verse is problematic for a number of reasons. He relies on a book, *Divre ha-yamim de-Moshe rabbenu*, which is of dubious authenticity, as he himself writes in his Exodus commentary. Secondly, as Sarah Kamin notes (*Jews and Christians Interpret the Bible*, pp. 84–85, note 31), Rashbam's interpretation of these verses seems far from both his general methodological approach and from the simple meaning of the verses. Rashbam integrates a peculiar and fantastic midrash into his commentary and calls it "*peshaṭ*."

Kamin suggests that Rashbam's primary goal in this passage may be to polemicize against Christian allegorical interpretations of our verses. According to Origen, for example, Moses' marrying the Cushite woman prefigures Jesus' "marriage" to the gentile Church. By saying that the wife mentioned here was a flesh and blood Cushite, Rashbam is opposing that allegory. By saying that the marriage was never consummated Rashbam is undercutting the "prefiguration" argument. If Moses' marriage to that Cushite woman was a sham and was never consummated, Christians would not want to claim it as a prefiguration of the relationship between Jesus and the gentile Church.

While Kamin's approach is creative and interesting, I am not convinced that Christians were on Rashbam's mind when he was writing this passage. Rashbam explicitly says that it is the "Cushite = Zipporah" equation that he is opposing. He is following his standard methodological approach in a number of ways: (1) he is criticizing Rashi for reliance on a midrash; (2) he is rejecting a non-literal reading of the word "Cushite."

Kamin's questions are still valid. Rashbam's approach—his reliance on such a strange midrash—is unusual. But I would argue that Rashbam has very little choice here. There is no clear and simple textually grounded explanation for our text. We learn here that Moses married a Cushite, a fact that is nowhere reflected in any other verse in the Bible. As Budd puts it: "The explanatory gloss of vs. 1, while meaningful at the time it was inserted, has proved more of a hindrance than a help to modern [or medieval; ML] scholars because of their lack of knowledge of the original circumstances."

In such a situation, the exegete has two choices: (1) to say that the word "Cushite" does not mean Cushite; or (2) to look for some extra-biblical support for the story of Moses marrying a real Cushite. Rashbam, reasonably enough, concludes that the *peshaṭ*-oriented exegete will not adopt the first method. In fact, when one examines either Rashi or iE's explanation of this text, one finds that their troubles do not end when they take the interpretive leap and say that Zipporah was the Cushite. They still then have to figure out what could be

12:2 ויאמרו הרק אך במשה THEY SAID: "WAS IT ONLY THOUGH MOSES [THAT THE LORD SPOKE]: In other words, they voiced [a] further [complaint] about Moses.[79] "Why should he lord it[80] over us? God has spoken to the Israelites through us, too [not just through him]."

---

wrong now, from Aaron and Miriam's perspective, with Moses' marriage to Zipporah, and they add various other "facts" with no textual basis into the narrative.

Rashbam does want, whenever possible, to interpret the Bible using only the Bible. But when that is not possible (as here), he resorts to whatever sources can help. If such sources remain true to the words of the text, he accepts them.

For Rashbam, *peshaṭ* is not an absolute category but a relative one. Every verse in the Bible has to have a *peshaṭ* meaning—the meaning that does the least damage to the words and to the context. Rashbam feels that the legend about the Cushite princess here best satisfies that criterion.

See also the *Be'ur* here who surveys all the attempts of traditional medieval commentators to explain our verse and then concludes that the true *peshaṭ* is the explanation offered by Rashbam (היותר אמיתי לפי פשוטו של מקרא הוא פי' הרשב"ם). So also JBS.

[79]Rashbam explains that the question in vs. 2, "Was it only through Moses that the LORD spoke . . .?" represents a separate complaint from what is described in vs. 1, "Miriam and Aaron spoke against Moses because of the Cushite woman he had married."

As Kamin (*ibid.*) notes, the syntax of verses 1 and 2 argues against Rashbam's understanding. The wording, "They spoke against Moses . . . and they said . . .," is most easily interpreted as meaning "They spoke against Moses and this is what they said when they spoke against him, 'Was it only through Moses . . .?'" Kamin sees the fact that Rashbam's explanation is at odds with the syntax as further evidence that, when commenting on this section, Rashbam "strays from his methodological approach," abandoning his standard dedication to *peshaṭ* because of his anti-Christian polemical agenda. (See note 78.)

True, the syntax suggests that the words of vs. 2 represent an elaboration of vs. 1. But the two verses are very different in content. All of the proposed ways of reading vs. 2 as an elaboration of vs.1 are weak. Generally they involve adding many elements to the text in order to make a connection. For example, both Rashi and iE connect vss. 1 and 2 in essentially the same manner:

> They spoke against Moses because of the Cushite woman whom he had married **and with whom he had stopped having intercourse,** saying, "Was it only through Moses that the LORD spoke? Has He not spoken through us too, **and still we did not stop having intercourse with our spouses?"**

Rashbam rejects the idea that the central theme here is the interconnection of prophecy and sexuality, a theme that is not reflected anywhere in the biblical text. Instead Rashbam opts not to add extraneous ideas to the verses in order to make the syntax smooth. This however does not prove that he "strays from his methodological approach." If Rashbam is focusing on a different aspect of *peshaṭ* (on content instead of on syntax), there is no proof here of a hidden polemical agenda.

Many moderns also interpret the two complaints as unconnected; see e.g. Noth and NJPSC. So also Mendelssohn (ויא שפראכן אונטר אנדרן) and the *Be'ur*.

[80]Rashbam's language, להתפאר עלינו, is an allusion to Ex. 8:5. See also Rashbam's commentary there.

בנו: means "[He spoke] *through* us."[81]

12:4 פתאום SUDDENLY [THE LORD CALLED TO MOSES, AARON AND MIRIAM]: I.e. right when they were speaking against Moses, [immediately God spoke to them,] even though that was not a usual time[82] for God to be addressing them.[83] Rather [God spoke to them at such an unusual time] because He wanted to rebuke them on account of [their insult to] Moses,[84] and because He wanted to honor Moses.

12:6 נביאכם: means "your prophecy."[85]

---

[81]In Rashbam's view, Miriam and Aaron claim that they, along with Moses, act as transmitters of God's word to the people. In this he opposes Rashi, who has Miriam and Aaron claim that they, just like Moses, were addressed by God. Rashi paraphrases the phrase דיבר ב- here as meaning "speak to" or "speak with" (לדבר עם). In other words, Miriam and Aaron said, "Did God speak only *to* Moses, did He not speak *to* us too?" As NJPSC notes, Rashbam's explanation—that דיבר ב- means to speak "through"— finds support in a number of other biblical passages (e.g. II Sam. 23:2). NJPSC, however, prefers Rashi's understanding. Like Rashbam, see NJPS.

[82]See Rashbam below ad vs. 7 where he says that Moses, on the other hand, was used to getting prophecy from God at any time of day. See note 88 below.

[83]Rashbam's explanation opposes the midrashic explanation of Rashi that "suddenly" means that Aaron and Miriam were summoned by God despite the fact that they were impure at that time, as a result of sexual activity. (Rashi's explanation is adapted from early midrashic sources. See e.g. Tanh. B *Metzora'* 6. Rashi's explanation may also be found virtually verbatim in Tanh. *Ṣav* 13, but it seems clear that a later copyist copied Rashi's comment into the text of Tanh. there. See the note on Rashi's commentary in the *Torat Ḥayyim* Pentateuch here.) Rashbam explains more simply and more contextually that "suddenly" means "immediately."

Rashbam's comment may be understood as a *peshaṭ*-like reworking of the midrash. The midrash claims that Aaron and Miriam were summoned at a time when they were unprepared for prophecy as a result of sexual activity. Rashbam also says that they were unprepared for prophecy—because they were not used to God revealing Himself to them in such a sudden manner. Like Rashbam, see iE and Nahm.

[84]The language here in Rashbam's commentary—לגעור בהם מפני משה—is unusual. Perhaps it should be emended to לגעור בהם בפני משה. Then Rashbam would be saying that "God wanted to rebuke them in Moses' presence." Rashbam's comment would then be explaining why Moses was called (in our verse) when God wanted to speak only to Aaron and Miriam (vs. 5). Moses was called so that he could hear the rebuke that God was delivering in his honor. (So also iE: ומשה שומע.) If that is the meaning of Rashbam's comment, then it should be seen as opposing the explanation of Rashi (ad vs. 5, s.v. ויצאו שניהם) that God's speech to Moses and Aaron was delivered outside of Moses' hearing.

[85]The two halves of this verse are both difficult. The general idea seems to be that other prophets cannot be compared to Moses. Rashbam here deals with how to explain the words אם יהיה נביאכם. The simple translation of the words is "if your prophet is." However, that

12:7 נאמן הוא [THROUGHOUT MY HOUSEHOLD] HE IS נאמן: I.e. he is firm and established [there] at any time of day.[86] [The word נאמן appears] in the same sense in the verse (Is. 22:23), "I will fix him as a peg in a strong (נאמן) place." A peg that has been fixed in a strong place [is firm and] will not easily fall.[87]

12:12 אל נא תהי כמת DO NOT BE LIKE THAT DEAD PERSON: In other words, for your own honor and for your own sake, do not be, you, yourself,[88] like that dead person. Which [dead person]? Some [dead] person who was born—i.e. בצאתו—coming out from the loins—i.e. מרחם אמו, FROM THE WOMB OF *HIS* MOTHER, i.e. the mother of the living brother. [Because in that case,] it is as if HALF OF THE FLESH of the living [brother] has been eaten away.[89]

---

translation does not fit into the verse well. Instead, Rashbam interprets נביאכם as if נבואתכם were written, i.e. "when your prophecy is divine . . .."

Rashbam does not deal with the second half of the verse, which presents even more difficulties. Probably he would understand the idea of the verse in this way: "[Even] when your prophecy is divine, it still is on a level below that of Moses."

Rashi paraphrases the wording as אם יהיו לכם נביאיכם, yielding the sense, "when you [the Jewish people?] have prophets, they are still on a level below that of Moses."

As Levine notes, the phrase is extremely difficult and no explanation of it is satisfying.

[86]I.e. as opposed to Aaron and Miriam who, according to Rashbam ad vs. 4, were used to receiving prophecies only at specific times of the day. See note 82 above.

[87]Rashbam offers this same explanation of the word נאמן or related words (e.g. אמונה) in his commentary to Ex. 17:12 and Deut. 28:59. See notes 6 and 7 on p. 82 of my Exodus volume.

See also Rashbam's commentary to Ex. 33:16 where he writes that Moses requested that he be "distinguished and separated from the people of Israel, that it will be known that I am נאמן לנביא ולמוכיח ויהיו שומעים לדברי." In my Exodus volume (p. 410), I translated that phrase "a trustworthy prophet and rebuker so that the people will listen to me." Based on Rashbam's comment here, it is possible that נאמן in that passage should also be seen as meaning fixed, permanent or established.

[88]Rashbam's emphatic and repetitive language is meant to clarify that he is opposing the reading of Rashi (s.v. אל נא תהי) and almost all other exegetes who see the form תהי as third-person feminine singular. As Rashbam explains at the end of his comment, he sees the form תהי here as second-person masculine singular. It is *not* (as Rashi would have it) that Aaron is saying something about Miriam ("Let her not be . . ."), but rather that Aaron is saying something to Moses ("Do not, you, be . . .").

Grammatically speaking, both explanations are valid. For a similar ambiguity in the Bible concerning a form that could be either second-person masculine singular or third-person feminine singular, see Lev. 19:13 (לא תלין). See N. Leibowitz, *'Iyyunim ḥadashim besefer Va-yiqra'*, pp. 240–241. See also Rashbam's commentary below on 17:25, s.v. ותכל, and note 47 there.

[89]Both the syntax of the biblical verse and the syntax of Rashbam's comment are very difficult. But the general meaning of the comment is clear. As NJPSC paraphrases Rashbam, "Let *you* be not like one dead, inasmuch as all who come from the same mother's womb partly die (when any brother or sister dies)."

In other words, since Miriam, who was born from the womb of Moses' mother, is now "dead,"[90] [it is as if] half of Moses' flesh has been eaten away.

אל נא תהי [is a second-person masculine singular form, not a third-person feminine singular. It means] "Do not, you, be like someone dead." Similarly [the form תהי is used for a second-person masculine singular verb in the verses] (Prov. 22:26) "Do not be (תהי) one of those who give their hand," or (*ibid.* 24:28) "Do not be (תהי) a witness without good cause," or (*ibid.* 23:20) "Do not be (תהי) of those who guzzle wine."[91]

NJPSC also claims that Rashbam changed the whole mood of Aaron's words from a plea to a rebuke. I would say that, according to Rashbam, Aaron is reminding Moses that it is in Moses' self-interest (לכבודך ובשבילך) to intercede on Miriam's behalf.

Later Jewish commentators do not adopt Rashbam's idiosyncratic reading.

[90]All explanations of this verse are premised on the equation of leprosy with death. See Rashi here who quotes the rabbinic maxim (which may well be based on our verse) that a leper is tantamount to a dead person (מצורע חשוב כמת; see e.g. Sifre here).

[91]Rashbam is, without doubt, correct that in those verses the phrase אל נא תהי must be interpreted as second-person masculine singular. Still Rashbam's prooftexts show only that his reading is possible, not that it is required. There are also verses in the Bible were the phrase אל נא תהי appears and it must be interpreted as third-person feminine singular. See e.g. Gen. 13:8.

שלח (Numbers 13–15)

13:2 כל נשיא בהם EACH ONE OF THEM SHOULD BE A נשיא—A VOLUNTEER: The true plain meaning is as follows. [God said to Moses,]

> You should choose all of these twelve men from among those Israelites whose hearts move (נשא) them[1] to go. You should make an announcement and ask[2] the people, "Which man[3] would be willing to go spy out the land?" You should take [your spies] from those who say that they are willing to go, and you should select twelve.

And [this should be done] because men who are fit to go [as spies] to a foreign country and [who are capable of] acting boldly[4] and taking some of the fruit of the land are [the type of] men who are neither afraid nor [easily] disheartened.[5] That is why an announcement had to be made [to find volunteers]. God did not designate them by name,[6] as He had designated the chieftains who counted the Israelites[7] or the chieftains through whom the land was apportioned in [the Torah portion] *'Elleh mas'e*.[8] Those were designated by name [by God.][9]

---

[1]"נשא אותם לבם." An allusion to Ex. 35:29.

[2]I have translated according to Rosin's emendation שתכריז לשאול את העם (instead of the difficult wording of the ms.: שתכוין את העם). Berzinsky also proposes an acceptable emendation: שתבחון את העם, which would yield the translation, "You should put the people to the test [by asking,] 'Which man would be willing . . .'."

[3]"מי האיש." An allusion to Deut. 20:5–8.

[4]An allusion to the language of vs. 20, below: "והתחזקתם—act boldly." See Rashbam's commentary there.

[5]Another allusion to Deut. 20:8.

[6]"לא נקבם בשמות." An allusion to Num. 1:17. See also Rashbam's commentary to 7:2.

[7]See Num. 1:5–17.

[8]See Num. 34:16–29.

[9]Rashbam's offers an unusual understanding of the text, suggesting that נשיא, in this context, does not mean "chieftain" or "tribal head" but "volunteer."

Rashbam's explanation helps to solve a number of problems in the text: (1) How were the spies chosen? The simple meaning of our verse is that the twelve men were given the job of spying due to their rank or position. Verse 3 suggests that these twelve people were chosen "by the LORD's command." But Deut. 1:22 ("I selected from you twelve men, one from each tribe") states that Moses selected the twelve spies himself. (2) If נשיא in our verse means "head of the tribe" as it is standardly understood, why are there so many lists of נשיאים in the book of Numbers? As Levine puts it, "This list of names differs radically from the other lists of *nesi'im* in Numbers." In chapter one there is one list, which is repeated in chapter 7. In chapter 34 there is a separate list, with only one name in common with our list and no names in common with the list of chapter 1.

כל נשיא בהם EACH ONE OF THEM A VOLUNTEER: The cantillation sign under the word כל proves [that] its interpretation[10] [is as I said]. [The fact that the word "כל—each" is separated from the word נשיא (normally translated "chieftain") by a disjunctive cantillation sign shows that the verse means,] "Each one of these twelve men should be a נשיא—i.e. should volunteer to go." [The word כל is also used] in the same way in the verse (Ps. 8:7) "You placed everything (כל) under his feet."[11]

Rashbam's solution is that נשיא need not mean tribal leader. Our chapter presents not another list of heads of tribes, but a list of people who volunteered, or better yet, a list of those twelve men whom Moses selected from among the volunteers.

The *Be'ur* is correct, however, when it says that Rashbam's explanation is far-fetched (והוא רחוק). I have found no further echoes of this interpretation—that נשיא means volunteer—in later or earlier commentaries, although NJPSC does quote it without comment. Nahm.'s approach has something in common with Rashbam's when he writes that God commanded Moses to send one person from each tribe, and commanded him that they should be נשיאים, and Moses in his wisdom chose these twelve. Nahm. also must have felt that each tribe had many people who could be called נשיאים. See also LT who interprets נשיאים here as meaning important people (גדולים). And see also Krinski, *Qarne 'or*, note ב, and Licht, here. Arguably the parallel passage in Deut. 1:23 ("I selected twelve of your men [אנשים] one from each tribe") also implies that the twelve were not really "chieftains."

[10]Rashbam does not often refer explicitly to the cantillation marks as a tool for the exegete, but he does consider them important. See RSBM, p. 87, and see also Kogut, *passim*. One other specific example of using the disjunctive nature of the *ṭipḥa* as an exegetical tool may be found in the commentary, attributed to Rashbam, on Eccl. 4:13, s.v. מסכן.

[11]In biblical Hebrew the word כל can serve at least two different syntactical roles: it can be an adjective meaning "each or "every," and it can be a pronoun, meaning "everybody" or "everything." In the phrase which Rashbam quotes from Psalms—כל שתה תחת רגליו—it is obvious that כל is not an adjective. It could not refer to "every שתה," as if the word שתה were a noun. Rather, כל is a noun meaning "everything," a word which is not "connected" to any of the words that follow. According to Rashbam, this is why it has a disjunctive accent.

Here in Numbers it is more likely that the phrase כל נשיא consists of a noun and an adjective—"every chieftain." Onq. reads our phrase that way, understanding it as "all the chieftains that are among them (כל רבא דבהון) [will go as spies]." Rashbam argues that since there is a disjunctive accent here, just as in Psalms 8, we must conclude that כל is not to be connected to the following noun, נשיא—chieftain. The phrase, according to Rashbam, should be understood as: "כל—all" of the aforementioned men should be "נשיא בהם—volunteers."

The syntax and precise meaning of the phrase כל נשיא בהם are still difficult. I agree with Rashbam's assumption that reading the phrase כל נשיא as meaning "every chieftain" causes as many problems as it solves. (See similarly Levine's comment: "the phrase *kol nasi' bahem* means not 'every chieftain among them' . . ..") But even if that is not the syntax, Rashbam's understanding of נשיא is still unusual.

Cf. iE's attempts to deal with the phrase. iE's syntactical analysis accords with Rashbam's: כל is not an adjective modifying נשיא. But he still understands the meaning of the phrase in its usual way: "each [one of the above men] shall be a chieftain among them [= among the Israelites]."

13:16 ויקרא משה להושע בן נון יהושע MOSES CALLED HOSEA THE SON OF NUN JOSHUA: [This does not mean that Moses now changed his name to Joshua; already before this event he was called Joshua.][12] Rather this is what the verse means:

That same person, Hosea the son of Nun, whom we mentioned above (vs. 8) and who was called "Hosea" by his family, that is the same person whom Moses named "Joshua" when Moses appointed him as his attendant[13] and put him in charge of his [= Moses'] household.[14]

That was their custom [to assign a new name to a person who was appointed to a new task, as a special assistant to a ruler]. So also (Gen. 41:45) "Pharaoh then [when he appointed him viceroy] gave Joseph the name Zaphenath-paneah," and (Dan. 1:7) "He named Daniel [when he was entering the king's service] Belteshazzar," and (Dan. 4:5), [where Nebuchadnezzar refers to] "Daniel, called Belteshazzar after the name of my god."[15]

13:18 וראיתם את הארץ מה היא SEE WHAT KIND OF COUNTRY IT IS: If its

---

[12]The text of Rashbam in the ms. (as reported by Rosin) must be defective, as it begins with the word "rather" (אלא). The words in square brackets above are a translation of Rosin's speculative emendation of Rashbam's text. See Rosin RSBM, p. 32, note 2, and Rosin's notes to the commentary here, note 12.

Hizq.'s comment to this verse parallels and copies Rashbam's to a large extent. Hizq.'s wording for the beginning of the comment is: "לא שקראו עתה יהושע אלא כך הפירוש —This does not mean that now he named him Joshua. Rather this is the meaning . . .."

Rashbam's explanation is understandable even without emendation, especially when compared with his parallel comments ad Gen. 1:5 and 41:45. Berzinsky suggests the reasonable emendation of simply erasing the one word אלא—rather.

[13]An allusion to the language of Ex. 33:11.

[14]An allusion to the language of Gen. 39:5.

[15]As noted above (note 12), Rashbam is reiterating here a comment that he made twice in his commentary on Genesis. See my Genesis volume, pages 36–37, and note 1 on page 37. See also p. 292 there.

Rashbam's comment here opposes Rashi's explanation (following Sot. 34b) that it was precisely at this time, just before the spies left on their mission, that Moses changed Hosea's name to Joshua. This name change reflected Moses' prayer that Joshua would be saved by God from the evil plots of the rest of the spies. Like Rashbam, see also JBS, Hizq. and the *Be'ur*.

There are minor inaccuracies in Rashbam's quotations of both verses in Daniel. See the discussion in my Genesis volume, p. 292, note 4.

frontier lands[16] have forests or prairies[17] or moist,[18] well-watered land. Because you will prepare the [appropriate] weapons of war depending on what you see in the land—[for example] to chop down[19] the forests [in order] to clear a path for your soldiers to march on.

[The purpose of gathering this information was *not* in order to decide whether to capture the land.] For they were confident that God would give them the land of Canaan. Still [they did] not [think that they would get the land] without effort [on their part,] but [they knew that it would be done] by means of a military campaign.[20]

---

[16]As Rashbam clarifies in his commentary below to vs. 19, he is dealing with an apparent redundancy: our verse (18) says "See what kind of country it is," and the next verse (19) reads "Is the country in which they dwell good or bad." Rashbam's explanation is that the word "country" (ארץ) has two different meanings. In the first verse, it refers to the frontier lands, the uninhabited lands at the entrance to Canaan that the Israelites will encounter when they first arrive. In the next verse, it refers to the "country *in which they dwell*," i.e. the inhabited parts of Canaan. See further commentary to vs. 19, and note 23 below.

[17]Judging by the context, Rashbam is using the adjective חלקה to describe land without trees. It is possible that such usage originates in Joshua 11:17. See Qimḥi's commentary there.

It is also possible that when Rashbam uses the adjective חלקה here, he means "flatlands." See e.g. Rashi's commentary to Is. 40:4 or 63:14.

[18]Rashbam uses the unusual adjective מטוננת here. See MK 6b.

[19]Rashbam's phrase here—לסתת את היערים—is unusual. The verb *s-t-t* is generally used with stone, not wood, and means to sharpen or polish, not to chop down. (See Rashi's comment to that effect ad BQ 93b: שפוי שייך בעצים וסתיתה באבנים ושניהן לשון תיקון שמתקנן ומחליקן.) From the context it appears that Rashbam is using the verb in a less standard way here, as meaning "to chop down trees."

Perhaps this usage was popular in northern France in Rashbam's days. See similarly *Maḥzor Vitry* 531:3: "סופו של ארז זה באים וסותתין . . . אותו ומסככין בו בתים—a cedar tree which in the end they will chop down (סותתין) . . . and use for roofing."

In his commentary to Ex. 20:21, Rashbam uses the word המסתתין in its standard sense, but there too there is some confusion between wood and other media. See note 42 on p. 222 of my Exodus volume.

[20]Again Rashbam uses an unusual phrase ערכי המלחמה. See his commentary to Ex. 17:11, and note 3 there.

This paragraph of the commentary introduces the major theme of Rashbam's comment to this verse and to the following verses. Rashbam is expressing his opposition to Rashi's approach to these verses.

Rashi (following a number of midrashic sources, e.g. Tanh. *Shelaḥ* 5) sees the entire request that spies be sent to the land as an inappropriate idea suggested by untrusting Israelites and grudgingly accepted by God. Presumably Rashi is attracted to that explanation partially because it helps to harmonize our text with the story in Deut. 1, but also because he sees the questions posed by Moses in vss. 18–20 as inappropriate. If God told the people that the land was good, why ask further? If God told the people that he would capture the land for them, why ask about the strength of the inhabitants?

החזק הוא ARE THE PEOPLE STRONG: All of this [information is being collected] to let them know in what way they should wage war against them.[21]

13:19 ומה הארץ אשר הוא יושב בה IS THE COUNTRY IN WHICH THEY DWELL GOOD OR BAD: [It is necessary to pose this question, even after posing the question above in vs. 18, "what kind of country is it?"] because the question, "what kind of country," mentioned above (vs. 18), referred to frontier lands, where there are no settlements.[22] Now [the question in our verse] concerns the settled [part of the] land, "is it good or bad?"[23] I.e. is it filled with many crops, so that they will find there all the good things[24] [that they might need during[25]] their battles? For [if they know that they will find such items there,] they will not have to prepare in advance[26] too many provisions for the campaign.[27]

Rashbam rejects this. God told Moses to send spies in vss. 1–2 and in vs. 3 it says that they went "by the LORD's command." Rashbam accordingly interprets the sending of the spies as reasonable, and even meritorious. But then he must answer Rashi's implied theological question: if God had promised to capture the land for the Israelites, what is the purpose of this information-gathering exercise?

Rashbam's answer is that, while it is true that God would help the Israelites capture the land, still they were expected to capture it in a natural manner, through a well-planned military campaign, which required reconnaissance. See this explanation offered at greater length by Nahm., in his commentary here to vs. 2, and by JBS at the end of his commentary to chapter 13. So also NJPSC.

[21]Rashbam is continuing his explanation of why these questions are appropriate. See note 20.

[22]Rosin writes (RSBM, p. 126; and see note 11 there) that Rashbam's comment here shows his acquaintance with the standard ways of protecting frontier areas in the Middle Ages.

[23]As noted above (note 16), Rashbam is addressing the issue of the apparent redundancy of the two similar questions in vss. 18 and 19. Most other exegetes also deal with this question, explicitly or implicitly. iE (and so also Rashi, in the printed editions) sees the first question as referring to the populace and the second as referring to the agriculture of the land. JBS, Luzzatto, the *Be'ur* and Licht all suggest that the first question should be seen as introductory—in general, check "what kind of country is it?"—followed by a detailing of the specific concerns. Rashbam's explanation appears to be unique

[24]Rashbam's reference here to finding "all good things" in the land when they capture it is an allusion to Deut. 6:11 and Neh. 9:25. That verse in Neh. may contain (as Licht suggests here) a number of allusions to our chapter, making it especially appropriate for Rashbam to allude to that verse in this context.

[25]I added the words "that they might need during" to the text. The phrase here— וימצאו בה כל טוב מלחמותם—appears to be clumsy Hebrew. (מלחמותם is not a legitimate grammatical form and, even if it is emended to מלחמתם or מלחמותיהם, the syntax of the phrase is strange.) There is probably some textual corruption here, although Rashbam's point is clear.

[26] Rashbam's language—*להקדים* להם צדה כל כך לעת מלחמה *מקודם*—is redundant. I assume that there is some corruption in the text.

[27] Rashbam explains that the information being sought does not demonstrate the faithlessness of the people. (As opposed to Rashi; see note 20 above.) It is legitimate that troops going into

הבמחנים "Are they living in OPEN CAMPS: or in fortified cities?" All of this [information is provided] in order [for them] to know whether they need to construct towers and a mound[28] in order to capture the cities.[29]

13:20 השמנה היא [IS THE COUNTRY] FAT [i.e. fertile]: [This question was posed] in order to [cause the spies] to tell the Israelites that they will find the land flowing with milk and honey, just as God had promised.[30]

והתחזקתם ACT BOLDLY: Take [the fruit of Canaan] like brave men. Do not be afraid of anyone.[31]

והימים ימי בכורי ענבים IT HAPPENED TO BE THE SEASON OF THE FIRST RIPE GRAPES: This is written here [in order to prepare the reader for the story of] the cluster of grapes that they [i.e. the spies] would take (in vs. 23).[32]

---

battle should know whether they require a large or a small amount of provisions. In fact, according to Rashbam's explanation of the question, the Israelites here are proving their faithfulness. They are so confident of capturing any storehouses that the enemy might have that they feel they can count on having those provisions.

[28]The phrase is an allusion to a number of verses in Ezek. (e.g. 4:2) in which "towers and a mound" (דייק וסוללות) are two of the necessary parts of a successful siege of a fortified city. Although the precise meaning of the phrase is uncertain, Rashbam uses it again in his commentary to Deut. 20:19, where he writes that wood is necessary for building "towers and a mound."

[29]Rashbam explains further the military purpose of the Israelites' reconnaissance efforts. When the spies brought back the report, the people were taken aback and began to express their lack of trust when they heard that the Canaanite cities were so well fortified. This could imply that, from the beginning, the purpose of asking whether the cities were fortified was to decide *whether* it would be possible to capture the land. Accordingly Rashbam emphasizes that trusting soldiers who are sure that they will be able to capture the land would still have legitimate use for such information.

[30]This final question about the land's fertility is much more difficult to explain as serving a military purpose and Rashbam therefore suggests instead that the question had a different purpose—to reinforce to the Israelites that they were coming to a country with extraordinary agricultural produce. See similarly Nahm.'s commentary to vs. 2, where he suggests that perhaps Moses knew how impressive the agriculture was in Canaan and that he asked about it so that the people would react with happiness and would joyfully continue on their path with renewed resolve.

[31]"לא תגורו מפני איש." A direct quotation from Deut. 1:17.

See note 32.

[32]In other words, this phrase is an example of "anticipation," a literary device in the Bible that Rashbam often points out to his readers. See the discussion in my Genesis volume, pp. 400–421 (on anticipation in general) and especially p. 404 (on our verse). See also Licht here who notes that our phrase appears out of place, as it interrupts the narrative. It appears right between the command to the spies and their performance of their task. Licht, like

13:22 ויבא עד חברון [*THEY* WENT UP (ויעלו) INTO THE NEGEV] AND *HE* CAME (ויבא) TO HEBRON: There is an *'aggadah* that appears [at first glance to represent] the plain meaning of Scripture which [explains that] the verse is referring to Caleb [who, according to this midrash, was the only one of the spies who came to Hebron]. For it says below (Deut. 1:36) [concerning Caleb] "to him I will give the land on which he set foot," and (Num. 14:24) "him will I bring into the land that he entered and his offspring shall hold it as a possession." So [the midrash says that the meaning of the singular verb in the phrase,] "*he* came (ויבא) to Hebron" is [that] Caleb [alone came there]. And [according to that same midrash] he prostrated himself at the grave of the forefathers [at the Cave of Machpelah in Hebron] and prayed that he would be saved [by God] from the evil advice of the [rest of the] spies. And we find that Joshua assigned Hebron to Caleb, as it is written (Josh. 21:12), "They gave the fields and the villages of the town [of Hebron] to Caleb the son of Jephunneh as his holding."[33]

But in any case, following the true plain meaning of Scripture[34] [the phrase "he came—ויבא to Hebron" means that] each and every one of the spies "comes"[35] to Hebron. We know this because the spies [other than Caleb] say

---

Rashbam, explains that at this point the text provides incidental information that will help the reader understand the continuation of the narrative.

Rashbam's approach to the end of this verse may be seen as opposed to that of Hizq. who connects the phrase "act boldly and take of the fruit" with the phrase "it happened to be the season of the first ripe grapes." Hizq. says that the latter phrase helps explain the former one: bravery was required because the Canaanites had increased protection in their vineyards during the grape-harvest season. Rashbam's theory of anticipation is that the significance of an individual phrase need not always be found *within* the verse where it first appears. Sometimes, for example here, the significance is found in the continuation of the story.

[33]Rashbam, uncharacteristically, provides here a long argument (which he will eventually reject) that ostensibly proves that a specific midrash really conforms to *peshaṭ*. The argument is based on three factors: (1) a grammatical anomaly in our verse—the shift to a singular verb, ויבא, where a plural was anticipated; (2) the fact that Caleb was promised that the land where *he* went would be his inheritance; and (3) the fact that Caleb eventually received Hebron as his inheritance. Putting these points together, the midrash concludes that Caleb must be the one who "comes," in the singular, to Hebron.

This midrash originates in Sot. 34b. It is cited here approvingly by Rashi and also by more *peshaṭ*-oriented exegetes like iE and Luzzatto.

[34]Rashbam's dismissal of the midrash from Sot. 34b may not be the only reason why he comments at such length here. He may also be rejecting the strange *peshaṭ* interpretation found in LT and JBS. These exegetes write that the understood subject of the verb ויבא must be "the road," yielding the sense "They went up into the Negev and it [the road] came to Hebron."

[35]In other words, the singular verb ויבא is used because each one of the spies came there, not because Caleb alone came there.

Rashbam's solution is that a singular is sometimes used when a plural is expected in order to convey the idea of "each and every one." He uses this explanation in several places;

(vs. 28) "we saw the children of Anak[36] there," [and the children of Anak lived] in Hebron.[37] It is also written [that they said,] (vs. 33) "there we saw the Nephilim, the children of Anak."[38]

לפני צען מצרים [NOW HEBRON WAS BUILT SEVEN YEARS] BEFORE ZOAN OF EGYPT: According to the plain meaning of Scripture,[39] it was built before Zoan and furthermore, it, the older city, was [even] more important than the newer city.[40]

Since the Israelites knew how important Zoan was, it was necessary to tell them that the cities of Israel were even more important.[41] Also, another reason for providing [the incidental information about] the antiquity of Hebron [was to explain] why there were "children of Anak" there, since they ["the children of Anak"] are from the days of old.[42]

---

see e.g. his commentary to Gen. 49:22 (and note 5 there), Ex. 32:29 (and note 40 there) and Ex. 35:25 (and note 13 there). iE too often offers this explanation. See e.g. his commentary to Gen. 27:29, Ex. 23:23 (longer commentary), Lev. 19:8 and Num. 24:8.

See similarly G.-K. 145l: "The plural of persons . . . is sometimes construed with the singular of the predicate, when instead of the whole class of individuals, each severally is to be represented as affected by the statement."

[36]Or "giants." We do not know how Rashbam understands the phrase בני ענק.

[37]Verse 22 says explicitly that the children of Anak lived in Hebron.

[38]Rashbam argues that the midrashic reading, while resembling *peshat*, ignores the facts of the story. Caleb could not have been the only one of the spies to visit Hebron, as the midrash suggests. The other spies report that they saw "the children of Anak," who we know lived in Hebron, proving that these spies, too, visited Hebron.

The *Be'ur* agrees with Rashbam. See, however, Luzzatto who supports the midrashic reading and dismisses Rashbam's objection, arguing that some "children of Anak" could have lived outside of Hebron, too.

[39]Rashbam is opposing the midrashic explanation of Rashi (following Sot. 34b) according to which Hebron, despite the simple meaning of the words here, was *not* as old as Zoan. The midrash reinterprets the verse as saying that Hebron נבנתה—was better or more fertile than Zoan. (See also Rashi there in Sot., s.v. מבונה.)

[40]See note 39. Since Rashi writes that Hebron was not older but just more important than Zoan, Rashbam writes that Hebron was both older and more important. So also Licht here.

[41]Rashbam displays historical sensitivity and reader awareness in this comment. Perhaps the significance of the Torah's words here, "Hebron was built seven years before Zoan of Egypt," escapes modern (and medieval) readers. Rashbam writes that the words were meaningful to the original readers of the text, the Israelites leaving Egypt, who knew of Zoan's antiquity and importance. See also Hizq.'s reformulation of Rashbam's comment. Hizq. writes that Egypt was used as the point of reference for describing Hebron "since they had just left there and they were experts [concerning Egypt] and they knew its [= Zoan's importance."

[42]Other commentators also note that the age of Hebron is emphasized here because of some connection between its antiquity and the fact that "children of Anak" live there. Slightly differing variations on this connection appear in the commentaries of JBS, Nahm., Luzzatto and Ehrlich.

13:30 ויהס [CALEB] HUSHED [THE PEOPLE]: He silenced them through his wisdom.[43]

13:33 מן הנפילים [THERE WE SAW NEPHILIM, CHILDREN OF ANAK DESCENDED] FROM THE NEPHILIM: I.e. from the first [Nephilim], as it is written in Genesis (6:4), "There were Nephilim in the land in those days."[44]

כחגבים LIKE GRASSHOPPERS: To someone who is much taller, a short person looks like a grasshopper, [a creature] which is very short. Proof [of this explanation] comes from the verse (Is. 40:22), "He who is enthroned above the vault of the earth so that its inhabitants seem like grasshoppers."[45]

14:9 סר צילם מעליהם THEIR "SHADE" HAS DEPARTED FROM THEM: means "they do not have any protection under which to seek refuge,[46] for already, ever since the time that God dried up the Red Sea, all the inhabitants of the land are quaking before us." That is what Rahab the harlot said (Josh. 2:9–11), and so it is written (Ex. 15:15) "all the inhabitants of Canaan are quaking."

---

[43]Rashi (following Sot. 35a) suggests that Caleb used a ruse to silence the people: he pretended to be giving a speech attacking Moses in order to get the people's attention. Rashbam simply says that by using his wisdom (in some unspecified manner, perhaps as embodied in his speech which follows), Caleb was able to get the people to stop murmuring. (As Licht notes, nowhere has the text said yet that the people were murmuring, but from the fact that Caleb had to silence them the implication is clear.) Others say that the word ויהס means "to silence by saying 'hush'." See iE (in the name of ibn Janaḥ) and NJPSC. Rashbam's use of the word בחכמתו (through his wisdom) shows that he sees Caleb's action as something more sophisticated than saying "hush."

[44]Rashbam is explaining the doubling here "Nephilim . . . from the Nephilim." He says that the Nephilim alive in Moses' days are the descendants of the original Nephilim, whom we know of from Genesis. His comment may be a *peshaṭ* reworking of Rashi's midrashic identification of the names of the ancestors of these Nephilim.

[45]In other words, the simile " like grasshoppers," means "tiny." See similarly JBS, Hizq. and the *Be'ur*.

[46]Rashbam's interpretation opposes that of Rashi who explains midrashically (following BB 15a) that the term "their shade" is a reference to the righteous people on whom the Canaanites had depended in the past, specifically a reference to Job who had just died. Rashbam contends that the reference is not to some internal problem in Canaan, but to the reaction of the Canaanites to the miracles wrought for the Israelites. The Canaanites were afraid and had lost their confidence. So also Hizq. The *Be'ur* explains that in biblical Hebrew a confident person who fears no enemies is said to be hidden in the shade. It can therefore be said of frightened people that "their shade has departed from them."

Cf. JBS who says that the "shade" of the Canaanites is a reference to God, who has now abandoned them, and see also Nahm. who says that the guardian angel of the Canaanites has abandoned them. See NJPSC where both of these explanations are cited approvingly.

14:14 ואמרו אל יושב הארץ הזאת THEY WILL SAY אל THE INHABITANTS OF THAT LAND: I.e. "they—the Egyptians—will say *concerning* (על)[47] the inhabitants of the land of Canaan." So [this speech] is fleshed out further on—that the Egyptians would say (vs. 16): "It must be because the LORD was powerless [against the Canaanites]."[48]

But now [i.e. before the text tells us *what* it is that the Egyptians will say about the Canaanites,] the text first explains [parenthetically] *why* the Egyptians will say those things.[49] It is because they have heard that You took them out [of Egypt] with great power[50] and with a pillar of fire and cloud,[51] all apparently done with abundant love and affection [for the Israelites].[52] Then, [if] You[53] (vs. 15) slew them [the Israelites] to a man,[54] THEY, i.e. the Egyptians,[55] WOULD SAY that it was not because of hatred[56] that You did this to them but

---

[47]So also Rashi. In general, Rashbam's explanation of these verses follows the basic pattern of Rashi's.

[48]Rashbam explains that the words "they shall say" in vs. 14 and "they shall say" in vs. 15 refer to the same speech, the speech that starts in vs. 16. So also Rashi. Cf. iE who disagrees.

While Rashbam and Rashi do not say so explicitly, their interpretation implies that the words that "they will say" are repeated because of the principle of repetitive resumption. After the narrative flow has been interrupted by telling us what the Egyptians are thinking, it is necessary to repeat the phrase "they will say" when the narrative resumes.

[49]This is the major contribution of Rashbam to the exegesis of these verses—his explanation of *why* there is an interruption between, on the one hand, the statement in vs. 14 that the Egyptians "will say" something, and, on the other hand, the actual words that they will say, which are reported only in vs. 16. Rashbam explains that the interruption is a parenthetical remark that provides the reason for what they will say.

In his explanation, Rashbam plays on the language of Ex. 32:12: למה יאמרו מצרים.

[50]An allusion to Ex. 32:11, another prayer of Moses with a similar theme about what the Egyptians would say if God destroyed the Israelites.

[51]An allusion to Ex. 14:24.

[52]The idea is found also in Rashi. Rashbam's phrase אהבה יתירה וחבה may be an allusion to *'Avot* 3:14, another text that describes God's special attitude to the Jewish people.

[53]In the printed texts of Rashbam's commentary, this comment concerning what the Egyptians would say about God alternates between referring to God in second person and in third person, apparently arbitrarily. I have translated all the references as second person, for ease of reading.

[54]Or perhaps, "if you slew them 'at a single blow'" (following Harrison). See Rashbam's commentary below on vs. 20, s.v. כדבריך, and note 63 there.

[55]Cf. iE who says that, in vs. 15, "they will say" refers to the Egyptians and the Canaanites and any other nations that will hear of the events that Moses describes.

[56]So also JBS.

There is a parallel prayer to this one in Deut. (9:26–29) in which Moses tells God that, if the Israelites are destroyed, the Egyptians will think that "God was powerless to bring them into the land." But, in that version of the prayer, Moses says that the Egyptians might also think that "ומשנאתו אותם—because He hated them He took them out to kill them in the wilderness." (See a similar line of argumentation in Moses' prayer in Ex. 32:11–13.)

as result of (vs. 16) מבלתי יכולת—[Your] POWERLESSNESS to fight against those thirty-one [Canaanite] kings.[57] So now "turn from Your blazing anger"[58] for the sake of Your Name, that it not be desecrated.[59]

14:17 יגדל נא כח ה׳ LET MY LORD'S STRENGTH: to show forbearance, BE GREAT. [Showing forbearance is a form of demonstrating one's strength,] as it is written (Prov. 16:32) "Better to be forbearing than mighty, to have self-control than to conquer a city."[60]

14:20 סלחתי: [Even though this form appears to be a past-tense verb, meaning "I forgave," it is actually a present-tense verb meaning,] "I now forgive." So similarly (Gen. 23:13), "נתתי—I am giving you the money."[61]

Here in Numbers, Rashbam and JBS note that Moses seems to have different concerns about what the Egyptians "might say" than he does in Deut. and Ex. Here he emphasizes that the Egyptians know of the miracles that God did for the Israelites, a theme which is absent from his prayers in Deut. and Ex.

Therefore, Rashbam and JBS conclude that Moses' argument here is: because the Egyptians know about all of God's kindness to the Israelites, they could *not* reasonably think that it was because of God's hatred that the Israelites were destroyed.

[57]The kings that were vanquished by Joshua. See Joshua 12:24.

Very similar wording, paraphrasing what the Egyptians were likely to say, is found in the midrash in NR 16: "[The Egyptians] would say, 'He was able to overcome us, but He is unable to overcome thirty-one [kings]'" (אומרים בנו היה יכול לעמוד בשלשים ואחד אין יכול לעמוד).

[58]Exodus 32:12.

[59]The last four words of Rashbam's comment—למען שמך שלא יתחלל—are found verbatim in Rashbam's explanation of Moses' similar prayer in Exodus 32. See notes 21 and 22 on page 397 of my Exodus volume. See also Rashbam's commentary to Gen. 32:13, and notes 1 and 2 on p. 204 there.

[60]The difficulty in our verse is: when asking God to have mercy and to refrain from destroying His people, Moses pleads, "Let Your strength be great." Saying this to God would usually mean asking God to display His awesome might (perhaps in a destructive manner, but, at a minimum, in an overpowering manner). Rashi says (following Sanh. 111a-b) that Moses is asking God to be "strong," by keeping His promises. Rashbam says that displaying restraint constitutes a sign of strength.

Rashbam's explanation—that self-control is a sign of power and strength—is a common idea in rabbinic literature (e.g. *'Avot* 4:1) and is well supported by the prooftext that he cites from Proverbs. Many other exegetes interpret the verse as Rashbam does. See e.g. iE, JBS, the *Be'ur* and NJPSC.

[61]Rashbam often makes the point that perfect forms may have a present-tense meaning in biblical Hebrew. See his *Dayyaqut* (Merdler's edition, p. 46), and his commentary to Gen. 1:29, 23:11, and 41:41.

See also notes 4 and 5 on p. 56 of my Genesis volume, where I point out that there Rashbam is not simply making a grammatical point. There he is also arguing against Rashi's reading of Gen. 23:13, where Rashi attributes significance to the use of the perfect נתתי.

כדבריך [I FORGIVE,] IN THE MANNER THAT YOU HAVE ASKED: [I.e. I will show my slowness to anger which you mentioned (vs. 18),] in that I will not "strike them with pestilence" (vs. 12) [all] at one time; I will rather grant them an extension[62] for forty years.[63]

Here, too, it is possible that Rashbam is arguing against the idea, preserved in Hizq.'s commentary, that סלחתי is actually to be understood in the past tense. Hizq. writes: "I forgave them in the past, at the time of the sin of the golden calf, but this time I will not forgive them; rather I will punish them." While this interpretation does not seem to appear in the extant works of any exegete before Rashbam, scholars believe that Hizq.'s work was a compilation of exegetical traditions, mainly from Northern France. Perhaps here too Hizq. preserved an interpretation older than Rashbam's, one against which Rashbam is reacting here.

[62]Rashbam's phrase, אאריך להם, is playing with the language of Moses' request (vs. 18) that God show himself as ארך אפים.

[63]There are a number of exegetical problems with this verse. The most serious one is that God says here, "I forgive" (סלחתי), but then, in vss. 22–35, He outlines a strict punishment: all the people above age 20 shall die in the wilderness over the next forty years. Did God then really forgive?

Above (note 61), I presented Hizq.'s creative but far-fetched solution: God did not say that he was forgiving this time. Rather He said "in the past I forgave (סלחתי), but not this time."

Rashbam's solution is that God promised to forgive in the specific manner that Moses had requested. Moses had asked that God be (vs. 18) ארך אפים, i.e. slow to anger, and not punish the people immediately. God had, in fact, said that he would (vs. 12) "strike them with pestilence," which would kill them off quickly. Moses' prayer (vs. 15) addressed this threat: he described what the other nations would think if God killed them כאיש אחד—i.e. "to a man" or perhaps "at a single blow" (following Harrison). God's answer, סלחתי, then meant that that original plan of immediate destruction had been abandoned. The evildoers would still be punished, but in a more compassionate manner (and one which was less obvious to the other nations), dying off slowly over the forty years of wandering in the wilderness.

Both iE and Nahm. offer versions of this same interpretation—that Moses' request had been for something less than total forgiveness and that God granted that request when He said סלחתי which means "I am delaying the punishment." See also NJPSC here, vs. 19: "Hebrew *salaḥ* implying not the absolution of sin, but the suspension of anger; that they not die immediately . . .." See also NJPSC, Excursus 32, on pp. 392–396.

The second exegetical problem with this verse is theological: what does it mean to say that God forgave כדבריך, as Moses said? Does this mean that God "obeys" Moses' words? In fact, a number of *midrashim* unabashedly highlight Moses' power over God. See e.g. DR 5:13: ["Moses says to God], 'Let us see who will win—You, God, or I?' . . . Whatever Moses decreed, God accepted."

Rashi's solution is that the phrase means "I am forgiving them *for the reason* that you mentioned," i.e. the damage to God's reputation. Rashi is reworking a number of midrashic sources which say that God said two things to Moses: (1) סלחתי—I forgive, and (2) כדבריך—the other nations would indeed say what you, Moses, said that they would say. See e.g. NR 16 (סלחתי כדברך שהם עתידים המצרים לומר כדבריך).

Rashbam's explanation is that the word כדבריך qualifies and limits the amount of "forgiveness" that God is granting. He promises to forgive them only כדבריך, *to the extent that* Moses mentioned, granting an extension and not punishing immediately.

14:21 ואולם: means "however."[64]

14:22 עשר פעמים [THEY TRIED ME THOSE] TEN TIMES: I.e. many [times].[65] So also [the number ten should not be taken literally in the verses] (Gen. 31:7) "[changing my wages] *ten* [i.e. many] times" or (Lev. 26:26) "*ten* [i.e. many] women shall bake" or (Job 19:3) "you humiliated me *ten* [i.e. many] times."[66]

14:33 רועים במדבר [YOUR CHILDREN] WILL GRAZE IN THE WILDERNESS: It appears to me that [the correct understanding of this verse is that] they will support themselves by going here and there, just as sheep do when grazing. In other words, they will roam to and fro in the wilderness.[67]

14:36–37 והאנשים אשר שלח משה THE MEN WHOM MOSES HAD SENT: and then, after he had sent them, וישובו—THEY HAD RETURNED, from the land

---

[64]Rashbam made the same comment concerning the word ואולם in his commentary to Gen. 28:19 and 48:19. See also his commentary to Ex. 9:15–16 and note 9 there.

See also S. Japhet, *The Commentary of Rabbi Samuel ben Meir (Rashbam) on the Book of Job*," pp. 213–215 and see the discussion in my article, "'Rashbam' on Job: a Reconsideration," *Jewish Studies Quarterly* 8 (2001), 80–104, especially pp. 81–82.

[65]Rashbam makes this point many times in his commentary—that the number ten (or seven) is not to be taken literally, but simply means "many." See commentary to Gen. 31:7 and Lev: 26:18 and 26:26. See also Andrew of St. Victor who notes here that both the number seven and the number ten in biblical Hebrew are not to be taken literally, but actually mean "many."

Here Rashbam's comment opposes Rashi who identifies those "ten times" that the Israelites tested God in the wilderness. Many rabbinic texts mention those "ten" tests, taking the number here literally. See e.g. *'Avot* 5:4.

Cf. JBS who writes that while sometimes words like "ten" are not literal numbers, specifically here that interpretation is *not* to be followed. The emphatic language זה עשר פעמים shows, according to JBS, that the number does not mean "many," and that is why the rabbis took the ten tests of God by the Israelites in the wilderness literally. From the list of examples that JBS cites, it appears that his comment is meant as criticism of Rashbam.

[66]In his commentary to Lev. 26:26, Rashbam makes the same point about Job 19:3.

In the commentary on Job attributed by Sara Japhet to Rashbam there is an interpretation of that verse that contradicts what is written in Rashbam's Torah commentary. See Japhet, p. 67, note 61, and see Rashbam's commentary to Lev. 26:26, and note 15 there.

[67]The *qal* of the Hebrew verb *r-'-h* may refer either to the action of the shepherd taking sheep to pasture, or to the action of sheep, grazing on grass. Rashbam prefers the latter interpretation of the metaphor in the verse: the Israelites are compared to grazing sheep, not to shepherds. Cf. iE who offers the shepherd interpretation instead.

See also Rashbam's commentary to Lev. 16:10 where he explains that the word מדבר means a grazing area, and see note 8 there.

of Israel,[68] and then, after they had returned, וילינו they HAD CAUSED [the community] TO MUTTER, as it is written above[69] (13:31–14:4), [those men] now died.[70]

דבה CALUMNY: [The word דבה] comes from [a geminate root, *d-b-b*, just like] (Song 7:10) "causing the lips of sleepers to speak (דובב)." So also the word רינה ("joy"), as in the phrase (Prov. 11:10) "when wicked perish there is joy (רינה)," comes from [the geminate root *r-n-n*, as in the phrase] (Job. 20:5) "the joy (רננת) of the wicked has been brief." So similarly [the word סיבה (cause),] in the phrase (I K 12:15) "for the cause (סיבה) was from God," is from סובב [i.e. from the root *s-b-b*].[71]

14:40 אל המקום אשר אמר ה׳ [WE ARE PREPARED TO GO UP] TO THE PLACE THAT THE LORD SPOKE OF: and to which God was referring when he said that we should go there to capture it.[72]

---

[68]Rashbam explains carefully that the word וישובו means that the spies returned from the land of Israel. He may be opposing the interpretation, found in both Nahm. (ad 13:32) and Hizq. (here), that the phrase וישובו וילינו means that they *once again* (שוב) caused the people to mutter.

Here Rashbam agrees with Rashi.

[69]Rashbam emphasizes that the muttering here is the same muttering that was mentioned above. It is not meant to describe a new further complaint. See note 68.

[70]Rashbam is explaining the syntax of vss. 36–37. He is saying that vs. 36 consists entirely of the subject of the sentence ("the men") and a relative clause modifying that subject: "*whom* Moses had sent and *who* had returned from the land and *who* had caused the community to mutter." The predicate begins (with a repetitive resumption of the word והאנשים) only in vs. 37: [those men] died.

So also Rashi.

[71]Rashbam makes an unarguable point about certain nouns which are derived from geminate roots. Rashbam often discusses geminate verbs and often uses the verb *s-b-b* as his paradigm. See my Exodus volume, p. 176, note 35, and see also commentary to Num. 17:20 below.

Rashi here also comments on the word דיבה and also cites the verse in Song 7 to explain the word.

[72]Theoretically, the phrase המקום אשר אמר ה׳ כי חטאנו could mean "the place to which God was referring when he said that we sinned there." Rashbam wants to direct us away from that reading. It means "the place concerning which God said [that we should go there and capture it]." The words כי חטאנו do not mean "*that* we have sinned," but "*because* we have sinned." The clause כי חטאנו is connected to the verb "ועלינו—we are going up," not to the verb "אמר—[God] said."

In most printed editions of Rashi, a similar comment may be found here. The comment is absent in the first edition printing of Rashi and in a number of Rashi mss. Accordingly it is difficult to say whether Rashbam is following Rashi or whether Rashbam was the first to explain the verse in this way.

כי חטאנו FOR WE SINNED: when we trusted the evil advice of the rest of the spies.[73]

14:41 והיא [WHY ARE YOU TRANSGRESSING THE LORD'S COMMAND?] IT: i.e. this course of action,[74] SHALL NOT SUCCEED.

14:43 כי על כן INASMUCH AS YOU HAVE TURNED: [The phrase כי על כן שבתם should be understood as if it were written] כי על כן אשר שבתם.[75] So also the phrase (Gen. 39:4), וכל יש לו נתן בידי should be understood as if it were written וכל אשר יש לו נתן בידי ("everything *that* he had he entrusted to me").[76]

---

[73]The phrase "עצת מרגלים" is a common rabbinic phrase. See e.g. Meg. 13a and see Rashi and Rashbam's commentaries to 13:22.

On Rashbam's understanding of the syntax, see note 72.

[74]The syntactical problem of our verse is that the pronoun והיא (it? she?) does not have a clear antecedent. The closest noun is פי ה'—God's "mouth" or "command." But there are two problems with saying that that is the antecedent: (1) it is unlikely that Moses is saying that God's command will not succeed, and (2) the noun פה is masculine and the verb תצלח is feminine.

Rashi's solution is to paraphrase והיא לא תצלח as "that which you are doing shall not succeed." In this way, Rashi solves the first issue, the theological one, but he does not address the second issue, the grammatical question. Rashbam attempts to deal with both by saying that the antecedent of והיא is the implied noun דרך, which is feminine. See also iE who suggests two other possible feminine nouns that could be seen as the implied antecedent of the pronoun והיא.

Modern grammarians would presumably find Rashbam's and iE's attempts to find a specific feminine antecedent here unnecessary. See e.g. G.-K. 135p ("The separate pronoun היא . . . sometimes refers in a general sense to the verbal idea contained in a preceding sentence"). So also the *Be'ur* here.

[75]Rashbam often makes this comment about the phrase כי על כן, meaning "inasmuch as." He is emphasizing that it does not mean "*that is why* you have turned," as the words might imply literally, but "*because* you have turned." See also his commentary to Gen. 18:5, and note 2 there, and commentary above ad Num. 10:31.

So also Rashi.

[76]Rashbam here is going beyond the claim that the specific idiom כי על כן would be better understood if one added the word אשר. Rashbam writes in his commentary to Gen. 18:5 that the word אשר is often implicit in biblical texts. Here he cites an example of the phenomenon. See also his commentary to Ex. 20:10, and note 13 on p. 216 of my Exodus volume.

Rashi interprets Gen. 39:4 (*ad loc.*) in the same way that Rashbam does here.

14:44 לא משו DID NOT MOVE: [The verb משו here] is like[77] the verb (Ex. 13:22), "לא ימיש—shall not move."[78]

15:20 כתרומת גורן [THE *FIRST* YIELD (ראשית) OF YOUR BAKING YOU SHOULD SET ASIDE] LIKE THE *TERUMAH* OF YOUR THRESHING FLOOR: [That *terumah*] is also called (Deut. 18:4) "the *first* fruits (ראשית) of your new grain."[79] So also this [gift to the priests, the *ḥallah*,] is called "the *first* yield of your baking."[80] So we learned in a Mishnah in *'Avodah Zarah* and in *Shabbat.*[81]

---

[77]It is debatable what Rashbam means when he writes that משו here is *מגזרת* לא ימיש. Merdler has shown (in her M.A. dissertation; see especially p. 131) that the word גזרה in Rashbam's grammatical terminology can mean three different things: (1) a גזרה in the modern Hebrew grammar sense—i.e. a paradigm such as the גזרה of final-*heh* verbs or of geminate verbs; (2) a *binyan* (i.e. *qal*, *nifal* etc.); or (3) a root.

Here it appears that Rashbam is using the term in the third sense. His comment could be translated: "[The verb משו] is from the same root as the verb (Ex. 13:22), לא ימיש—shall not move."

If he were using it in the second sense, and equating the *binyan* of משו and ימיש, then he would be contradicting his own commentary to Ex. 13:22, where he writes that ימיש there is a *hifil* form (while משו here must be *qal*). See note 40 on page 136 of my Exodus volume.

[78]Rashbam's grammatical point is unarguable. It is possible that he emphasizes this point since he wishes to distance himself from Menaḥem who combines the roots *m-sh-h* and *m-v-sh* into one verb in his *Maḥberet*. See both Rashi and Rashbam to Ex. 2:10, and note 25 on page 26 of my Exodus volume.

[79]On ראשית as a reference to *terumah* (or "heave-offering"), see also Rashbam's commentary to Num. 5:9, and note 8 there.

[80]See also Rashi and many other exegetes who, like Rashbam, explain our verse as making an explicit comparison between the rules of *terumah* and the rules of *ḥallah.*

[81]It is hard to identify the texts that Rashbam is referring to. Rosin was unable to find a Mishnah in either *'Avodah zarah* or in *Shabbat* that was relevant. He emended the Hebrew letters ע"ז to עד' and said that the reference was to Mishnah *'Eduyot* 1:2. He also suggested that Rashbam's reference to *Shabbat* was to BT *Shabbat* 15a.

Those texts do say something about *ḥallah*, but they say nothing about *terumah*. There are, however, a number of classical rabbinic texts that compare *terumah* to *ḥallah* explicitly or implicitly. See e.g. (among others) Mishnah Hal. 1:9, BT Meil. 15b or Sifre Num. 110. Unfortunately none of these texts appears to be named in the printed text of Rashbam.

Another possible solution to the problem would be to attach the cryptic words וכן שנינו בע"ז ובשבת to the commentary to vs. 22, instead of vs. 20. In this reading, all the words of the commentary would make sense, although some might need minor emendations.

Rashbam would then be saying that a Mishnah (in *Horayot* 2:3) teaches us that the verses (22f.) here are referring to idolatry, and to other infractions that incur the punishment of *karet*. The words, וכן שנינו, the technical words for referring to a Mishnah, would now be pointing the reader to a Mishnah that is pertinent to these verses. The words בע"ז (= בעבודה זרה) would mean "concerning the sin of idolatry," and would not be a reference to the tractate

15:22 וכי תשגו IF YOU INADVERTENTLY [FAIL TO OBSERVE ONE OF THE COMMANDMENTS]: The rabbis explained that this verse applies to a person who worshipped idolatrously by accident. [They interpreted] the portion in Leviticus (4:13–21) concerning [an accidental sin in] a matter that "escapes notice" as a reference to [infractions of] all other commandments [for which the penalty is] *karet* ("cutting off").[82]

15:23 את כל אשר צוה ה׳ אליכם ביד משה EVERYTHING THAT THE LORD HAS ENJOINED UPON YOU: They will [ultimately] end up transgressing all the rules of the Torah inadvertently [after they transgress this one specific commandment]. This is a reference to idolatry. For whoever worships idolatry denies all the commandments.[83]

---

of that name. The word ובשבת would refer to the parallel discussion of the issue of *karet* in BT Shab. 69a. See note 82.

[82]A number of classical rabbinic sources say that the verses in Lev. 4 refer to an accidental infraction, that, had it been done on purpose, would have incurred the penalty of *karet*. See for example Mishnah Hor. 2:3. In BT Shab. 68b-69a, Rabbi Joshua ben Levi explains that the principle is derived from a comparison of our verse in Numbers, a verse which he sees as referring to idolatry, with the verses in Leviticus 4:13f.

Like Rashbam, see Rashi who attempts to justify the rabbinic claim that our verses refer to an inadvertent infraction of the laws of idolatry. Rashi finds proof for that claim here in vs. 22. Rashbam, in the continuation of his commentary to this chapter, finds his proof for the same claim in vss. 23 and 30. See below.

[83]The difficulty in these verses is that the text does not specify which sins are being committed. It would be problematic to say that the phrases ולא תעשו את כל המצוות האלה (vs. 22) and את כל אשר צוה ה׳ אליכם mean that the penalty here is applied only to someone who transgresses *all* the commandments. Equally problematic would be the alternative suggestion—that כל here means a transgression of *any* of the laws of the Torah (see NJPS). See Nahm.'s displeasure with iE who (at least according to Nahm.) understands the verse that way.

Rashbam's reading of these verses conforms to the standard halakhic approach. (So also his commentary to Lev. 6:23, referring to our verses.) However, instead of bringing proof from vs. 22 as the classical sources do (see Rashi, following Hor. 8a), Rashbam cites vs. 23 as proof. These verses must be referring to idolatry, he says, because it is an infraction that leads to transgressing "everything that the LORD has enjoined upon you." See also Rashbam's next comment, s.v. מן היום.

Rashbam's comment here—that the person who worships idols will ultimately end up transgressing all the rules of the Torah *inadvertently*—resembles Rashi's comment (following Sifre Numbers 111) that anyone who believes in idols has denied the entire Torah. But the difference is significant. Rashi (and his sources) say that *believing* in idolatry is tantamount to rejecting the whole Torah. But they also say that our verses are dealing with the *inadvertent* idolater. Rashbam reformulates the rabbinic statement to make more sense here in the context: an inadvertent idolator will end up breaking all the laws of the Torah inadvertently.

מן היום אשר צוה ה׳ והלאה [EVERYTHING THAT THE LORD HAS ENJOINED UPON YOU] FROM THE DAY THAT THE LORD GAVE HIS COMMANDMENT AND THENCEFORTH: All of the commandments were given *after* (Ex. 20:2–3) "I am [the LORD your god]" and "You shall not have [any other gods],"[84] for they were the first [commandments].[85]

15:30 ביד רמה . . . מגדף [THE PERSON WHO] ACTS DEFIANTLY . . . AND REVILES [THE LORD]: This is a reference to the sin of idolatry, according to the plain meaning of Scripture.[86]

---

[84]In other words, the phrase, "from the day that the LORD gave His commandment and thenceforth," means all the rules given since the time that God started to give rules. The Decalogue is the first set of laws given by God and the first laws of the Decalogue are about idolatry.

Rashbam's interpretation looks similar to Rashi's but there is a difference. Both exegetes are trying to answer the question: what "mistake" is vs. 22 talking about. Both agree that the mistake is idol worship. Rashi explains that since the text refers both to a rule that God "commanded Moses" (at the end of vs. 22) and to a rule that God "spoke to you" (at the beginning of vs. 23), and since the midrash (Mak. 24a and *passim*) teaches that God spoke the first two commandments of the Decalogue directly to the Israelites, the commandment referred to here must be the law against idolatry. See Hor. 8a and the commentary of pseudo-Rashi there, s.v. איזו היא מצוה. (On the authorship of that commentary, see Grossman, *Ḥakhme Ṣorfat*, p. 216, note 275.)

Rashbam, like Rashi, believes that the reference here is to the first two commandments of the Decalogue, but *not* because of the midrash about what the Israelites heard directly from God's speech. Instead, he explains that the phrase, "from the day that the LORD gave His commandment," itself means "from the beginning of the Decalogue."

In many classical rabbinic sources, vs. 23 is seen as expanding the idolater's culpability and guilt. Rashi says that the verse means that the idolater has also transgressed the words of the prophets. Sifre says it means that the idolater has also transgressed the words of the commandments to the forefathers. Rashbam accepts the idea of expanding the idolator's guilt, but suggests simply that transgressing the first laws given by God leads to transgressing the later ones too.

[85]Note Rashbam's language here—that the laws of the Decalogue are the first laws given to the Israelites. This theme appears a number of times in Rashbam's commentary. See similarly commentary to Gen. 26:5 and commentary to Ex. 15:25–26, and note 77 there.

[86]Rashi offers two interpretations to our verse. According to the first, our verse continues the discussion of the rules of idolatry. According to the second (following Ker. 7b), our verse switches away from the theme of idolatry and teaches that someone who curses God will get the penalty of *karet*. This second interpretation was so popular in rabbinic literature that the technical term in halakhic writing for a person who curses God is מגדף. See e.g. Mishnah Sanh. 6:4.

Rashbam's comment is his way of saying that *peshaṭ* considerations support only Rashi's first alternative. The undefined sin which involves "reviling God" must be seen as connected to the theme of vss. 22–31, idolatry.

15:34 כי לא פורש [HE WAS PLACED IN CUSTODY,] FOR IT HAD NOT BEEN SPECIFIED [WHAT SHOULD BE DONE TO HIM]: I.e. which mode of execution [should be used].[87]

15:38 ציצית [The word ציצית means one thing in verse 38 and another in vs. 39.[88] In vs. 38 it means] "a group of hanging threads," as in the phrase (Ezek. 8:3), "[He grabbed me] by the hairs (בציצת) of my head."[89] [However in vs. 39 the meaning is different.] והיה לכם לציצית IT—i.e. the ציצית mentioned in vs. 38—SHALL BE FOR YOU AS "something to look at," because you will see it.[90] [The word ציצית in vs. 39 should be connected to the idea of seeing;] so also (Song 2:9) "peering (מציץ) through the lattice."[91] So I found also in the Sifre.[92]

The rabbis [also[93]] explained the phrase פתיל תכלת—A THREAD OF BLUE [as connected to the theme of "seeing"]: "Blue is like the [color of the]

---

[87]So also Rashi (following Sifre Numbers 114), iE and many others. The point that they are making is that the Israelites surely must have known that the death penalty had been legislated for Sabbath infractions. (See e.g. Ex. 31:14.) So the only way of interpreting the doubt here about "what should be done to him" is that the Israelites did not know which of the (four rabbinic) methods of execution applied in this case.

[88]In other words, there is a pun here. "You should make ציצית and they should be ציצית" means "you should make hanging threads and they should be seen."

[89]Rashi (based on Men. 42a) also cites the same prooftext. Still it appears that there is a difference between their interpretations of vs. 38. Rashi (in his first interpretation) says that ציצית is the word for "the corner," from which the threads hang. Rashbam says that ציצית refers to the hanging threads themselves. See notes 90 and 91.

[90]I.e. the word ציצית should be seen as connected to the words "וראיתם אותו—you shall look at it," in vs. 39. So also Rashi.

See also note 94 below.

[91]Rashbam's interpretation again looks like Rashi's but is different. Rashi offers two *alternative* interpretations of ציצית in vs. 38—connecting it either to the idea of "threads" or to the idea of "seeing." Rashbam says that the text is purposely punning; in vs. 38 it means "threads" while in vs. 39 it means "seeing."

So also JBS. See similarly NJPSC: "Possibly *tsitsit* in this phrase should be rendered 'ornament, something to look at'—from the verb *hetsits*, 'peek, glimpse'." See also Rashbam's commentary to Ex. 28:36, concerning the word ציץ.

[92]Rashbam must be saying that he found in Sifre the prooftext from Song of Songs, but not the interpretation that he is offering.

Both Rashi and Rashbam cite the same prooftext from Song. In Sifre, that prooftext is cited as a reference to the way God looks upon the Israelites, not to the way the Jew is to look at the ציצית.

[93]Rosin has added the word וגם in square brackets to the text of Rashbam's commentary here. The commentary would also be understandable without that word. But if Rosin is correct—that this comment is connected to the previous one—that fact is significant. See note 94.

sea, the [color of the] sea is like the [color of the] sky, and the [color of the] sky is like [the color of] the Throne of Glory."[94]

[94]Rashbam's quotation is found in a number of places in rabbinic literature. See e.g. Sifre Numbers 115 and Men. 43b.

But why does Rashbam, uncharacteristically, cite a midrashic explanation of the significance of the color blue? Rosin's explanation (see previous note) is the simplest. Rashbam's comment here is a continuation of his previous comment, on "seeing." When one looks at the ציצית one is looking at a blue thread, and that is like looking at God's Throne.

Another more complicated explanation of this section is that when Rashbam says הציצית הזה יהיה לכם לראייה שתראו אותו, he means "the ציצית shall be for you as something to look at, so that you will see Him [= God!]," instead of "because you will see it." If the theme of this comment is "seeing God," then it makes sense that Rashbam would cite that midrash from Sifre and Men. 43b.

See also a further statement on that same page of the Talmud (Men. 43b) by Rabbi Simeon b. Yoḥai that implies that looking at the ציצית helps one "see" God. See also Rashi's commentary there, s.v. כתיב הכא וראיתם אותו, where Rashi explains that the words "you shall see אותו," mean, according to Rabbi Simeon, "you shall see the Shekhinah."

On Rashbam's attitude to seeing God, see commentary to Gen. 48:8 (and note 3 there), Ex. 24:11 (and note 17 there) and 33:18 (and note 20 there), Lev. 16:2 (and note 4 there) and Num. 4:20 (and note 37 there).

קרח (Numbers 16–18)

16:1 ויקח קרח KORAH TOOK: [The word "ויקח—took" should be understood] as in the verse (Gen. 12:5) "Abram took (ויקח) Sarai his wife and Lot . . .."[1] Here also "Korah . . . and Dathan and Abiram took." [It is to be understood that the implied direct object of "took" is] "a large number of people," to such an extent that (vs. 2) two hundred and fifty [people] stood with them before Moses [in rebellion].[2]

16:2 קריאי מועד THOSE CHOSEN IN THE ASSEMBLY: [Like the phrase (1:16) "קרואי העדה—the elected of the assembly."][3] The people who are called

[1]Rashbam is arguing against an interpretation which originates in Tanh. (*Qoraḥ* 1) and which appears in some versions of Rashi (but not in the first edition). That interpretation is that Korah "took with words"—i.e. convinced or persuaded important people (ראשי סנהדראות) to join the cause of the rebellion.

Rashi feels that *l-q-ḥ* generally has a literal, physical meaning—either "purchase" or "take in one's hand." When those explanations do not fit, Rashi says that it means "to persuade." See e.g. Rashi ad Gen. 2:15, Lev. 8:2 and Num. 8:6.

Rashbam here is saying that the verb *l-q-ḥ* can mean "to take" in a non-physical sense, somewhat like the verb "to lead." Rashbam cites Gen. 12:5 (a verse where Rashi does not comment on the abstract use of *l-q-ḥ*) to show that Rashi's explanation that *l-q-ḥ* implies persuasion is unnecessary.

[2]The verb ויקח is a transitive verb in the Bible and there is no clear direct object for it in our verse. Rashi (following Onq.) suggests that here the verb is intransitive, and it means that Korah separated himself from the people. See also ibn Janaḥ (cited by iE) who sees the verb as intransitive, meaning "to start up," or something similar. So also Nahm.

As noted in note 1, Tanh. (and a second opinion in some versions of Rashi) says that the implied object of the verb "took" or "persuaded" is "the leaders of the Israelites" (ראשי סנהדראות). Rashbam suggests that the implied object is "a large number of people." See similarly iE and JBS. See also Qara (cited in Berliner's *Peleṭat Soferim*, p. 22). Licht also adds a similar understood direct object and says that he is interpreting "as Rashbam does" (although his understanding of Rashbam differs slightly from mine). See also the list of proposed solutions to the problem of the word ויקח in NJPSC, pp. 312–313, note 2.

[3]The reading in the ms.—קרואי עדה קוראים ושולחים בשבילם—is clearly faulty. Rosin emends to: קריאי מועד כמו קרואי העדה קוראים ושולחים בשבילם. My translation is based on that emendation. A more simple solution might be that Rashbam was commenting on the words קריאי מועד but a copyist recorded them incorrectly as קרואי עדה. If that is the case, then the added text in the square brackets above would be unnecessary.

and sent for on the day of assembly, the day set for judging[4] between people.[5]

16:4 ויפל על פניו [MOSES HEARD] AND HE FELL ON HIS FACE: to pray.[6] There, [while he was praying to God,] he received instructions [to say] the things that he later said to Korah.[7]

---

[4]Rosin claims (RSBM, p. 126; and see note 12 there) that when Rashbam wrote this comment, he had in mind the medieval German institution of "*Gerichtstage*," or "days of judging." But this theory may be unnecessary, since classical rabbinic texts also mention special days on which judging takes place. See e.g. Mishnah Ket. 1:1 and the *beraita* cited in BT BQ 82a.

[5]Cf. iE who says that קריאי מועד are people who are called to the Tent of Meeting (the אהל מועד). See also Rashbam's commentary to Lev. 23:2.

[6]Many commentators discuss why Moses fell on his face. According to Rashi (following Tanh.), Moses had already prayed so many times following sins committed by the Israelites that he felt *unable* to pray this time. Rashi apparently sees Moses' falling on his face as an act of despair. Since he could *not* pray, he fell on his face. Rashbam disagrees squarely with Rashi and says that the text simply means that Moses prayed.

iE offers two options—either that Moses fell on his face as the result of a prophetic spell or else that he did so "of his own volition." In his commentary to vs. 22 below, iE clarifies that falling on one's face is a way of praying. JBS says that Moses fell on his face because of shame. Luzzatto says that Moses fell on his face to ask permission to pray.

Like Rashbam, see NJPSC and the second opinion in Hizq. See also Levine's note to 14:5.

A similar interpretive problem arises at verse 14:5, where Moses and Aaron both fall on their faces. Rashbam comments only here (and not on the first place where this phrase occurs in the Torah), presumably because here is the place where Rashi comments.

[7]There are two ways of understanding Rashbam's comment to this verse. He may have a theological agenda and/or he may be introducing a theme that appears again in his commentary—trying to remove blame from Moses for the death of so many Israelites.

If his comment has a theological agenda, then Rashbam is addressing the issue that many exegetes deal with in the continuation of this chapter: Is Moses acting under divine orders/guidance or is he acting independently? Nowhere does it say that God told Moses to set up a contest with "fire pans" (vss. 5–7). Nowhere does the Bible say that Moses was promised by God that Korah and his followers would be swallowed up by the ground. Perhaps Moses was acting independently, in a sense forcing God's hand, and God, after the fact, agreed to Moses' initiatives.

In *'Iyyunim* (pp. 238–242), N. Leibowitz outlines three approaches to this issue: one, that Moses acted as God told him; a second, that Moses acted out of his own initiative (an approach which she attributes to Joseph Albo); and a third, a compromise position, that Moses received no explicit instructions from God but acted as a result of divine inspiration. That last position is found here in Nahm.'s commentary (ad vs. 5). Before offering his own approach, Nahm. writes that "some say" that Moses prayed (in vs. 4) to God for instructions and that, even though those instructions are not recorded, he did receive explicit directions from God. As the narrative unfolds here and the text describes Moses' actions, we learn what Moses must have heard from God. While Nahm. did not have access to Rashbam's Torah commentary, the position that Nahm. describes is the one that Rashbam advocates.

16:11 לכן אתה וכל עדתך TRULY YOU AND ALL OF YOUR COMPANY: are the ones WHO have BANDED TOGETHER AGAINST THE LORD.[8]

16:12 לא נעלה WE WILL NOT APPEAR [lit. "WE WILL NOT GO UP"]: to you [i.e. "we will not appear before you"] for judgment. Verbs related to "going up" (עלייה) are commonly used for appearing before judges. [For example] (Deut. 25:7), "his sister-in-law shall appear (ועלתה; lit. 'shall go up') before the elders," or (Jud. 4:5) "the Israelites would appear (ויעלו; lit. 'would go up') before her for judgment" or (Ruth 4:1) "Boaz had gone up (עלה) to the gate" [to appear before the ten elders].[9]

Rashbam, in general, tries not to portray Moses as acting in an independent and forceful manner. See e.g. commentary above to 11:21 (and note 52 there) and commentary to Ex. 19:23 (and note 42 there) and to Ex. 32:19 (and note 28 there).

An alternative (but not necessarily contradictory) understanding of Rashbam's comment here is that he is preparing the readers for his comments to 16:28, 16:29 and 17:6. There he defends Moses against the accusation that he invented a contest that led to the death of so many Israelites. See commentary there, and notes 24, 25 and 32 below.

[8]Rashbam is reacting to the difficult syntax of this phrase. A literal translation yields a sentence fragment, not a sentence: "Truly you and all your company who have banded together against the LORD."

A number of solutions have been offered. Mendelssohn translates the phrase as a hanging threat, a purposeful use of a sentence fragment. "You and all your company who have banded together against the LORD . . . [be warned!]." Rashi offers a similar explanation to a similar apparent sentence fragment in Gen. 4:15: "Truly anyone who kills Cain . . .." Luzzatto suggests, in the name of one of his students, the possibility that the word נועדים should be understood as if it were written twice, yielding the sense "You . . . who have banded together, have banded together against the LORD." iE in one of his two explanations, reads הנועדים as if נועדים were written, yielding the full sentence, "You and all your company band together against the LORD." Rashbam says that the connective verb "are" is to be understood. See similarly Everett Fox's translation: "Truly (it is) you and your entire community that come-together against YHWH."

The text of Rashi's commentary seems to be corrupt, so his position is unclear. According to the notes in the *Torat Ḥayyim* Pentateuch (Num. 16:11, note 45), Nahm.'s understanding of Rashi yields an interpretation similar to Rashbam's.

[9]Rashi does not really explain what the verb "to go up" means in this context. He simply points out (following Tanh. and NR 18:10) the dramatic irony: they said "we will not go up," not realizing how true it was. Indeed, they would not "go up"—i.e. rise in status—as they had hoped. iE offers a number of suggestions, including a very prosaic one—that the Tent of Meeting might have been on higher ground than the rest of the Israelite camp. LT says that going to the east, in the direction of the Tent of Meeting, is considered "going up."

Rashbam's explanation, that "going up" refers to appearing before a judge, seems to be his innovation. It was later accepted by Hizq., the *Be'ur*, NJPSC and Levine.

16:13 גם השתרר ALSO LORD IT OVER US: The word "גם—also" in the Torah is often "reversed" [i.e. not placed at the appropriate spot in the verse.[10] The words of the phrase כי תשתרר עלינו גם השתרר should be read as if written] כי גם תשתרר עלינו השתרר.[11] So also the phrase (Ex. 12:32) וברכתם גם אותי—[lit. "bless me also," should be understood as if written] וגם תברכו אותי ("also bless me").[12] Similarly, the phrase (Gen. 29:30) ויאהב גם את רחל [lit. "he loved Rachel also," should be understood as if written] וגם אהב את רחל ("he also loved Rachel").[13] The phrase (Num. 22:33) גם אותך הרגתי [lit. "I would kill you also," should be understood as if written] גם הרגתי אותך ("I would also kill you").[14]

16:14 העיני האנשים ההם תנקר WILL YOU GOUGE OUT THE EYES OF THOSE MEN: I.e. "Do you think that those men who are complaining about you do not have any eyes to see this failure [of yours]? You took us out of Egypt, a good land, to die in the wilderness. I.e. YOU DID NOT fulfil your promise to bring us TO 'A LAND FLOWING WITH MILK AND HONEY'; instead of that, they will [all] die during these forty years in the wilderness.[15] And that is the reason why לא נעלה WE WILL NOT APPEAR before you."

---

[10]Rashbam makes this point concerning the word גם in the Bible on a number of occasions. See commentary to all the passages that he lists in this comment.

[11]As Levine notes, the syntactical sequence found in this phrase is rare. The midrashically minded have explained that the phrase תשתרר גם השתרר implies two different types of "lording it" over the Israelites. Before the days of Rashbam, LT wrote: "you lorded it over us in Egypt and you are doing it again in the wilderness." See also iE and Hizq. who interpret the phrase as referring not just to one type of "lording," but to the ways that both Moses and Aaron allegedly lorded it over the Israelites. Rashbam counters that the placement of the word גם is arbitrary and insignificant; the verse really means "you took us out of Egypt to kill us and you also lord it over us."

Like Rashbam, see the *Be'ur* here.

[12]Rashbam's comment on the verse in Ex. 12 is difficult. See the discussion in note 2, p. 175, of my Genesis volume and note 67, p. 116, of my Exodus volume.

[13]As I noted in my Genesis volume (p. 174, note 4), Rashbam is rejecting the understanding that "He loved Leah, but he loved Rachel even more." Rashbam prefers to see the verse as saying "He cohabited with her [= Rachel], and he also loved her."

[14]Rashbam opposes the understanding that the angel there is telling Balaam: "I will kill you also," i.e. just as I have already killed someone else, I will kill you too. See note 16 there.

[15]Rashbam's comment here is partially in agreement with Rashi's. Both of them highlight the connection between vs. 13 and vs. 14. Back in Egypt, Moses had promised to bring the Israelites into a land flowing with milk and honey and had told them that that was why they should leave Egypt. Now Moses and God have declared that the Israelites will die in the wilderness. Was that actually Moses' nefarious plan all along?

But Rashbam disagrees with Rashi about how to read the last clause of vs. 14. Rashi sees it as a new thought: "even if you threaten to gouge out our eyes, we will not come to you." Rashbam sees this phrase as a continuation of the same thought. "Do you think that we

[The speakers[16] first] made a general statement, then they provided the details and then they repeated the general statement. First they said [in vs. 12] WE WILL NOT APPEAR." Then they explained why [in vss. 13 and 14, up until the last phrase]. Then [in the last phrase of vs. 14] they repeated the general statement, [as if to say,] "that is why WE WILL NOT APPEAR."[17]

16:15 אל תפן DO NOT TURN: [The form תֵּפֶן comes] from the root *p-n-h*, just as the form וַתֵּרֶב, in the phrase (Gen. 43:34), "Benjamin's portion was larger (וַתֵּרֶב)," [comes from the root *r-b-h*]. From the phrase "Do not turn yourself—אל תפנה,"[18] one says [in the apocopated form] אל תֵּפֶן. From [the *hifil* form,]

---

are so blind that we have not noticed that the promises you made will never be fulfilled?!" Or, as NJPSC phrases it, "Do you think that you can pull the wool over our eyes?!"

Both Rashi's and Rashbam's interpretations are cited by iE as possibilities. Like Rashbam, see also Hizq. and the *Be'ur*.

[16]Rashbam uses singular verbs in this sentence and in the next one. He means something like "the text generalizes and then it specifies . . . ." I have translated in the plural for ease of understanding.

[17]Rashbam appears to be the first classical exegete to comment on the ostensible redundancy here—that Dathan and Abiram say the same words, "we will not appear," both at the end of vs. 12 and at the end of vs. 14. Rashbam says that this is acceptable style. See also NJPSC which describes our verses as being framed by an inclusio.

Rashbam uses a common interpretive category from rabbinic literature כלל ופרט וכלל "a general statement followed by details followed by a summary general statement." The category originates in the well-known *beraita* at the beginning of the Sifra that begins "Rabbi Yishmael says" (the *beraita* that has become part of the daily synagogue liturgy). This category of textual analysis is used in the Talmud and in *midreshe halakhah* dozens of times. (See e.g. Eruv. 27b or Mekhilta *Ba-ḥodesh* 8 [re Ex. 20:14].) Rashi also uses it in his commentary (e.g. ad Deut. 14:26).

Rashbam, however, uses the category in a new and unprecedented way. For the classical rabbinic texts, כלל ופרט וכלל is a category with halakhic implications. Whenever a list appears in a legal text in the Torah in a כלל ופרט וכלל form, the item(s) that constitute(s) the פרט are to be interpreted as archetypes, according to the *midrash halakhah*'s understanding.

Rashbam appears to be the first exegete to use the principle of כלל ופרט וכלל in the interpretation of a narrative, non-legal passage of the Torah, as a category of literary analysis, not of halakhic exegesis. See also Rashbam's commentary to Ex. 30:34 (pp. 388–389 of my Exodus volume, and note 29 there) where Rashbam interprets a legal verse of the Torah in a כלל ופרט וכלל manner, but, as I noted there, does not attribute legal significance to the pattern. Rashbam uses the כלל ופרט וכלל pattern for literary interpretation of the text in the same way that he uses the כלל ופרט pattern (e.g. ad Gen. 1:27 or Ex. 2:15) and in the same way that he uses the פרט וכלל pattern (e.g. ad Deut. 20:5).

Rashbam often points out literary patterns without discussing their significance. See my forthcoming article in the volume, *With Reverence for the Word*, edited by Jane McAuliffe and Barry Walfish.

[18]Since it is not clear what Rashbam thinks is the correct "elongated" form of תֵּפֶן, I did not vocalize the word תפנה above. There are two possible ways to vocalize it.

"Do not cause something else to turn—אַל תְּפַנֶּה," one says [in the apocopated form] אַל תֶּפֶן.[19]

לא חמור אֶחָד מהם נשאתי I HAVE NOT TAKEN ONE ASS FROM THEM: "I did not take from them even one ass, as other leaders who lord over the people would have done, so why do they accuse me of lording it over them?"

If the vocalization were לא חמור אַחַד מהם, then one would explain the words as meaning "I have not taken the ass of even one of them." [But the word אַחַד in other verses means "one of,"] as in the phrase (Gen. 26:10), "one of (אַחַד) the people," or (at the end of this verse) "I DID NOT WRONG ANY ONE OF (אַחַד) THEM."[20]

In his edition, Rosin vocalizes the word as תִּפָּנֶה. If Rosin is right, then Rashbam's opinion is the one generally accepted by grammarians today—that תֶּפֶן is the apocopated imperfect form of the *qal* of a final-*heh* root. See similarly G.-K. 75p. In my notes on Genesis and Exodus, I assumed that that was the only way to understand Rashbam's comments. See commentary to Gen. 43:34 (and note 2 there) and to Exodus 39:32.

Since then, R. Merdler has published a new edition of Rashbam's *Dayyaqut*. There (p. 3, and note 9 there) and in her M.A. dissertation (pp. 83–84), she shows convincingly that, when Rashbam wrote *Dayaqqut*, he analyzed both the form תִּפֶן and the form וַתֵּרֶב as apocopated forms of the imperfect of the ***nifal***. Modern grammarians would dismiss this position, but it is clearly what Rashbam thought when he wrote his grammar book. We do not know which came first—the grammar book or the Torah commentary, despite Merdler's attempts (Introduction to her edition of *Dayyaqut*, pp. ד-ז) to prove that the grammar was written later. In any case, if, when he wrote his Torah commentary, Rashbam had the same opinion that he expressed in *Dayyaqut*, then the text above should be vocalized, as Merdler writes, "From the phrase 'Do not turn yourself—אַל תִּפָּנֶה,' one says [in the apocopated form] אַל תִּפֶן." Similarly, one would have to assume that Rashbam here sees וַתֵּרֶב as the apocopated form of a *nifal*. Merdler reports that in the parallel discussion in *Dayyaqut*, the form was vocalized in the ms. that she used: וַתֵּרָבֶה.

Rashbam continues his discussion of apocopated imperfect forms below in his commentary to 17:25. It is possible that here he is anticipating or setting up his opposition there to Rashi's comment. Rashbam there will argue that וִיבַל is a *piel* form, not a *qal* (or a *nifal*) as Rashi's comment there would imply. If one combines Rashbam's comments here and there, Rashbam has taught us how to distinguish *piel* forms from *qal* (or *nifal*) in the apocopated imperfect.

[19]This last statement of Rashbam, concerning *hifil* forms, is clear and unarguable. It is also parallel to the discussion in *Dayyaqut* (Merdler's edition, pp. 2–3). Although the form תֶּפֶן does not appear in the Bible, the comparable *hifil* form וַיֶּפֶן does (Jud. 15:4).

[20]Rashbam is opposing the interpretation offered by Rashi and Onq. (לא חמרא דחד מנהון שחרית—"I did not take the donkey of any one of them"), later found in Mendelssohn's translation and in NJPS. Like Rashbam, see Nahm., Everett Fox ("Not [even] one donkey of theirs have I carried off") and Noth ("I have not taken one ass from them")

Rashbam's grammatical argument appears very strong, although the *Be'ur* dismisses it and argues that the cantillation signs support Rashi.

16:22 א-להי הרוחות [O GOD,] THE GOD OF SPIRITS [OF ALL FLESH, WHEN ONE MAN SINS WILL YOU BE WRATHFUL WITH THE ENTIRE COMMUNITY]: [Moses calls God the "God of spirits" here, as if to say,] "You know the spirits and the minds of the rest of the people. [You know] that **they** did not sin.[21]

16:25 וילך אל דתן ואבירם [MOSES ROSE] AND WENT TO DATHAN AND ABIRAM: In case they would repent.[22]

16:28 כי לא מלבי [THE LORD SENT ME TO DO ALL OF THESE THINGS;] THEY WERE NOT OF MY OWN DEVISING: When I introduced them[23] to the offering of incense, when I said (vs. 17), "You and Aaron, each of you take his fire pan . . .," [it was at God's suggestion].[24]

At first glance it appears that Rashbam contradicts himself in his commentary to BB (47a, s.v. הוה ממטי). There he quotes our verse and Onq.'s translation without comment, ostensibly implying that he accepts the translation that he opposes here. But he is addressing a different issue in BB. There his only purpose is to cite Onq.'s use of the word שחרית here, as part of his (albeit weak) attempt to explain the word שחוור in that talmudic text. The syntactical question of how to read the word אחד was not relevant to Rashbam in his comment on that talmudic phrase.

[21]In other words, "since You have such excellent information about them, You know who is guilty and who is not. Accordingly, there is no reason for You to inflict punishment on the whole community, as You implied (in vs. 21) that You would do."

Rashbam's comment is an abridgement of Rashi's, following Tanh. *Qoraḥ* 7.

[22]In other words, despite the fact that God had said in the previous verse that everyone should leave the camp of Dathan and Abiram (implying that God was about to destroy them), Moses still made a last-minute attempt to save them, if they would only repent. Rashbam's approach follows that of NR 18:12 and other midrashic sources. See also Sanh. 110a and Ps.-Jon. here ("לאוכחא—to rebuke Dathan and Abiram").

See the *Be'ur* here, who quotes Rashbam's explanation and then says that there is another explanation. After God told Moses (vs. 24) that everyone should leave Dathan and Abiram's camp, Moses went there (vs. 25)—not to appeal to Dathan and Abiram, but to tell everyone else to leave (vs. 26).

[23]In other words, Moses is saying: "When I created this test and suggested that people who were not priests should offer incense, i.e. when I introduced (שחינכתים) non-priests to the offering of incense, I was acting under orders from God." The phrase לחנך בקטורת is common in rabbinic literature (although not in the same precise sense that Rashbam uses it). See e.g. Sifre Numbers 143.

Hizq., who appears to be quoting Rashbam, has a different reading: שהבחנתים בקטורת, yielding the meaning "When I put them to the incense test." Berzinsky suggests reading שהבחנתים here in Rashbam, too.

[24]Rashbam's comment here continues the theme of his comment to vs. 4 and leads into his explanation of 17:6. Moses assures the Israelites (and Rashbam assures his readers) that Moses is not acting as a free agent; he is following God's orders. Since this test will have

16:29 לא ה' שלחני [IF THESE MEN DIE AS OTHER MEN DO . . ., then] IT WAS NOT THE LORD WHO SENT ME: Rather it was I who did it to them when I charged them to offer incense.[25]

16:30 ואם בריאה IF THE LORD CREATES SOMETHING: [I.e. brings about something] new in the world—[that they will die in a way] that differs from the death of Nadab and Abihu.[26] The phrase is similar to the verse (Jer. 31:21), "For the LORD creates (ברא) something new in the earth."[27]

---

disastrous results—leading to the death of 250 people whom Moses told to offer incense—Moses defends himself by saying even before the fact that this contest was not his idea.

Rashbam is opposing Rashi. According to Rashi, Moses is telling the assembled that back when he appointed Aaron and his descendants as priests, he, Moses, was not acting on his own initiative, but was simply following God's instructions. (Nahm. [on vs. 29] expands Rashi's approach further. Moses is attempting to prove that in *everything* that he does he should be seen as God's agent.)

According to Rashi, the progression of Moses' thoughts in vss. 28–29 is: "You might think that I appointed Aaron as a priest on my initiative. I did not. When you see the miracle connected to the incense test, you will realize that God is on my side." According to Rashbam, the progression is: "You might think that I thought of this test on my own. I did not. When you see the miracle connected to the incense test you will realize that the test was God's idea, not mine." According to Rashi, then, the continuation of the narrative is a form of ordeal. If the results are miraculous, that will prove that Moses acted, on an entirely different issue, according to God's orders. But Rashbam says that the incense test is not an ordeal to prove Moses right. It is God's way of punishing wayward Israelites. The miracle will prove that God intended for them to die.

See further Rashbam's commentary to 16:29, 16:30 and 17:6, and notes 25 and 32 below.

[25]Rashbam offers an unusual explanation of this phrase. To be understood, it must be read together with his comments to 16:30 and 17:6.

Generally the phrase in our verse is understood as meaning: "If these men die a natural death—i.e. if nothing happens to them when they offer the incense and they go on living as long as most people do—then that will be proof against me, proof that I was not acting according to God's instructions." So e.g. Rashi.

Rashbam however suggests (as we can see from his comment on 17:6) that the phrase means: "If these men die in the manner that people who illegitimately offer incense normally die, then you can blame me, Moses, for having been responsible for their death. That will prove that it was all my idea that they offer incense and that they die as a punishment. I then will be culpable."

While Rashbam's explanation of vss. 28–29 is far-fetched, it does connect the end of chapter 16 with 17:6. It makes the Israelites' complaints in 17:6 more understandable, as the miracle did not take place the way that Moses said it would. Moses had promised in vs. 30 that the offenders would die by being swallowed up in the ground, but in vs. 35, 250 of them die a different sort of death.

[26]See note 25.

[27]While the precise meaning of the verse in Jeremiah is uncertain, it is clear that "creation" there simply means something unprecedented and surprising.

16:34 נסו לקולם ALL OF ISRAEL FLED AT THEIR CRIES: For they screamed as they fell [into the earth]. So it is written (Jer. 49:21),[28] "At the sound of their downfall the earth shakes."[29]

17:5 כאשר דבר ה' ביד משה לו [(4) ELEAZAR TOOK THE COPPER FIRE PANS . . . AND THEY WERE HAMMERED INTO PLATING, (5) AS A REMINDER . . . SO THAT NO OUTSIDER SHOULD PRESUME TO OFFER INCENSE . . . AND SUFFER THE FATE OF KORAH AND HIS BAND] AS THE LORD HAD COMMANDED HIM THROUGH MOSES: [This last phrase, "as the LORD had commanded him through Moses,"] is connected to (vs. 4) above. I.e. "Eleazar the priest took the copper fire pans" from among the charred remains, "AS THE LORD HAD COMMANDED HIM—i.e. Eleazar—THROUGH MOSES." [This is true,] for God really did command Moses (vs. 2), "Order Eleazar son of Aaron the priest to remove the fire pans . . . ."[30]

Rashbam's interpretation of the "בריאה—creation," here is similar to Rashi's first interpretation. It is opposed to the midrashic understanding cited by Rashi as his second explanation (following e.g. *'Avot* 5:6 and Sanh. 110a) that God had actually created the "mouth of the earth" that swallowed up Korah during (or at the end of) the original six days of the creation of the world.

[28]Rashbam's quotation of the verse (לקול מפלתך) differs slightly from MT (מקול נפלם).

[29]Rashbam's interpretation opposes that of Rashi who says that the phrase נסו לקולם means that the people ran away because of the קול היוצא על בליעתן. This could mean either that *the report* of the swallowing up of Dathan and Abiram caused Israelites to flee, or (as Mizraḥi understands it) that they fled because of *the noises* that were made by the earth when it opened its mouth to swallow Korah. For some reason Rashi is avoiding the simple explanation found here in Rashbam—that the noise is the shrieking of the people being swallowed. See Mizraḥi who suggests that Rashi rejected that explanation since, so he argues, shrieking of that nature does not cause people to run away but rather causes them to come closer to see what is happening.

Like Rashbam, see JBS and Hizq. Hizq. misquotes the verse in Jer. the same way that Rashbam does, clearly showing the dependence of his commentary on Rashbam's. See also NJPS: "fled at their shrieks." In NR 18:19, one retelling of the story has those being swallowed up yelling, "Moses, save us!"

Rashbam uses the prooftext from Jeremiah to argue against the explanation that the "קול—voice" related to falling refers to noises emitted *by* the earth. In the verse in Jeremiah, the voice or noise is not caused by the earth, but it is rather what affects the earth.

[30]Rashbam's interpretation opposes both explanations offered by Rashi. Rashi first says that the word לו refers to Aaron; the phrase is to be connected to the immediately preceding clause, "let him not be like Korah." The progression of thoughts, according to Rashi, is: "Do not let anyone offer incense illegitimately, lest he suffer the fate of Korah, which would happen כאשר דבר ה' ביד משה לו, i.e. because God had commanded Moses to give this prerogative לו, only to Aaron." (According to the citation from Qara's Torah commentary in Berliner's *Peleṭat Soferim*, p. 21, Rashi learned this explanation from Joseph Qara.) After that explanation, Rashi writes that the midrashic reading (e.g. Tanh. *Ṣav* 11) understands לו as a

17:6 אתם המיתם את עם ה' YOU HAVE BROUGHT DEATH ON THE LORD'S PEOPLE: "We admit concerning Dathan and Abiram who were swallowed up [in an unprecedented manner] that [that proves that] they were sinners [and that is why they died in that spectacular manner]. But the other two hundred and fifty men died in the same way that Nadab and Abihu died [after they too offered incense without authorization].[31] You are responsible for their death [i.e. the death of the two hundred and fifty men] since you commanded them to offer an [unauthorized] incense offering."[32]

---

reference to Korah. "Let him not be like Korah and not suffer the fate כאשר דבר ה' ביד משה לו, the fate that Moses had pronounced for Korah at God's command." Rashbam disagrees and says that לו refers to Eleazar.

Rashi attempts to support his first explanation as the *peshat* by arguing that the phrase דבר ל- always means "speak concerning" or "speak for the sake of," but not "speak to." Rashi offers this same rule three other times in his Torah commentary. In two of the cases (ad Gen. 28:15 and Ex. 4:16), Rashbam explains the phrase in the same way that Rashi does. (Ad Gen. 24:7 Rashbam does not comment on the phrase דבר ל-.) Considering all the evidence, it seems that even though Rashbam agrees with Rashi on two individual occasions about the meaning of the words דבר ל-, he does not accept Rashi's rule, that that is *always* what those words mean. See Nahm.'s reasoned arguments against Rashi's exegetical rule in his commentary to Gen. 24:7 ("ואין החילוק הזה אמת—this distinction is not true").

Most exegetes follow Rashbam's understanding of the verse. See e.g. JBS and Nahm. See also NJPS which moves the clause כאשר דבר ה' ביד משה לו in their translation from the end of vs. 5 to the beginning, in order to make Rashbam's understanding of the verse clearer. Cf. the *Be'ur* who argues for Rashi's explanation, arguing that the cantillation signs do not accord with Rashbam's interpretation.

[31]Rashbam notes the striking similarity in language between the description of the death of the 250 men (16:35), "A fire went forth from the LORD and consumed the two hundred and fifty men offering the incense," and the description of the death of Nadab and Abihu (Lev.10:2), "A fire went forth from the LORD and consumed them" (when they were offering improper incense). This comparison is noted already in Tanh. B. *'Aḥare* 1, and is commented upon by many moderns (e.g. Noth and NJPSC).

[32]Rashbam is continuing here his commentary to 16:28, 16:29 and 16:30. There he explains that Moses promised that the unusual and unprecedented manner in which, he said, the evildoers would die would prove that it was God, not Moses, who was responsible for their death. They would die as a punishment from God, not because Moses was getting back at them and entrapping them. Now Rashbam notes that (in vss. 32–33) actually only Dathan and Abiram and some hangers-on died in the unprecedented manner that Moses had predicted (in vs. 30). The death of the 250 other men resembles the death of other illegitimate offerers of incense, as described in Lev. 10.

Like Rashbam, see Nahm. who also argues that it is only about the 250 men that the Israelites complain, not about those who were swallowed up into the ground. See similarly iE and NJPSC: "It was you two who devised the incense test by which they lost their lives."

This comment of Rashbam is another instance where he chooses to describe the Israelites' complaints as understandable. See the discussion in note 53 below.

17:10 הֵרֹמּוּ REMOVE YOURSELVES: [The form הֵרֹמּוּ] is [a *nifal* imperative masculine plural form from a hollow root] on the pattern of [הִמּוֹלוּ, in the phrase] (Jer. 4:4) "Be circumcised (הִמּוֹלוּ) for the LORD." Because of the letter *resh* in the word הֵרֹמּוּ, the *ḥiriq* vowel [in the first syllable of the standard form, הִמּוֹלוּ] becomes an "ay"[33] vowel. Just as the form בֵּרֵךְ [is the proper form,[34] and not] בִּרֵךְ.[35]

Above (16:21), God says to Moses and Aaron "Separate yourselves (הבדלו)." Here he says to them "Remove yourselves (הֵרֹמּוּ)" which implies a further degree of separation, now needed because the "wrath" [i.e. the plague; see vs. 11] had already begun.[36]

17:11 ושים קטורת [MOSES SAID TO AARON "TAKE THE FIRE PAN . . .] AND ADD INCENSE": To let it be known that incense, which causes death when handled by non-priests, is a source of life in the hands of priests.[37] [This was done so that people would] know that they [= the priests, the sons of Aaron] are the ones who are entitled to perform the divine service.[38]

---

[33]Rashbam's grammatical terminology here is unusual. He refers to a *ḥiriq* as a *ḥiriq* (not an "i" vowel), but he refers to a *ṣere* as an "ay" vowel. Rashbam does know the word *ṣere*; see his commentary to Gen. 49:5 or Ex. 16:23.

[34]Rashbam's language, כמו ברך ברך, is strange but the meaning of the comment is clear both from context and from a comparison with his commentary on Gen. 49:5.

[35]As far as it goes, Rashbam's grammatical explanation is unobjectionable. The *ḥiriq-ṣere* vowel change before a *resh* that should have taken a *dagesh* is a common phenomenon. See e.g. G.-K. 27f.

But the more difficult aspect of this grammatical form remains unexplained—the fact that there is a *dagesh* in the *mem* of הֵרֹמּוּ. Comparison to the form הִמּוֹלוּ does not explain that *dagesh*. Rashbam does not address this question.

Cf. the explanation in G.-K. 72dd.

[36]Rashbam's explanation may be directed against that of LT. Like Rashbam, LT feels that הֵרֹמּוּ implies greater distancing than הבדלו, but he argues that the continuing deterioration of the Israelites' behavior has caused God to request this time that Moses and Aaron move even further away from the people than he requested last time. Rashbam says instead that the escalating language is a function of the greater danger. In 16:21 God uses the weaker language of separation since at that point he was just threatening to punish the Israelites. Here the plague had already begun, so God tells Moses and Aaron to get very far away.

[37]This same idea—that the same incense which just caused death in the previous chapter is shown here to be an agent of life—may be found in a number of midrashic sources (e.g. Mekhilta *Va-yassa'* 6) and in Rashi, in his final comment to vs. 13. So also JBS. See note 38.

[38]Rashbam is reworking the midrashic sources that were mentioned in note 37. In the Mekhilta and in Rashi (and in other sources listed in *Torah shelemah*, p. 79, note 37), the reason that incense was chosen as the agent of healing was that some people were disparaging the incense ("מרננים על הקטורת" or some similar phrase). Rashbam says that incense was chosen in order to prove the legitimacy of the priests, the children of Aaron, i.e. to stop the

17:13 ויעמד בין המתים ובין החיים HE STOOD BETWEEN THE DEAD AND THE LIVING: Because the destroyer (המשחית)[39] did not cross the place of the burning of the incense.[40]

17:17 קח מאתם מטה מטה TAKE FROM THEM ONE STAFF FROM EACH [CHIEFTAIN]: [God said,] "Since the Israelites are complaining about the incense, saying that it 'brought death on the LORD's people,' and that it does not prove that I have chosen the priests, I will give them a different proof so that they will not be able to undermine the priesthood. [That proof is] that his [= Aaron's] staff will flower at My command."[41]

17:20 והשיכותי I WILL STILL: [The word והשיכותי] is from [the root *sh-k-k*, the same root as שככה in the phrase] (Est. 7:10), "the king's anger subsided (שככה)." Similarly the form "הסיבותה—you turned"[42] is from the root *s-b-b*.[43]

---

disparaging of the priesthood. In that way Rashbam connects this verse well to the general theme of chapters 16 and 17.

Many moderns follow Rashbam's explanation. See e.g. NJPSC ("The same incense that causes destruction when used by unauthorized persons averts destruction when used by authorized persons") and Luzzatto (on vs. 10).

[39]Rashbam appropriately uses the language of Ex. 12:23, which, like our passage, describes a death-dealing force that stops when the appropriate apotropaic ritual is performed.

[40]Or, as NJPSC paraphrases Rashbam's comment: "The destroyer could not pass beyond the place of the incense offering."

Rashbam's approach opposes Rashi's midrashic explanation (following Tanh. *Teṣavveh* 15) which sees in the phrase "He stood between the dead and the living" a reference to Aaron confronting the Angel of Death and arguing with him (and, in Tanh., physically restraining him). Rashbam says more simply that Aaron was protecting those who were still alive. He stood at the edge of the area that the plague had ravaged and somehow that stopped the plague from going further.

[41]Rashbam has already explained that the people accused Moses of using the incense test as a way of killing off his opponents. See commentary to 16:28–29 and 17:6, and notes 24, 25 and 32 above. Rashbam now explains that our text is a continuation of the theme of the previous verses—an attempt to prove the legitimacy of the priesthood.

Cf. Hizq. who tries to explain why two different forms of proof (the incense and the staff) are needed. One, he argues, is to prove the legitimacy of the Levites and one is to prove the legitimacy of the priests, the sons of Aaron. Rashbam says more simply that, as NJPSC puts it, "more persuasion is necessary" to establish the legitimacy of Aaron and the priests.

[42]Based on the parallel passage in Rashbam's grammar book, *Dayyaqut* (Merdler's edition, p. 13), Rashbam is referring here to the usage in I Kings 18:37. Both here and there he spells the word הסיבותה with a *yod*; in MT it does not have a *yod*.

[43]Rashbam makes this same (reasonable) grammatical point, concerning the same two forms, in his grammar book. (See note 42.) There he is trying to help his readers distinguish between *hifil* perfect forms of hollow verbs and of geminate verbs. The forms are, as Rashbam shows there, similar but not identical.

17:23 ויצא פרח ויצץ ציץ ויגמל שקדים IT [= the staff] HAD BROUGHT FORTH SPROUTS, PRODUCED BLOSSOMS, AND BORNE ALMONDS: According to the plain meaning of Scripture, it appears that when Moses took the staff out, he found that it had brought forth sprouts and nothing else. That is why it says [in the first half of the verse, before the *'etnaḥta'*, only that] "Aaron's staff had sprouted." However afterwards [i.e. after Moses took the staff out to show to the Israelites], the staff "produced blossoms" in view of all the Israelites. And then it also "bore almonds."

For if that had been the case from the beginning[44] [i.e. if the staff had blossomed, sprouted and borne almonds *before* Moses picked it up], then the sprouting and the blossoming would not have been seen [by anyone]. And then there would be no reason for the text to write "[Aaron's staff] had sprouted," [since no one had seen the sprouting]. Rather [the text would have written "Moses entered the Tent of the Pact and there] the staff of Aaron of the house of Levi had borne almonds."[45]

See Levine who also uses the passage in Esther to explain our form והשיכותי. See also Rashbam's commentary to Num. 14:36. As I pointed out in note 71 there, Rashbam often discusses geminate verbs and often uses the verb *s-b-b* as his paradigm.

[44]Rosin reports that the manuscript has a reading that does not make sense: שכן הוא העניין תחילה והנה לא היתה נראית לא הפריחה ולא הניצה. I have translated according to the modest emendation proposed by Ashkenazi, who changed the words שכן הוא to שאילו כן היה. Rosin writes that such an emendation is impossible ("לא יתכן") and proposes his own emendation which adds an entire line to the text conjecturally: שכן הוא העניין בפירות האילן שאם הכל היה בבת אחת אם כן כשהוציאו משה נגמר כל אותו העניין תחילה . . . Rashbam's idea is the same with either reading.

[45]Rashbam's argument here is based on two points:

(1) There is a redundancy in the verse. In the first half or the verse (before the *'etnaḥta'*) it says that Aaron's staff "sprouted." In the second half of the verse it says that Aaron's staff "sprouted, blossomed and bore fruit."

(2) When the verse says that the staff "brought forth sprouts, produced blossoms and bore almonds," it must be describing a miracle that the people could see. Yet if all three of these steps had already taken place when Moses showed them the staff, the people would be able to see only the final stage—the almonds. It would be impossible for them to see the two earlier stages of sprouting and blossoming once the staff had produced its fruit. So what miracle did the people see?

Rashbam then explains that when Moses picked it up, only the first stage—sprouting—was complete. He showed it to the people, and they too saw the sprouting. While they were looking at it, it quickly progressed from the sprouting stage to the blossoming stage and to the stage of bearing fruit.

Like Rashbam, see the *Be'ur*. Luzzatto quotes one of his students who disputes with Rashbam, arguing that sprouts, blossoms and fruits could reasonably all be on one branch at the same time, on different parts of the branch.

17:25 לאות לבני מרי [TO BE KEPT] AS A LESSON TO REBELS: In the coming generations who might wish to rebel, like [King] Uzziah.[46]

ותכל תלונותם REMOVE THEIR COMPLAINTS: [The verb וּתְכַל is a transitive verb in the *piel*. The phrase means] "remove the complaints of the Israelites."[47]

---

[46]Rashbam continues to use the theme of authorized and unauthorized incense use in his interpretation. (See commentary to 16:28–30, 17:6 and 17:17, and notes 24, 25, 32 and 41 above). The staff of Aaron is to be kept as a reminder to someone who might choose to rebel and who might think that incense may be offered by someone who is not a descendant of Aaron. Rashbam's example is King Uzziah who was not a priest and who, according to II Chr. 26:16f., attempted to offer incense himself. He was then chastised by the priests and punished by God with leprosy.

Rashbam knows that Rashi, too, has also just mentioned King Uzziah in his commentary to vs. 23. There, Rashi sees the word "שקדים—almonds" as a veiled allusion to leprosy. Rashbam disagrees with Rashi about the significance of the almonds. His use of the example of King Uzziah is also for a purpose quite different from Rashi's.

While Rashbam writes that the staff is a lesson לדורות, for future generations, the more common understanding is that the lesson is for the rebellious Israelites of Moses' own generation (see e.g. DR 2:8) and that the rebelliousness that concerns the Bible is the continued rejection of the legitimacy of the priesthood (e.g. Rashi here). See e.g. Gray here who suggests that "בני מרי—sons of rebellion" is an insulting play on the name of the people "בני ישראל—sons of Israel." Perhaps Rashbam, ever mindful of Christian claims about the sins of the Jews, preferred to see the insulting term applied to an individual sinning Israelite (King Uzziah) and not to the people as a whole. See also note 53 below.

Cf. however Rashbam's commentary to 20:8, s.v. ודברתם (and see note 10 there), where Rashbam explains בני מרי in the standard manner, as a reference to the rebelliousness of the Israelites in the wilderness.

[47]Rashbam's comment opposes that of Rashi. Rashi explains that the word ותכל is an intransitive verb whose subject is תלונותם—"their complaint(s) will cease."

There are two problems with Rashi's explanation. First of all, ותכל is a singular verb and תלונותם is a plural noun. (In some versions of Rashi's printed commentary there is a section where Rashi tries to explain how he solves that problem. The explanation is unclear and probably not part of the original commentary.) Secondly, it is not clear what *binyan* Rashi thinks that the verb ותכל is. See e.g. Luzzatto here: "it is troubling that Rashi did not notice that ותכל here is a *piel*."

Rashbam argues that the verb is a transitive *piel* verb and that the form is not, as Rashi would have it, third-person feminine singular, but rather second-person masculine singular. (Those two forms are always indistinguishable in the imperfect in Hebrew, except on the basis of context.) The phrase means, "you, Moses, should remove their complaints," not "their complaints will cease." For a similar dispute between Rashi and Rashbam, see their commentaries to Num. 12:12 and my note 88 there.

Like Rashbam, see Luzzatto, the *Be'ur* and Noth ("that you may make an end of their murmurings"). And see Heidenheim, *Havanat ha-miqra'* here, who says that it is impossible that Rashi would offer such a weak and ungrammatical explanation. Heidenheim offers a new version of part of Rashi's text and a new understanding of the rest which results in an explanation that is identical to Rashbam's.

Similarly the word צו[48] [is an apocopated form of the word] צוה.

17:27–8 אבדנו WE ARE LOST: [As it says above,] (16:33) "They [= the company of Korah] were lost (ויאבדו) from the midst of the congregation."

[In other words, the Israelites said,] "If that [= the fate of the company of Korah] is the case, then ALL OF US (כלנו) will keep dying every day." Why? Because (28) EVERYONE WHO SO MUCH AS DRAWS NEAR [TO THE LORD'S TABERNACLE DIES. In other words, they were concerned that] each and every person who either drew near to the Tabernacle to guard it or who, along with the Levites, drew near to the vessels of the Tabernacle, was going to die. [They had this concern] because they had not yet received a warning from

---

A number of moderns explain as Rashi does (i.e. that the phrase means "their complaints will cease"), some by emending the vocalization of the verb or of the noun or of both (NJPSC [p. 315, note 48], Licht, Gray) and some by saying that ותכל, as vocalized, is "the jussive of the *qal* stem of the root *k-l-h*: 'let it cease'" (Levine).

An interesting alternative explanation is offered by Seforno, who suggests, like Rashbam, that the word ותכל is a transitive *piel* verb, but that it is, as Rashi says, a third-person feminine singular form. The subject of the verb is neither Moses nor "their complaints," but rather the word, משמרת. The sense is: "Put aside the staff as a safekeeping (משמרת). That safekeeping will remove (ותכל) the complaints of the Israelites." In theory, it is possible that Rashbam understands the syntax in that same creative way, but if he did, I imagine that he would have said so more clearly.

[48] Rashbam's point in citing this example here is very unclear.

One possible explanation of the comparison (ותכל/ותכלה, צו/צוה) would be as follows. The form ותכל is a voluntative, expressing a wish about a future action ("*may* you remove" or "you *should* remove," not the indicative "you *will* remove"). In that sense, it is similar to an imperative form, which also expresses a desire about the future. Perhaps Rashbam in saying, then, that in all such forms of non-indicative *piel* future verbs from final-*heh* roots, the *heh* drops out and so does any sign of doubling of the last letter of the root. In future *indicative* forms of the verb, though, the *heh* and the *dagesh* do appear. If that is what Rashbam is saying, his point is solid and unarguable. (See G.-K. 201, 48f, 48k, 75bb and 75cc.) Still it seems unlikely that Rashbam really did categorize imperatives and voluntatives together.

There may be a mistake here in the ms. (or perhaps in Rosin's transcription). There is a parallel passage to ours in Rashbam's commentary to Gen. 35:16. There, in an attempt to explain the form וַתְּקַשׁ, Rashbam says that it is a shortened form of the word וַתְּקַשֶּׁה, and he says that that change is like "ותצו ותצוה, ותכס ותכסה"—i.e. like the change of וַתְּצַוֶּה to וַתְּצַו, and like the change of וַתְּכַסֶּה to וַתְּכַס. It would make sense for the same example of shortening, ותצוה/ותצו, to have originally been part of Rashbam's commentary here too. Rashbam would then be saying that in shortened forms of the *piel* imperfect of final-*heh* verbs, whether with or without *vav ha-hippukh*, the *heh* drops out and there is no doubling of the second letter of the root.

Some copyist might have substituted here the words כמו צו מן צוה for a text that originally had read כמו ותצו מן ותצוה. That copyist might have been attracted to such a hypercorrection, since the form ותצו does not appear in the Bible.

God [on this matter]; all that they had heard [so far] was the verse (1:51, 3:10 and 3:38) "any outsider who draws near shall be put to death."[49] That is why they receive, in the continuation of this text, that [specific] warning (18:4), "No outsider [זר; i.e. non-priest] shall draw near to you," and [then they receive a reiteration of the promised penalty] (18:7) "any outsider who draws near shall be put to death." So [now that they have been warned], from now on they will not draw near and they will not die.[50]

In the Torah portion, *'Emor 'el ha-kohanim*, where it is written (Lev. 21:17) "Speak to Aaron and say, 'No man of your offspring throughout the ages who has a defect shall draw near to offer the food of his God'," even there it is only the blemished [priests] who were disqualified. The text there does not disqualify "outsiders" (i.e. non-priests). And the disqualification in the following section[51] [in Leviticus] (22:3), "Say to them, 'Any man who draws

---

[49] Rosin's text reads here: שעדיין לא התרה בם הק' שעדיין לא נכתב והזר הקרב יומת. I have emended to שעדיין לא התרה בם הק' שעדיין לא נכתב אלא והזר הקרב יומת (adding the word אלא).

Unemended the text would be translated, "[They had this concern] because they had not yet received a warning from God [on this matter], for the verse (18:7) 'any outsider who draws near shall be put to death' had not yet been written." This reading is impossible. It is inconceivable that that is what Rashbam is saying. True, 18:7 "Any outsider who draws near shall be put to death" had not yet been written. But the identical phrase has appeared already three times in the book of Numbers (1:51, 3:10 and 3:38).

Some further proof for my emendation may be adduced from Hizq.'s commentary here. Hizq.'s comment seems to be a reworking of Rashbam's and the final words of his comment read: "וכסבורים שעדיין לא נאמר והזר הקרב יומת רק בבעלי מומין—they thought that when the verse 'the outsider who draws near shall be put to death' appeared beforehand [e.g. 1:51], it was referring only to blemished [priests, about whom we know from Lev. 21 that they may not 'draw near']."

For an explanation of the meaning of Rashbam's comment as emended, see note 53.

[50] Rashi, like Rashbam, also sees our verses as connected to the following chapter. The people are concerned that the laws related to the Tabernacle are so strict that they are certain to lead to many deaths. Accordingly God clarifies them in the next chapter.

Rashi does not explain why people are suddenly concerned about Tabernacle violations. Rashbam, however, connects our verses not just forward to chapter 18, but also backwards to the Korah story. The people say "we are lost," echoing the fact that the company of Korah was lost (16:33). See also Onq. who goes far beyond his role of translator and attempts to connect the people's complaint "we perish, we are lost, all of us lost," to the events of the previous chapters. See also Licht who describes verses 27–28 as the verses that provide the transition from the Korah story to the laws that follow.

[51] Rashbam uses the word פרשה in this comment in two very different ways. First he refers to the פרשה—i.e. the Torah portion—*'Emor 'el ha-kohanim.* Then he refers to a text that appears בפרשה שלאחריה. That phrase must be understood as referring to the following "section" of the book of Leviticus, the unit of text following the unit that discusses blemishes of the priests (but still in the same Torah portion).

near . . . [shall be cut off]’,” is referring to someone who, when impure, eats holy food.[52] But we have not yet seen [a text prescribing] the death penalty for outsiders who do holy work in the Tabernacle or [with] its vessels.[53]

---

[52]See Rashbam’s commentary to Lev. 22:2 and 22:3, and notes 12 and 13 there.

[53]Rashbam’s comment (following my emendation; see note 49 above) argues as follows. The people’s concerns were that they were told on many occasions so far that outsiders who come near the Tabernacle would die and they actually saw evidence a number of times that that happened. But they had never, in halakhic terms, been “warned.” The text had never formulated a negative commandment “do not do X.” According to halakhic principles, it is not sufficient for the text to say “he who does X shall die.” The Torah also has to say specifically “do not do X.” In that sense, Rashbam’s comment here may be seen as a reworking of the section in Sifre Numbers 116, concerning 18:4: “ וזר לא יקרב אליכם למה נאמר לפי שהוא אומר והזר הקרב יומת ענוש שמענו אזהרה מנין ת״ל וזר לא יקרב אליכם—why does the text have to say, ‘no outsider shall draw near to you’? Since it is written ‘the outsider who draws near shall die,’ we know that there is a punishment. But where was the warning given? In the verse—‘no outsider shall draw near to you’.” (The phrase, “ענוש שמענו אזהרה מנין—we know that there is a punishment [for this infraction]; but where is the ‘warning’ given about this infraction?” is very common in rabbinic literature. See e.g. Sanh. 54a.) See also Hizq.’s commentary to 18:7, s.v. והזר.

Alternatively, it is possible to understand Rashbam’s comment even without such technical halakhic analysis. Rashbam might be saying that the Israelites had never received specific instructions about what had been prohibited; all they had learned was that undefined outsiders would die for the unclear crime of “drawing near.” They were then justifiably afraid since they did not know who was or was not an outsider.

Rashbam surveys verses on the subject that had appeared in previous books of the Torah. He finds that there were verses in earlier biblical passages that formulated a restriction, “do not draw near,” but he explains that those verses outlawed only very specific forms of “drawing near.” The standard non-priest Israelites had never yet received an explicit warning “do not draw near.”

Rashbam has now explained the progression of chapters 16, 17 and 18. Some Israelites, who should not have drawn near, died (in chapter 16). Other Israelites complained (in chapter 17) that they did not know and had never been told what it was that they should not do. Accordingly, in chapter 18, God formulated a negative commandment giving the Israelites a specific warning. (While Rashbam does not attempt to make the legal section of chapter 19 part of his connected narrative explanation, he does assert in his commentary to 20:8 and 20:10 that the story of that chapter is based on various themes introduced in chapter 17. See commentary there.)

Rashbam’s explanation understands the complaint of the Israelites here in vss. 27 and 28 not as petulant and carping but as something essentially understandable. This continues the theme that we have already seen in the commentary to vss. 6 and 25, where Rashbam justifies to some extent the behavior of the Israelites. Their complaint in vs. 6, “You have brought death on the LORD’s people” is understandable, for the death of the Korah’s company did *not* follow the pattern predicted by Moses. (See also commentary to 16:29, and note 25 there.) The Israelites are *not*, following Rashbam’s understanding, the people who are called “rebels (בני מרי)” in vs. 25. And their complaint here is based on the fact that, halakhically speaking, they have not yet received sufficient instruction from God.

18:1 ויאמר ה' אל אהרן אתה ובניך . . . וזר לא יקרב . . . והזר הקרב יומת [ACCORDINGLY] THE LORD SAID TO AARON, "YOU AND YOUR SONS . . . (4) NO OUTSIDER SHALL DRAW NEAR TO YOU . . . (7) ANY OUTSIDER WHO DRAWS NEAR SHALL BE PUT TO DEATH: Now I have given them a warning concerning the death penalty [for an outsider drawing near]. Now there is no reason for them to worry that (17:28) "Anyone who so much as draws near [shall die]." I have now forbidden them from drawing near and I have made them liable for the death penalty [if they do so].[54]

18:7 עבודת מתנה [I WILL MAKE YOUR PRIESTHOOD] A SERVICE OF DEDICATION: [Since only the priests are required to do the Temple work, it is now clear that the Israelites] are exempt from such work. Since they are not obligated to do it, they will no longer draw near for [now they know that] ANY OUTSIDER WHO DRAWS NEAR SHALL DIE.[55]

We have already encountered Rashbam attempting to minimize the sinfulness of the Israelites. See commentary to 10:33–11:1 (and notes 25 and 29 there), and to 11:7 (and note 31 there) and to 21:5, below (and note 31 there). Polemical considerations—an attempt to refute Christian claims that the Jews have always been wayward and unbelieving—may be responsible, at least in part, for Rashbam's positive portrayal of their behavior. Cf. however commentary to 20:8 and 20:10, s.v. ויאמר, and see note 10 there.

[54]Rashbam continues the explanation that he began in his commentary to 17:27–8. See note 53. See also commentary to vs. 27, below, and the end of note 62 there.

From the way that Rashbam quotes parts of vss. 1, 4 and 7 in the beginning of this comment, it appears that the meaning of his explanation is: From the juxtaposition of "Aaron and his sons," and "no outsider shall draw near," we now have for the first time the Torah's definition of who should not draw near. An "outsider" has now been defined as anyone who is not a descendant of Aaron.

Rashbam's explanation is opposed to Rashi's. Ad vs. 4, Rashi argues that that verse represents a new command to the priests. The priests, according to Rashi, are being told that they too have the responsibility of keeping the outsiders away from the Temple service. Rashbam interprets these verses as instruction—in fact the first detailed instruction—to *the Israelites* of what they are not allowed to do. Note Rashbam's language "הזהרתים . . . אסרתים . . . חייבתים—I have given *them* a warning . . . I have forbidden *them* . . . I have made *them* liable." Rashbam's explanation may also be seen as opposed to the explanation later offered, for example, by NJPSC, that our verses are a warning to the priests that they should not encroach beyond the permitted areas.

[55]Rashbam continues and concludes his explanation, which began in his final comment on chapter 17. See note 53 above.

The phrase עבודת מתנה is difficult. The translation above ("a service of dedication") follows NJPS, but it is not clear what Rashbam thinks that it means.

The purpose of Rashbam's comment is not to explain that phrase but to explain the juxtaposition of thoughts here. Verse 7 says that the Temple service is the priests' responsibility. It says further that any outsider who draws near shall die. Rashbam attempts to show the connection between those ideas by explaining the verse as compassionate, not as

18:8 לך נתתים למשחה I HAVE GIVEN THEM TO YOU AS AN 'ANOINTMENT': I.e. [for the priests, the holy portions shall be] like a sign that is given to great people, who are anointed [to signify] that they will rule.[56]

18:9 מן האש [THIS SHALL BE YOURS FROM THE MOST HOLY SACRIFICES,] FROM THE FIRE: [I.e. these holy portions—] the parts that remain [separate] from the fire—[shall be yours] after the burning of the *'emurim*.[57]

אשר ישיבו לי [ANY *'ASHAM*] THAT THEY RETURN TO ME: [This phrase should be understood in the same way as] (5:8), "the *'asham* that is being returned to the LORD [shall go] to the priest," i.e. as a reference to [the restitution of] something that was stolen from a convert who has no heirs [and accordingly the restitution is given to the priests].[58]

---

threatening. The non-priests are being told that they have no Temple duties; therefore they should now rest assured that they will be able to avoid the stiff penalties for "drawing near" illegitimately. Now the text has addressed the concerns that the Israelites expressed in 17:27–28, as Rashbam explains them there.

[56] See note 39 to Lev. 7:35, and the discussion there about the word משחה, when it does not have the literal meaning of "anointing."

It is not clear whether Rashbam has a consistent explanation of the word when it is not referring to a physical act of anointing. Here he tries to stay close to the literal sense. The word itself *means* "anointing," but when the verse says that the emoluments are the priests' משחה, that phrase should be understood as a metaphor. This explanation is opposed to that of Rashi who writes (following Sifre Numbers 117) both here and in other passages that the word משחה *means* something like "greatness" or "increase."

[57] The *'emurim* are those parts of a sacrifice that are not to be eaten but are burnt on the altar.

The difficulty of the phrase, "these shall be yours . . . from the fire," is that it sounds as if parts that are offered on the altar's fire shall be given to the priests. As *Gur Aryeh* puts it, that could not be the explanation, for anything that is consigned to the fire is "God's" entirely and the priests would receive none of it. Parts of the sacrifices go *either* to the fire of the altar *or* to the priests, but not to both. As NJPSC writes (p. 315, note 27), the expected reading here would be מאשי or מאשי ה', yielding the sense "this is their share which comes from my sacrifices." Some exegetes, e.g. iE, attempt to explain מן האש as if מאשי were written.

Rashbam explains that "from the fire" means those parts that remain separate from the fire. His explanation, practically speaking, reaches the same conclusion as that of Rashi (מן האש: לאחר הקטרת האשים—'from the fire' i.e. after the sacrifices have been burnt). But Rashbam tries to read this explanation into the word "from." His explanation is the same as that of Onq. (מותר מן אישתא). So also JBS.

[58] So also Rashi here (following Sifre). See also Rashbam's commentary to 5:6, 5:7 and 5:8 and notes 4, 5 and 7 there.

18:12 כל חלב יצהר ANY OF THE 'FAT' OF THE OIL: As in the phrase (vs. 30), "when you lift up the 'fat' from it."[59]

18:19 ברית מלח A COVENANT OF 'SALT': It appears to me [that "salt" here] means "lasting." So one should also interpret the verse (II Chr. 13:5) "gave David kingship—to him and his sons—by a covenant of 'salt'," [i.e. by an everlasting covenant]. One must interpret [the word "salt" in] those verses in a contextually appropriate manner.[60] But [the word "salt" in the verse] (Lev. 2:13) "do not omit the 'salt' of your covenant with God," means salt, literally.

"A covenant of salt" means a covenant that continues and lasts over the generations.[61]

---

[59]Rashbam has attempted to explain one obscure phrase by citing another similar but equally obscure phrase. He has not said what he thinks the word "fat" means in either of these verses. He seems to understand "fat" as a reference to the *terumah* ("heave-offering"), following the common rabbinic explanation. See e.g. Bekh. 53b.

Rashbam cites vs. 30 because there the verb that is used concerning the "fat" is תרימו, which he sees, apparently, as a reference to *terumah*. If my explanation of this comment is correct, then Rashbam is disagreeing with Rashi ad Bekh., *ibid.*, s.v. תן חלב, where Rashi says that our verse refers to *terumah* while vs. 30 refers to *ma'aser*.

Rashbam's comment is strange in that the presumed major point of the comment—that "fat" means *terumah*—is not explicitly written at all.

[60]The phrase פתרונו לפי עניינו is Rashbam's common phrase for an interpretation that is based primarily on context. See e.g. commentary to Gen. 41:23. See also Rashbam's use of the similar and more traditional phrase דבר הלמד מעניינו in his commentary to Lev. 19:26, and see note 52 there.

[61]Rashi offers two different explanations, here and in Leviticus, of what covenant God made with salt. In Leviticus he says that at the time of the creation of the world, God made a promise to salt that it would later be used in the Temple rites. Here Rashi says that God made a covenant with salt that it would be one type of food that would last and would never spoil.

Rashbam does not refer to any covenant between God and salt. Here, he says, a covenant is made with the priests. Calling the covenant a "salt covenant" is simply a way of saying that is it a lasting one. A similar explanation appears in the commentary attributed to Rashi to II Chr., *ibid.* That commentary was not written by Rashi (see Grossman, *Ḥakhme Ṣorfat*, p. 182) but did originate from Northern French exegetical circles in or around Rashi's days.

There is a subtle difference between Rashbam's approach to our verse and the approach of other exegetes who note the similarity of language in our verse and in Lev. 2:13. Ps.-Jon., for example, explains that in Leviticus a covenant was made that salt would be used on sacrifices and a commitment was made that that regulation was unchangeable. When our text says that a "salt covenant" was made with priests, it is assuming that we know what was written in Leviticus 2. Our text is saying that a covenant that is just as immutable as the salt covenant of Leviticus has made been here, in Numbers, with the priests. Ps.-Jon.'s explanation has had a certain popularity over the years. It is found in the Numbers commentary of Rashbam's Christian neighbor and contemporary, Andrew of St. Victor, and appears also in some moderns (e.g. Levine).

18:27 כדגן מן הגורן AS WITH NEW GRAIN FROM THE THRESHING FLOOR: [When the Levites receive tithes, the gift that they give to the priests from those tithes (vss. 26–27) shall have the same status as the *terumah* that is given directly to the priests by the farmers in the form of "new grain from the threshing floor." About that *terumah*, we know already that] there is a negative commandment concerning [a non-priest who eats] it. For in the Torah portion *'Emor 'el ha-kohanim*, it is written, in the section about *terumah* (Lev. 22:10), "no lay person shall eat of the holy things."[62]

Rashbam would disagree. According to Rashbam our text is understandable even by someone who does not know the Leviticus text. The word "salt" means salt, literally, only in the Leviticus passage. Here the word means "lasting" or "continuing." As NJPSC puts it, "Salt is a symbol of permanence, and a 'salt covenant,' therefore, means an unbreakable covenant."

[62]See Rashbam's commentary, and note 16 there.

The simpler way of understanding our verse is that it is saying to the Levites that when you give to the priests a tenth of the tenth that you receive, your action will be seen to be as meritorious as the actions of farmers who give *terumah* from their crops directly to the priests. Rashbam, however, follows the halakhic line of exegesis. According to that explanation, the verse relates to the restrictions concerning tithes, not to the merit of those who give tithes. It says that the same restrictions that apply to the farmer's *terumah* apply also to the "tenth of a tenth" given by the Levite. Yet Rashbam refines and reworks that interpretation somewhat.

A number of rabbinic texts see our verse as providing a blanket comparison of the rules of the Levites' "tenth of a tenth" with the rules of *terumah*. See e.g. Git. 30b-31a and Men. 54b-55a. In that spirit, Rashi, in his commentary to this verse, provides a long list of laws that apply equally to both types of priestly gifts. Rashbam confines the comparison to one law—the law that non-priests may not eat *terumah* and may also not eat the "tenth of a tenth" that the Levites give to the priests. See also note 63.

Rashbam is then continuing the theme of interpretation that he has been pursuing consistently in the commentary to the last three chapters. As he explains in his commentary to 17:27–8, the people want precise information about what they, the non-priests, are and are not allowed to do when it comes to holy items. Rashbam explains the beginning of chapter 18 as a direct reaction to their desire for clearer information. Here he explains the end of chapter 18 as providing further details about the restrictions that apply to non-priests. See commentary to 17:27–28 and 18:1, and notes 53 and 54.

Note also that Rashbam points out here that the outsider who eats the "tithe of the tithe" is covered by the לאו—the negative commandment—found in Lev. 22:10. Again Rashbam is continuing the theme of his comment to 17:27–28 and 18:1, where, as I explained in the notes, he shows his concern that every restriction on lay people vis à vis holy items has to be covered by some specific negative commandment.

18:32 לא תחללו YOU MUST NOT PROFANE [the *terumah*, LEST YOU DIE]: By eating [the *terumah*] while [you are] impure.[63]

[63]In Lev. 22:2, a similar phrase, "lest they profane," appears in a context of priests and holy items. Rashbam writes there that that reference is to sacrificial meat or other *sancta* eaten by an impure priest. See also Rashi there, ad vs. 9. Here Rashbam offers that same explanation for the phrase "you must not profane." I presume that it is the similarity of the language of this verse and Lev. 22:2 that causes Rashbam to interpret as he does.

Rashbam unfortunately does not specify which holy food would be profaned by eating it in a state of impurity. The immediate context shows us that the text is addressed to Levites. They are supposed to receive tithes and then give some of that tithe to the priests. The part that they keep, they are told (vs. 31), "you and your household may eat anywhere." Rashi baldly presents the universal halakhic position—that Levites are allowed to eat their tithes even while impure—when he tells us (ad vs. 31) that "eating it anywhere" means even in a cemetery. It is unlikely that Rashbam would be disputing that halakhic understanding. Presumably he is saying here that if an impure person were to eat the "tithe from the tithe," the part that is given to the priests, that would be a form of "profaning" that would be punishable by death (at the hands of heaven, according to the rabbis).

Rashbam's comment, then, is a continuation of his comment to vs. 27. There, as I explained in note 62, Rashi argues that vs. 27 teaches us that "tithe of a tithe" is totally similar to *terumah*. The same laws apply to them: laws concerning outsiders eating them, laws concerning eating them while impure and various other laws. Rashbam explains vs. 27 much more specifically. He says that the verse compares the "tithe of a tithe" to *terumah* only in regards to one restriction—that outsiders may not eat them. Now Rashbam says that the restriction concerning not defiling "tithe of a tithe" by eating it when impure is found here in vs. 32, not, as Rashi would have it, in vs. 27.

Rashi does not really tell us how he understands the term "profaning" in our verse. Cf. iE who says that this verse describes the Levite who eats his tithes without separating a "tithe from the tithe."

חוקת (Numbers 19:1–22:1)

19:2 זאת חקת התורה THIS IS THE LAW OF THE RITUAL (*TORAH*): Below the text explains which ritual (*torah*) it is referring to. There (vs. 14) it says, "This is the ritual (*torah*): if a person dies in a tent . . .."

In other words [our verse is saying that] the law for that ritual—the one concerning which [God] said to Moses "this is the ritual . . ."—is to take A RED HEIFER in order to perform the purification ritual for a person who becomes impure through touching or carrying or being in the same tent as (vs. 14) "a person who dies in a tent."[1]

19:5 לעיניו [THE COW SHALL BE BURNED] AT HIS: Eleazar's, SIGHT.[2]

19:13 עוד טומאתו בו HIS IMPURITY IS STILL UPON HIM: Even though he already immersed [in a *miqveh*].[3]

---

[1]It is not certain how Rashbam is interpreting the words חוקה and תורה here. However, he is certainly rejecting some common midrashic understandings of these words. He is not interpreting חוקה as a reference to a law that has no (obvious) reason to it, the common explanation in rabbinic literature. In that, he is opposing the interpretation of Rashi here (following a number of rabbinic sources, e.g. *Yoma'* 67b). The same difference of opinion between Rashi and Rashbam about the word חוקה appears in their commentaries to Gen. 26:5, Ex. 15:25 (and see note 77 on pp. 166–167 of my Exodus volume) and Lev. 19:19 (and see note 34 there).

Rashbam is also opposing the various midrashic traditions that attribute some grand significance to the use of the word תורה here, e.g. seeing the laws of this chapter as being the essence of the Torah. See e.g. Pesiqta Rabbati 14, concerning the word תורה in our verse, or Ber. 63b, concerning the word תורה in vs. 14.

Like Rashbam's explanation of our verse, see JBS and Hizq. ad vs. 14.

[2]The syntax of the verse is unclear. It is possible to interpret both the verb ושחט, at the end of vs. 3, and ושרף here as meaning that Eleazar must do the slaughtering and the burning of the red heifer himself. Rashbam follows the common halakhic understanding that these actions need not be performed by Eleazar or even by a priest; they simply must be done in Eleazar's presence. Rashi says the same thing concerning the verb ושחט in vs. 3. Rashbam's comment about the verb ושרף may be seen as a reworking of the comment of Sifre here. See similarly iE.

[3]The phrase "his impurity is still upon him" appears to be redundant. The Sifre here does careful midrashic analysis of each word of the phrase and offers a convoluted midrashic explanation: Each of the ostensibly redundant words here teaches that each and every step of the purification process is required in order for the process to work. A person who was sprinkled once but not twice or who was sprinkled twice but has not immersed would still be impure.

19:16 וכל אשר יגע על פני השדה AND IN THE OPEN, ANYONE WHO TOUCHES [A BODY]: In other words, someone who enters a tent where there is a dead body will become impure even without touching that body. However, "in the open," i.e. not in a tent, one cannot become impure except by touching [the dead body].[4]

19:22 והנפש הנוגעת THE PERSON WHO TOUCHES: another person who [had previously] touched a dead body SHALL BECOME IMPURE UNTIL THE EVENING. This is because a corpse is considered the most infectious source[5] of impurity.[6]

20:1 ותמת שם מרים MIRIAM DIED THERE: [She died] IN THE FIRST MONTH of the fortieth year, at the end [of the years of wandering in the wilderness]. For her brother Aaron died [right] after her in the fifth month of "the fortieth year after the Israelites had left Egypt," as it is written in the Torah portion *'Elleh mas'e*.[7]

Rashbam's comment is identical to that of Rashi. Both simplify the midrashic explanation. They say that someone who attempts to become pure using the standard method of removing impurity—immersing in a *miqveh*—will not succeed. To remove the most serious form of impurity—from contact with the dead—the red heifer ceremony is required.

[4]The ostensible difficulty of our verse is that the words "in the open" are not necessary. Anyone who touches a corpse becomes impure, whether it is in the open or under a roof. Rashbam explains that the words are written in order to emphasize that when the corpse is "in the open," touching it is the only way to become impure.

The printed editions of Rashi's commentary here have two possible explanations for the phrase על פני השדה. The first is a midrash (following the opinion of Rabbi Aqiva in Sifre Numbers 127) that this ostensibly redundant phrase teaches us that the person who touches various parts of a grave or its marker (גולל ודופק) becomes impure. Then Rashi offers his *peshaṭ* explanation, which is the same explanation found here in Rashbam. If the printed editions of Rashi's commentary are correct, then Rashbam is supporting Rashi's second, *peshaṭ* explanation, and disputing with his midrashic one.

However, in a number of old manuscripts and in the first printing of Rashi's Torah commentary, the second, *peshaṭ* explanation of the verse does not appear. If that is the correct version of Rashi's commentary, then Rashbam completely disagrees with Rashi. Perhaps Rashbam's *peshaṭ* explanation was added by some later hand to the text of Rashi's Torah commentary.

[5]Literally "the father of the father of [all] impurities" (אבי אבות הטומאה).

[6]Rashbam's explanation represents the plain meaning of the text. His comment is the same as that of Rashi, and the language of the comments is also very similar. The explanation is also found in AZ 37b.

[7]See Numbers 33:36–38.

The difficulty in our verse is that only the month of Miriam's death is given, and not the year. In theory, she could have died in any one of the forty years of wandering in the desert.

20:8 קח את המטה TAKE THE STAFF: From before the Pact.[8]

ודברתם אל הסלע SPEAK TO THE ROCK [TO YIELD ITS WATERS]: The reason that God commanded [them] to take the staff was not because He wanted them [to use the staff in order] to hit the rock,[9] as he had done in Rephidim, where it says (Ex. 17:6), "Strike the rock and water will issue from it." Rather He told them to take the staff in order to serve as a visual reminder of their stubborn rebelliousness, as it is written: [the staff was] (17:25), "to be kept as a

---

Rashbam does not explain his logic here in detail but the argument presumably proceeds as follows. In Numbers 33, in the list of the Israelites' travels, the stop after "the wilderness of Zin, that is Kadesh" is Mount Hor. At Mount Hor, Aaron dies "in the fortieth year after the Israelites had left Egypt, in the fifth month." Numbers 20:1 says that Miriam died in "the wilderness of Zin, which is Kadesh." Since this is the stop that immediately preceded Mount Hor, Rashbam concludes that she too died in that same year, four months before Aaron.

See iE and Nahm. here and Seder Olam Rabba 10, who all say, along with Rashbam, that Miriam died in the fortieth year.

[8]Rashbam's next comment clarifies that he sees the staff of our verse as being the same staff of Num. 17:19–25. There Aaron's staff is placed "before the Pact" (in vss. 19 and 25) and "before the LORD, in the Tent of the Pact" (in vs. 22). In vs. 25 there we are told that Moses returned that staff to be "before the Pact" permanently. Here, Moses and Aaron are told to take "the" staff, and in the following verse they take it from "before the LORD." This linguistic link is what causes Rashbam to connect the two staffs. So also iE (on vs. 9) and Hizq. here.

Cf. Levine here who says that the staff referred to in this narrative must be the famous מטה א-לוהים of the book of Exodus, the staff with which the miracles were performed in Egypt. So also NJPSC, which says that our text may be referring to the staff of Numbers 17, but "it was more likely the rod of Moses, which had been employed in the performance of God's miracles." iE apparently feels that the מטה א-לוהים of Exodus and the staff of Numbers 17 are both the same staff. See his commentary to 17:17 and 20:9.

[9]Rashbam presumably has heard or read some commentator who argued just that: that the fact that God told Moses and Aaron to take the staff with them shows that God intended them to use that staff to hit the rock. Accordingly, whatever their sin was, it was *not* the fact that they hit the rock. They were supposed to do that. See e.g. Nahm. who, around a century after Rashbam, argues that position passionately.

It is hard to know where Rashbam encountered that explanation but it was definitely around in his days. In his commentary here, iE, Rashbam's slightly younger contemporary, quotes a number of different explanations—all of which he rejects—about what sin was committed here. According to more than one of those explanations, there was nothing wrong with Moses hitting the rock; that was what was expected. Most of the explanations to which iE alludes that make that suggestion are hard to identify, but iE does specifically mention Rabbi Moses Gikatilla as one exegete who felt that way.

lesson to the rebels."[10] But it is through speech—talking to the rock—[that they were] to get the rock to yield its waters. [That is the meaning of] YOU SHALL BRING OUT WATER FROM THE ROCK—i.e. by talked to the rock.

20:10 ויאמר להם שמעו נא המורים HE SAID TO THEM, "LISTEN YOU REBELS: [for you are rebels,] just as this staff with the almonds on it proves, for it is (17:25) 'to be kept as a lesson to the rebels'[11] SHALL WE GET WATER FOR YOU OUT OF THIS ROCK?" At the time when he lifted up his hand with the staff [to show it to the people,[12]] HE HIT THE ROCK with it[13] TWICE. Then, in anger and rage, he said to them, "Did you think[14] that we would get water out of this rock for you?"

> [An alternate explanation:][15] Moses said[16] those words because he had doubts. He was mistaken about the meaning of what God had said to him (vs. 8), "take the staff," [because] he did not trust that by talking to the rock he would succeed in getting water from it. Rather he thought that [he would have to] hit [the rock] with his staff, as he had done in Rephidim (Ex. 17:6). As for the fact that God had said to him (vs. 8),

---

[10]Both here and in his comment to the next verse, Rashbam interprets the phrase בני מרי from Num. 17:25 as a reference to the rebelliousness of the Israelites in the wilderness. This comment appears inconsistent with his comment to Num. 17:25. See note 46 there.

[11]See note 10.

In note 53 to the commentary on 17:27–28, I noted that Rashbam explains that the narratives in chapters 16 and 17 and the laws in chapter 18 flow in an understandable progression. Rashbam does not try to explain the place of chapter 19 in this progression, but here he does connect chapter 20 to the progression that he noted in those earlier chapters.

[12]As Rashbam just explained in his previous comment.

[13]Rashbam paraphrases our verse slightly in order to deal with a perceived vagueness in the verse. Verse 11 reports two actions: Moses lifted his *hand*; Moses hit the rock with his *staff*. Rashbam emphasizes that the word "במטהו—with his staff" should be connected to both actions. He lifted up his hand *with his staff* and then hit the rock *with his staff*. The phrase "to lift up one's hand with one's staff" may be found in Ex. 8:13.

Rashbam's interpretation may be directed against the midrashic explanations that see "lifting one's hand" as an allusion to taking an oath. See *Midrash Tehillim* 106:7 and Ps.-Jon. here ad vs. 8.

[14]Our texts of Rashbam's comment read "סבורים אתם," which would be more accurately translated "*do* you think." However, that reading confuses the sequence of actions in Rashbam's comment.

In the commentaries of both JBS and Hizq., Moses' question is paraphrased: ההייתם סבורים שמן הסלע הזה נוציא לכם מים. Following that reading, the sequence of actions is perfectly clear. A small emendation of Rashbam's comment brings the text in line with their more reasonable formulation.

[15]I have labeled the continuation of the comment here "an alternate explanation" and I have indented this section of the commentary, since it seems that another hand has added this second explanation into the commentary. See note 20 below where I offer my arguments.

[16]Berzinsky proposes an emendation here: ומספק עשה, instead of ומספק אמר, yielding the translation, "Moses did those things because he had doubts."

"*Talk* [to the rock]," he thought that talking to the rock meant hitting it. That is why he hit the rock twice—just like [a person who is acting] in anger and rage—for he was in doubt, and he reasoned, "If the rock gives forth water [after I hit it,] well and good. If not, I will talk to the rock afterwards."

God supported Moses' actions after the fact,[17] [allowing] the water to flow from the rock when he hit it. Nevertheless, Moses was punished [for his error], for God is very strict with righteous people.[18] That is the meaning of what God said (vs. 12), "Because you did not trust Me enough to make Me holy [before the people of Israel]," by speaking to the rock. For God is very strict with righteous people, even for [departing from expected behavior] by a hair's breadth.

Because I, the interpreter, know that Moses, our rabbi, could not have transgressed God's word except inadvertently, that is why I have to interpret[19] this way—that Moses, our teacher, was mistaken.[20]

---

[17]This same phrase, that God הסכים על ידי משה, may be found in Shab. 87a, in a context that discusses actions that Moses took out of his own initiative. See also the use of the phrase in Rashbam's commentary to Gen. 24:33.

[18]The concept that God expects a higher standard of behavior from the righteous and will punish them even for relatively minor infractions is common in rabbinic literature. In his commentary to the phrase בקרובי אקדש in Lev. 10:3 Rashbam argues against those who interpret that phrase as meaning that God exacts a higher standard from the righteous. See also Rashbam's commentary to Ex. 29:43 (and see note 25 there), where again Rashbam rejects an explanation of Rashi's that reads into a verse the idea that God exacts a higher standard from the righteous and punishes them for minor infractions. See also Rashi's commentary to Ps. 99:9. See also Rashi and Rashbam on vs. 13, s.v. ויקדש בם, and notes 21 and 22 there. And see Tanh. *Balaq* 20, where the phrase is used about the punishment of Moses (but not about the sin recorded in our chapter).

[19]The phrase "אני זקוק לפרש—I have to interpret" does not appear anywhere else in Rashbam's Torah commentary but does appear more than once in his Talmud commentary. See e.g. ad BB 106b, s.v. אמר רב.

[20]While there is nothing explicit in the text of the commentary itself here that indicates an addition into the commentary, I feel confident in proposing that a second, more conservative hand has added this second explanation of Moses' sin into the text of Rashbam's commentary. Perhaps a copyist or a student was not pleased with the explanation that Moses sinned and was punished for displaying unwarranted anger. (See e.g. Nahm.'s vituperative comments against Maimonides [*Shemonah peraqim* 4] who says just that.)

There are a number of signs in this section that a second opinion has been interpolated into Rashbam's commentary.

(1) Rashbam never refers to himself as אני המפרש (I, the interpreter) in the middle of his commentary. He does speak at times in the first person, generally when he wishes to contrast his interpretation with older or more traditional ways of explaining a text. (See e.g. commentary to Ex. 16:15, Lev. 4:23 and Num. 6:3.) There are also a number of interpolations into Rashbam's commentary that are introduced by the words ואני הצעיר ("But I, the young [i.e. the unworthy copyist,] say that . . ."; see e.g. in Rosin's edition ad Gen. 45:28 and ad Deut. 2:14). Once, Rosin identifies, reasonably to my mind, a text that begins with the words ואני שמעתי ("But I heard . . .") as being an addition of a second hand into the commentary. (See Rashbam's commentary to Deut. 3:13, p. 203 in Rosin's edition, and Rosin's notes there.) Here I would argue that we have another example of an interpolation that uses the

20:13 ויקדש בם AND HE [= GOD] WAS SANCTIFIED THROUGH THEM: I.e. [He was sanctified] in any case,[21] through the water [that flowed miraculously] even though they had not spoken to the rock.[22]

---

word אני (twice!) in a contrastive manner, presenting this second explanation of the text as an alternative to the first.

(2) As noted in note 18 above, Rashbam has distanced himself a number of times in his commentary from interpretations of texts that read into the Torah the concept—common to other exegetes—of God exacting a higher standard of behavior from the righteous and punishing them severely for minor infractions. See also Rashbam's commentary below on vs. 13, and note 22 there.

(3) Rashbam has also rejected another common portrayal of Moses, where he acts as a free agent and then God "supports Moses' actions after the fact." See e.g. commentary to Num. 16:4, and note 7 there. In the three places in the Torah where the rabbis (Shab. 87a) suggest that Moses acted independently and then God supported him, Rashbam does not follow their line of interpretation.

(4) The strongest argument, to my mind, in favor of seeing in Rashbam's comment here two different explanations from two different hands is that the explanations are best understood as contradictory and mutually exclusive. The first commentator says that there was a good reason why God told Moses to take the staff even though he was not supposed to hit with it. That commentator also feels that Moses understood what he was to do: he took the staff that was meant to remind rebels about the uselessness of rebellion and he held it up and said "Listen you rebels." Then the second commentator tells us that Moses was not sure what to do with the staff. The first commentator says that Moses behaved "in anger and rage" (דרך כעס וחמה). The second commentator says that Moses did not know what he was supposed to do. He hit the rock twice because he was unsure of whether that was called for. His behavior only appeared to be motivated by anger (כעין כעס וחמה), but was actually מספק, because he was in doubt. Acting because of anger (explanation 1) and acting because of doubt (explanation 2) are two incompatible explanations.

[21]By "in any case," Rashbam means that God was sanctified through the miracle of the water despite the fact that Moses and Aaron had not performed the miracle in the correct way.

[22]Rashbam's interpretation opposes that of Rashi and iE who both argue that ויקדש בם means that God was sanctified through "them"—i.e. through Moses and Aaron. Rashi explains that God punished Moses and Aaron strictly and the strict punishment of offenders leads to greater sanctification and fear of God.

This comment (s.v. ויקדש בם) is part of the original commentary. The postulated interpolation of the second hand into the commentary, which began in the comment to vs. 10 (see note 20), has now finished. In disagreeing with Rashi here, Rashbam is rejecting the very idea that was contained in the interpolated section in the commentary to vs. 10, namely, that strict divine punishment leads to God's greater sanctification. (See e.g. Yev. 121b and BQ 50a.)

Throughout his commentary on this section, Rashbam never minimizes Moses' sin. Accordingly, if God was sanctified, it must have been despite Moses' sin and not because of it (and not because of the punishment that Moses received for his sin.)

Like Rashbam, see also Nahm. and Hizq.

See also Rashbam ad Lev. 10:1–3 where Rashbam again prefers the idea of God being sanctified through miracles (there a divine fire descending from heaven) over the idea of God being sanctified by the strict administration of punishment. See especially note 32 there.

20:17 לא נשתה מי באר WE WILL NOT DRINK WATER FROM ANY WELL: that belongs to you. Water was a precious commodity for nations who lived in that country.[23]

דרך המלך [WE WILL FOLLOW] THE KING'S HIGHWAY: I.e. the path for travelers, the one that is designated for everyone [to use].[24]

---

[23]Rashbam is pointedly disagreeing with Rashi's comment to this verse. Rashi (following Tanh. B. *Ḥuqqat* 35) says that the verse means that the Israelites actually *did* offer to drink the water of the Edomites. This interpretation flies in the face of the simple meaning of the words "we will not drink water from any well."

Presumably, Rashi is attracted to that explanation because it solves a problem that arises when our verse is compared to Deut. 2:28–29. Here in Numbers, the Israelites promise the Edomites that they will not drink water from any of their wells. But in Deuteronomy, Moses asks Sihon to sell water to the Israelites who would pass through his territory, "just as the descendants of Esau did for me." So Rashi concludes that here the Israelites really promise not to drink water from their *own* well—i.e. they promise to buy water from the Edomites.

Rashbam interprets the verse according to the simple meaning. He addresses the conflict between our verse and the verse in Deut. in his commentary there, by saying that the "Edomites" of Numbers 20 are not the same people as the "descendants of Esau" in Deut. As for why the Israelites had to promise not to drink Edomite water, Rashbam points out that water is a precious commodity in that part of the world. I would read these words as Rashbam's response to Rashi's suggestion that the nicest thing that the Israelites could do for the Edomites was to *buy* their water (not to refrain from depleting their water supply).

Like Rashbam, see iE, JBS and (with a slight twist) Hizq. A careful reading of JBS and Hizq. shows that they too are trying to explain how it could be that the Edomites would be concerned about their water supply (since they, like Rashi and Rashbam, lived in countries with plenty of water). On the other hand, iE, the world traveler, who was well acquainted with many arid countries, feels no need to explain why Edomites might be concerned about the depletion of their water supply.

[24]The ostensible difficulty in the phrase is that the promise to go on the king's highway might not appeal to the king, who might wish to keep people from trespassing on his property.

Again Rashi offers an unusual explanation of the text, one that strays from the simple meaning of the words. He says that Moses' promise that the Israelites would stay on the דרך המלך means that they would muzzle their animals. It is unclear why Rashi was attracted to that midrashic explanation (from Tanh. B., *ibid.*). Perhaps he is saying that the Israelites promised that their animals would not stray from the middle of the road: being muzzled, they would have no reason to stray, for they would not be able to eat anything growing on the roadside. So for Rashi, the phrase "on the king's highway" means on that highway itself, not on its shoulders.

For Rashbam the phrase means, "on a major thoroughfare, open to all." According to Rashbam, the Israelites promised to confine their travel to routes that were, in any case, meant for the public. They were not asking for permission to use roads that were normally restricted.

A number of other classical Jewish exegetes suggest that "on the king's highway" simply means "on whatever highway the king would like us to use." See e.g. iE (in his second explanation) and Seforno.

21:1 יושב הנגב . . . דרך האתרים [THE CANNANITE KING OF ARAD WHO] DWELT IN THE NEGEV [HEARD THAT THE ISRAELITES WERE COMING] BY THE WAY OF אתרים: I.e. [by the same route used by] the תרים—the spies.[25] For there [concerning the spies,] it is written (13:17), "Go up by way of the Negev," and (13:29), "Amalek dwell in the Negev." The Canaanites lived near them [i.e. near the Amalekites, in the Negev,] as it is written (Num. 14:43), "The Canaanites and the Amalekites are there facing you."

[The *'aleph* in the word] אתרים [is not part of the root; it] is like [the *'aleph* in the words] אפרוח—chick,[26] אתמול—yesterday[27] and אזרוע—arm.[28] Often the letter *'aleph* at the beginning of a word is a prefix[29] [to the root].

21:2 והחרמתי I WILL PROSCRIBE THEIR TOWNS: The chattels therein will be dedicated to God.[30]

---

[25]Rashbam's explanation is the first of two explanations offered here by Rashi. It originates in Onq. and in Sifre Numbers 82. The latter source presents that explanation and then mentions the objection raised by Rabbi Simeon b. Yoḥai: דרך התרים לא נאמר כי אם דרך האתרים —the text does not say that they came on the route of the תרים (which could be interpreted as referring to the spies) but rather on the route of the אתרים. Perhaps it is in order to counter this objection that Rashbam adds his grammatical explanation which defends Rashi's reading. The *'aleph* in אתרים, Rashbam says, need not change the meaning of the word, just like the *'aleph* in אתמול or אזרוע does not change the meaning of those words.

See NJPSC, which writes that the meaning of אתרים is "unknown," and notes that the explanation of Rashi and Rashbam may be found also in the Greek translations of Aquila and Symmachus. Most moderns see אתרים as a place name, although it has not been identified satisfactorily.

[26]E.g. Deut. 22:6. The root is clearly *p-r-ḥ* and, the *'aleph* is "added" as Rashbam says.

[27]E.g. Ps. 90:4. In biblical Hebrew the standard form is תמול, appearing nineteen times in the Bible. The form אתמול appears only three times.

[28]See e.g. Jer. 32:21. The form אזרוע appears in the Bible only twice, while the form זרוע appears over forty times. G.-K. (19m) explains the *'aleph* of אזרוע as "prosthetic."

[29]Rashbam's language—באין לשמוש—is similar to the common later Hebrew term for prefixed and suffixed letters, אותיות שימוש. It seems that Rashbam uses this terminology only here and in one passage in his grammar book, *Dayyaqut* (Merdler's edition, p. 31), where the term is used twice in the same passage. Rashi uses the term more often. See e.g. his commentary to Ex. 9:17, 15:18 and Deut. 32:26.

In his grammatical discussions, Qimḥi uses the term אותיות שימוש in contradistinction to the term אותיות נוספות. The former means letters that are added to the root and that in some way change the meaning or serve a grammatical purpose. The latter simply means a letter that is "added" or "extra" and that serves no particular purpose. Rashbam apparently uses the term אותיות שימוש in both senses.

[30]So also Rashi. This explanation—that the *ḥerem* mentioned here means that the chattels in the captured city will become Temple property—appears to be the simple meaning of the text. See the note here in NJPS: "I.e. utterly destroy, reserving no booty except what is deposited in the Sanctuary; see Josh. 6:24."

21:5 הקלקל [WE HAVE COME TO LOATHE THIS FOOD WHICH IS] קלקל: I.e. this dry, white[31] food, like the color of bdellium,[32] as in the phrase (Ezek. 21:26), "shiny (קלקל) arrows."[33] In the vernacular, *luisant*.[34]

21:8 וראה אותו [IF ANYONE WHO WAS BITTEN] LOOKS AT IT, [HE SHALL RECOVER]: For he will look to the heavens above.[35]

21:11 בעיי העברים [THEY ENCAMPED AT] THE עיים OF ABARIM: עיי means "ruins," as in the phrase (Jer. 26:18), "Jerusalem shall become heaps of ruins (לעיים)," or (Mi. 1:6) "into a ruin (לעי) in open country."[36]

It is possible that Rashbam and Rashi are both explaining how this promise of executing a *ḥerem* differs from the standard way in which Israelites were commanded to treat captured Canaanite cities. See e.g. Deut. 20:16–17, where the verb *ḥ-r-m* is used and where it appears to mean the total annihilation of the populace. Rashbam and Rashi therefore explain that the *ḥerem* when applied to the cities of Num. 21 includes a dedication of all their captured chattels to the Sanctuary.

On *ḥ-r-m*, see also Rashbam's commentary to Num. 5:10, and note 11 there.

31 See Ex. 16:31 and Rashbam's commentary and note 59 there. See also commentary to Num. 11:7 (and see note 30 there), where again Rashbam emphasizes that the manna was dry and white.

In general, Rashbam's explanation of this verse is unique and finds little or no support in later exegesis. The common understanding of לחם קלקל among both classical and modern exegetes is that it means "miserable food." Rashbam may have been attracted to his explanation in order to portray the people's complaints in a more positive light. See similarly commentary above ad 17:27–28, and note 53 there.

32 See Num. 11:7 and Rashbam's commentary and notes 30 and 31 there.

33 The prooftext from Ezekiel is not persuasive since that verse is difficult. NJPS translates it as "He has shaken arrows." Rashbam quotes the Ezekiel verse again in his commentary to 22:7. There his explanation is easily understood, but it does not seem to be in consonance with what he writes here.

As Rosin notes here (note 6), Rashbam's explanation is ultimately dependent on Menaḥem's *Maḥberet*, s.v. *q-l*. See also Rashi's commentary to Ezek 21:26.

Probably the best prooftext for the position of Rashbam and Menaḥem is Ezek. 1:7, "their sparkle was like the luster of burnished bronze (נחושת קלל)" (if we can assume that קלל there and קלקל here and in Ezek. 21 have the same root). See also the commentary on Eccl. attributed to Rashbam, ad 10:10, where the word קלקל there is explained as meaning "polished," and is connected to קלל in Ezek. 1.

34 I.e. "shining" or "glistening." Rashi offers that same Old French gloss in his commentary to Arakh. 10b, s.v. ממורק, and says that it is equivalent to the Hebrew קלל.

35 Rashbam's explanation is a shortened version of Rashi's who, following Mishnah RH 3:8, explains that the whole purpose of building the copper serpent and placing it high up was to force the Israelites to lift up their eyes towards heaven and then subjugate their hearts to the will of God.

36 Rashbam's explanation is somewhat similar to that of Rashi. Rashi says that עיים means ruins but he adds that he does not know why this place is called "ruins." He suggests further

21:14 על כן יאמר CONCERNING THIS IT IS SAID: I.e. mention of those journeys[37]—when they [the Israelites] made an about-face[38] and took a detour around the land of Edom (as it is written [Deut. 2:1] "we encircled Mount Seir for many days") and came back so far that they reached the well that was described above[39] (20:11)—may be found in the record of their praises of God;[40] [there] they praised God for the miracles at the Sea of Reeds[41] and for the miracles which were performed for them at wadi Arnon[42] and for the well.

---

that the root of the word עיים consists of only one Hebrew letter (*'ayin*) and that עיים and יעה ("pan" or "scraper"; e.g. Ex. 38:3) come from the same root. Presumably Rashbam would reject much of what Rashi writes, but he does agree that the word means "ruins," and he adds prooftexts to support this explanation.

[37]The verse is difficult and has been explained in many ways. Rashbam's commentary is very similar to that of Rashi. One of the few differences is that Rashbam says that "על כן—concerning this" is a reference to all the recent journeys of the Israelites in the wrong direction (21:10–13), while Rashi says that it is a specific reference to the last encampment of the Israelites, "beyond the Arnon" (21:13).

[38]The phrase חזרו לאחוריהם to describe the Israelites' travels here is found also in Rashi's commentary to 21:4.

[39]Rashbam says that the reference to a well in these verses (16, 17 and 18) is to the well that was described above in chapter 20. That would appear to be the simple meaning of the words (vs. 16), "this is the well concerning which God said to Moses, 'Assemble the people that I may give them water'." Very similar language appears in 20:8. Like Rashbam, see Hizq. ad vs. 18.

Rashbam is opposing the midrashic explanation offered here by Rashi. Rashi (ad vs. 15, s.v. ואשד, and ad vss. 16 and 17; following Tanh. *Ḥuqqat* 20) provides a detailed description of the miracles that God performed for the Israelites at Wadi Arnon, killing many of the Israelites' enemies. According to Rashi and the midrash, after their death (out of the sight of the Israelites), the well of the Israelites went miraculously into the wadi to remove body parts of the dead enemies and to display them to the Israelites. This explanation adds so much to the text that it surely offends Rashbam's sense of *peshaṭ*.

See also note 43 below.

[40]Rashbam's phrase here, "בספירת דברים שמשבחו להקב"ה—the record of their praises of God," is his paraphrastic explanation of the words in the verse, בספר מלחמות ה'. Rashbam and Rashi understand the phrase in the same manner. Neither wishes to explain the phrase as a reference to another book, *The Book of the Wars of the LORD*, presumably because no such ancient book is known to them (or to us). Cf. iE and Nahm. who both explain that there was a book by that name in ancient days and, as iE says, "many [old] books have been lost and we no longer have them." See Luzzatto's criticism of iE and his defense of Rashi and Rashbam.

In *Recherches augustiniennes* 24 (1989), p. 234, Berndt notes the similarity of Andrew of St. Victor's explanation here to that of Rashbam.

[41]It appears that Rashbam mentions the Sea of Reeds in his commentary here because he interprets the word בסופה as referring to ים סוף. So also Onq. and Rashi, s.v. את והב. This does not appear to be the plain meaning of Scripture. Nahm., for example, explains the word as meaning a storm. NJPS sees Suphah as a place name (following ibn Janaḥ; see Levine).

[42]Uncharacteristically Rashbam does accept the idea that some unspecified miracles were performed for the Israelites at Wadi Arnon, despite the fact, discussed in note 39 above, that

The phrase (below, vs. 17) "Then Israel sang this song" [about a well], is also [a reference to the well mentioned in chapter 20. The text says that the Israelites sang about the well *then*, i.e. only] when they saw the well now [a second time, after they doubled back]. The first time [that they encountered the well] they did not sing about it, because Moses and Aaron were punished concerning it then.[43]

את והב: means the same thing as את יהב, [i.e. the gift (יהב) that you received] from God. [The word והב should be understood in] the same [way] as [the word יהב in the phrase,] (Ps. 55:23), "Put your burden (יהב) on the LORD."[44]

Similarly, [in Hebrew roots we often find alternations between the letters *vav* and *yod*.] From the word "יהיה—he will be," [with a *yod*, comes the form הֹוֶה with a *vav*, as in the phrase] (Eccl. 2:22) "what comes (הֹוֶה) to a man";[45] from [the root *y-q-sh*, with a *yod*, as in the phrase] (Jer. 50:24) "I have set a snare (יקושתי) for you, O Babylon, and you were trapped," [comes the form תִּוָּקֵשׁ, with a *vav*, as in the phrase] (Deut. 7:25), "lest you be ensnared (תִּוָּקֵשׁ) thereby";[46] [from the root *y-r-'*, to fear, with a *yod*,] one finds [the form תִּוָּרֵא,]

---

he opposes Rashi's midrashic explanation of the miracles performed at Wadi Arnon by the Israelites' well.

[43]As noted above in note 39, Rashbam disputes Rashi's understanding of the well in these verses. According to Rashbam, the reference is to the Israelites returning to the well of Numbers 20, the well that Moses and Aaron created by hitting a rock.

In most but not all versions of Rashi's commentary there is a comment here in which Rashi muses about the question of why there would be a poem about the miraculous well of the Israelites specifically at this point in the narrative (מה ראה ליכתב כאן). Rashi then answers that it must be that the poem is not really about the well itself, but about the role that the well played in the (midrashic) miracles that took place at Wadi Arnon. It is presumably in order to argue with that comment that Rashbam explains why it is appropriate that specifically at this point in the text there is a poem in praise of the well.

Rosin (note 14) argues that Rashbam's explanation must be seen as a mistake (נזדמן טעות לרבנו). According to Rosin, the chronology is impossible. Wandering around Mount Seir must have taken place before Moses' and Aaron's sin at the rock. So it is impossible, says Rosin, to say that the Israelites returned to the rock of Num. 20 after wandering around Mount Seir, since the story of the rock had not taken place yet. Perhaps such chronological concerns were what motivated Rashi to explain the well of this chapter so midrashically. However, I am not convinced that the chronological assumptions that Rosin makes are necessarily shared by Rashbam.

[44]I am not sure how Rashbam understands the word יהב in the verse in Psalms, but I have translated it following NJPS.

[45]Rashbam cites the same example to make a similar point in his commentary to Ex. 3:14–15 (page 38 in my Exodus volume).

[46]Rashbam cites the same example to make a similar point in his commentary to Gen. 45:11 (p. 315 in my Genesis volume).

with a *vav* replacing the *yod*,[47] [in the phrase] (Ps. 130:4) "so that You may be feared (תִּוָּרֵא)." So also the form וָהֵב [in our verse] is from the root *y-h-b*.[48]

21:18 שרים [THE WELL WHICH WAS DUG BY] THE CHIEFTAINS: I.e. by Moses And Aaron.[49]

וממדבר מתנה AND FROM MIDBAR TO MATTANAH: According to the plain meaning of Scripture, all these [words][50] are names of places where the Israelites traveled and encamped.[51]

21:27 על כן יאמרו המושלים THAT IS WHY THE SEERS SAY: They prophesied about the wars of Sihon (and Og)[52] before they took place. מושלים means those who speak their prophecies in the form of parables, like Balaam and his colleagues.[53]

---

[47]This same phrase, ויו תחת יוד, appears also in Rashbam's *Dayyaqut* (Merdler's edition, p. 4). Rashbam often discusses this question in *Dayyaqut*. See e.g. pp. 8–10 there.

[48]Few scholars would agree with what Rashbam says about the word והב in our verse. (Most see it as a place name.) But the rest of Rashbam's grammatical excursus is in accord with generally agreed upon scholarship. The letter *vav* and the letter *yod* do alternate in a number of grammatical forms. See e.g. G.-K. sections 69 and 73.

A similar but shorter grammatical explanation (discussing only nouns, not verbs) is found in Rashi here.

[49]So also Rashi. Rashbam, as noted above (notes 39 and 43), differs with Rashi about the question of which well is being described here. But they do agree that the term שרים must refer to Moses and Aaron.

[50]I.e. Midbar and Mattanah, in this verse, and, in the next verse, Nahaliel and Bamoth.

[51]Rashbam is taking issue with the midrashic explanations of these words as references to events and not to places. See e.g. Rashi here, following the Targum.

For a similar dispute between Rashi and Rashbam, see Rashbam's commentary to Deut. 1:1 (where he makes the point twice in the same verse).

[52]I would propose emending the text of Rashbam's commentary to read מלחמת סיחון (the wars of Sihon), not מלחמת סיחון ועוג (the wars of Sihon and Og). The phrase מלחמת סיחון ועוג would have to mean the wars that the Israelites waged against Sihon and Og as described in this chapter. The phrase מלחמת סיחון could, theoretically, still mean the war when the Israelites defeated Sihon (vss. 23–25) but it could also mean the war that took place earlier, in which Sihon captured Moabite territory (i.e. the war alluded to in vs. 26). That last explanation is the only one that makes sense here.

Both Rashi and Rashbam (here and in his BB commentary [ad 78b, s.v. מאי דכתיב]) explain that the poem that appears here describes the way that Moabite territory was captured by Sihon in the war that he had waged once against the "first Moabite king" (vs. 26). Moderns generally follow this line of interpretation.

[53]Or perhaps, "those who express their prophecies in poetry, like Balaam and his colleagues."

21:28 עד מואב CONSUMING AR OF MOAB: The name of the royal city of Moab was Ar.[54]

21:30 וַנִּירָם means "we threw them out"[55] from where they were. [Just like] (Deut. 3:6) "We proscribed them (ונחרם אותם)."

[ונירם should be understood as a first-person plural *vav*-consecutive imperfect verb, with a third-person plural pronominal suffix.] Just as from the root *n-ṭ-h* the form [in the imperfect] is "וַנֵּט—we pitched [a tent]," so also from the root *y-r-h* the form [in the imperfect] is "וַנִּיר—we shot." [With the addition of a pronominal suffix, the form becomes] וַנִּירָם, which is the same as [the more expected form] וַנִּירֵם.[56] The form (Is. 56:3) "יַבְדִּילַנִי—he will separate me," is the same as [the more expected form,] יַבְדִּילֵנִי. The form (Ex. 14:11) "להוציאָנו—to take us out," is the same as [the more expected form,] להוציאֵנו.

[There are two words that look extremely similar in the second half of this verse: ונירם and ונשים.] ונירם just like "ונשים—we wrought desolation" is a *vanifal* form [i.e. a first-person plural imperfect *vav*-consecutive verb].

Instead of saying, as most moderns would, that the word מושלים here refers to poets who described the events of the war *after* they took place, both Rashi and Rashbam say that the מושלים here are prophets who *predicted* the outcome of the war before it took place. They both say that the reference is to Balaam and his colleagues. The explanation is not very attractive on the *peshaṭ* level, but it is presumably based on the fact that in the Balaam cycle, which begins in the next chapter, the verb *m-sh-l* is used about Balaam's prophecies seven times. The verb appears in the Torah only here, in the Balaam cycle, and once in Deut. (28: 37). Cf. iE and the *Be'ur* who explain that the reference is to poets. Cf. also Nahm. who interprets מושלים as meaning rulers.

[54] Onq. translated our phrase as: "קטילו עמא דשרו בלחית מואב—killing the people who lived in *leḥayat* of Moab." Rashi (s.v. אכלה) then says that there was a city-state in Moab, whose Hebrew name was Ar and whose Aramaic name was *Leḥayat*. Most scholars would dispute Rashi's understanding of Onq. Onq., according to Jastrow, is saying that the fire devoured "the *fortresses* (לחית) of Moab." (See also NJPSC, p. 318, note 50, which says that Onq. presumably understands the word ער as if the word "ערי—cities" were written.)

Rashbam says simply that Ar is the name of the royal city in Moab. Probably Rashbam means that this is the Moabite name of the city, not, as Rashi would have it, the *Hebrew* name.

[55] As many scholars have noted, the form ונירם is extremely difficult. See e.g. the comments of NJPSC ("This verse is an insoluble crux") and the *Be'ur* ("המילה הזאת אינה נמלטת מזרות—there is something unavoidably strange about this word").

[56] See the *Be'ur* here, who rejects the interpretation offered here by Rashbam, precisely because the form that appears in the text is not וַנִּירֵם. Rashbam, knowing of this objection, attempts to deal with it by proving that the suffix ending with an *a* vowel is not so rare.

See similarly G.-K. 58f, who writes that, when the verb is imperfect or an infinitive, the expected connecting vowel before the pronominal suffix is *e*. In 60d, G.-K. notes that there are many exceptions to that rule; often that vowel will become an *a* instead of an *e*.

If the Targum were correct about the interpretation of this word [that it is a noun, not a verb], the word would have to be vocalized וְנִירָם, with a *sheva* under the *vav*.[57]

22:1 מעבר לירדן ירחו [THE ISRAELITES ENCAMPED . . .] ACROSS THE JORDAN FROM JERICHO: In other words, across the Jordan and opposite Jericho. Not at the bottom of the Jordan and not at the top, where Israelites lived.[58]

The phrase "across the Jordan" is appropriately written[59] after[60] they [i.e. the Israelites] had crossed [to the west side of] the Jordan. From their point of

---

[57]The Targum, Rashi and many other exegetes say that the word ונירם consists of the noun ניר, preceded by a *vav*, meaning "and," and followed by a suffix meaning "theirs." In other words, ונירם means "and their ניר." The word ניר would then mean their "dominion" or "lands" or "royalty." Rashbam's objection to that explanation is clear and unarguable. See similarly the *Be'ur* and NJPSC which note this problem.

Rashbam's explanation is later offered by Qimḥi (*Shorashim*, s.v. *y-r-h*) and by NJPS ("we have cast them down"). G.-K. also explains the form that way, with hesitation, in 76f, but seems to prefer the suggestion that the text is corrupt. See G.-K. *ibid.*, and 69r.

[58]It is hard to know what Rashbam's image of the land of Israel was. See e.g. Rashbam's commentary to Ex. 23:31 (and my note 78, on p. 294, there). And see also his commentary to Deut. 1:1. Rosin suggests that "not at the bottom of the Jordan" means "not opposite the Dead Sea," and "not at the top" means not at the northern part of the Jordan River, where various sources pour into the Jordan. The distinction between being "opposite Jericho" and being "opposite the Dead Sea" is tenuous (since the locations are so close), but possible.

See also Berzinsky's emendation, at the end of note 61 below.

[59]Rashbam's wording here, ראוי ליכתב, appears, in this or a similar form, in many places in his commentary. See e.g. his commentary to Gen. 23:2, 41:21, Ex. 11:4 and Num. 4:10. Rashbam uses this phrase when he wishes to defend the actual wording of the biblical text, by providing the reason why it was written that way. Based on those uses, it is not possible that he is using the words here in a subjunctive sense: "It would have been appropriate for this phrase to have been written." See further notes 60 and 61 below.

[60]The "best" printed editions of Rashbam's commentary available today all read: ראוי ליכתב מעבר לירדן *לאותם* שעברו את הירדן. However, that reading is based on a conjectural emendation by Rosin, who tells us (in note 13 here) that the ms. that he used (and that is unfortunately now lost) reads ראוי ליכתב מעבר לירדן *לאחר* שעברו את הירדן. The early printed editions of Rashbam (and recent ones that did not make use of Rosin's work) have that second reading and that is the one that I translated above. I am convinced that Rosin's emendation is based on his desire to make Rashbam's comment here seem less heterodox.

view the plains of Moab [on the east side of the Jordan] are called "across the Jordan."[61]

[61]The simple meaning of Rashbam's comment here is that this verse was written after the Israelites had crossed the Jordan River, i.e. after Moses' death. Rosin, as mentioned in note 60, tried to avoid this understanding by changing the text. Even according to his emendation, it is still hard to imagine why Moses would have written a text that would be properly understood only לאותם שעברו את הירדן—i.e. by those Jews who in the future, years after the text's composition, would cross the Jordan River. (See Rosin's unconvincing attempt in note 13, to explain that Rashbam makes this argument—that Moses wrote the Torah specifically for an audience that did not yet exist—in other texts too.)

There is some slight evidence that Rashbam's approach to the authorship of the Torah was "heterodox," i.e. that he did not espouse the widely (but not universally) accepted traditional Jewish belief that Moses wrote every word of the Torah. For instance, his attitude to the meaning of the phrase "עד היום הזה—until this very day" (e.g. ad Gen. 19:37) is somewhat daring. (See the discussion by Uriel Simon in *Tehillah le-Moshe: Biblical and Judaic Studies in Honor of Moshe Greenberg*, ed. by M. Cogan, B. Eichler and J. Tigay, p. 199*.) However, nowhere else in the Torah commentary as we have it does Rashbam takes a position inconsistent with Mosaic authorship of the Torah.

An interesting reference to Rashbam's supposedly heterodox attitude to the authorship of the Torah appears in *Moshav Zeqenim*, a Tosaphist collection of Torah commentaries that appears in a number of different versions. One version of *Moshav Zeqenim*, Paris ms. 260, quotes Rashbam as claiming that the verses that begin (Gen. 36:31) "These are the kings who ruled in Edom before any king ruled in Israel," were written many years after Moses' death, in the days of the Judges (פירש רשב"ם שפרשה זו נכתבה בימי שופטים). See Y. Lange, "*Sefer Moshav Zeqenim 'al ha-Torah ketav yad Paris*," in *Ha-ma'ayan* 12:4 (1972), p. 83. (I am grateful to Uriel Simon [*ibid.*, note 52] for drawing this source to my attention.)

To be sure, Rashbam in his Genesis commentary offers a very "orthodox" explanation of that passage. (See my Genesis volume, p. 236, and note 4 there.) But the combined evidence of all these passages suggests that Rashbam, like his younger contemporary ibn Ezra, was open to and perhaps offered explanations of Torah texts that implied that Moses might not have authored the entire Torah.

There is one more emendation of Rashbam's words here that should be mentioned. Berzinsky suggests a small change here—reading the word ליושבי, instead of מיושבי in the beginning of this comment. That text would then yield the translation:

> Not at the bottom of the Jordan River, and not at the top. The phrase "across the Jordan" is appropriately written for those who live in the land of Israel, after they had crossed [to the west side of] the Jordan.

This emendation has two benefits. It smoothes over the difficult syntax of the text of Rosin's manuscript, ולא למעלה מיושבי ארץ ישראל. It also possibly tones down the heterodoxy of the comment.

בלק (Numbers 22:2–25:9)

22:3 ויקץ מואב MOAB WAS DISGUSTED: [The word קצתי means] the same [here] as in the phrase (Gen. 27:46) "קצתי בחיי—I am disgusted with my life."[1]

22:4 ילחכו [NOW THIS HORDE] WILL LICK CLEAN: all the crops and all the food.[2]

22:5 ארץ בני עמו IN THE LAND OF HIS: i.e. Balak's, PEOPLE.[3]

22:6 את אשר תברך WHATEVER YOU BLESS: through prophetic powers [SHALL BE BLESSED].

Even Balak understood that Balaam was [only] a prophet [i.e. someone who had insider information about the future, not someone who caused events to occur in the future]. When he foretold the future he did so through prophecy or through divination—that is why he was called in Joshua (13:22), "Balaam the diviner." But [Balak wanted to hire him in any case], because he thought that his [= Balaam's] prayers and sacrifices would be efficacious [in helping Balak to carry out his plan to harm the Israelites].[4]

---

[1]So also Rashi here and Rashbam ad Ex. 1:12. See note 16 there.

[2]The precise meaning of the image here is debatable. Rashi (following Tanh. *Balaq* 3) sees the image of "licking clean" as implying a curse. Nahm. explains it as a military image. Rashbam follows the same approach as that of LT, who explains that the Moabites were *not* concerned about being captured for they understood that that was not the Israelites' plan. But they were concerned about economic hardships from the Israelites' travels through their land.

[3]The phrase "*his* people" is ambiguous. Most *peshat*-oriented exegetes say that it refers to Balaam's people. In other words, Balak sent messengers to retrieve Balaam from *Balaam's* home territory. See e.g. iE, Nahm. and Hizq. Rashi and Rashbam both follow the explanation of Tanh. (*ibid.*, 4)—that Balak sent to summon Balaam who was living at that time in *Balak's* territory.

The *Be'ur* attempts to argue for Rashbam's understanding as follows: the Torah explains how Balak knew about Balaam. Balak knew all about him, since Balaam lived in the territory of his—Balak's—people.

[4]A simple reading of the verses might suggest that Balak and Balaam have different understandings about Balaam's powers. Balak thinks that Balaam's words can affect the future. Balaam then constantly reminds Balak that he only serves as God's mouthpiece. He cannot change what will be; all he can do is pass on prophecies about the future that have come to him from God. (See e.g. 22:18, 22:38, and 23:12.)

22:7 וקסמים בידם [THE ELDERS OF MOAB AND THE ELDERS OF MIDIAN SET OUT] WITH DIVINATION TOOLS IN THEIR HANDS: They brought [all] kinds of divination tools to Balaam, lest he say, "I [cannot predict the future since I] do not have the [appropriate] divination tools."[5] So it is written (Ezek. 21:27), "In his right hand he divined concerning Jerusalem . . . (*ibid.*, vs. 26) shaking arrows,[6] consulting teraphim and inspecting the liver [of a sacrificed animal]."[7]

22:14 הלך עמנו [BALAAM REFUSES] TO GO WITH *US*: For we are insignificant in his eyes.[8]

Rashbam attributes more sophisticated religious thinking to Balak. According to Rashbam, Balak understood all along that Balaam could not change the future with his powers. But he did hope that Balaam, as a prophet, could influence the deity, in the same manner that, for example, God says (Gen. 20:7) that since Abraham is a prophet, his prayer will be efficacious in influencing God to change the outcome of a future event. See also Rashbam's comment there in Genesis and my note there (pp. 81–82).

In general, Rashbam's portrayal of both Balaam and Balak is more positive than the one usually found in midrashic and Jewish exegetical literature. See especially Rashbam's comments ad 24:1, and note 58 there.

[5]The difficulty in the verse is: why would the emissaries have to take divination tools with them when going to visit a professional diviner?

Rashi presents two answers to the question, the one found here in Rashbam (which originates in Tanh. *Balaq* 5) and a more midrashic one. Rashbam, typically, opts for the one interpretation of Rashi's which to him seems closer to the plain sense of Scripture.

[6]Rashbam quotes this same phrase—קלקל בחצים—above in his commentary to 21:5. As I noted there (in note 33), it is unclear what Rashbam is proving in that comment. Here the reference is clearer: it is about shaking or shooting arrows as a form of divination. On using arrows for divination, see e.g. Git. 56a.

[7]Rashbam appears to have been the first commentator on Numbers to cite these verses in Ezekiel in order to show what constituted appropriate divination tools in the biblical world. So also iE and Hizq. iE, like Rashbam, points out that our verse appropriately speaks of "divination tools in their *hands*," in the same way that the verse in Ezekiel describes how "in his right hand he divined."

[8]Rashbam's comment looks like Rashi's comment to vs. 13, but there is a significant difference.

In vs. 13, Balaam says to the emissaries that he will not go with *them*. Rashi (following Tanh. B. *Balaq* 9) says that Balaam was bargaining in a haughty manner. He said, "I refuse to go with *you*," but he implied that he would go with other, more important people.

Rashbam offers a very similar explanation, but in his commentary on vs. 14, not on vs. 13. Rashbam says nothing about what Balaam meant when he said "I refuse to go with you." But he says that when the emissaries *reported* in vs. 14 that "Balaam refuses to go with *us*," *they* were saying—perhaps correctly, perhaps incorrectly—that Balaam was holding out for more special treatment.

Rashbam's reworking of the midrashic source appears to be unique.

22:15 [BALAAM SENT OTHER DIGNITARIES] רבים: i.e. more numerous,[9] and נכבדים: more important and more respected than the first [group of emissaries].

22:22 כי הולך הוא [GOD WAS ANGRY] THAT HE WAS GOING: willingly, i.e. that he was eager to curse them, even though he knew that God did not approve.[10]

22:25 ותלחץ את רגל בלעם [THE ASS] SQUEEZED BALAAM'S FOOT: And that is how he became lame, as it is written (23:3), "he went about שפי—lame."[11]

22:33 אולי נטתה מפני HAD (אולי) SHE TURNED AWAY PAST ME: The word אולי in the Bible is always to be interpreted [as referring to something that will occur or that might occur, or that might have occurred already,][12] just like the

---

[9]Rashbam is avoiding the interpretation of רבים as meaning either "many" or "dignified." He says that the word in this context means "more numerous." So also NJPS and most moderns.

[10]This verse has traditionally troubled the exegetes. Since, in vs. 20, God gave Balaam permission to go with the emissaries, why was God now angry that he was going with them?

Rashbam's answer is similar to Rashi's both in idea and in wording, but there is a small difference. Rashi says that God was angry that Balaam was eager to *go*, even though God had hinted to him that He was not pleased with the idea of Balaam going. (Rashi prepared his readers for this explanation by explaining God's permission to go, in vs. 20, in a very grudging manner.) Rashbam says that God was angry that Balaam was eager to *curse* the Israelites, not that he was eager to go.

[11]Twice in his commentary to Genesis, Rashbam writes that Balaam was made lame when his foot was crushed into the wall. See his commentary to Gen. 29:30 and 32:29. This explanation is based on one opinion in the Talmud (Sot. 10a) about the meaning of the difficult phrase below in 23:3, וילך שפי. See also Rashbam's commentary (and note 18) there.

Both in his commentary to Gen. 32:29 and in his commentary to Ex. 4:14, Rashbam discerns a pattern of punishments which God gives to those who go to a place to which God does not want them to go, or to those who refrain from going somewhere that God told them to go. Three of the four characters he discusses (Jacob, Moses and Balaam) are punished by something related to their legs, a fitting punishment for "going" inappropriately. Arguably the fourth example, too, the sin of Jonah who ran away, is part of the same pattern. While nothing specific happened to Jonah's legs, his mobility was restricted even more when he was swallowed up by the great fish. I am very grateful to my friend, Rabbi Shmuel Klitsner, for sharing with me this insight on these comments by Rashbam.

[12]Neither Rashi nor Rashbam explains the word אולי in this passage in its most common adverbial meaning of "perhaps." Both of them see אולי here as a conjunction, introducing a contrary-to-the-fact conditional subordinate clause. The structure of the verse (a subordinate conditional clause introduced by אולי, followed by the main clause, introduced by כי עתה) is very similar to that of vs. 29 above: "If (לו) I had a sword in my hand [a contrary-to-the-fact

word "אם—if," or like the word "אילו—had . . . .."[13] Those who interpret [אולי in] this verse [as meaning "had she *not* shied away because of me,"] like [the word לולא in] the phrase (Gen. 43:10), "had we not (לולא) dawdled," or the phrase (Gen. 31:42) "Had not (לולי) the God of [my father . . . been with me]," are mistaken.

Rather אולי here is to be understood [as introducing a clause with a positive verb, not a negative one,] as in the phrases (Lam. 3:29) "perhaps (אולי) there is hope," or (Amos 5:15) "perhaps (אולי) the LORD of Hosts will be gracious," or (Gen. 43:12) "perhaps (אולי) it was a mistake."[14]

This is what the angel said [to Balaam]:

> (32) WHY HAVE YOU BEATEN YOUR ASS these three times? You did not behave properly, for (33a) SHE HAD TURNED AWAY *BEFORE ME* (לפני) THESE THREE TIMES. Each time that she turned away it was לפני—before she reached me, never מפני—i.e. she never went past me. (33b) HAD SHE TURNED AWAY מפני, AFTER [passing] ME, i.e. had her turning away taken place after [passing] me (מפני) and not before [reaching] me (לפני), in other words had she passed me on the road and gone beyond me, then I would have killed you. You would not have gotten away with the minor injury of the crushing of your leg. Rather I would even HAVE KILLED YOU. She, though, would not have been damaged for I WOULD HAVE SPARED HER, just as she now survives [undamaged]. [She would not have been harmed by me] for *she* would not have sinned [even had she passed me against my will]. It would

---

conditional subordinate clause, introduced by לו], then I would kill you [the main clause introduced by כי עתה]."

Thus Rashi and Rashbam agree about the syntactical reading of our verse: "אולי she shied away from me, I would have killed you." The difference between their interpretations is that Rashi sees אולי as meaning "had she *not* shied away," while Rashbam says that it means "*had* she shied away." Rashi is following the opinion of Menaḥem (*Maḥberet*, s.v. אולי) and his opinion is accepted by NJPS here: "If she had not shied away from me, you are the one that I should have killed." So also Onq., iE and JBS.

Rashbam disagrees and argues that the text would have used the word לולא if it meant "had she *not*." Rashbam sees אולי נטתה as equivalent to אילו נטתה—"*had* she shied."

The distinction that Rashbam makes between, on the one hand, אולי and אילו, and, on the other hand, לולא, is reminiscent of another distinction made by Rashbam's brother, Rabbenu Tam. According to Tos. Meg. 21a, s.v. אלמלא, Rabbenu Tam claimed that the word אלמלי and the word אלמלא have a similar difference in meaning. The latter has a negative meaning built into it ("If . . . had *not*, then . . ."), the former does not ("If . . . *had*, then . . . ").

[13]The word אילו, while very common in mishnaic Hebrew, is rare in the Bible. It appears twice in Eccl. In the Eccl. commentary attributed to Rashbam by Japhet, the exegete explains one of those passages (6:6) as meaning "had . . .," but he explains the other one (4:11) in a midrashic manner (אילו = אוי לו—woe is to him).

[14]Rashbam is not saying that אולי here is to be understood as it is in those verses, i.e. as meaning "perhaps." All he is saying is that just as the word "not" is not built into the meaning of אולי in those verses, so it is not part of the meaning of אולי here either.

have been *you* who sinned against me [had she passed me against my will,] for you [were the one who] hit her three times [to goad her to pass me].[15]

גם אותך הרגתי: [should be understood as if] גם הרגתי אותך [were written].[16] So also the phrase (Ex. 12:32) וברכתם גם אותי—[lit. "bless me also," should be

---

[15]Rashbam's interpretation of the verse is forced. To his credit, it should be noted that he pays careful attention to the verse's variation of language, from ותט *לפני* to נטתה *מפני*. To the best of my knowledge he is the only exegete to note and explain that distinction. But his claim that the phrase נ-ט-ה מפני means "to go past" is not convincing.

In the final analysis, the difference between Rashi and Rashbam is very small. Rashi says that the idea of the two clauses is: "Had the ass not turned away upon seeing me, I would have killed you." Rashbam says that the complete thought is: "Had the ass turned away after passing me, I would have killed you." Either way the angel is saying that had the ass passed the angel and not turned away, then the angel would have killed Balaam. The only issue is whether אולי should be seen as equivalent to לולא ("had not") or to אילו ("had").

[16]In other words, we should avoid an overly literal reading of the phrase גם אותך הרגתי as meaning "I would have killed you, too," implying that the angel had killed someone else and now was threatening to kill Balaam, too. This phrase should be read as if גם הרגתי אותך were written, meaning "I would have also killed you (instead of just injuring your leg)."

In several places, Rashbam writes that the placement of the word גם is not always significant. Twice previously in his Torah commentary he has cited our verse as an example of the principle. See commentary to Gen. 29:30 and Num. 16:13.

Rashbam here may be specifically opposing the midrashic tradition that says that the angel really meant "I would have killed you, too." According to that midrash, the angel said, "killed you, *too*," because he had already killed the ass. The phrase as a whole means, "I would kill you, Balaam, too, and then bring the ass back to life (החייתי)." See e.g. Tanh. B. *Balaq* 14.

Rashi's accepts part but not all of the midrashic explanation. He accepts (s.v. ואותה החייתי) the midrashic claim that the angel *had* killed the ass already. Rashbam rejects that claim, and that is why he writes specifically, "for I WOULD HAVE SPARED HER, just as she now survives [undamaged]." Both Rashi and Rashbam understand that "I would have spared her" has a subjunctive sense to it. Rashi says that it means, "I did not spare her, but I would have if. . . ." Rashbam says that it means, "I spared her, and I would have spared her also even if. . . ."

Rashi mysteriously says that even though the angel had already killed the ass, the meaning of גם אותך הרגתי is *not* "I would have killed you, too, [the way I killed the ass]." Rashi says, like Rashbam, that the phrase means גם הרגתי אותך, meaning "I would have also killed you" (instead of just delaying you. Rashi does not concur with Rashbam that Balaam was lamed when his leg was squeezed against the wall.)

Rashi's explanation of the unusual syntax of גם אותך הרגתי is similar but not identical to Rashbam's. Rashi labels the phrase a מקרא מסורס, one of dozens of verses in the Torah concerning which Rashi says that the syntax has to be reworked. Rashbam never uses that term in his Torah commentary. Here (and in a number of similar passages related to the word גם) he says that there is something about the word גם specifically that justifies what appears to be its unusual placement.

understood as if] וגם תברכו אותי ("also bless me") [were written].[17]

23:3 וילך שפי HE WENT ABOUT שפי: I.e. lame.[18] It is related to [the word שופו, in the phrase (Job 33:21)], "ושופו עצמותיו—his bones are crushed."[19] Both of these verbs are from a final-*heh* root [i.e. *sh-p-h*].[20]

23:7 ינחני: [Even though the imperfect form is usually used for an action in the future, yielding the sense, "he will lead me," here it should be understood as describing an action in the past, as if the form were the perfect,] הנחני—"he led me."[21]

מהררי קדם FROM THE HILLS OF THE EAST: [The phrase, "hills of the East," is] in parallelism [with the phrase "from Aram"], for it is written (Is. 9:11), "Aram in the East."[22] In other words, "he [Balak] went to great troubles [to

[17]Rashbam's comment on the verse in Ex. 12 is difficult. See note 2, p. 175, of my Genesis volume, and note 67, p. 116, of my Exodus volume.

[18]This explanation is found four times in Rashbam's Torah commentary. See note 11 above.

There is no consensus about the meaning of שפי. It may be a reference to some form of divination. Rashi says that it means "alone." iE and Luzzatto say that it means that Balaam went to some high place. As noted above, Rashbam's explanation is found in the Talmud (e.g. Sot. 10a). It is also mentioned by Ḥayyuj, ibn Janaḥ and Qimḥi, although some of them suggest that it means that Balaam's spirit was crushed, not his leg. It was later accepted by Hizq.

[19]Based on his remarks here, it seems that Rashbam believes that the word שופו in the verse in Job means "crushed," although this is not a standard translation.

[20]The grammarians listed in note 18 all identify the root in the same manner, and they all mention the possibility that the word is related to ושופו in Job. Moderns (e.g. B.D.B.) agree.

In the Job commentary that Japhet attributes to Rashbam, the exegete also states clearly ad 33:21 that the root of ושופו is *sh-p-h*. See the discussion by Japhet on p. 230 of her *Rashbam on Job*.

[21]Rashbam often notes that a verb that appears to be one tense would actually be best understood in another tense. See e.g. the discussion in *Dayyaqut* (Merdler's edition, p. 46). See also Japhet's excursus on the subject in her *Rashbam on Job*, pp. 262–267. See also below, commentary ad 23:9 and 24:17, where Rashbam says that an imperfect form can refer to a present-tense action.

[22]Rashbam's comment may be opposing the midrashic reading found in Tanh. B. *Balaq* 17 that explains מהררי קדם as meaning "from the heights where I used to be." Balaam is then seen as complaining that Balak was responsible for Balaam's diminution in honor.

Rashbam is not the only exegete to say that קדם here simply means "the East." See e.g. Onq. and iE. But he is, I think, the first exegete to specifically identify the parallelism in the verse. This idea is later found in many exegetes; see e.g. Hizq. and the *Be'ur*. It is possible that Rashbam reads this poetic verse in the same way that NJPS does:

From Aram has Balak brought me
Moab's king from the hills of the East.

That reading ignores the cantillation signs, which mark the phrase, "Balak, Moab's king," as one unit.

bring me] from a faraway land, and for naught,[23] for it will do him no good."[24]

זַעֲמָה [GO] VILIFY [ISRAEL]: It appears to me[25] [that the proper vocalization of this word is] with a *pataḥ* [under the *zayin*], as it is an imperative form.[26] The form [that appears in our biblical texts,] זֹעֲמָה with a *ḥolam* [following the *zayin* is inappropriate here, because that form] is a feminine [singular active participle, meaning] "she vilifies." It would be like the forms (Deut. 4:24) "consuming (אֹכְלָה) fire," or (Jud. 4:4) "she judged (שֹׁפְטָה) Israel."

23:8 לא זעם ה' GOD DID NOT VILIFY: them.[27] In other words, He did not let His anger loose on them. [The verb זעם here is a transitive verb,] as in the verse (Mal. 1:4), "the people the LORD זעם," which means "the people *whom* the LORD vilified." It means unleashing anger[28] onto someone else.[29]

---

[23]So also Qara, cited by Berliner in *Peleṭat Soferim*, p. 23.

[24]So also the *Be'ur*, verbatim.

[25]Berzinsky suggests emending נ"ל (= נראה לי—it appears to me), to צ"ל (= צריך להיות—the text must read).

[26]As Esh writes (p. 87): "Here Rashbam appears to advocate a vocalization for which he cannot adduce manuscriptal evidence." In other words, Rashbam appears to be proposing a conjectural emendation of the standard vocalization of MT, based solely on his understanding of the rules of Hebrew grammar. See also Rashbam's commentary to Ex. 23:24 and note 61 on p. 291 of my Exodus volume. See also Rosin, RSBM, p. 59. See also the discussion on pp. 93–94 of Merdler's M.A. dissertation. It is possible that Rashbam knew of a textual tradition, now lost, that vocalized the word זַעֲמָה, and that in this comment Rashbam is supporting that tradition. However, that explanation seems unlikely.

This specific form זַעֲמָה appears also in Rashbam's *Dayyaqut* (Merdler's edition, p. 21). There he simply assumes that that is the correct form in our verse.

For a defense of the reading of MT, see G.-K. 63p and 64c.

[27]Particularly in later Hebrew but occasionally in the Bible, too (e.g. Ps. 7:12), the verb זעם is intransitive and means "to be angry." Rashbam therefore emphasizes that here it must be a transitive verb. It means "to vilify," and its object is "them," or "Israel."

[28]Rashbam uses the word הכעים in this comment in a non-standard way. Generally the word means "to cause someone else to become angry." Rashbam uses it in the sense of "to release anger onto another person."

Often Rashbam uses the paradigm of *hifil* simply as a way of saying that a specific verb is transitive. There is one passage in *Dayyaqut* (Merdler's edition, p. 45) where Rashbam labels a verb "לשון מפעיל" even though he realizes that it is *piel*. All he is saying is that the verb is transitive. So here also he is saying that זעם, although often an intransitive verb, can be used transitively.

[29]Rashbam supports his explanation of זעם by comparing it to כעס. Especially in post-biblical Hebrew they are synonyms, intransitive verbs meaning "to be angry." So Rashbam points out that just as the verb כעס can take on a transitive meaning, so also the verb זעם can and does. (The analogy is imperfect, since כעס in *qal* is always intransitive.)

Rashbam may be opposing the midrashic tradition that says that Balaam's cursing power was based on his ability to calculate the precise hour when God was in an angry mood

23:9 כי מראש צורים אראנו FOR I SEE THEM FROM THE MOUNTAIN TOPS: [This verse and the ones that follow] explain the reason why God did not vilify them and why He did not want to curse them. Because FROM THE MOUNTAIN TOPS, on which I am currently standing,[30] I see them, and from the top of the hill I see[31] that they are alone; no other nations are counted or intermingled among them.[32] And [I also see that] they have countless numbers of small children.[33] (For only those over twenty years of age were counted.[34]) That means that their [total] numbers must be extremely high, for (vs. 10) WHO CAN COUNT THE DUST OF ISRAEL. That is why God does not want to curse

---

("זועם," in the language of Ps. 7:12). Balaam's problem was that at the specific time that he needed God's anger, God never became angry. Since "לא זעם ה'—God never became angry," despite the fact that usually God has a moment of anger every day, that is why Balaam could not curse the Israelites effectively. See Rashi's comment here, following Sanh. 105b. According to Rashbam, the verse means simply that since God did not vilify the Israelites, Balaam was powerless to curse them.

[30]Rashbam opposes Rashi's interpretation (following Tanh. *Balaq* 12) of the phrase "from the mountain tops" as an allegorical reference to the heroic roots of the Jewish people, which Balaam now sees prophetically. Rashbam says much more simply that Balaam went to a high spot to see the Israelites. Rashbam's comment may originate with Qara. See the citation in Berliner's *Peleṭat Soferim*, p. 23. So also iE and Nahm. See similarly commentary below ad 24:20 (and see note 89 there), where again Rashi explains the phrase וירא את עמלק as referring to Balaam seeing a prophecy about Amalek, while Rashbam says that Balaam literally saw Amalek.

[31]Two ostensibly future forms appear in this verse: "אראנו—I will see them" and "אשורנו—I will gaze upon them." Rashbam paraphrases both of them with the same present-tense verb, "I see (them)." So also Rashi and many other exegetes. See also Rashbam above ad vs. 7, s.v. ינחני, and note 21 there, and see also Rashbam ad 24:17, s.v. אראנו.

[32]This is Rashbam's paraphrase of the second half of the verse, "a people that dwells apart, not reckoned among the nations." Many commentators attribute great significance to these words (and they are often quoted even today as a statement about the Jews' uniqueness). They are seen as a blessing that Balaam gave, against his will, to the Jewish people. See e.g. Sanh. 39a-b (whenever the nations are mentioned in the Bible, the Jews are not included), LT here (only the Jews will merit the world to come) and Rashi here (a number of different explanations about the way that the Jews are unique and separate). See also Qara (as cited in Berliner's *Peleṭat Soferim*, p. 23) who suggests that dwelling "apart" actually means being secure, and impervious to cursing.

Rashbam, predictably, offers a more prosaic contextual explanation. Verse 10 describes the counting of the Israelites. Verse 9 introduces the theme when Balaam says that the count is a count of Israelites alone. Since they are wandering through the wilderness, no one has had a chance to intermingle with them.

[33]In his commentary to vs. 10, Rashbam explains that he sees the words רובע ישראל as a reference to the children of the Israelites.

[34]See e.g. Num. 1:3.

them,[35] as it is written concerning Nineveh (Jon. 4:11),[36] "Should I [God] not care about Nineveh, that great city, in which there are more than one hundred and twenty thousand persons who do not yet know their right hand from their left?" [I.e. God said that he did not want to destroy the Ninevites, because] even if the adults sinned, what sin did the children commit?[37]

23:10 רובע ישראל [WHO CAN NUMBER] THE רובע OF ISRAEL: The seed of Israel. [Children are appropriately called רובע,] since people are created through the process of copulation (רביעה).[38]

23:19 לא איש א-ל GOD IS NOT MAN: [Balaam said to Balak:] "He [God] would not [behave] like a man, retracting His blessing in such a short time. They

---

[35]God does not want Balaam to curse the Israelites because the number of casualties from that curse would be enormous. There are multitudes of Israelites there in the wilderness within Balaam's gaze.

[36]Rashbam's exegesis of this verse is shocking. As mentioned above, these verses are generally seen as a blessing that Balaam gave, against his will, to the Jewish people. The blessing in this verse is generally understood as a compliment to Israel on its large numbers, or as a wish that those large numbers will continue. Rashbam, however, sees this verse not as a compliment to Israel, but as a reason why God does not want Balaam to curse the people. Because of Israel's large numbers, and particularly its large number of innocent children, God has mercy on Israel. When Rashbam points out that God's mercy here is similar to the mercy He showed for the Ninevites, Rashbam is reversing what is traditionally seen as a compliment to Israel and equating Israel with the evil (or at least foolish) Ninevites.

[37]The quotation, "even if the adults sinned, what sin did the children commit?" is taken verbatim from the Talmud (*Yoma'* 22b) but it has been removed entirely from its context. There the thought that innocent children should not die is attributed to King Saul, who offers that argument as an excuse for the fact the he had not destroyed Amalek entirely. God, according to the Talmud, then told Saul that his mercy was misplaced and inappropriate.

Here Rashbam uses that same phrase as a paraphrase of the words of God Himself at the end of Jonah.

Rashbam interprets the phrase "who do not [yet] know their right hand from their left hand" as a reference to children. So also Rashi and Qimḥi in Jonah. See also Uriel Simon (in the *Miqra' le-Yisrael* commentary on Jonah [1992]) who writes that there is no reasonable way to interpret that phrase except as a reference to children (דומה שאין מנוס מלבאר . . . שהכוונה ב'אדם' היא לקטנים).

[38]Rashbam's comment continues and offers support for his explanation of the previous verse.

Rashbam's interpretation is a reworking of the midrashic explanation of the Talmud (Nid. 31a). There our phrase is explained as meaning that God counts the Israelites' acts of copulation (רביעיותיהם). In his commentary to 24:3, s.v. שתם העין, Rashi quotes that explanation (as one alternative). Here, though, Rashi reworks that midrash and says that רובע means "children," and that children are called רובע because of the way that they are created. Rashbam follows Rashi's lead.

The word רובע is very difficult. See the variety of explanations and emendations suggested in NJPSC.

[the Israelites] have not sinned since the time of the blessing that I bestowed on them earlier today."[39]

ויכזב WOULD HE LIE?: I.e. how could he lie and renege for no reason? ויתנחם: should [also] be read as a [rhetorical] question, i.e. HOW COULD HE CHANGE HIS MIND? ולא יעשה [WOULD HE SPEAK] AND NOT ACT?: is [also to be read as] a [rhetorical] question.[40]

23:20 הנה ברך לקחתי NOW I HAVE RECEIVED TO BLESS [THEM]: [Balaam said:] "Now, today, I have already received [instructions][41] to bless them.[42] And [furthermore, וּבֵרֵךְ:] He already blessed them, and לא אשיבנה, I will not reverse that blessing."[43]

---

[39]Rashbam's interpretation opposes that of Rashi and LT. They say that Balaam is telling Balak here that God cannot renege on the commitments that he made to the Israelites, e.g. to bring them to Canaan.

Rashbam's explanation is much simpler. It does not require assuming that either Balaam or Balak was privy to God's promises to the Israelites. Rashbam notes that we are now dealing with Balaam's second speech (in vss. 18–24; the first speech was vss. 7–10) about the Israelites, i.e. with Balak's second attempt, in one day, to get Balaam to curse them. Balaam is simply telling Balak that since nothing has changed over the last few hours, there is no reason to expect God to be more willing to curse the Israelites now than He was a few hours ago.

[40]Rashbam emphasizes that all of the stichs of our verse are to be read as rhetorical questions, expecting the answer "No." The entire verse says, in a number of different ways, that God never changes his mind.

His explanation opposes that of Tanh. *Va-yera'* 13, which claims that the first half of the verse says that God will not change his mind when he has promised to do something good for people (even if the people later are found to be undeserving). According to Tanh., the second half of the verse should be read not as a rhetorical question, but as an affirmative statement: "He [God] says that He will do [certain] things and then He does *not* do them." What that means is that God sometimes promises to bring punishments but subsequently revokes the punishment.

[41]Rashbam does not explain how he interprets the difficult word לקחתי here. I assume that he understands it the same way that Rashi does, namely "to receive instructions" or "to take upon oneself."

[42]My translation here follows the text as it appears in the (usually inferior) editions that preceded Rosin's. Those printings do not have the redundant word לברכם found in Rosin's edition: הנה לקחתי לברך אותם היום כבר לברכם והוא ברך אותם כבר.

[43]Rashbam's interpretation follows Rashi's. The word בָּרֵךְ in the beginning of the verse is interpreted as an infinitive, while the word וּבֵרֵךְ, two words later, is seen as a past-tense verb, the subject being God. Both Rashbam and Rashi say that אשיבנה means to reverse or to retract, and they both explain that אשיבנה has the feminine ending נה because the understood object is the feminine noun "ברכה—blessing."

The form וּבֵרֵךְ is a past-tense verb, like the form חֵרֵף, in the phrase (Prov. 17:5) "affronts (חֵרֵף) his Maker."[44]

23:21–3 לא הביט און HE SEES NO INIQUITY IN JACOB: He [God] does not wish to punish them even when they sin. So it is written (Job 11:11), "He saw iniquity, but did not scrutinize it."[45] "לא הביט—He does not see" means "He does not *want* to see."[46]

ותרועת מלך: [means] THE KING'S [= God's] friendship [is with the Israelites], because He dwells among them.[47] [The word תרועה refers to friendship,] as in the phrase (Prov. 18:24), "There are friends to keep one company (להתרועע)."[48]

---

[44]In other words, the form is a *piel* perfect form. The vowel following the letter *vet* is a *ṣere*, and not the standard *ḥiriq*, because the letter following is a *resh*, just as the first vowel of חֵרֵף is a *ṣere*, and not a *ḥiriq*.

Rashbam's comment appears to be an abridgement of Rashi's. Rashi explains at length that the word is not to be confused for a noun. Both Rashbam and Rashi cite the same form חֵרֵף as proof (although they each cite a different verse where it appears). Like Rashbam and Rashi, see iE, Seforno and others.

[45]The verse in Job is difficult and there is not one accepted interpretation. A common understanding is the one reflected in NJPS: "When He sees iniquity does He not discern it?" That explanation would hardly prove Rashbam's point. In the commentary to Job attributed to Rashbam by Japhet there is an explanation only of the first half of the verse, and it does not shed light on the second half.

Rashi also says that God does not "scrutinize" (להתבונן) the iniquities, using the precise verb that Rashbam cites from Job. Perhaps Rashi has that verse in mind, although he does not cite it.

[46]Rashi offers two explanations for the phrase. First he says that it is to be explained the way Onq. interpreted it—that God sees no iniquity among the Israelites because there is none to see. So also Qara (as cited in Berliner's *Peleṭat Soferim*, p. 23). JBS also expands on this explanation: Balaam is hinting to Balak that if he would only succeed in getting the Israelites to sin, God would see the iniquity and would gladly curse the Israelites. (See JBS here and ad 31:8.)

In his second explanation, Rashi (following Tanh. *Balaq* 14) offers an alternative explanation, one that he considers a pleasing midrash that accords with the *peshaṭ* (אחרי פשוטו הוא נדרש מדרש נאה). That explanation is that God does not look carefully at the sins of the Israelites.

Rashbam's explanation is very close to Rashi's second explanation. It is possible that Rashbam is purposely reworking the language of Rashi's comment. Rashi's phraseology might imply that God does not see Israel's iniquity; the language of his source (Tanh.) says even more clearly that God does not look at the sins. Rashbam says that God does not *want* to look too closely.

[47]The phrase "because He dwells among them," is a paraphrase of Onq.'s translation of the phrase that Rashbam is explaining. See Rashi who also refers to Onq.'s explanation.

[48]Both Rashi and Rashbam explain that the word תרועה here is unconnected to its standard meaning of blowing a ram's horn. Each uses a different text to prove the point.

And why does God dwell among them, and why does He have affection for them? (23) כי לא נחש ביעקב FOR THERE IS NO AUGURY IN JACOB.[49] [Balaam explained:] "They are not soothsayers and diviners[50] like us, nor do they consult ghosts or familiar spirits.[51] Rather כעת יאמר ליעקב ולישראל מה פעל א-ל, i.e. since the Divine Presence is among them, the prophets can tell Jacob and Israel today what God is doing and what He has decreed for the future. That is why they do not need soothsayers and diviners."[52]

[The phrase] כעת יאמר [means] that which will happen כעת—i.e. at some time tomorrow or after a number of days or years—is told to them today by a prophet.

The phrase כעת always refers to [predictions of] the future. So it is written in the story of Manoah's wife, [who said to her husband] (Jud. 13:23), "'Had the

---

For exegetes who see תרועה here as a reference to a blast of a ram's horn, see e.g. iE and LT.

[49]JBS says that our verse means that soothsaying *against* the Israelites—as a way of cursing them—will not be efficacious. Rashi, on the other hand, writes that our verse means that since there is no soothsaying found *among* the Israelites, that is why the Israelites are worthy of blessing. Rashbam's explanation is fairly similar to Rashi's, but Rashbam also connects this verse with vs. 21. God (21) has a special relationship with the Israelites because (23) there are no soothsayers among them.

[50]The phrase מעוננים וקוסמים is an allusion to Deut. 18:14.

[51]The phrase שואל אוב וידעוני is an allusion to Deut. 18:11.

[52]Rashbam's last phrase here, "they do not need soothsayers and diviners," is found virtually verbatim in Qara (cited by Berliner, *Peleṭat Soferim*, p. 23).

Rashi offers two explanations of this verse. First he suggests that the verse refers to a future promise of what *will be said* of the Israelites. In other words, Balaam is predicting something positive about the Israelites that has not yet happened. Rashi's alternate explanation is that יאמר means "it is *now* said." The phrase then would mean that in order to know God's will, Israel needs no soothsayers, as they have prophets who can tell them what God wants. In other words, Rashi's first explanation interprets the phrase solely about future events. Rashi's second explanation interprets it solely about present events.

Rashbam's explanation is similar but not identical to that second explanation. Rashbam sees יאמר as meaning "it is now said." But he sees the word כעת as a reference to the future. (See the continuation of his comment.) Rashbam's wording emphasizes that the phrase כעת יאמר has a connection to the present and to the future. יאמר means "now it is said," but כעת is not an adverb modifying the verb יאמר. Rather כעת is an adverb modifying the verb פעל, and the phrase means "what God will do *in the future* (כעת)." Cf. JBS who says explicitly that כעת means here and now, and see Qara (*ibid.*) who says that כעת means "whenever" Israel requires information about the future, prophecy is available for them.

Rashbam's interpretation is forced. The logic also appears circular. God dwells among the Israelites because they do not consult soothsayers. They do not consult soothsayers because God dwells among them and makes His will known to Israelite prophets. To his credit, Rashbam does succeed in linking verses 21 and 23 in a reasonable manner. Like Rashbam, see iE, who interprets the general idea of the verse the same way, but does not explain the word כעת in the way that Rashbam does.

LORD meant to take our lives'—now—'He would not have accepted a burnt offering and a meal offering from us . . . and he would not have made such an announcement to us כעת' i.e. he would not have made an announcement to us concerning the birth of our son, which he told us would take place כעת—i.e. next year.[53] Rather we can be certain that we will live and that [the prophecy concerning] our son will be fulfilled. For if we were to die, how could we have a son next year?"

In the same way [one should interpret the word כעת as a reference to the future in the phrase] (II Kings 4:16), "כעת חיה[54] you will be embracing a son."

24:1–2 [ולא הלך כפעם בפעם] לקראת נחשים: [BALAAM DID NOT, AS ON PREVIOUS OCCASIONS, GO] IN SEARCH OF AUGURY: by going from place to place [looking for the most propitious spot][55] so that he might succeed in cursing them. Rather, from this point on he intended[56] to bless them with all his heart. And for this reason, it is written here that (2) ותהי עליו רוח א-לוהים THE SPIRIT OF GOD CAME UPON HIM: i.e. the spirit of the Divine Presence came upon him[57] with love and with affection.[58]

---

[53]Rashbam's explanation of that phrase is not the standard one. Generally the phrase is understood as meaning, "If God was planning to kill us, why did he *now* (כעת) make this dramatic announcement to us about the future?"

[54]Rashbam does not clarify here how he understands the phrase כעת חיה there. See his commentary to Gen. 18:10. It is not clear to me that Rashbam's two interpretations, here and in Genesis, are consistent.

[55]The idea that Balak and Balaam were searching for the best spot from which to curse the Israelites is the simple meaning of the text in 23:13 above.

[56]A number of midrashic sources attempt to read even these verses as saying that Balaam was still trying to curse the Israelites, but God forced him to bless them nonetheless. See e.g. *Tanna' deve Eliyyahu Rabbah* 21. For that reason Rashbam emphasizes that Balaam is at this point a changed man who is eager to bless the Israelites. See notes 57 and 58.

[57]Rashbam is opposing the Talmud's understanding of our verse (or at least, the Tosaphists' explanation of the Talmud's understanding of our verse). In BB 60a, the Talmud says that when Balaam saw the modest way that the Israelites' tents were aligned, he said "the Israelites are therefore worthy that God's Presence should descend upon them." The Tosafot (s.v. ראויין) say that the Talmud is explaining the last words of our verse—ותהי עליו רוח א-לוהים—as meaning that God's Spirit descended *on the Israelite people* (not on Balaam). The Zohar (3:21) also explains the phrase as referring to the Israelites. Presumably this midrashic explanation is meant, at least in part, to minimize Balaam's prophecy. Rashbam, on the other hand, emphasizes that Balaam was graced with true prophetic vision. See note 58.

[58]Rashbam notes that both Balaam's actions (in 24:1) and God's response (24:2) are described here by the text in language that differs from the way that Balaam's preparations and prophetic visions are described in previous chapters. Rashbam says that Balaam's improved behavior is the reason why God rewards him with a higher form of prophetic vision.

Rashbam's language describing Balaam's prophecy—that God appeared to him מאהבה ודרך חיבה—is shocking when compared to the standard attitude of Jewish exegesis

24:3 שתום העין: means "with an open eye." [In other words Balaam] sees divine visions.[59] [The word שתום refers to something open,] as in the Mishnah (AZ 5:4) "until he opens (שישתום) it and then closes it."[60]

24:4 אשר מחזה שדי יחזה WHO BEHOLDS VISIONS FROM THE ALMIGHTY: at times נופל—PROSTRATE, i.e. lying down at night, and at other times גלוי עיניים—WITH OPEN EYES. [Balaam says this,] because now he was receiving prophecies [even] during the daytime. [The word נופל in this

---

towards Balaam. Cf. e.g. Rashi here, who reinterprets Balaam's change of heart in vs. 1 (he still wanted to curse them, but was going to try an indirect method) and downplays the significance of the phrase ותהי עליו רוח א-לוהים. Rashbam's reading clearly is more anchored in the biblical text, which, on the *peshaṭ* level, is trying to say something positive about Balaam in these verses. Rashi, in standard midrashic manner, wishes to portray Balaam as consistently evil.

It is instructive to compare Rashbam's comment here with Nahm.'s. Nahm. arrived independently at the same explanation of the connection between vss. 1 and 2: Balaam behaved better and then received a truer form of prophetic vision from God. But Nahm. does not present this idea in the startling language that Rashbam does: "The Spirit of the Divine Presence came upon him with love and with affection." It is my assessment that from time to time, when Rashbam opposes a common midrashic tradition, he purposely phrases his comment in such a way that he knows will be irritating for proponents of midrash. (See e.g. commentary and notes to Ex. 2:3, 12:29 and 21:6 [s.v. אל הדלת], and below ad Num. 30:11.) A portrayal of Balaam as the beneficiary of God's affection and love would be very discomfiting for any loyal follower of Rashi.

It should be noted that there exists among ancient *midrashim* a tradition that portrayed Balaam as a great prophet. See e.g. Sifre Deut. 357. That midrash claimד that Balaam was an even greater prophet than Moses. See also Nahm.'s "reinterpretation" of that surprising midrash in his comment to our verse.

[59]The *hapax legomenon* שתום is difficult. Rashi offers two explanations, both of which, consistent with his previous comments, say something negative about Balaam. Rashbam's explanation is more contextual. All the phrases about Balaam in the following verse describe his prophetic ability to hear and see things that others do not see. Accordingly, it makes sense that this phrase should too. See iE who also notes that the context determines the meaning of this difficult word.

[60]Rashi cites the same prooftext from the Mishnah but manages to turn the phrase שתום העין into an insult of Balaam: "the one with the pierced or disfigured eye." Nahm. also cites the same prooftext, and claims further that Onq.'s understanding of שתום here is based on that Mishnah. Nahm. alludes to the methodological difficulty of using rabbinic Hebrew to establish the meaning of a biblical Hebrew word. Generally, Rashbam also is not keen to do so, but does so when he finds no alternative. See the discussion in the appendix to my Genesis volume, pp. 422–424.

Like Rashbam, see the *Be'ur*. See Gray (pp. 361 and 366–7) who lists a number of moderns who interpret the way that Rashbam did, although Gray himself disagrees.

verse means "lying down,"] as in the phrase (I Sam. 31:8) "prostrate (נופלים)," i.e. lying, "on the field,"[61] concerning Saul [and his sons].[62]

24:6 כנחלים נִטָּיוּ LIKE PALM GROVES[63] THAT STRETCH OUT: [The verb נִטָּיוּ is a *nifal* form from the root *n-ṭ-h*; it is equivalent to] ננטיו.[64] It means arranged in a straight pattern.[65]

---

[61]Rashbam's citation of the verse in I Sam. is inexact. There the corpses do not fall על פני השדה. There are a number of biblical references, though, to corpses falling על פני השדה; see e.g. Jer. 9:21.

[62]Just as in his comments to the previous verses of this chapter, Rashbam again interprets a phrase about Balaam in a more positive manner than most classical Jewish exegetes do. Rashi, in his first explanation, says (following Onq.) that the phrase means that only when Balaam was prostrate did he receive divine visions. In other words, his eyes were "open," prophetically speaking, only when he was prostrate. Rashi's second explanation (following *'Aggadat bereshit* 11; see also Rashi ad Gen. 17:3) says that Balaam was always knocked prostrate by the prophetic experience. See also Nahm. ad vs. 1: " הנפילה בבלעם פחיתות שלא יסבול הנבואה—'falling' is a sign of Balaam's [prophetic] inferiority as he cannot withstand the [intensity of] prophecy." There is another tradition of negative interpretation of this phrase that is found in Sanh. 105a-b, according to which the word נופל alludes to inappropriate sexual activity by Balaam.

iE offers the explanation later reflected in the NJPS translation: "Prostrate, but with eyes unveiled." This explanation is more positive, in that it says that Balaam can see prophetically even though he is prostrate.

But Rashbam's explanation is even more positive. He says, continuing the theme of his commentary to vss. 1–2 (and see note 58), that "now" Balaam has risen to a higher level of prophecy, and is able to see prophecies either by day or by night.

Another explanation of this phrase as describing Balaam's vast prophetic powers may be found in the unusual midrash found in Sifre Deut. 357, mentioned above in note 58. Again Nahm. (in his commentary to vs. 1) attempts to explain away the positive description of Balaam that that midrash attaches to our phrase.

[63]The translation of כנחלים is from NJPS. It is difficult to know what Rashbam thought that this word meant. He may think that the word means "rivers" or "brooks," its most common meaning in the Bible.

[64]Rashbam's grammatical point is the standard explanation of the form. So also iE.

[65]The meaning of the image here is open to many interpretations. Rashi says that נטיו means that the tents of the Israelites reached to far-away places, like rivers that traverse large areas. Onq. suggests that כנחלים נטיו means that the Israelites are like rivers that gain strength.

I would tentatively suggest that Rashbam is again taking issue with the midrashic explanation of the Talmud about the tents of the Israelites. As noted above in note 57, the Talmud (BB 60a) says that Balaam saw the modest way that the Israelites' tents were aligned — purposely *not* in straight rows—in order to ensure that no Israelite could see into another's tent. Rashbam, on the other hand, explains that in our verse Balaam is praising the Israelites for having tents that are מיושרים, i.e. arranged in straight lines.

כאהלים LIKE ALOES: [אהלים here means aloes,] as in the phrase (Ps. 45:9), "myrrh and aloes (ואהלות)."[66]

In the form כַּאֲהלים—like aloes [and in the next form in this verse "כַּאֲרזים—like cedars] beside the water," there is a *pataḥ* vowel [in the first syllable,] because that vowel comes in place of a *sheva* vowel.[67] Similarly the form (Is. 44:4) "כַּעֲרבים—like willows by watercourses." But the form כָּאֲרזים[68] in the phrase (Song 5:15), "stately as the cedars," has a *qameṣ* vowel [in the first syllable,] because it contains a definite article,[69] "as *the* cedars (כְּהָאֲרזים)."[70]

24:7 וירום מאגג מלכו THEIR KING: i.e. Saul,[71] SHALL ARISE ABOVE AGAG. All kings of the Amalekites are called Agag, just as all kings of the Egyptians are called Pharaoh and the kings of the Philistines are called Abimelech, and the kings of Jerusalem are called Melchizedek or Adonizedek.[72]

---

[66]So also Rashi and iE. The exegetes want to ensure that this word is not confused with the word אוהליך—your *tents*, which appears in the previous verse. See NJPSC's suggestion that the text is purposely punning by switching from the word for tents to the similar word for aloes.

[67]A lengthier explanation of this point may be found in Rashbam's *Dayyaqut* (Merdler's edition, p. 48). G.-K. (102d) has a different explanation of the form's development, but his conclusions are the same as Rashbam's.

[68]This is the primary purpose of Rashbam's comment here—to explain why the word כארזים here is vocalized with a *pataḥ* vowel in the first syllable but in Song is vocalized with a *qameṣ* vowel in the first syllable.

[69]Rashbam uses the unusual word מבורר here to describe a noun that is "defined" (i.e. a noun with a definite article). He also does that in *Dayyaqut* (e.g. pp. 48–49 in Merdler's edition).

[70]So also Rashbam in *Dayyaqut* (Merdler's edition, p. 48). See similarly G.-K. 35n.

[71]So also Rashi and iE.

I have translated the text as it appears in Rosin's edition. I am convinced, though, that the text is faulty. My speculative emendation would be to remove the word "שאול—i.e. Saul." See note 72 for my rationale.

[72]In his commentary to Gen. 41:10 (pp. 281–282 of my Genesis volume), Rashbam makes his point much more clearly. He writes that Egyptian kings from different periods of history (Abraham's, Joseph's, Moses') are all called Pharaoh; kings of the Philistines from different periods (Abraham's, David's) are called Abimelech; kings of Jerusalem are called Melchizedek (in the days of Abraham and David) and the similar name, Adoni-Zedek, in the days of Joshua. (For references, see notes in Genesis.)

In his commentary to Genesis, Rashbam writes further that " של עמלק אגג בימי משה וירום מאגג מלכו ובימי שאול אגג מלך עמלק—Kings of Amalek are called Agag, both in Moses' days (Num. 24:7), 'their king shall arise above Agag,' and in Saul's days (I Sam. 15:8), 'King Agag of Amalek'." In other words, Rashbam says explicitly in his Genesis commentary that our verse, "their king shall arise above Agag," is a reference to an Amalekite king in Moses' day, not a prophecy about King Saul. So the Genesis commentary contradicts what Rashbam ostensibly writes in the beginning of his commentary to our verse—that Balaam is describing in a prophetic passage the future king of Amalek who will be vanquished by Saul.

24:8 תועפות: means strength. So also in the phrase (Ps. 95:4), "the strength (תועפות) of the mountains is his."[73]

24:14 איעצך "LET ME ADVISE YOU: [I.e. give you] advice[74] on how to trip them up.[75] For I know WHAT THIS PEOPLE WILL DO TO YOUR PEOPLE[76] IN DAYS TO COME. But now in the near future, in your own lifetime, there is no need for you to be afraid of them."

And the advice was [for the Moabite women to seduce Israelite men, as it is written] (Num. 31:16), "Yet they [the women] were the very ones who, at Balaam's suggestion, [induced the Israelites to trespass against the LORD]."

Furthermore, I would rule out the possibility that Rashbam changed his mind after writing his Genesis commentary and now, when writing his Numbers commentary, feels that the verse is about the Agag of Saul's days. I do not think that there is any reasonable way to read the end of Rashbam's commentary to this verse as anything other than a reiteration of what Rashbam said in his Genesis commentary. In other words, either the end of Rashbam's comment to this verse or the beginning must be emended. And since the end of the comment is (a) much longer and (b) in consonance with the Genesis commentary, removing the word שאול from the text seems to be the preferred emendation.

If I am correct, then Rashbam's comment here was specifically meant to oppose Rashi's explanation that Agag here is the name of a king who will be born a few hundred years after Balaam's prophecy. As Nahm. writes here, "רחוק הוא שיקרא הנביא שם הרשע בטרם נוצר בבטן—it is far-fetched to think that the prophet [= Balaam!] would give a name to this evil man before he was even conceived."

[73]So also Rashi and iE ad Num. 23:22 and in Psalms. Aside from the citation in Psalms, the word appears once more in the Bible, in Job 22:25. There again Rashi and iE say that it means strength. All of these commentaries should be seen as opposed to the midrashic explanation that תועפות means "angels." See e.g. *Midrash Tehillim* 78.

Most moderns explain the word as meaning "horns," here. iE mentions that possibility in his commentaries both to Numbers 23 and to Psalms 95.

[74]Most moderns would say that the word איעצך here means "let me *inform* you [what this people will do to your people in days to come]." In other words, this phrase is not referring to any advice, just as there is no specific reference to any advice in the continuation of Balaam's poem. So also Nahm. See Qara (cited in Berliner's *Peleṭat Soferim*, p. 23, and in Heidenheim's *Havanat ha-miqra'*, here) who says that the word איעצך is appropriately used despite the fact that there is no advice here. According to Qara, the word עצה simply means something that is said and that one does not want many people to hear. Rashbam, however, goes along with the midrashic approach of Rashi (following Sanh. 106a) and says that Balaam did offer real advice to Balak at this point.

[75]The phrase עצה להכשילם is taken directly from Rashi.

[76]Rosin emended the text, adding the word יהיה—leading to the following translation: "I know that what the people will do to your people will be [only] in the days to come." His emendation, however, seems superfluous.

Moses wrote about this advice in an elliptical manner, for Balaam said it to Balak in a whisper.[77] The advice was accordingly not known [widely] until Moses spoke of it explicitly at the appropriate time.[78]

24:17 אראנו: [does not mean I *will* see it,[79] but] right now I see future events,[80] but ולא עתה—they will NOT take place NOW.[81]

כל בני שת [SMASHING THE FOUNDATIONS OF] ALL THE CHILDREN OF SETH: Following the plain meaning of Scripture, this refers to the [actions of the anticipated] messianic king.[82]

---

[77]Rashbam is answering the obvious (but unarticulated) question: "If Balaam told Balak that he would give him advice, why does that advice not appear in the continuation of Balaam's speech?" The idea that Balaam whispered these words to Balak is first found in Qara (cited by Berliner, *Peleṭat Soferim*, p. 23). As noted above (note 74), Rashbam did not accept all of Qara's explanation of this phrase.

[78]I.e. once the war with the Midianites had taken place and the Midianite women were captured, Moses, at that point, had to point out to the Israelites that those Midianite women had seduced Israelite men "at Balaam's suggestion" (בדבר בלעם). Only at that point in the text does Moses make Balaam's advice explicit.

Rashbam's conception of Moses' editorial role is interesting. The words כאן סתם משה את העצה imply that Moses, when editing Balaam's speeches for inclusion in the Torah, decided not to include those words that were spoken in an undertone.

[79]See comment above ad 23:7, s.v. ינחני.

[80]Rashi says that "אראנו—I see *it*," refers to seeing the greatness of the Jewish people. Rashbam says more simply that it means "I see the future."

[81]There is a subtle difference between the explanations of Rashi and Rashbam for this phrase. Rashi says that ולא עתה means "לא עתה היא אלא לאחר זמן—it *is* not now but in the future." Rashbam says, though, that ולא עתה means "it *will not be*" in the near future, but only in the much more distant future. Rashbam may be preparing us for his dispute with Rashi about the meaning of the next phrase of the verse. See note 82.

There is a strong similarity between the wording of Rashbam's comment here and the comment of Andrew of St. Victor. Andrew (p. 191) first quotes the Vulgate's translation of the verse, *videbo* (I shall have seen; future perfect) and then says: "In Hebrew the text says 'I shall see it,' [*videro*, future tense] which is to say, 'I see [*video*, present tense] what his future is, and it is "not now" but in the distant future'." The similarity is noted by Berndt, *Recherches augustiniennes* 24 (1989), p. 235.

[82]Rashbam's explanation opposes that of Rashi who says that Balaam's prophecy here was fulfilled by King David. See the long discussion in iE, who agrees with Rashi, and says that there is no heterodoxy involved in saying that the reference here is to David, and not to the messiah. Presumably he says that because someone has argued that explaining the verse about David would be a sign of lack of belief in the messiah.

Rashbam says that the prophecy does refer to the messiah. He does not tell us why he considers the messianic reading the *peshaṭ*. I would speculate that his logic is that David never did destroy the foundations of all "the children of Seth," particularly if one explains "the children of Seth" as meaning all of humanity. (So Onq. and Rashi. See also Rashbam's

24:18 יְרֵשָׁה HEREDITARY: יְרֵשָׁה is [an adjectival form,][83] like שְׁמֵנָה—fat[84] or [שְׂבֵעָה in the phrase (Prov. 27:7)], "a sated (שְׂבֵעָה) person." [יְרֵשָׁה means] *eritere* [in Old French].[85]

24:19 וירד מיעקב AND FROM JACOB . . . SHALL RULE: [In other words,] a man from "Jacob" [i.e. the Jewish people] will rule over all kingdoms.[86]

והאביד שריד מעיר AND HE WILL WIPE OUT ANY SURVIVOR FROM IR:[87] [I.e. anyone who survives] from Edom. As it is written (Obad. 18), "No survivor shall be left from the house of Esau, for the LORD has spoken."[88]

24:20 וירא את עמלק HE SAW AMALEK: He could see them from the place where he was standing.[89]

---

commentary below ad vs. 23. So also Andrew of St. Victor, who adds, however, that the verse could not really mean that the messiah would smash *all* of humanity. Rather he will smash only those who have "oppressed God's people.")

See also Maimonides (MT, *Melakhim* 11:1) who explains the individual phrases of our verse as referring, in an alternating manner, to King David and to the messianic king.

[83]Cf. iE who says that the form יְרֵשָׁה is a noun.

[84]See e.g. Num. 13:20.

[85]*Héréditaire* in modern French.

[86]The phrase וירד מיעקב is syntactically clumsy, but there is general agreement that it means what Rashbam says it means.

Rashi sees this phrase as the transitional phrase between the previous verses (that describe the accomplishments of King David) and the next verses (that describe the anticipated messianic king). Rashi explains וירד מיעקב as meaning that yet another man from Jacob, other than King David, will be a ruler in the future. Rashbam does not agree, since he feels that the same messianic king is being described throughout vss. 17–19.

[87]It is impossible to know whether Rashbam saw the word עיר here as a place name or as the simple Hebrew noun that means "city." I have translated following NJPS. If his interpretation is that the word עיר means "city," then Andrew of St. Victor is echoing his comment when he writes (p. 191), "Jacob will destroy those who remain in the cities of Edom."

[88]Rashbam's comment is similar to that of Rashi. Both say that the verse describes total victory over the Edomites. Rashi says that the word מעיר is a specific reference to *the* city of the Edomites (whom he identifies as the Christians/Roman Empire), i.e. Rome. Rashbam says simply that the reference is to "Edom."

See NJPSC which, like many moderns, suggests that our verse may be a prediction of an Israelite victory over the Moabites. However NJPSC notes that the language of Obadiah, in the verse quoted here by Rashbam and Rashi, shows that the author of Obadiah understood our verse in Numbers as referring to the Edomites.

[89]Rashbam opposes Rashi's understanding here, in the same way that he did above ad 23:9, s.v. כי מראש צורים אראנו. (See note 30 there.) Rashi says that וירא את עמלק means that Balaam here "saw" prophetically the downfall of Amalek. Rashbam, on the other hand, says that Balaam literally saw Amalekites, presumably from the high spot where he was standing.

Like Rashi, see iE. Like Rashbam, see Nahm.

ראשית גוים AMALEK IS THE FIRST NATION: [This phrase should be understood] as the Targum explains it.[90]

24:21–22 איתן מושבך YOUR ABODE IS SECURE: [In other words,] you [the Kenites] imagine that your abode *will be* secure [forever] and that בסלע קנך—YOUR NEST *will last* [safely] IN THE ROCKS [forever]. What you imagine will not come to pass. (22) Rather[91] in the future[92] KAIN WILL BE REMOVED[93] to a very distant place to which[94] אשור תשבך—i.e. the place to which the Assyrian kingdom[95] will exile you as captives.[96]

---

[90]The Targum explains the phrase: "ריש קרביא דישראל הוה עמלק—Amalek was the first to wage war against the Israelites." So also Rashi.

[91]Rashbam sees the first words of vs. 22, כי אם, as meaning "rather." Based on this, Rashbam explains that the Kenites' thoughts in vs. 21 will *not* come true. Vs. 22 then begins by saying "כי אם—Rather, this shall be the case . . .."

Rashbam is opposing Rashi's understanding that vs. 22 continues the thought of vs. 21. The Kenites, according to Rashi, really do have a certain strength and security, and that strength will later help them when they are exiled. See note 96.

[92]The translation "in the future" is based on Rosin's speculative emendation אלא אחר כן. The ms. (as reported by Rosin) reads אלא אשר כן, an incomprehensible phrase. Berzinsky suggests erasing the words אשר כן, yielding the simple translation, "What you imagine will not be. Rather, KAIN WILL BE REMOVED."

[93]Rashbam understands the word לבער as meaning to "remove." That is the way that the *piel* of the verb *b-'-r* is standardly used in rabbinic Hebrew. See e.g. Jastrow, s.v. *b-'-r*.

[94]Rosin has added a word and a half to Rashbam's commentary here. Instead of לבער קין עד מקום רחוק, Rosin suggests the reading לבער קין עד מה? המקום רחוק. If Rosin is right then Rashbam is explaining the syntax of the last part of the verse the same way that Rashi does. The text asks עד מה—i.e. how far will the Kenites be exiled? And then it answers אשור תשבך—as far as the Assyrians will exile them.

I have translated above without Rosin's added text. I do not know how Rashbam understands the syntax of עד מה אשור תשבך, but I see no reason to assume that he accepts Rashi's understanding of the syntax since he clearly rejects Rashi's understanding of the idea here. See note 96.

[95]Rosin suggests that Rashbam has added the feminine noun, מלכות—kingdom, to his paraphrase of the verse in order to explain why the feminine verb תשבך is used. See iE who also deals with this problem.

[96]Rashi says that the end of this verse constitutes comfort to the Kenites. The Kenites will be taken into exile but not very far. They will only go as far as the Assyrians take them, and they will later return to their land along with the Israelite captives. Like Rashi, see also JBS. They both cite I Sam. 15 as proof that the Kenites received special treatment and that their destiny was separate from that of the Amalekites.

Rashbam opposes that reading. Our verse, he says, is not comforting the Kenites, and is not continuing the thought of the previous verse. The Kenites (21) might think that they are secure, but (22) they will be taken into captivity "to a very distant place."

24:23 אוי מי יחיה ALAS WHO CAN SURVIVE: when opposed by the messianic king, when God בשומו, grants to him all of these powers, to (vs. 17) "smash the foundations of all the children of Seth."[97]

24:24 וצים SHIPS: [צים should be understood] like (Is. 33:21) "a mighty ship (צי)." *Dromont*[98] in the vernacular; i.e. a large boat (בורני).[99]

25:3 ויחר אף [THE LORD] BECAME ANGRY: [God's anger manifested itself in that] a plague began among the people.[100]

25:4 והוקע אותם [TAKE ALL THE LEADERS OF THE PEOPLE] AND EXECUTE THEM: I.e. execute the sinners.[101] [והוקע should be understood] as in the

---

[97]As NJPSC notes, our verse is very difficult and "a literal rendering is incomprehensible."

Rashi says that the reference in this verse is to the Assyrians who were just mentioned in the previous verse. The meaning is something like "Who can withstand the actions of King Sennacherib?"

Rashbam sees our verse as a summary of vss. 17–22. All of those verses describe, according to Rashbam, how the messianic king will overcome the nations. Our verse then concludes "Who can withstand the powers granted by God to the messiah, the powers that he will use to overcome the nations?" Rashi cannot explain our verse that way as he has viewed some of the previous verses—the ones about the Kenites—as expressing a prophecy about a positive destiny.

[98]A battle ship. So Rosin and B. Heller, in MGWJ 82, p. 132. Cf. Darmesteter and Blondheim, p. 43, "*une sorte de navire*," and Andrew of St. Victor (p. 192), "*genus navium*."

[99]Rashbam, as he occasionally does, tells us nothing about how to understand this extremely difficult verse and simply comments on one word, not the hardest one in the verse. He explains the word צים by referring to the word צי in Isaiah. He translates the word צים both into Old French and into rabbinic Hebrew. All of these points, with the exception of the Old French gloss, are found already in Rashi's commentary here. The explanation of צי in Isaiah as a בורני גדולה is found in the Talmud (RH 23a). Rashi there provides the same Old French gloss that Rashbam offers here.

On בורני, see Jastrow.

[100]So also Rashi.

The plague is actually not mentioned in the biblical text until vs. 8, when it stops. Rashbam feels the need to mention the plague right away, because, as he has told his readers on more than one occasion, he feels as the Talmud says (Zev. 102a) that when the Torah mentions God's anger (חרון אף), a perceivable effect always ensues. God's "anger" is never simply an emotion. Accordingly, Rashbam feels obliged to explain here what "The LORD became angry" really means. See Rashbam's commentary to Gen. 32:29, to Ex. 4:14 (and note 8 there) and above ad 22:25 (and note 11 there).

[101]The difficulty is clear. The verse seems to say that Moses is to take all the leaders of the Israelites and kill them. Why? Were all the leaders guilty of idolatry?

Rashbam follows the solution of Rashi. Despite what the syntax implies, the only ones executed were the sinners. The leaders were gathered, but the instruction, "execute them," does not refer to the leaders, but only to the implied antecedent, "the sinners." So also iE. All phrase (II Sam. 21:6), "and we will hang them (והוקענום) in Gibeah of Saul." The word can mean hanging and killing.[102]

25:6 ויקרב אל אחיו HE BROUGHT [THE MIDIANITE] NEAR HIS BROTHERS: for sexual purposes. [The verb "ויקרב—he brought (her) near" is] like (Lev. 18:6) "do not come near to uncover nakedness."[103]

25:8 אל הַקֻּבָּה INTO THE TENT: [The word הַקֻּבָּה] means tent, [while the similar word at the end of the verse,] קֳבָתָהּ, means "her stomach," like the word (Deut. 18:3) "והקֵּבָה—and the stomach."[104]

---

these exegetes are rejecting the opinion of Rabbi Judah (Tanh. *Balaq* 19) that all the leaders were executed, even those who were not idolaters, since they failed in their role of leading the people to proper behavior.

Like Rashbam, see also Andrew of St. Victor (p. 192).

[102]Rashi's explanation of this word conforms more closely to halakhic norms. In rabbinic Judaism, hanging is not a method of putting a criminal to death, but a way of displaying the criminal's dead body after he or she has been executed in another manner. Rashi tries to explain what crime the miscreants committed here, and why their crime merited both the death penalty and the further penalty of hanging the dead corpse.

Rashbam notes that הוקענום in II Samuel means "to put to death through hanging" and he understands that this is what our verse means, even if that does not conform with later *halakhah*.

[103]As NJPSC notes, the text does not explain at all why Zimri brought the Midianite woman near his brothers. Rashbam sees here an allusion to a sexual meaning; perhaps it means that Zimri attempted to involve his brothers in the indiscretion. See also Hizq. who expresses the same idea more graphically (ויקרב . . . לשון הפעיל מענין שכיבה).

Rashbam is opposing the explanation that the phrase, "he brought the Midianite near his brothers before Moses," is a reference to a legal consultation. Zimri, according to the Talmud (Sanh. 82a) and Rashi, came to Moses publicly for a mocking halakhic consultation ("Moses, is this woman permitted or forbidden to me? Should you say forbidden, who allowed *you* to marry a Midianite?"). That midrash is based in part on seeing the phrase ויקרב אל as implying a legal consultation. See e.g. Num. 27:5: "Moses brought (ויקרב) their case before (אל) the LORD."

[104]Like Rashi, Rashbam notes here that there is a pun in this verse. The similar words הַקֻּבָּה and קֳבָתָהּ have different meanings. Rashi and Rashbam agree that the first means "tent." They also both say that the second word means "stomach" and they cite the same prooftext from Deut. But Rashi (following Sanh. 82b) adds that "stomach" here is really a euphemism for the female genitalia. (So also Hizq.) For Rashi, Zimri and Cozbi received the appropriate punishment of being stabbed through their sexual organs. For Rashbam, such a conclusion is not supported by the text.

Rashbam's commentary to the Torah portion פנחס (Numbers 25:10–30:1) has never been found.

מטות (Numbers 30:2–32:42)

30:2–3 וידבר משה אל ראשי המטות MOSES SPOKE TO THE HEADS OF THE ISRAELITE TRIBES: When I was in the city of Loudun[1] in Anjou, I was asked [if I could answer the following question] using [only the methodology of] the plain meaning of Scripture:

> Where have we ever seen a [legal] section of the Torah that begins in this manner? It does not say anywhere above that "The LORD spoke to Moses saying, 'If a man makes a vow . . .'." Why then does this section begin with Moses' speech, [the content of] which is not explicitly described as originating from God?[2]

---

[1]See Urbach, *Ba'ale ha-Tosafot*, p. 46; Gross, *Gallia Judaica*, p. 259; Golb, *The Jews in Medieval Normandy* (Cambridge, 1998), p. 228, note 21.

[2]The questioner is asking about the unusual introduction to the laws about vows and oaths. Why here, and nowhere else in the Torah, does Moses tell the laws to "the heads of the tribes"? And why does Moses say "This is what the LORD commanded," when our passage is actually the first time that the laws are mentioned in the Torah?

Many commentators pose some or all of these questions. Rashi (following Sifre Numbers 73) says that actually there is no difference between the way in which the laws of oaths were taught to the Israelites, and the way that all other laws were taught to them. Our verse is paradigmatic; all laws that Moses received from God he taught first to the heads of the tribes and then to all of the Israelites. And why is that process described here, specifically? Rashi answers that its placement here teaches us (through a *midrash halakhah*) a technical rule about who is qualified to annul vows.

Nahm. also confronts the question and suggests that either some of the rules of vow annulment have to be known only by those doing the annulling, or that it might be best that the rank and file not know at all that vows may be annulled, so that they continue to take vows seriously. Nahm. also points out that Moses, when speaking to the heads of the tribes, must have been simply relaying God's words to them (even though those words are never recorded in the text). He argues that vs. 17 makes that point clear.

Rashbam has his own original approach to the question, but he does not articulate a precise answer to the question addressed to him by the residents of Loudun. Rashbam is saying that Moses was concerned that the Israelites might not understand the rule of 29:39 properly, the rule that says that freewill offerings in the Temple will be offered on the pilgrimage festivals. Accordingly Moses (of his own initiative?) decided to go to the heads of the tribes and teach them the different time limits that apply to different types of vows. Rashbam thus answers the question, "Why did Moses tell the laws to the heads of the tribes here?" He does not explain why Moses did it here and nowhere else. He also does not explain

This is what I answered:

It is written above (Num. 29:39), "These you should offer to the LORD on your holidays, in addition to your votive and freewill offerings," which you [also] have to bring during one of the three pilgrimage festivals[3] because of [the halakhic concept of] "do not make it overdue,"[4] as it is explained in tractate *Rosh ha-shanah*.

So Moses went and spoke to "the heads of the tribes," i.e. to the judges, [asking them] to teach the rules about vows to the Israelites.[5] Moses said to

---

why the Torah does not explicitly tell when or where Moses learned these laws from God. Much of his comment is a detailed digression about time limits of vows.

Rashbam's comment also takes issue with Rashi on one further point. According to Rashi, the purpose of the previous verse (30:1) was to separate the themes of chapters 29 and 30 (להפסיק הענין). Rashbam says here that, according to the *peshaṭ*, chapter 30 must be read as a continuation and elaboration of one detail in chapter 29.

[3]On fulfilling a sacrificial vow during a pilgrimage festival, see also Rashi ad Num. 29:39. See also Rashbam's commentary ad Deut. 16:2.

[4]The phrase בל תאחר is the rabbinic Hebrew rephrasing of the words of Deut. 23:22, "When you make a vow to the LORD your God, do not delay (לא תאחר) in fulfilling it."

The Talmud in RH 4a explains that when a person vows to bring a sacrifice to the Temple, he or she must bring it before three pilgrimage festivals have gone by. If that is not done, then the infraction of בל תאחר, of delaying the fulfillment of a vow, has taken place.

[5]In order to understand how different Rashbam's approach is from all the other Jewish exegesis of this verse, it is necessary to give a short introduction (modeled on Maimonides' MT, *Nedarim* 1:1–2).

The word נדר can have two very different meanings in halakhic literature. Often it means one of two specific categories of oaths that are meant to restrict a person's behavior. If a person says "Tomatoes are קונם for me," i.e. tomatoes are as forbidden for me as sacrificial meat, then the person has enunciated a נדר. Practically speaking, such a vow is very similar to declaring "I swear that I will eat no tomatoes." But the latter phrasing—where the *person* is the subject of the promise—is called a שבועה, while the declaration, "Tomatoes are קונם for me," in which the *tomatoes* are the subject, is called a נדר.

A second totally unrelated use of the word נדר is to describe one type of promise to bring an animal as a sacrifice to the Temple. A person who says "I take upon myself to bring a sacrifice to the Temple," has enunciated a נדר. (If the commitment was formulated in the terms "I declare this specific animal to be a [future] sacrifice," then that promise is called a נדבה, not a נדר.)

Every rabbinic exegete whom I have seen, other than Rashbam, interprets our verse as referring to the first type of נדר, the type that Maimonides calls נדרי איסר, the נדר that forbids a certain type of activity for a specific human being. In fact, Maimonides uses our verse in his introduction to the rules of נדרים to make this distinction. Numbers 30:2, says Maimonides, is the paradigm verse for נדרי איסר, the type of נדר that restricts human behavior.

Rashbam's innovation is to say that נדר in our verse should be understood using the second definition of נדר, namely a promise to bring a sacrifice to the Temple. Thus the word נדר here is used in the same sense that it was used three verses earlier, in 29:39. So also Luzzatto.

them, "God commanded [through] me that the Israelites should offer their votive and freewill offerings on the pilgrimage festivals, so that their vows will not be delayed. Accordingly [I must teach you now that] IF A MAN MAKES A VOW TO THE LORD—[that he will offer] a sacrifice, OR IF HE SWEARS TO MAKE SOMETHING FORBIDDEN [FOR HIMSELF] in [a vow of] self-denial,[6] [then] לא יחל דברו." This [last phrase] refers to the vow [to offer a sacrifice]. It means that he should not delay his vow until after the pilgrimage festivals, as God commanded them [in 29:39].

For that is what יחל means ["to delay" or "to wait"], as in the phrase (Jud. 3:25), "he waited (ויחל)[7] a long time," or (Gen. 8:10), "he waited (ויחל) another seven days," or (Ps. 130:7), "Israel shall wait (יחל) for the LORD," which means to await and anticipate Him. Anyone who says that it [= the word יחל, in our verse] means to desecrate is, following the plain sense of Scripture, mistaken.[8]

[The next clause of the verse,] ככל היוצא מפיו יעשה HE MUST CARRY OUT ALL THAT HAS CROSSED HIS LIPS, refers to [the second type of promise in the verse], "if he swears [making something forbidden for himself]." [In that case, there is no standard maximum time for the vow;] he should fulfill whatever it was that he said when he swore, following the time frame that he himself specified, whether short or long.[9]

---

[6]The phrase לענות נפש is from vs. 14.

There are two phrases in our verse: ידור נדר and השבע שבועה. The distinction between them, according to Rashbam, is that the first refers to promises to bring a sacrifice to the Temple, while the second refers to vows that restrict behavior. All prior halakhic exegetes said that both phrases refer to vows that restrict behavior. According to them, each one of the phrases refers to one of the two categories of restrictive vows: vows formulated as "X is קונם to me," and vows formulated as "I will not do X." (See note 5.)

[7]MT reads ויחילו, "they waited."

Esh (p. 88) discusses whether this reading might reflect a different text tradition, or whether it is a simple error (or as Esh puts it, a *lapsus memoriae)*. I am confident that it is just that.

[8]Rashbam's interpretation of יחל as meaning "to delay" is yet another innovation of his. So also Hizq. (Most other exegetes interpret it as meaning to break one's pledge.) He assumes that just as the phrase (in Deut. 23:22) לא תאחר means, halakhically speaking, "do not delay beyond the third pilgrimage festival," so also the phrase "לא יחל" here means the same thing.

See the criticism of Y. Shapira (in *Ha-rekhasim le-viq'ah* here) who says that Rashbam's proofs are poor. The examples he cites, according to Shapira, are of waiting with anticipation for something to happen, not of forgetting and delaying to do something.

When Rashbam says that other readings are mistaken, he is opposing Rashi, or, at a minimum, he is saying that Rashi's interpretation is midrash, not *peshaṭ*. iE, Nahm. and almost all halakhic exegetes follow Rashi's approach.

[9]I.e. unlike the first kind of vows in this verse—vows to offer a sacrifice, vows which have a legislated time frame related to the three pilgrimage festivals—vows of the second type, oaths

Proof of the matter [that our verse is referring both to sacrificial vows, which have a specific time frame, and to oaths of self-denial, which do not, comes from] Moses' elaboration on these two categories in a similar manner in Deuteronomy. [There (23:22–24) he explained] "(22) If you make a vow to the LORD your God [which means a vow to offer a sacrifice, as in our verse] do not delay its fulfillment [until after the pilgrimage festivals] . . . ."[10] [Then the verse which follows,] (24) "You must fulfill what has crossed your lips [in the manner that you vowed] . . .," is [referring to the second type of promise, the oath of self-denial,] just like [the second clause in our verse], "or if he swears."[11]

30:11 ואם בית אישה נדרה IF SHE MAKES A VOW WHILE IN HER HUSBAND'S HOUSEHOLD: [In this verse, we see that a husband can annul vows that his wife makes after marriage.] However, above (vs. 7) it is written, "[IF SHE SHOULD MARRY] WHILE HER VOW IS UPON HER." That verse [must be] about vows that were made before marriage. We can [then] conclude [from the contrast between vs. 7 and vs. 11], that, following the plain meaning of Scripture, [vss. 7–9 must be teaching] that a husband has the power to annul [his wife's] vows, [even vows] from before [their marriage].[12]

---

of self-denial, have no standard time frame. Whatever the person said in the oath determines the time requirement.

Rashbam understands our verse as having an "A-B-A-B" structure. The two types of vows are listed—(A) to bring a sacrifice and then (B) to restrict one's behavior—and then the text mentions the relevant time factor for each one: (A) In the case of a vow to bring a sacrifice, do not delay [beyond the third pilgrimage festival]. (B) In the case of a vow to restrict behavior, observe the vow for however long you said that you would. See Touitou in *Tarbiz* 48, p. 273, end of note 142.

[10]Rashbam's prooftext is well chosen. The phrase there כי תדר נדר is virtually the same as כי ידר נדר in our verse. There the halakhic exegetes all say that it means to vow to offer a sacrifice and they say further that the vow must be fulfilled before three pilgrimage festivals have gone by.

Rashbam says that, following the *peshaṭ*, the phrase means the same thing here. He could argue further that the phrase "to vow a vow" appears often in the Bible in the sense of taking upon oneself some cultic obligation to God. See e.g. Num. 6:21 and 21:2, Deut. 12:11, Judges 11:30, I Sam. 1:11, II Sam. 15:7, Is. 19:21, Jon. 1:16 and Eccl. 5:3. There is no biblical verse (with the possible exception of ours) in which the phrase certainly means "to restrict oneself through a נדר."

[11]Rashbam explains that vs. 24 in Deut. is referring to the second type of promise, the promise to restrict one's behavior. That is why the text there says that one must fulfill the vow in the manner that one said. There is no fixed time limit, no point at which the automatic rule of "do not delay" would kick in.

[12]For the continuation there reads, "(9) he thereby annuls her vow that was in force."

Rashbam realizes well that he is offering an explanation of the *peshaṭ* that contradicts *halakhah*. He uses a minor variation on a standard talmudic maxim to advocate an interpretation that is diametrically opposed to standard *halakhah*. The Talmud says on more than

30:16 ואם הפר יפר אותם אחרי שמעו IF HE ANNULS THEM AFTER [THE DAY] HE HEARS: [I.e. if he annuls the vows on a day subsequent to his hearing,[13] i.e. on a day when he no longer has a right to annul them,] but his wife does not know that he had [already] heard [the vows on a previous day, and she therefore does not know that he no longer has the power to annul them], then ונשא את עונה, HE SHALL BEAR HER GUILT [if she subsequently transgresses the vow, thinking that her husband's annulment had been efficacious. This is] because the vows were not annulled. Her sin is unintentional for she did not know whether or not her husband had already heard [the vows on some day previous to the day that he attempted to annul them].[14]

31:5 וימסרו [FOR THE CAMPAIGN, A THOUSAND FROM EACH TRIBE] WERE HANDED OVER: against their will. For God had said [to Moses that once this campaign was finished,] (vs. 2) "then[15] you shall be gathered to your kin."[16] [This explanation is from a] *midrash 'aggadah.*[17]

---

one occasion that אין הבעל מיפר בקודמין—a husband does *not* have the right to annul vows that predate the marriage. (See e.g. Git. 35b and Ned. 72a.) Rashbam quotes the talmudic saying here, but leaves out the negative. Instead he writes: הבעל מיפר בקודמין—the husband *does* have the right to annul his wife's vows that predate the marriage. On Rashbam's tendency to phrase a unique or a heterodox explanation in a confrontational manner, see note 58 above to 24:1–2, s.v. ותהי עליו.

For an explanation of the logic of the talmudic reading, see Nahm. ad vs. 7. See also NJPSC, which explains the talmudic position, but also says that the *peshat* must be as Rashbam explains. Like Rashbam, see iE and JBS ad vs. 7.

[13]A husband may annul his wife's vow only during the first day after the time that he heard it. See vs. 8 and see Ned. 76b. If he waits more than one day after hearing the vow and then annuls it, the vow continues to be in effect.

[14]Cf. iE who explains that the verse is saying that a husband who forces his wife to break a vow shall incur guilt for doing so. See Nahm. who writes that iE is wrong (ואינו נכון) and explains the verse as Rashbam does. So also, with minor variations, JBS and Hizq.

Compare also Rashbam's explanation of the phrase here, "ונשא את עונה—the husband shall bear his wife's guilt," with his explanation of the phrase (Num. 5:31), והאשה ההיא תשא את עונה. That phrase means, according to Rashbam (see note 25 there), that that husband has *no* responsibility for his wife's punishment; the responsibility there is entirely hers.

[15]Rashbam quotes vs. 2 as reading ואחר. MT reads אחר. See the discussion in Esh, p. 87.

[16]Since the troops did not wish to hasten Moses' death, they did not volunteer for battle on their own. They had to be "handed over," against their will.

[17]So also Rashi, following Sifre Numbers 157.

In the entire Torah commentary, this is the only time that Rashbam labels a specific interpretation as a *midrash 'aggadah* and offers that midrashic interpretation as his only explanation of the verse. It is possible that a later copyist added this comment.

31:12 את השבי THE CAPTIVES: i.e. the human beings. ואת המלקוח THE BOOTY: i.e. the animals. ואת השלל THE SPOIL: i.e. the chattels.[18]

31:13 אל מחוץ למחנה [MOSES . . . CAME OUT TO MEET THEM] OUTSIDE THE CAMP: So that those returning from the war would not enter the camp, because of [their] impurity from [contact with] dead bodies.[19]

31:23 אך במי נידה יתחטא EXCEPT THAT THEY [the utensils] MUST BE CLEANSED WITH WATERS OF LUSTRATION: from [the ashes of] a red heifer, in order to purify them from [their contact with] a dead body. All of the other things [listed in this verse—"passing though fire" and "passing through water"—are meant to make the utensils kosher for foodstuffs. These latter actions] cleanse the utensils from the forbidden foods that were absorbed in them.[20]

---

[18]Rashbam's comment to this verse is similar to Rashi's comment to vs. 11. They agree about the meaning of שבי (= humans) and מלקוח (= animals), although Rashi adds that at times (e.g. in vs. 11) the word מלקוח alone is used and then it means "humans and animals."

Rashi and Rashbam differ about the meaning of שלל. Rashi feels that שלל applies only to two specific types of chattels—clothes and jewelry. All other chattels captured in war are, according to Rashi, called בז. Rashi's claim is difficult. The noun בז as a type of spoil of war appears only once in the Torah (vs. 32 below) and there is no reason to say that it means "chattels other than clothes and jewelry" there. Rashbam's explanation that שלל simply means "chattels" seems more reasonable. Even Rashi's standard staunch defender, the *Mizraḥi*, says that he does not know why Rashi interprets the word that way, and that it makes more sense to say that שלל means chattels in general.

[19]Rashbam's interpretation opposes that of Rashi who claims (following Sifre Numbers 157) that Moses and his entourage went outside of the camp in order to stop certain Israelites from taking unauthorized booty.

Like Rashbam, see Hizq. and NJPSC among others.

[20]Standard *halakhah* says that two things have to be done to a used food utensil that a Jew acquires from a non-Jew before the Jew can use it for food. It has to undergo a process to make it kosher—expunging, halakhically-speaking, the non-kosher food absorbed in the utensil. This is usually done with boiling water or fire. Beyond that, the utensil also has to be immersed in a *miqveh* (ritual bath). This latter rule applies according to standard *halakhah*, to any utensil, used or new, that a Jew acquires from a non-Jew.

Rashi offers two explanations of our verse. One of them, following AZ 75b, explains that our verse is legislating those two separate processes described in the previous paragraph. The phrase במי נידה יתחטא means, according to this midrash, that, before use, the utensil must be cleansed in a *miqveh*, i.e. in the same type of water that a *niddah*, a menstruant woman, uses for purification.

Rashi himself realizes that that explanation is not the simple interpretation of the verse. (He also may feel that since *halakhah* considers the immersing of a utensil in a *miqveh* before use to be a *rabbinic* rule, it does not make sense to claim that that idea is included in the meaning of a *biblical* verse.) He accordingly offers a second explanation, which he labels

31:49–50 עבדיך נשאו את ראש . . . ולא נפקד ממנו איש "YOUR SERVANTS HAVE COUNTED . . . AND NOT ONE OF THEM WAS LOST: in a plague [as a result of the count].[21] That is why (50) WE BROUGHT AN OFFERING TO THE LORD . . . TO MAKE EXPIATION FOR OUR PERSONS: For before we were counted, we had made a vow [to bring that offering], so that the plague would have no power over us.[22] And for that reason, God commanded that that offering be assigned (Ex. 30:16) 'to the service of the Tent of Meeting'."

[Verses 49–50 here follow the pattern of Ex. 30:12–16.] For we saw [there] in the Torah portion *Ki tissa'*, [that the Torah says] (Ex. 30:12) "so that

---

peshaṭ. That explanation is the one that Rashbam offers—that במי נידה יתחטא refers to cleansing the utensil not for purposes related to the laws of kosher food, but for purposes of ritual purity. According to that explanation, מי נידה does not mean a *miqveh*. Rather it means here what it means in Num 19 (vss. 9, 13, 20 and 21): water that is mixed with the ashes of a red heifer, and that is used for the removal of ritual impurity that comes from contact with a dead body.

To make his explanation perfectly clear, Rashbam emphasizes that our verse relates to two distinct areas of Jewish law. The utensil is "passed through fire" for the sake of the laws of kosher food. The utensil is cleansed with מי נידה to remove the ritual impurity that resulted from contact with a dead body, following the laws of Numbers 19.

[21]The standard explanation of the phrase is that they, as NJPSC puts it, "discovered that Israel had not suffered a single casualty" in the war. So JBS and Nahm.

Rashbam understands the verse very differently. He says that the concern here is that counting the Israelites might have led to a plague against them. The verse then means, "Though we counted the people, no one died as the result of a plague." See the story of David's counting of the Israelites in II Sam. 24. See also Ex. 30:12, which dictates what the Israelites should do in order to ensure that no plague comes upon them when there is a count of the people. Rashbam's explanation of verses 49–50 is based on his view that these verses are parallel to that legal section in Ex. 30:12–16, as he explains in the continuation of this comment.

Besides opposing the standard explanation of the phrase, Rashbam's explanation opposes the midrash that says that the phrase ולא נפקד ממנו איש means that no man who went to war engaged in any sexual sin. (See Shab. 64a, and Rashi there, s.v. לא נפקד.)

[22]The standard explanation would be that after their miraculous victory without casualties, the people knew that they should present an offering to God. So Nahm. But Rashbam's interpretation here explains why the people felt that they had to do something so that "expiation may be made for our persons." The identical phrase is used in Ex. 30:15.

This explanation is opposed to the Talmud's attempt (*ibid.*) to say that even if the Israelites committed no sexual sin, they had to do penance for illicit sexual thoughts when they were at war. Rashi alludes to that explanation in his comment to vs. 50, s.v. וכומז ("לכפר על הרהור הלב של בנות מדין—to do expiation for the licentious thoughts of [the Israelite soldiers concerning] the Midianite women"). In that sense, Rashbam's explanation is opposed to Rashi, too. According to Hizq., Rashi here quotes those midrashic talmudic texts here at greater length, but in our editions of Rashi only the one allusion is found.

See Nahm. who also tries to rationalize, without recourse to midrash, the need here for expiation.

no plague will come upon them when they are counted . . ., (30:16) take the expiation money from the Israelites and assign it to the service of the Tent of Meeting. It shall serve the Israelites as a reminder [before the LORD]." Accordingly here also (in Numbers 31:54) "They brought it to the Tent of Meeting as a reminder . . . before the LORD."[23]

I heard this explanation from my teacher, my father Rabbi Meir.[24] It is the correct one.

32:17 חושים: means HURRIEDLY.[25] So also (Ps. 55:9) "I would quickly find (החישה)[26] a refuge for myself."

---

[23]Rashbam's explanation is later adopted by Hizq. It is cited also by JBS who does not accept it.

[24]This is the third and last time that Rashbam makes reference to his father in his Torah commentary. No honorific for a dead person is attached to the name, but it is unlikely that Rabbi Meir was still alive. (According to Grossman, *Ḥakhme Ṣorfat*, p. 169, Rabbi Meir died around 1140.) The wording of Rashbam's commentary to Gen. 37:2 makes it clear that Rabbi Meir was no longer alive; Rashbam calls himself the son of Rabbi Meir זצ"ל—may the memory of the righteous be a blessing. In his commentary to Gen. 25:32 Rashbam quotes an interpretation in the name of his father "מ"כ" = מנוחתו כבוד—"may he rest in honor." [In my Genesis volume, p. 137, I mistakenly understood מ"כ as meaning מעלת כבודו, and translated it as "his eminence."] מ"כ is the standard honorific that Rashbam uses, at least ten times in his BB commentary (e.g. ad 79b, s.v. דרך שובכו) about his grandfather Rashi, who was certainly dead when Rashbam wrote that commentary.

The lack of an honorific such as זצ"ל or מ"כ here is probably due to the fact that copyists were not always careful to preserve such terms. On this point I take issue with Professor Avraham Grossman who argues (*ibid.*, p. 28) that Rashbam's Torah commentary was written in the 1120s. In a personal communication, Professor Grossman wrote to me that he feels that the fact that Rashbam mentioned Joseph Qara in his commentary without using ז"ל or some similar honorific title makes it likely that his commentary was written before Qara's death, around 1130. However, I believe that the commentary was written almost twenty years later, after Rabbi Meir's death. See also note 30 to Num. 4:10.

[25]So also Rashi, iE and most exegetes.

[26]In his notes here Rosin writes that, in the ms. that he used, Rashbam cites this verse in Psalms as including the word החישה, not MT's אחישה. This is most likely a copyist's error.

מסעי (Numbers 33–36)

33:1 אלה מסעי THESE ARE THE TRAVELS: The text repeats [each of the place names when it enumerates] the travels and the encampments, in order to make the location of each of the encampments clear.[1]

33:49 ויחנו על הירדן . . . בערבות מואב THEY ENCAMPED BY THE JORDAN . . . IN THE STEPPES OF MOAB: There,[2] (50) THE LORD SPOKE TO MOSES IN THE STEPPES OF MOAB AT THE JORDAN NEAR JERICHO.

33:55 לשיכים בעיניכם NAILS IN YOUR EYES: The word שיכים means the same as "thorns" or "nettles," which sting the eyes.[3] So it is written (Hos. 2:8) "I

---

[1]There are two possible ways of understanding what the issue is that Rashbam is addressing here. He may be asking why this chapter is written at all, since many or most of the Israelites' travels have already been recorded. Alternatively, he may be asking why the particular repetitive style of this chapter was used. Using the style of "they traveled from A and encamped at B, they traveled from B and encamped at C, they traveled from C etc . . .," the result is that the text here repeats every place name.

Rashi and various midrashic sources address the first question and it is likely that Rashbam's interpretation is meant to oppose theirs. Rashi offers two midrashic explanations. According to each of those explanations, the length of the text shows the love of God for the Jewish people in a different way. LT asks the direct question, "Why were these travels recorded?" and answers that the list taught the Israelites about God's miracles and about their own poor behavior, or perhaps the list teaches us about the miracles that God will do for us in the future.

Characteristically, Rashbam gives a more prosaic answer: the list teaches us where the Israelites encamped.

See Rashbam's comment above ad 11:35. There Rashbam explains that the redundant listing of travels and encampments in this chapter clarifies which places the Israelites really *stopped* at, not just which places they passed through.

[2]Rashbam is explaining the redundancy between vss. 48 and 49. Verse 48 tells us that "they traveled from the hills of Abarim and encamped in the steppes of Moab." Then vs. 49 repeats that they "encamped . . . in the steppes of Moab." Rashbam understands that vs. 48 is the original narration. Vs. 49 should be read together with vs. 50: "(49) When they had encamped at the steppes of Moab, then (50) the LORD spoke to Moses . . .."

Rashbam's explanation is opposed to that of Rashi who (following Eruv. 55b) sees our verse as teaching about the size of the Israelite encampment in the wilderness.

[3]Most exegetes agree with Rashbam about the meaning of שיכים. See e.g. Rashi. Rashbam may be arguing against LT, who sees שיכים as related to the word for knife, and sees our verse as meaning that any Canaanites who are not killed by the conquering Israelites will end

will hedge up (סך) your road with thorns." Proof can be adduced from [a similar verse in] the book of Joshua where it is written (23:13), "They shall become a snare and a trap for you, a scourge (ולשוטט) in your side and thorns (ולצננים) in your eyes."

(לשוטט is connected to the word "שוטים—whips," as in the phrase [I Kings 12:11], "My father flogged you with whips [שוטים]," or [Prov. 26:3] "a whip [שוט] for a horse.")[4]

So also the word "ולצנינים—and as thorns" [in our verse and in Joshua] refers to a type of thorn that harms humans.[5]

Menaḥem ben Saruq categorized the word [ולצנינים, here] together with [the word מצנים, in the phrase] (Job 5:5), "ואל מצנים יקחהו." But I explain [the word מצנים, there] as meaning ["cold,"][6] the same as in the phrase (Prov. 25:13), "like the coldness (כצנת) of snow." For there the verse reads:[7] אשר קצירו רעב יאכל ואל מצנים יקחהו ושאף צמים חילם—in other words "Highwaymen who are hungry, naked—[which is the meaning of the word] צנים[8]—and thirsty will carry off their wealth."

---

up attacking the Israelites with weapons. Rashbam explains that the verse describes a potential irritation from those nations, not a military threat.

I have divided Rashbam's comment above into four paragraphs. Its basic outline is as follows: (1) an explanation of שיכים; (2) an aside about the meaning of שוטט in the parallel verse in Joshua; (3) an explanation of the word צנינים here and in Joshua; and (4) a side argument against Menaḥem, who believed that the word מצנים in Job 5:5 meant the same thing as צנינים here.

[4]Rashbam is opposing Rashi's commentary to Joshua, where Rashi suggests that לשוטט means to roam about looking for booty. Moderns concur with Rashbam.

[5]Rashbam's interpretation opposes LT which understands ולצנינים in our verse as related to the word for cold (צינה). See note 6.

'Rashbam's comment may also be opposed to Rashi who saw ולצנינים as an image of closing people in with a fence of thorns, not of irritating them with sharp thorns.

[6]In other words, Rashbam is disagreeing both with LT and with Menaḥem, each of whom suggests that מצנים in Job and ולצנינים in Numbers mean the same thing. LT says that they both mean "cold." Menaḥem says that they both mean "thorns." Rashbam says that one means "cold" and the other means "thorns."

[7]Rashbam's literal translation of the verse would likely be: "Since his harvest will be eaten by the hungry, it will be taken by naked people, and the thirsty will take their wealth." As noted by NJPS, the verse is difficult and its meaning is uncertain.

[8]The assumption is that people who are naked—i.e. who have insufficient clothing—are cold.

The interpretation of the word מצנים in the Job commentary that Japhet attributes to Rashbam (ואל מצנים: ואל אותו הניצול מצנים ומגנים של רשעים) is not consonant with the interpretation offered by Rashbam here. The explanation in that Job commentary follows Rashi's commentary on that verse.

33:56 כאשר דמיתי WHAT I PLANNED: I.e. what I had thought[9] TO DO TO THEM—that which I commanded you (Deut. 20:16), "Do not let a soul remain alive." But you spared them (מותירים)[10] and let them remain alive. [Accordingly] I WILL DO TO YOU [what you were supposed to do to them]—I will not let *you* remain alive.[11]

34:2 זאת הארץ אשר תפל לכם בנחלה THIS IS THE LAND THAT SHALL FALL TO YOU AS YOUR PORTION: My grandfather, our teacher [Rashi], explained [this text] and drew [maps of] the boundaries.[12] Still I will explain in brief.

First the text explains the southern border [of the land of Israel], then its western border—for the Great Sea is its western border—then the northern border and then the eastern one.[13]

34:3 על ידי אדום: means near Edom.[14]

---

[9]See also Rashi's commentary to Est. 4:13, where he explains the *piel* of the verb *d-m-h* as being synonymous with the verb *ḥ-sh-b*, to think.

[10]Using the language of vs. 55, "the ones whom you allow to remain (תותירו)."

[11]So also JBS and Nahm.

[12]In recent years there has been increased interest in Rashi's maps. See Avraham Grossman's *Ḥakhme Ṣorfat*, p. 207, note 254, and the literature cited there, especially the article of Mayer Gruber. Both Gruber and Grossman feel that we have now found Rashi's original drawings. They both see this comment of Rashbam as one of the important texts that prove that Rashi really did draw maps of the land of Israel.

[13]In Rashi's uncharacteristically long comment on these verses, he does not point out this simple fact—that the text progresses in the order: south, west, north and east. It is clear, though, that Rashi did understand the borders of the land in that manner.

[14]In post-biblical Hebrew there is a fairly consistent distinction between the phrases על יד (beside) and על ידי (by means of, through). In the Bible, the distinction is sometimes found, but not always. Here clearly the distinction is not germane; על ידי here means "near" or "beside," just as Rashbam writes.

Curiously Rashi does not comment on the phrase על ידי אדום here; from his paraphrase of the verse, though, it is clear that he understands it as Rashbam does, i.e. "beside Edom (אצל אדום)." (See also Rashi ad Jud. 11:26.) Rashi comments more than once in his Torah commentary (e.g. ad Ex. 2:5 and Num. 13:29) on the phrase על יד, explaining why it means "beside." Arguably that phrase does *not* require explanation; readers of post-biblical Hebrew (= Rashi's audience) immediately know what it means. Rashbam never comments on the phrase על יד, but he comments here on the phrase על ידי, which appears to be anomalous.

Cf. iE here who equates על יד and על ידי, but suggests that יד in both of those phrases really means "place," yielding here the meaning "at the place of Edom." See also iE ad Deut. 2:37 and 23:13.

34:4 ונסב לכם THE BORDER WILL TURN: [I.e. at that point] the border protrudes. [However the phrases that say concerning the border that] ויצא and ועבר [mean that the border] goes straight without zigzagging.[15]

34:5 והיו תוצאותיו הימה AND IT: i.e. the southwestern border SHALL TERMINATE AT THE SEA.[16]

34:6 וגבול ים AND THE WESTERN BORDER: In other words, "and the western border is what?[17] THE GREAT SEA SHALL BE FOR YOU the western border."[18]

The rabbis explained[19] [that the ostensibly redundant word[20]] וגבול

---

[15]Rashbam's interpretation opposes that of Rashi who says that both the word ונסב and the word ויצא refer to protrusions of the border. Like Rashbam, see NJPSC.

[16]I have translated using the text found in the usually inferior printings before Rosin's edition: והיו תוצאותיו הימה: גבול דרומית מערבית. In the ms. that Rosin used, the word גבול appeared as וגבול. In order to make sense of that text, Rosin adds four words: וגבול [דרום כלה שם בקרן] דרומית מערבית. In any case the meaning of Rashbam's comment is essentially the same.

[17]Rashbam and Rashi explain the apparently redundant syntax of the beginning of the verse the same way. They also both point out that the word ים means "west" the first time it appears in the verse and means "sea" the second time.

[18]Once again (see note 16) I have translated using the text found in the usually inferior printings before Rosin's edition: "והיה לכם הים הגדול"—לגבול מערב. The ms. Rosin used read וגבול instead of לגבול, forcing Rosin to add another word to the commentary to try to get it to make sense: "והיה לכם הים הגדול וגבול": [גבול] מערב. According to that reading, Rashbam is suggesting that the meaning of the word וגבול is "as the western border." According to the translation that I used above, "as the western border" is simply part of Rashbam's paraphrase, not an explanation of the word וגבול.

[19]Git. 8a. So also Rashi.

As explained in the previous note, Rashbam may have already offered one explanation of the word וגבול and, if that is the case, now he would be offering a second, more midrashic suggestion. Alternatively he may be giving here his one and only explanation of the word. When Rashbam uses a phrase like "חכמים פירשו—the rabbis explained," it can be either to introduce a traditional midrash that he wishes to contrast with his own *peshaṭ* (e.g. ad Ex. 21:34 and 25:18) or to introduce a comment of the rabbis that he is offering as his one and only gloss of the phrase at hand (e.g. ad Lev. 1:15 and 10:16).

[20]Or perhaps, the rabbis explained that the redundant letter *vav* at the beginning of the word וגבול applies to the territorial waters of the land of Israel.

Rashbam generally says that redundancies are the source for midrashic explanations (see e.g. his commentary to Gen. 1:1) but he does not often provide specific explanations of how the redundancy led to a specific midrash in the way that he does here. See commentary to Num. 5:10, and note 15 there.

teaches us to include [within the borders of the land of Israel] the "*nesim*[21] in the sea"—i.e. the islands of the sea.[22]

34:7 תתאו: means "draw a line [for a border]"; it is related to the meaning of boundary and border.[23]

35:5 אלפים באמה TWO THOUSAND CUBITS: One thousand cubits is "yard" (מגרש) and the rest [beyond the yard] is for fields and vineyards.[24]

35:11 והקריתם: means "you shall prepare."[25]

35:14 את שלש הערים תתנו מעבר לירדן THREE CITIES YOU SHOULD DESIGNATE BEYOND THE JORDAN: Those are the cities [of refuge] which Moses, while still alive, set aside, as it is written (Deut. 4:41), "Then Moses set aside . . . ."[26]

35:31 ולא תקחו כפר YOU MAY NOT ACCEPT A RANSOM [FOR THE LIFE OF A MURDERER]: allowing him to exempt himself through a monetary payment.[27]

---

[21]Rosin records that in the ms. the word is vocalized: נֵיסים. The word in the talmudic text definitely means "islands," as Rashbam says, and may be derived from the Greek. See Jastrow, s.v. ניסא.

[22]Rashbam explains the unusual wording of the talmudic passage by quoting a biblical Hebrew phrase, איי הים (Est. 10:1). So also Rashi ad Git., *ibid.*, s.v. והנסין.

[23]Rashbam's interpretation opposes that of Rashi who says that תתאו means to turn, or to change the angle. Like Rashbam, see iE ad vs. 10. See also NJPS: "draw a line."

[24]So also Rashi (following Sot. 27b).

The problem in our verse is that vs. 4 says that each Levite city should have a "yard" (מגרש) around it that extends "a thousand cubits outside the town wall all around." Then vs. 5 says to measure *two* thousand cubits from the town in each direction. For other solutions, see e.g. Nahm. and NJPSC.

[25]So also Rashi (following Sifre Numbers 159). Cf. iE who explains the verb as connected to the noun קריה—city. The word is difficult: it is the only use of the root *q-r-h* in *hifil* in the Bible.

[26]Vss. 1 and 11 of our chapter make it clear that these instructions from God about "cities of refuge" were delivered "in the steppes of Moab, on the Jordan, near Jericho," just before the people were about to cross over to the west side of the Jordan. As Hizq. says: חסר כאן המעשה—it is surprising that the text does not tell us that this instruction was fulfilled right away, before they crossed the Jordan. Rashbam points out (and later Hizq. too) that the fulfillment of the instructions is recorded in Deut. See Rashbam's comment there for an explanation of why Deut. was an appropriate place for the execution of the law to be recorded.

[27]So also Rashi, verbatim (following Sifre Numbers 161).

35:32 עד מות הכהן UNTIL THE DEATH OF THE PRIEST: I.e. the high priest.[28]

Following the plain meaning of Scripture, this means [that the murderer must stay in the "city of refuge"] until the chief judge dies. This is the like [the idea of] (Is. 14:17), "who never released his prisoners to their homes."[29]

35:33 כי אם בדם שֹׁפְכוֹ EXCEPT BY THE BLOOD OF HIM WHO SHED IT: I say that it is appropriate that [the form שֹׁפְכוֹ here] has a *ḥolam* vowel,[30] because of its meaning here "except by the blood of the man who spilled blood."

36:6 לטוב בעיניהם [THEY MAY MARRY] ANYONE THEY WISH: Following the plain meaning of Scripture, [this means anyone] from their tribe.[31]

---

[28]In some printed editions this comment of Rashbam appears before the comment on vs. 31. If that is the case then Rashbam is commenting on vs. 25, rather than on verse 32, and his comment begins simply by quoting the words of that verse, עד מות הכהן הגדול.

My translation is based on Rosin's edition. See also Rosin, RSBM, p. 41, note 3.

[29]Chapter 14 of Isaiah describes the downfall of the king of Babylon. Once he has been humiliated, people will wonder: was this the great king who had had such total control of his country? One of the phrases used to describe the former power of the king is that he "never released his prisoners to their homes." Rashbam is intimating that since the Israelite High Priest is also charged with preserving the good order of society, his duties include making sure that people who belong in prisons stay there. It would therefore be a disgrace to the High Priest if these accidental murderers were set free. Once he has died, there would be no disgrace involved in declaring a general amnesty. (Rashbam's idea is expressed at greater length and much more clearly by Hizq. ad vs. 25.)

Rashbam is opposing the various midrashic explanations—two of which are quoted by Rashi ad vs. 25—of how the murderer achieves atonement through the death of the High Priest. According to Rashbam the law is meant to preserve the dignity of the highest member of the executive branch of Israelite society.

[30]Rashbam is distinguishing between our form, שֹׁפְכוֹ, and the form שָׁפְכוֹ, which would mean "his shedding" or "his spilling." (That precise form does not appear anywhere in the Bible, but the similar form "בְּשָׁפְכְךָ—your spilling" appears in Ezek. 9:8.) One might make a similar distinction in biblical Hebrew between שֹׁמְרוֹ—his guard, and שָׁמְרוֹ—his guarding.

Rashbam's grammatical point is clear and unarguable. So also iE. See also Rashbam ad Gen. 26:35, 27:19 and 38:9; ad Ex. 14:5; and ad Lev. 26:35. See also his *Dayyaqut* (Merdler's edition, p. 41).

[31]The Talmud in BB 120a discusses the alleged contradiction between the statement that Zelophehad's daughters could marry "anyone they wanted" and the statement that follows immediately, "however they must marry into the family of their father's tribe." The Talmud suggests that actually, by law, Zelophehad's daughters could marry any Israelite. The second half of this verse simply *suggests* to them that it might be better if they marry someone from their own tribe.

Rashbam opposes that midrash and says that, according to the *peshaṭ*, the two phrases taken together mean that (as NJPS puts it), "They may marry anyone that they wish, provided they marry into a clan of their father's tribe."

BIBLIOGRAPHY

I. CLASSICAL AND MEDIEVAL SOURCES

Abraham ben Moses Maimonides. *Perush ha-Torah.* Ed. by S. D.Sassoon. London, 1959.

Abarbanel, Don Isaac. *Perush.* 4 volumes. Tel-Aviv and Jerusalem, 1954/55–1959/60.

Andrew of St. Victor. *Commentary on the Heptateuch.* In *Corpus Christianorum,* volume 53. Edited by Charles Lohr and Rainer Berndt. Turnhout, 1986.

The Apocryha and Pseudepigrapha of the Old Testament in English. Ed. by R. H. Charles. 2 volumes. Oxford, 1913.

Ashkenazi, Shelomoh Zalman. *Qeren Shemuel.* Frankfort, 1727.

Babylonian Talmud. Vilna, 1881.

Bereschit rabba'. Ed. by J. Theoodor and C. Albeck. Berlin, 1903–36.

———. Ed. by M. Mirkin. Tel Aviv, 1957.

Bet ha-midrash. Ed. by A. Jellinek. Second edition. 6 volumes. Jerusalem, 1938.

Da'at zeqenim mi-ba'ale ha-tosafot. In the standard editions of the Hebrew Bible.

Dunash ben Labrat. *Teshuvot.* Ed. by H. Filipowski. London, 1855.

Friedlander, M. *Ibn Ezra on Isaiah.* London, 1873.

Ibn Janaḥ, Jonah Abu'l-Walid Merwan. *Sefer ha-shorashim.* Ed. by A. Neubauer. Oxford, 1875.

———. *Sefer ha-riqmah.* Ed. by M. Wilensky. Jerusalem, 1964.

Ibn Kaspi, Joseph. *Mishneh kesef.* Pressburg, 1904/5.

Joseph Bekhor Shor. *Perush leḥamishah ḥumshe Torah.* 3 volumes. Jerusalem, 1977–8.

Kasher, M. M. *Torah shelemah.* Jerusalem and New York. 1926/7– .

Maimonides, Moses. *The Guide of the Perplexed.* Translated by S. Pines. Chicago, 1963.

———. *Mishneh Torah.* 5 volumes. New York, 1947.

Mekilta derabbi Ishmael. Ed. by J. Z. Lauterbach. 3 volumes. Philadelphia, 1933–5.

Menaḥem ibn Saruq. *Maḥberet.* Ed. by H. Filipovski. London, 1854.

Midrash bereshit rabbati. Ed. by Ch. Albeck. Jerusalem, 1940.

Midrash ha-gadol. Genesis. Ed. by M. Margulies. Jerusalem, 1947.

Midrash leqaḥ ṭov. Ed. by S. Buber. 2 volumes. Lemberg, 1878.

Midrash rabba'. 2 volumes. Vilna, 1878.

Midrash Samuel. Ed. by S. Buber. Cracow, 1893.

Midrash sekhel ṭov. Ed. by S. Buber. 2 volumes. Lemberg, 1899.

Midrash Tanḥuma. 2 volumes. Jerusalem, 1971–2.

Midrash Tanḥuma ha-qadum veha-yashan. Ed. by S. Buber. Vilna, 1883.

Midrash Tehillim. Ed. by S. Buber. Reprint edition: New York, 1947.

Mishnah. Ed. by Ch. Albeck. 7 volumes. Jerusalem, 1952–9.

Moses ben Naḥman. *Perush 'al ha-Torah.* Ed. by Ch. Chavel. 2 volumes. 5th edition. Jerusalem, 1969.

Nissim of Marseilles. *Ma'ase Nissim.* Ed. by H. Kreisel. Jerusalem, 2000.

Palestinian Talmud. Krotoshin, 1866.

Perush Avraham ibn Ezra 'al ha-Torah. Ed. by Y. Krinski. 5 volumes. [=*Ḥumash meḥoqeqe Yehudah*]. Reprint edition: Jerusalem, 1961/2.

———. Ed. by A. Weiser. 3 volumes. Jerusalem, 1976.

Perushe ha-Ḥizquni 'al ha-Torah. Ed. by Ch. Chavel. Jerusalem, 1981.

Perush ha-Torah lerav Shemuel ben Ḥofni Gaon. Ed. by E. Greenbaum. Jerusalem, 1979.

Pesiqta Rabbati. Ed. by M. Ish Shalom. Tel Aviv 5723.

Pirqe derabbi Eliezer. Jerusalem, 1973.

Qara, Joseph. *Perush 'al nevi'im rishonim.* Ed. by S. Eppenstein. Jerusalem, 1972.

Qimḥi, David. *Perush 'al Bereshit.* Jerusalem, 1974/5.

———. *Perushim 'al ha-Tanakh.* In the standard editions of the Hebrew Bible.

———. *Sefer ha-shorashim.* Reprint edition: Jerusalem, 1967.

———. *Mikhlol.* Jerusalem, 1966.

Rashi. *Perushim 'al ha-Tanakh.* In the standard editions of the Hebrew Bible.

———. Commentaries on the Talmud. In the standard editions of the Babylonian Talmud.

———. *Rashi 'al ha-Torah.* Ed. by A. Berliner. Jerusalem, 1962.

———. *Perush 'al ha-Torah.* Ed. by Ch. Chavel. Jerusalem, 1982.

Rashbam. *Perush 'al ha-Torah.* Ed. by David Rosin. Breslau, 1882.

———. *Perush 'al ha-Torah.* Ed. by A. Bromberg. Tel Aviv, 1964/5.

———. *Sefer Dayyaqut.* Ed. by L. Stein. In *Jahrbuch des Traditionstreuen Rabbinerverbandes in der Slovakei.* Trnava, 1923.

———. *Sefer Dayyaqut.* Ed. by R. Merdler. Jerusalem, 1999.

———. *Perush Rashbam ha-qaṣar lefereq ḥezqat ha-batim.* Edited by Mordekhai Laib Katzenelenbogen. Jerusalem, 1985.

Seder 'olam. Ed. by A. Marx. Berlin, 1903.

Seforno, Ovadiah. *Perush 'al ha-Torah.* Ed. by W. Gottlieb. Jerusalem, 1980.

Sifra de-be Rab. Ed. by I. H. Weiss. Vienna, 1862.

Siphre ad Deuteronomium. Ed. by L. Finkelstein. Berlin, 1939.

Siphre ad Numeros. Ed. by H. S. Horovitz. Leipzig, 1917.

Targum Onqelos. Ed. by A. Sperber. Leiden, 1959.

———. Ed. by A. Berliner. Berlin, 1884.

Targum Pseudo-Jonathan. Ed. by M. Ginsburger. Berlin, 1903.

Torat Ḥayim: Ḥamishah ḥumshe Torah. 7 volumes. Jerusalem, 1986–1993.

Tosefta. Ed. by M. S. Zuckermandel. Jerusalem, 1938.

———. Ed. by S. Lieberman. New York, 1955– .

Wertheimer, S. A. *Bate Midrashot*. 2 volumes. Jerusalem, 1950–3.

Yalqut Shimoni. New York, 1925/6.

II. SECONDARY LITERATURE ON MEDIEVAL JEWRY AND MEDIEVAL EXEGESIS

Abecassis, Deborah. *Reconstructing Rashi's Commentary on Genesis from Citations in the Torah Commentary of the Tosafot.* McGill University doctoral dissertation, 1999.

Abraham, M. "*Commentaire de R. Joseph Bekhor-Shor sur le Lévitique.*" REJ 77 (1923): 41–59.

Bacher, W. *Ha-Rambam parshan ha-miqra'*. Budapest, 1896.

Baer, I. "*Rashi veha-meṣi'ut ha-hisṭorit shel zemano.*" In *Sefer Rashi.* Ed. by Y. Maimon (Fischmann). Pages 129–164. Jerusalem, 1956.

Baron, S. W. *A Social and Religious History of the Jews.* Second edition. Philadelphia, 1952– .

Berger, D. *The Jewish-Christian Debate in the High Middle Ages.* Philadelphia, 1979.

———. "On the Image and Destiny of Gentiles in Ashkenazic Polemical Literature" [Heb.]. In *Facing the Cross: The Persecutions of 1096 in History and Historiography.* Ed. by Yom Tov Assis, Jeremy Cohen, Aharon Kedar, Ora Limor and Michael Toch. Jerusalem, 2000. Pages 74–91.

Berger, M. *The Torah Commentary of R. Samuel ben Meir.* Harvard University doctoral dissertation, 1982.

Berliner, A. *Letoledot perushe Rashi.* In *Sefer Rashi.* Ed. by Y. Maimon (Fischmann). Jerusalem, 1956.

———. *Peleṭat soferim.* Breslau, 1872.

Berndt, Rainer, "*Les interprétations juives dans le Commentaire de l'Heptateuque d'André de Saint-Victor.*" In *Recherches augustiniennes* 24 (1989) 119–240.

———. *André de Saint-Victor: exégète et théologien.* Paris 1991.

Berzinsky, Jacob H.. *Quntres tiqqune ṭa'uyot ha-defus beferushe ha-Rashbam zaṣal 'al ha-Torah.* New York, 1934. Microfilm version from Yeshivah University Library.

Bland, Kalman. *The Artless Jew.* Princeton, 2000.

Breuer, Edward. *The Limits of Enlightenment.* Cambridge, 1996.

Cohen, G. *The Book of Tradition.* Philadelphia, 1967.

Dahan, Gilbert, "*Juifs et chrétiens en occident médiéval: La rencontre autour de la Bible (XIIe–XIVe siècles)*" *Revue de synthèse* 110, 1 (1989): 3–31.

———. *Les intellectuels chrétiens et les juifs au moyen age*. Paris, 1990.

Darmesteter, A. and Blondheim, D., *Les gloses françaises dans les commentaries talmudiques de Raschi*. Paris, 1929.

Esh, S. "Variant Readings in Medieval Hebrew Commentaries: R. Samuel ben Meir (Rashbam)." *Textus* 5 (1966): 84–92.

Friedlander, M. *Essays on the Writings of Abraham ibn Ezra*. London, 1877.

Funkenstein, Amos. "*Ha-temurot bevikkuaḥ ha-dat she-ben yehudim lenoṣerim ba-me'ah ha-12*." *Zion* 33 (1968): 125–144.

Geiger, A. "*'Al devar ḥakhme Ṣorfat mefarshe ha-Torah*." In *Qevuṣat ma'amarim*. Ed. by S. Poznanski. Warsaw, 1910. Pages 169–177.

———. *Toledot ha-Radaq*. *Ibid*. Pages 131–153.

———. *Parschandata*. Leipzig, 1855.

Gelles, Benjamin. *Peshaṭ uderash befarshanuto shel Rashi*. Jerusalem, 1992.

Ginzberg, Louis. *Legends of the Jews*. 7 volumes. Philadelphia, 1909.

Golb, N. *Toledot ha-yehudim be-'ir Rouen biyeme ha-benayim*. Tel Aviv, 1976.

———. *The Jews in Medieval Normandy*. Cambridge, 1998.

Goldenberg, Robert. "Review of *Rashbam's Commentary on Exodus*." *Journal of Biblical Literature* 1999: 736-737.

Gross, H. *Gallia Judaica*. Paris, 1897.

Grossman, A. *Ḥakhme 'ashkenaz ha-rishonim*. Jerusalem, 1981.

———. *Ḥakhme Ṣorfat ha-rishonim*. Jerusalem, 1995.

Guedemann, Moritz. *Ha-Torah veha-ḥayyim biyeme ha-benayim beṢorfat veAshkenaz*. Warsaw, 1897.

Halperin, Herman. *Rashi and the Christian Scholars*. Pittsburgh, 1963.

Halkin, A. S. "The Medieval Jewish Attitude Toward Hebrew." In *Studies and Texts*. Ed. by A. Altman. Cambridge, 1963.

Halivni, D. W. *Midrash Mishnah and Gemara*. London, 1986.

———. *Peshat and Derash*. New York, 1991.

Harris, Robert A., *The Literary Hermeneutic of Rabbi Eliezer of Beaugency*. Jewish Theological Seminary of America doctoral dissertation, 1997.

Heineman, I. *Darke ha-'aggadah*. Jerusalem, 1949.

———. *Ṭa'ame ha-miṣvot besifrut yisrael*. Jerusalem, 1956

Herzog, P. "Review of Krinski's *Meḥoqeqe Yehudah*." ZDMG 64 (1910): 219–238.

Japhet, Sara. *The Commentary of Rabbi Samuel ben Meir (Rashbam) on the Book of Job*. Jerusalem, 2000.

———. *Ha-miqra' bere'i mefarshav: sefer zikaron le-Sarah Kamin*. Jerusalem, 1994.

——— and R. Salters. *The Commentary of Rabbi Samuel ben Meir (Rashbam) on Qoheleth*. Jerusalem, 1985.

Kamin, Sarah. *Jews and Christians Interpret the Bible*. Jerusalem, 1991.

———. *Rashi: peshuṭo shel miqra' umidrasho shel miqra'*. Jerusalem, 1986.

Lasker, Daniel J. *Jewish Philosophical Polemics Against Christianity in the High Middle Ages*. New York, 1977.

Lockshin, Martin. *Rabbi Samuel ben Meir's Commentary on Genesis: An Annotated Translation*. Lewiston, 1989

———. *Rashbam's Commentary on Exodus: An Annotated Translation*. Atlanta, 1997.

———. "Tradition or Context: Two Exegetes Struggle with Peshat." In *From Ancient Israel to Modern Judaism*. Ed. by J. Neusner, E. Frerichs and N. Sarna. Volume 2. Atlanta, 1989: 173–186.

———. "Truth or *Peshaṭ*: Issues in Law and Exegesis." In *Law Politics and Society in the Ancient Mediterranean World*. Ed. by B. Halpern and D. Hobson. Sheffield, 1993. Pages 271–279.

———. "The Connection Between Rabbi Samuel ben Meir's Torah Commentary and Midrash Sekhel Tov" [Heb.]. In *Proceedings of the Eleventh World Congress of Jewish Studies*. Jerusalem, 1994. Division A. Hebrew Section: 135–142.

———. "'Rashbam' on Job: A Reconsideration." *Jewish Studies Quarterly* 8 (2001): 80-104.

Loewe, R. "The 'Plain' Meaning of Scripture in Early Jewish Exegesis." In *Papers of the Institute of Jewish Studies*. Ed. by J. G. Weiss. Jerusalem, 1964. Pages 140–185.

Margaliot, A. "*Ha-yaḥas she-ben perush ha-Rashbam leferush ha-Ra'va' 'al ha-Torah.*" In *Sefer Asaf.* Ed. by U. Cassutto. Jerusalem, 1953. Pages 357–369.

Melamed, E. *Mefarshe ha-miqra'*. Jerusalem, 1975.

———. "*Ṭa'ame ha-miqra' bedivre parshane ha-miqra'.*" In *Meḥqare ha-mercaz leḥeqer ha-folklor*. Jerusalem, 1970. Pages 185–189.

Merdler, Ronela, *Dayyaqut me-rabbenu Shemuel: Diyyun be-sefer ha-diqduq umasqanot*. Master's Dissertation: Hebrew University of Jerusalem, 1995.

———. *Dayyaqut me-rabbenu Shemuel, mahadurah biqqortit*. Jerusalem, 1999.

Moore, Rebecca. *Jews and Christians in the Life and Thought of Hugh of St. Victor*. Atlanta, 1998.

Parkes, James. *The Conflict of the Church and the Synagogue*. London, 1954.

Posnanski, Adolf. *Schiloh*. Leipzig, 1894.

Poznanski, Samuel. *Perush 'al Yeḥezqel utere 'asar lerabbi Eliezer mi-Beaugency*. Warsaw, 1913.

Preuss, Julius, *Biblical and Talmudic Medicine*. Translated by Fred Rosner. New York, 1978.

Rosen, Michael S. *The Hebrew Commentary on Job in Manuscript Jewish Theological Seminary N. Y. L. 778 Attributed by Some to R' Samuel ben Meir—An Analysis of its Sources and Consideration of its Authorship*. Doctoral dissertation. London, 1994.

Rosenthal, E.I.J. "*Anti-Christian Polemic in Medieval Bible Commentaries.*" JJS 11 (1960): 111–135.

Rosin, David. *R. Samuel b. Meir als Schrifterklärer*. Breslau, 1880.

Rosner, Fred. *Medicine in the Bible and Talmud*. New York 1995.

Sarna, Nahum. "Hebrew and Bible Studies in Medieval Spain." In *The Sephardi Heritage*. Ed. by R. Barnett. London, 1971. Pages 323–366.

Segal, N. *Parshanut ha-miqra'*. Jerusalem, 1971.

Simon, U. "*Ledarko ha-parshanit shel ha-Ra'va' 'al pi sheloshet be'urim lefasuq 'eḥad.*" In *Bar-Ilan Annual* 6 (1968): 92–138.

———. "*Ra'va' veRadaq: Shete gishot lishe'elat mehemanut nosaḥ ha-miqra'.*" *Ibid.* Pages 191–238.

———. "Review of Weiser's *ibn Ezra 'al ha-Torah.*" *Qiryat Sefer* (1976): 646–658.

Smalley, Beryl. *The Study of the Bible in the Middle Ages.* Notre Dame, 1964.

Spicq, C. *Esquisse d'une histoire de l'exégèse latine au moyen age.* Paris, 1944.

Spiegel, Shalom. *The Last Trial.* New York, 1969.

Talmage, Frank. *David Kimhi: The Man and the Commentaries.* Cambridge, 1975.

———. *Apples of Gold in Settings of Silver: Studies in Medieval Jewish Exegesis and Polemics.* Edited by Barry Walfish. Toronto, 1999.

Ta-shma, Israel. *Ha-sifrut ha-parshanit la-Talmud 1000–1200.* Jerusalem, 1999.

Touitou, E. "*'Al shiṭato shel Rashbam beferusho la-Torah.*" *Tarbiz* 48 (1979): 248–273.

———. "*Shiṭato ha-parshanit shel Rashbam 'al reqa' ha-meṣiut ha-hisṭorit shel zemano.*" In *Studies in Rabbinic Literature Bible and Jewish History.* Ed. by Y. Gilat, Ch. Levine and Z. Rabinowitz. Ramat-Gan, 1982. Pages 48–74.

———. "*Peshaṭ va'apoligeṭiqah beferush ha-Rashbam lesippure Moshe she-ba-Torah.*" *Tarbiz* 51 (1982): 227–238.

———. "*'Al ḥeqer parshanut ha-miqra' ha-yehudit-ṣorfatit.*" *Tarbiz* 51 (1982): 522–526.

Urbach, Ephraim. *Ba'ale ha-tosafot.* Second edition. 2 volumes. Jerusalem, 1980.

Walter, G. *Joseph Bechor Schor der letzte nordfranzösische Bibelexeget.* Breslau, 1890.

Weiss, P. R. "*Ibn Ezra ha-Qara'im veha-halakhah.*" *Melillah* I-IV (1944–50).

Zucker, M. "*Lefitron ba'ayat lamed bet middot.*" PAAJR 23 (1954).

III. MODERN LITERATURE AND COMMENTARIES ON THE BIBLE

Alter, Robert. *The Art of Biblical Narrative*. New York, 1981.

———. *The Art of Biblical Poetry*. New York, 1985.

———. "A Literary Approach to the Bible." *Commentary* 60 (1975): 70–77.

———. "Biblical Narrative." *Commentary* 61 (1976): 61–67.

Auerbach, E. *Mimesis*. Bern, 1959.

Buber, Martin. *Darko shel miqra'*. Jerusalem, 1964.

Buber, Martin and Rosenzweig, Franz. *Die Schrift und ihre Verdeutschung*. Berlin, 1936.

Fokkelman, J. P. *Narrative Art in Genesis*. Amsterdam, 1975.

Gerstenberger, Erhard S. *Leviticus*. Translated by Douglas W. Stott. Louisville, 1996.

Gesenius' Hebrew Grammar. Ed. by E. Kautzch and translated by A. E. Cowley. Oxford, 1974.

Good, E. M. *Irony in the Old Testament*. Philadelphia, 1965.

Gray, George, *A Critical and Exegetical Commentary on Numbers* (ICC). Edinburgh, 1903.

Gros Louis, K.R.R., editor. *Literary Interpretations of Biblical Narratives*. 2 volumes. Nashville, 1974 and New York, 1981.

Harrison, R.K. *Numbers: An Exegetical Commentary*. Grand Rapids, 1990.

Heidenheim, Wolf. *Sefer Torat ha-Elohim . . . im perush Havanat hamiqra'*. Reprint edition: Bene Beraq, 1997.

Hoffmann, David. *Sefer Va-yiqra'*. Translated from the German. Jerusalem, 1954.

Jouon, Paul. *Grammaire de l'Hébreu biblique*. Rome, 1923.

Kugel, James. *The Idea of Biblical Poetry*. New Haven, 1981.

Leibowitz, Nehama. "*Darko shel Rashi behava'at midrashim beferusho la-Torah.*" In her *'Iyyunim ḥadashim besefer Shemot*. Jerusalem, 1970. Pages 497–524.

———. *'Iyyunim Ḥadashim besefer Va-yiqra'*. Jerusalem, 1983.

Levine, Baruch. *The JPS Torah Commentary on Leviticus*. Philadelphia, 1989.

———. *Numbers 1–20: a new translation with introduction and commentary*. New York, 1993.

Licht, Jacob. *Perush 'al sefer Bemidbar*. 3 volumes. Jerusalem, 1985–1995.

Luzzatto, S. D. *Perush Shadal 'al ḥamishah ḥumshe Torah*. Philadelphia, 1964.

Mendelssohn, Moses. *Netivot ha-shalom*. Translation and Commentary on the Torah. Fürth, 1801.

Milgrom, Jacob. *The JPS Torah Commentary on Numbers*. Philadelphia, 1990.

———. *Leviticus 1–16: a new translation with introduction and commentary*. New York, 1991. [Further volumes of this commentary were published only after the research was completed for this book.]

Noth, Martin. *Leviticus: A Commentary*. Translated from the German by J.S. Anderson. Philadelphia, 1965.

———. *Numbers: A Commentary*. Translated from the German by James D. Martin. Philadelphia, 1968.

Orlinsky, Harry. *Notes on the New Translation of the Torah*. Philadelphia, 1964.

Sarna, N. "The Anticipatory Use of Information as a Literary Feature of the Genesis Narrative." In *The Creation of Sacred Literature*. Edited by R. E. Friedman. University of California, 1981. Pages 76–82.

Shapira, Yehudah Leib. *Ha-rekhasim leviq'ah*. Reprint edition: Vilna, 1888.

Talmon, S. *Darke ha-sippur ba-miqra'*. Jerusalem, 1965.

———. "The Presentation of Synchroneity and Simultaneity in Biblical Narrative." *Scripta Hierosolymitana* 27 (1978): 9–26.

Weiss, Meir. *Ha-miqra' kidemuto*. Jerusalem, 1962.

www.ingramcontent.com/pod-product-compliance
Lightning Source LLC
Chambersburg PA
CBHW022009300426
44117CB00005B/106
9781930675261